Greg Byrd, Lynn Byrd and Chris Pearce

Cambridge Checkpoint Mathematics

Coursebook 8

CAMBRIDGE
UNIVERSITY PRESS

CAMBRIDGE
UNIVERSITY PRESS

University Printing House, Cambridge CB2 8BS, United Kingdom

One Liberty Plaza, 20th Floor, New York, NY 10006, USA

477 Williamstown Road, Port Melbourne, VIC 3207, Australia

314–321, 3rd Floor, Plot 3, Splendor Forum, Jasola District Centre, New Delhi – 110025, India

79 Anson Road, #06–04/06, Singapore 079906

Cambridge University Press is part of the University of Cambridge.

It furthers the University's mission by disseminating knowledge in the pursuit of education, learning and research at the highest international levels of excellence.

www.cambridge.org
Information on this title: www.cambridge.org/9781107697874

First published 2013
20 19

Printed in Spain by GraphyCems

A catalogue record for this publication is available from the British Library

ISBN 978-1-107-69787-4 Paperback
ISBN 978-1-108-61595-2 Paperback with Cambridge Online Mathematics (1 Year)
ISBN 978-1-108-70915-6 Cambridge Online Mathematics Checkpoint 8 (1 Year)

Cover image © Cosmo Condina concepts/Alamy

Introduction

Welcome to Cambridge Checkpoint Mathematics stage 8

The *Cambridge Checkpoint Mathematics* course covers the Cambridge Secondary 1 mathematics framework and is divided into three stages: 7, 8 and 9. This book covers all you need to know for stage 8.

There are two more books in the series to cover stages 7 and 9. Together they will give you a firm foundation in mathematics.

At the end of the year, your teacher may ask you to take a **Progression test** to find out how well you have done. This book will help you to learn how to apply your mathematical knowledge and to do well in the test.

The curriculum is presented in six content areas:

- Number
- Measure
- Geometry
- Algebra
- Handling data
- Problem solving.

This book has 18 units, each related to one of the first five content areas. Problem solving is included in all units. There are no clear dividing lines between the five areas of mathematics; skills learned in one unit are often used in other units.

Each unit starts with an introduction, with **key words** listed in a blue box. This will prepare you for what you will learn in the unit. At the end of each unit is a **summary** box, to remind you what you've learned.

Each unit is divided into several topics. Each topic has an introduction explaining the topic content, usually with worked examples. Helpful hints are given in blue rounded boxes. At the end of each topic there is an exercise. Each unit ends with a review exercise. The questions in the exercises encourage you to apply your mathematical knowledge and develop your understanding of the subject.

As well as learning mathematical skills you need to learn when and how to use them. One of the most important mathematical skills you must learn is how to solve problems.

When you see this symbol, it means that the question will help you to develop your problem-solving skills.

During your course, you will learn a lot of facts, information and techniques. You will start to think like a mathematician. You will discuss ideas and methods with other students as well as your teacher. These discussions are an important part of developing your mathematical skills and understanding.

Look out for these students, who will be asking questions, making suggestions and taking part in the activities throughout the units.

Contents

Acknowledgements

The publisher would like to thank Ángel Cubero of the International School Santo Tomás de Aquino, Madrid, for reviewing the language level.

Cover image © Cosmo Condina concepts/Alamy

p. 7*b* pressureUA /iStock; p. 18*tl* Jon Arnold Images Ltd/Alamy; p. 18*mr* Maksim Toome / Shutterstock; p. 18*br* forestpath/ Shutterstock; p. 26*b* ilyast/ iStock; p. 31*b* Antonio Mo/Iconica/Getty Images; p. 37*b* Christopher Steer/ iStock; p.38*b* DAJ/ Getty Images; p. 44*mr* Chris Ryan/OJO Images/Getty Images; p. 44*b* NASA; p. 46*tr* Lynn Byrd; 46*mr* Aspen Photo/Shutterstock; p. 63*m* dundanim/Shutterstock; p. 83*t* Diego Cervo/Shutterstock; p. 83*mr* Francesco Dazzi/Shutterstock; p. 83*br* Peter Kirillov/Shutterstock; p. 93*mr* mbbirdy/iStock; p. 95*tr* pidjoe/iStock; p. 95*mr* Liz Van Steenburgh/Shutterstock; p. 95*br* Aleksandar Petrovic/iStock; p. 114*ml* a40757/ Shutterstock; p. 114*bl* Pakhnyushcha/ Shutterstock; p. 129*tr* Portrait Essentials / Alamy; p. 140*mr* RosetteJordaan/ iStock; p. 140*br* Mark Bowden/iStock; p. 143*b* Ferenc Szelepcsenyi/ Shutterstock; p. 146*tr* kryczka/ iStock; p. 147*br* design56/ Shutterstock; p. 158*br* Geoff Brightling / Peter Minister/Dorling Kindersley

l = left, *r* = right, *t* = top, *b* = bottom, *m* = middle

1 Integers, powers and roots

The first primes are 2 3 5 7 11 13 17 19 23 29 …

Prime numbers have just two factors: 1 and the number itself.

Every whole number that is not prime can be written as a product of prime numbers in exactly one way (apart from the order of the primes).

$8 = 2 \times 2 \times 2 \quad 65 = 5 \times 13 \quad 132 = 2 \times 2 \times 3 \times 11$
$2527 = 7 \times 19 \times 19$

It is easy to multiply two prime numbers. For example, $13 \times 113 = 1469$.

It is much harder to do the inverse operation. For example, 2021 is the product of two prime numbers. Can you find them?

This fact is the basis of a system that is used to encode messages sent across the internet.

The **RSA cryptosystem** was invented by Ronald Rivest, Adi Shamir and Leonard Adleman in 1977. It uses two large prime numbers with about 150 digits each. These are kept secret. Their product, N, with about 300 digits, is made public so that anyone can use it.

If you send a credit card number to a website, your computer performs a calculation with N and your credit card number to encode it. The computer receiving the coded number will do another calculation to decode it. Anyone else, who does not know the factors, will not be able to do this.

Key words

Make sure you learn and understand these key words:

integer
inverse
multiple
common multiple
lowest common multiple (LCM)
factor
common factor
highest common factor (HCF)
prime number
prime
factor tree
power
index (indices)
square
cube
square root
cube root

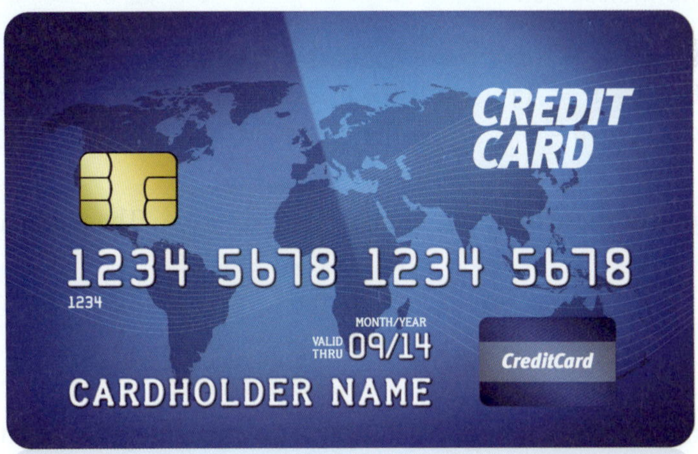

Prime numbers more than 200 are 211 223 227 229 233 239 241 251 257 263 269 271 … …

1.1 Arithmetic with integers

Integers are whole numbers. They may be positive or negative. Zero is also an integer. You can show integers on a number line.

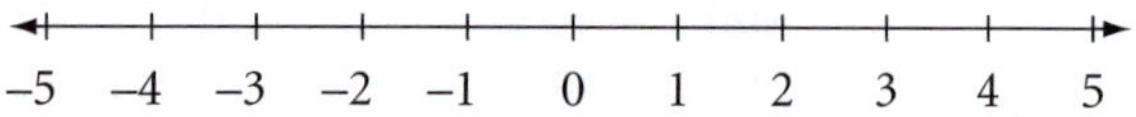

Look at the additions in the box to the right. The number added to 2 decreases, or goes down, by 1 each time. The answer also decreases, or goes down, by 1 each time.

$2 + 3 = 5$
$2 + 2 = 4$
$2 + 1 = 3$
$2 + 0 = 2$
$2 + -1 = 1$
$2 + -2 = 0$
$2 + -3 = -1$
$2 + -4 = -2$

Now see what happens if you subtract. Look at the first column.

The number subtracted from 5 goes down by 1 each time. The answer goes <u>up</u> by 1 each time. Now look at the two columns together.

You can change a subtraction into an addition by adding the **inverse** number. The inverse of 3 is –3. The inverse of –3 is 3.
For example, $5 - -3 = 5 + 3 = 8$.

$5 - 3 = 2$	$5 + -3 = 2$
$5 - 2 = 3$	$5 + -2 = 3$
$5 - 1 = 4$	$5 + -1 = 4$
$5 - 0 = 5$	$5 + 0 = 5$
$5 - -1 = 6$	$5 + 1 = 6$
$5 - -2 = 7$	$5 + 2 = 7$
$5 - -3 = 8$	$5 + 3 = 8$

Worked example 1.1a

Work these out. **a** $3 + -7$ **b** $-5 - 8$ **c** $-3 - -9$

a $3 + -7 = -4$	Subtract 7 from 3.	$3 - 7 = -4$
b $-5 - 8 = -13$	The inverse of 8 is –8.	$-5 - 8 = -5 + -8 = -13$
c $-3 - -9 = 6$	The inverse of –9 is 9.	$-3 - -9 = -3 + 9 = 6$

Look at these multiplications.

$3 \times 5 = 15$
$2 \times 5 = 10$
$1 \times 5 = 5$
$0 \times 5 = 0$

The pattern continues like this.

$-1 \times 5 = -5$
$-2 \times 5 = -10$
$-3 \times 5 = -15$
$-4 \times 5 = -20$

You can see that negative integer × positive integer = negative answer.

Now look at this pattern.

$-3 \times 4 = -12$
$-3 \times 3 = -9$
$-3 \times 2 = -6$
$-3 \times 1 = -3$
$-3 \times 0 = 0$

The pattern continues like this.

$-3 \times -1 = 3$
$-3 \times -2 = 6$
$-3 \times -3 = 9$
$-3 \times -4 = 12$
$-3 \times -5 = 15$

You can see that negative integer × negative integer = positive answer.

Here is a simple rule, which also works for division.

When you multiply two integers:
if they have same signs → positive answer
if they have different signs → negative answer

Worked example 1.1b

Work these out. **a** 12×-3 **b** -8×-5 **c** $-20 \div 4$ **d** $-24 \div -6$

a	$12 \times -3 = -36$	$12 \times 3 = 36$	The signs are different so the answer is negative.
b	$-8 \times -5 = 40$	$8 \times 5 = 40$	The signs are the same so the answer is positive.
c	$-20 \div 4 = -5$	$20 \div 4 = 5$	The signs are different so the answer is negative.
d	$-24 \div -6 = 4$	$24 \div 6 = 4$	The signs are the same so the answer is positive.

Warning: This rule works for multiplication and division. It does not work for addition or subtraction.

Exercise 1.1

1 Work out these additions.
a $3 + -6$ **b** $-3 + -8$ **c** $-10 + 4$ **d** $-10 + -7$ **e** $12 + -4$

2 Work out these additions.
a $30 + -20$ **b** $-100 + -80$ **c** $-20 + 5$ **d** $-30 + -70$ **e** $45 + -40$

3 Work out these subtractions.
a $4 - 6$ **b** $-4 - 6$ **c** $6 - 4$ **d** $-6 - 6$ **e** $-2 - 10$

4 Write down additions that have the same answers as these subtractions. Then work out the answer to each one.
a $4 - -6$ **b** $-4 - -6$ **c** $8 - -2$ **d** $-4 - -6$ **e** $12 - -10$

5 Work out these subtractions.
a $7 - -2$ **b** $-5 - -3$ **c** $12 - -4$ **d** $-6 - -6$ **e** $-2 - -10$

6 Here are some addition pyramids. Each number is the sum of the two in the row below it.
Copy the pyramids. Fill in the missing numbers.

In part **a**, $3 + -5 = -2$

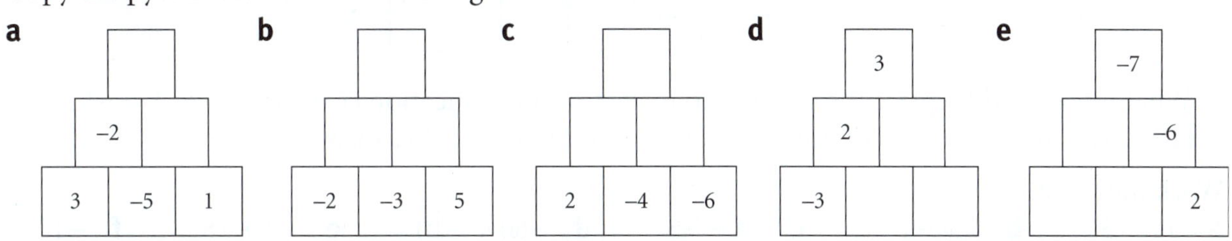

7 Here is a subtraction table. Two answers have already been filled in: $4 - -4 = 8$ and $-4 - 2 = -6$.
Copy the table and complete it.

		second number				
	−	**−4**	**−2**	**0**	**2**	**4**
first number	**4**	8				
	2					
	0					
	−2					
	−4				−6	

8 Work out these multiplications.

a 5×-4 **b** -8×6 **c** -4×-5 **d** -6×-10 **e** -2×20

9 Work out these divisions.

a $20 \div -10$ **b** $-30 \div 6$ **c** $-12 \div -4$ **d** $-50 \div -5$ **e** $16 \div -4$

10 Write down two correct division expressions.

a 4×-10 **b** $-20 \div 5$ **c** -20×5 **d** $-40 \div -8$ **e** -12×-4

11 Here are some multiplications. In each case, use the same numbers to write down two correct division expressions.

a $5 \times -3 = -15$ **b** $-8 \times -4 = 32$ **c** $-6 \times 7 = -42$

12 Here is a multiplication table. Three answers have already been filled in.

×	−3	−2	−1	0	1	2	3
3						6	
2							
1		−2					
0							
−1	3						
−2							
−3							

a Copy the table and complete it.
b Colour all the 0 answers in one colour, for example, green.
c Colour all the positive answers in a second colour, for example, blue.
d Colour all the negative answers in a third colour, for example, red.

13 These are multiplication pyramids. Each number is the product of the two in the row below it.
Copy each pyramid. Fill in the missing numbers.

The product is the result of multiplying two numbers
In part **a**, $2 \times -3 = -6$

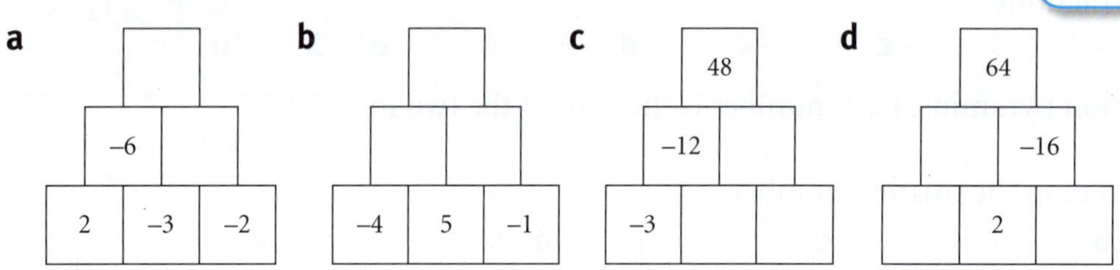

14 a What integers will replace the symbols to make this multiplication correct? $\bigcirc \times \Delta = -12$
b How many different pairs of numbers can you find that give this answer?

15 Work these out.

a 5×-3 **b** $5 + -3$ **c** $-4 - -5$ **d** $-60 \div -10$ **e** $-2 + 18$ **f** $-10 - 4$

16 Write down the missing numbers.

a $4 \times \square = -20$ **b** $\square \div -2 = -6$ **c** $\square - -5 = -2$ **d** $\square \times -3 = 12$
e $-2 + \square = 2$ **f** $\square - 4 = -3$

1.2 Multiples, factors and primes

The **multiples** of 6 are 6, 12, 18, 24, 30, 36, …, …

The multiples of 9 are 9, 18, 27, 36, 45, 54, …, …

The **common multiples** of 6 and 9 are 18, 36, 54, 72, …, …

The **lowest common multiple (LCM)** of 6 and 9 is 18.

The **factors** of a number divide into it without a remainder.

The factors of 18 are 1, 2, 3, 6, 9 and 18.

The factors of 27 are 1, 3, 9 and 27.

The **common factors** of 18 and 27 are 1, 3 and 9.

The **highest common factor (HCF)** of 18 and 27 is 9.

$6 \times 1 = 6$ $6 \times 2 = 12$ $6 \times 3 = 18$ … …
$9 \times 1 = 9$ $9 \times 2 = 18$ $9 \times 3 = 27$ … …

18 36 54 … … are in both lists of multiples.

$3 \times 6 = 18$ so 3 and 6 are factors of 18

Some numbers have just two factors. Examples are 7 (1 and 7 are factors), 13 (1 and 13 are factors) and 43. Numbers with just two factors are called **prime numbers** or just **primes**. The first ten primes are 2, 3, 5, 7, 11, 13, 17, 19, 23 and 29.

Worked example 1.2a

a Find the factors of 45. **b** Find the prime factors of 48.

a The factors of 45 are 1, 3, 5, 9, 15 and 45.

$45 = 1 \times 45$ so 1 and 45 are factors. (1 is always a factor.)
Check 2, 3, 4, … in turn to see if it is a factor.
2 is not a factor. (45 is an odd number.)
$45 = 3 \times 15$ 3 and 15 are factors.
4 is not a factor.
$45 = 5 \times 9$ 5 and 9 are factors.
6, 7 and 8 are not factors. The next number to try is 9 but we already have 9 in the list of factors. You can stop when you reach a number that is already in the list.

b The prime factors of 48 are 2 and 3.

You only need to check prime numbers.
$48 = 2 \times 24$ 2 is a prime factor. 24 is not.
$48 = 3 \times 16$ 3 is a prime factor. 16 is not.
5 and 7 are not factors.
Because 7×7 is bigger than 48, you can stop there.

Worked example 1.2b

Find the LCM and HCF of 12 and 15.

The LCM is 60.

The multiples of 12 are 12, 24, 36, 48, [60], …, ….
The multiples of 15 are 15, 30, 45, [60], 75, …, …
60 is the first number that is in both lists.

The HCF is 3.

The factors of 12 are 1, 2, [3], 4, 6 and 12.
The factors of 15 are 1, [3], 5 and 15.
3 is the largest number that is in both lists.

Exercise 1.2

1 Find the factors of each number.
   a 20 b 27 c 75 d 23 e 100 f 98

2 Find the first four multiples of each number.
   a 8 b 15 c 7 d 20 e 33 f 100

3 Find the lowest common multiple of each pair of numbers.
   a 6 and 8 b 9 and 12 c 4 and 14
   d 20 and 30 e 8 and 32 f 7 and 11

4 The LCM of two numbers is 40. One of the numbers is 5. What is the other number?

5 Find:
   a the factors of 24 b the factors of 32 c the common factors of 24 and 32
   d the highest common factor of 24 and 32.

6 List the common factors of each pair of numbers.
   a 20 and 25 b 12 and 18 c 28 and 35
   d 8 and 24 e 21 and 32 f 19 and 31

7 Find the HCF of the numbers in each pair.
   a 8 and 10 b 18 and 24 c 40 and 50
   d 80 and 100 e 17 and 33 f 15 and 30

8 The HCF of two numbers is 8. One of the numbers is between 20 and 30. The other number is between 40 and 60. What are the two numbers?

9 31 is a prime number. What is the next prime after 31?

10 List the prime numbers between 60 and 70.

11 Read what Xavier and Alicia say about the number 91.

Who is correct? Give a reason for your answer.

12 73 and 89 are prime numbers. What is their highest common factor?

13 7 is a prime number. No multiple of 7, except 7 itself, can be a prime number. Explain why not.

14 List the prime factors of each number.
   a 12 b 15 c 21 d 49 e 30 f 77

15 a Write down three numbers whose only prime factor is 2.
   b Write down three numbers whose only prime factor is 3.
   c Write down three numbers whose only prime factor is 5.

16 Find a number bigger than 10 that has an odd number of factors.

17 Find a number that has three prime factors.

1.3 More about prime numbers

Any integer bigger than 1, that is not prime, can be written as a product of prime numbers.

Here are some examples.

$84 = 2 \times 2 \times 3 \times 7$ $\quad$ $45 = 3 \times 3 \times 5$ $\quad$ $196 = 2 \times 2 \times 7 \times 7$

You can use a **factor tree** to find and show factors.

This is how to draw a factor tree for 120.

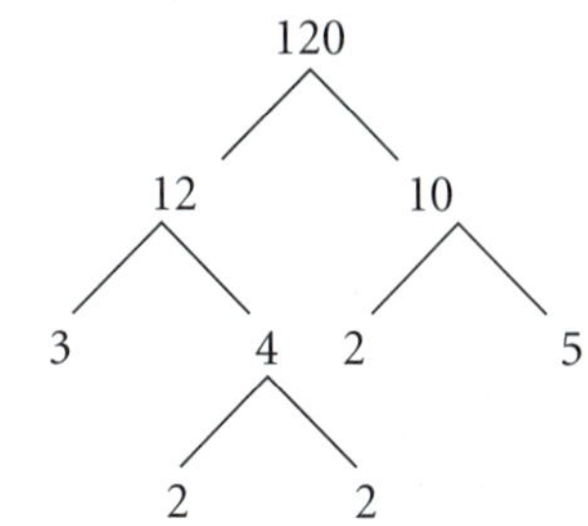

1 Draw branches to two numbers that multiply to make 120. Here 12 and 10 are chosen.
2 Do the same with 12 and 10. $12 = 3 \times 4$ and $10 = 2 \times 5$
3 3, 2 and 5 are prime, so stop.
4 $4 = 2 \times 2$ so draw two branches.
5 Stop, because all the end numbers are prime.
6 Multiply all the numbers at the ends of the branches.

   $120 = 2 \times 2 \times 2 \times 3 \times 5$

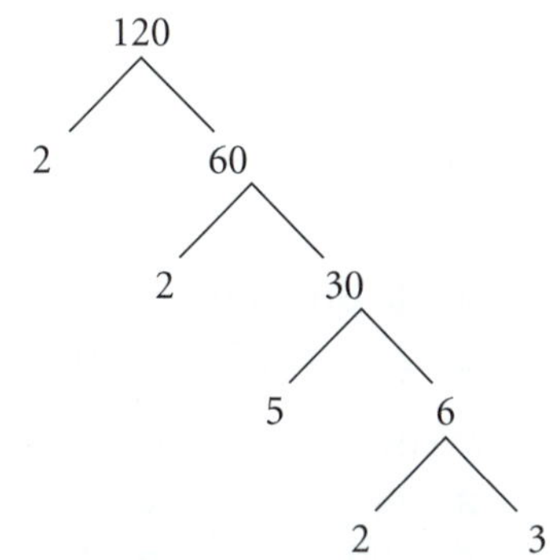

You can draw the tree in different ways.

Here is a different tree for 120.

The numbers at the ends of the branches are the same.

You can write the result like this. $\quad 120 = 2^3 \times 3 \times 5.$

The small number ^{3} next to the 2 is called an **index**. 2^3 means $2 \times 2 \times 2$.

Check that these are correct.

$60 = 2^2 \times 3 \times 5$ $\quad$ $75 = 3 \times 5^2$

You can use these expressions to find the LCM and HCF of 60 and 75.

For the LCM, take the larger frequency of each prime factor and multiply them all together.

LCM $= 2^2 \times 3 \times 5^2 = 4 \times 3 \times 25$

$= 300$

$60 = \boxed{2^2} \times \boxed{3} \times 5$

$75 = 3 \times \boxed{5^2}$

Two 2s, one 3, two 5s

For the HCF, take the smaller frequency of each prime factor that occurs in both numbers and multiply them all together.

HCF $= 3 \times 5$

$= 15$

$60 = 2^2 \times \boxed{3} \times \boxed{5}$

$75 = \boxed{3} \times 5^2$

No 2s, one 3, one 5

Exercise 1.3

1 Copy and complete each of these factor trees.

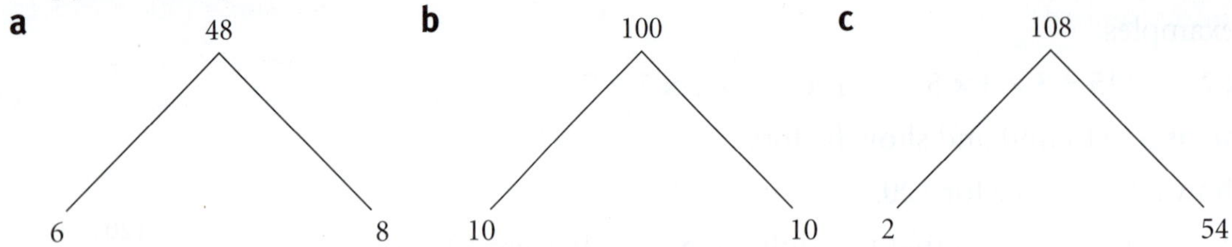

2 **a** Draw a <u>different</u> factor tree for each of the numbers in question **1**.
   b Write each of these numbers as a product of primes.
   i 48   **ii** 100   **iii** 108

3 Match each number to a product of primes.
One has been done for you.

20 • ———	• $2^2 \times 5$
24 •	• $2 \times 3 \times 7$
42 •	• $2^2 \times 3^2 \times 5$
50 •	• 2×5^2
180 •	• $2^3 \times 3$

4 Write down the number that is being represented.
   a $2^2 \times 3 \times 5$ **b** 2×3^3 **c** 3×11^2 **d** $2^3 \times 7^2$ **e** $2^4 \times 3^2$ **f** $5^2 \times 13$

5 Write each number as a product of primes.
   a 24   **b** 50   **c** 72
   d 200   **e** 165   **f** 136

You can use a factor tree to help you.

6 **a** Write each number as a product of primes.   **i** 45   **ii** 75
   b Find the LCM of 45 and 75.
   c Find the HCF of 45 and 75.

7 **a** Write each number as a product of primes.   **i** 90   **ii** 140
   b Find the LCM of 90 and 140.
   c Find the HCF of 90 and 140.

8 37 and 47 are prime numbers.
   a What is the HCF of 37 and 47?   **b** What is the LCM of 37 and 47?

1.4 Powers and roots

A number multiplied by itself several times is called a **power** of that number. You use **indices** to show powers.

> The plural of index is indices: one index, two indices.

Here are some powers of 5.

$5^2 = 5 \times 5 = 25$ This is five **squared** or the square of five.

$5^3 = 5 \times 5 \times 5 = 125$ This is five cubed or the **cube** of five.

$5^4 = 5 \times 5 \times 5 \times 5 = 625$ This is five to the power four.

$5^5 = 5 \times 5 \times 5 \times 5 \times 5 = 3125$ This is five to the power five.

The square of 5 is $5^2 = 25$.

Therefore the **square root** of 25 is 5 and you write this as $\sqrt{25} = 5$.

The cube of 5 is $5^3 = 125$.

Therefore the **cube root** of 125 is 5 and you write this as $\sqrt[3]{125} = 5$.

> $\sqrt{\ }$ means square root.
> $\sqrt[3]{\ }$ means cube root.

5 is not the only square root of 25.

$(-5)^2 = -5 \times -5 = 25$ so 25 has <u>two</u> square roots, 5 and -5.

$\sqrt{25}$ means the positive square root.

125 only has one integer cube root. -5 is <u>not</u> a cube root because $-5 \times -5 \times -5 = -125$.

Square numbers have square roots that are integers.

Examples: $13^2 = 169$ so $\sqrt{169} = 13$ $19^2 = 361$ so $\sqrt{361} = 19$

Try to memorise these five cubes and their corresponding cube roots:

$1^3 = 1$ so $\sqrt[3]{1} = 1$ $2^3 = 8$ so $\sqrt[3]{8} = 2$ $3^3 = 27$ so $\sqrt[3]{27} = 3$

$4^3 = 64$ so $\sqrt[3]{64} = 4$ $5^3 = 125$ so $\sqrt[3]{125} = 5$

Exercise 1.4

1 Find the value of each power.
a 3^2 **b** 3^3 **c** 3^4 **d** 3^5

2 Find the value of each power.
a 10^2 **b** 10^3 **c** 10^4

3 10^6 is one million and 10^9 is one billion.
Write down these two numbers in full.

> Over one billion people live in India.

4 In each pair, which of the two numbers is larger?
a 3^5 or 5^3 **b** 2^6 or 6^2 **c** 5^4 or 4^5

5 **a** N^3 is 27. What number is N?
b 6^M is 1296. What number is M?

6 Can you find two different integers, A and B, so that $A^B = B^A$?

7 Write down <u>two</u> square roots for each of these numbers.

a 9 **b** 36 **c** 81 **d** 196 **e** 225 **f** 400

8 Read what Maha says about her number. What could her number be?

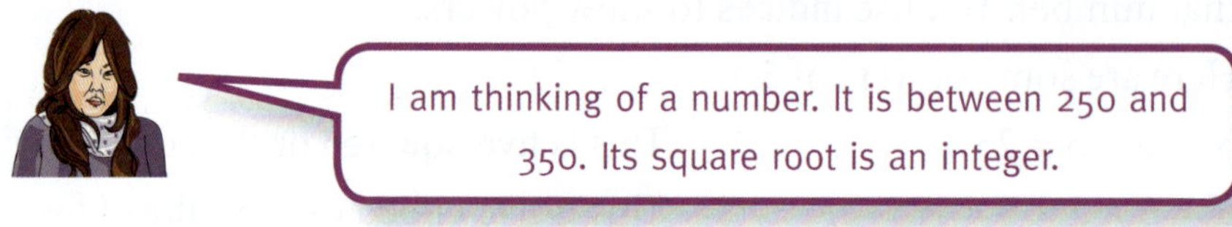

9 Read what Hassan says about his number. What is the largest possible value of his number?

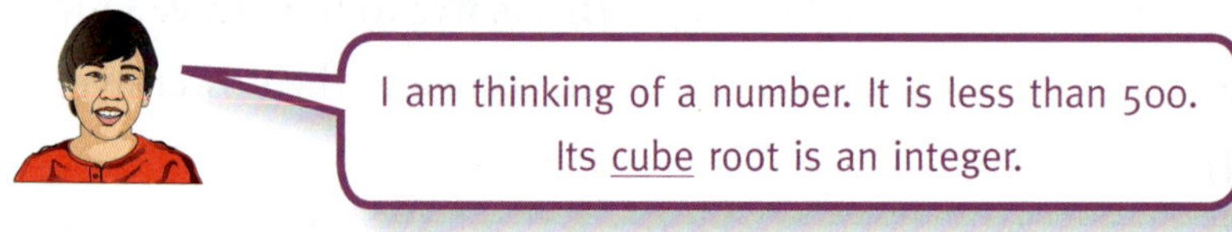

10 Find the value of each of these.

a $\sqrt{100}$ **b** $\sqrt{400}$ **c** $\sqrt[3]{27}$ **d** $\sqrt[3]{125}$ **e** $\sqrt[3]{1000}$

11 Read what Oditi says about her number. Find a possible value for her number.

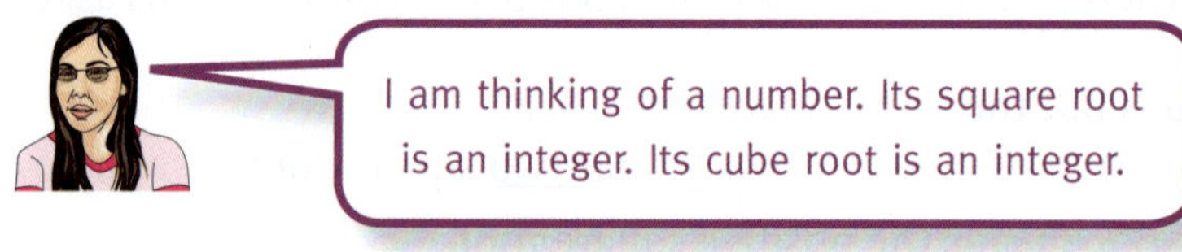

12 $2^{10} = 1024$. Use this fact to find:

a 2^{11} **b** 2^{12} **c** 2^9

13 **a** Find the value of each expression. **i** $1^3 + 2^3$ **ii** $\sqrt{1^3+2^3}$

b Find the value of $\sqrt{1^3+2^3+3^3}$. **c** Find the value of $\sqrt{1^3+2^3+3^3+4^3}$.

d Can you see an easy way to work out the value of $\sqrt{1^3+2^3+3^3+4^3+5^3}$? If so, describe it.

Summary

You should now know that:

- ★ You can multiply or divide two integers. If they have the same sign the answer is positive ($-5 \times -2 = 10$). If they have different signs the answer is negative ($-5 \times 2 = -10$).
- ★ You can subtract a negative number by adding the corresponding positive number.
- ★ You can find multiples of a number by multiplying by 1, 2, 3, etc.
- ★ Prime numbers have just two factors.
- ★ You can write every positive integer as a product of prime factors.
- ★ You can use the products of prime factors to find the lowest common factor and highest common multiple.
- ★ 5^4 means $5 \times 5 \times 5 \times 5$.
- ★ Positive integers have two square roots.
- ★ $\sqrt{49} = 7$ and $\sqrt[3]{64} = 4$.

You should be able to:

- ★ Add, subtract, multiply and divide integers.
- ★ Identify and use multiples and factors.
- ★ Identify and use primes.
- ★ Find common factors and highest common factors (HCF).
- ★ Find lowest common multiples (LCM).
- ★ Write a number in terms of its prime factors, for example, $500 = 2^2 \times 5^3$.
- ★ Calculate squares, positive and negative square roots, cubes and cube roots.
- ★ Use index notation for positive integer powers.
- ★ Calculate accurately, choosing operations and mental or written methods appropriate to the numbers and context.
- ★ Manipulate numbers and apply routine algorithms, for example, to find the HCF and LCM of two numbers.

End-of-unit review

1 Work these out.

a $5 + -3$ **b** $-3 - 5$ **c** $-8 + -7$ **d** $3 - 13$ **e** $-7 - 7$

2 Work these out.

a $2 - -5$ **b** $-3 - -4$ **c** $12 - -5$ **d** $-5 - -12$ **e** $-9 - -9$

3 Work these out.

a -3×-9 **b** $8 \div -4$ **c** -20×4 **d** $-30 \div -5$ **e** $-16 \div 8$

4 Copy and complete this multiplication table.

×	−2	3	5
−4			
−3			
6			30

5 Here is a number chain. Each number is the <u>product</u> of the previous two numbers.

$-1 \longrightarrow -2 \longrightarrow 2 \longrightarrow -4 \longrightarrow \square \longrightarrow \square$

Write down the next two numbers in the chain.

6 Find all the factors of each number.

a 42 **b** 52 **c** 55 **d** 29 **e** 64 **f** 69

7 **a** Find two prime numbers that add up to 40.

b Find another two prime numbers that add up to 40.

c Are there any more pairs of prime numbers that add up to 40? If so, what are they?

8 Write each of these numbers as a product of its prime factors.

a 18 **b** 96 **c** 200 **d** 240 **e** 135 **f** 175

9 Use your answers to question **8** to find:

a the highest common factor of 200 and 240

b the highest common factor of 135 and 175

c the lowest common multiple of 18 and 96

d the lowest common multiple of 200 and 240.

10 Find the square roots of each number.

a 25 **b** 81 **c** 169 **d** 256

11 Find the value of each number.

a $\sqrt{64}$ **b** $\sqrt[3]{64}$

12 In computing, 2^{10} is called 1K. Write down as a number:

a 1K **b** 2K **c** 4K.

13 **a** Read Shen's comment. What mistake has he made?

b Correct the statement.

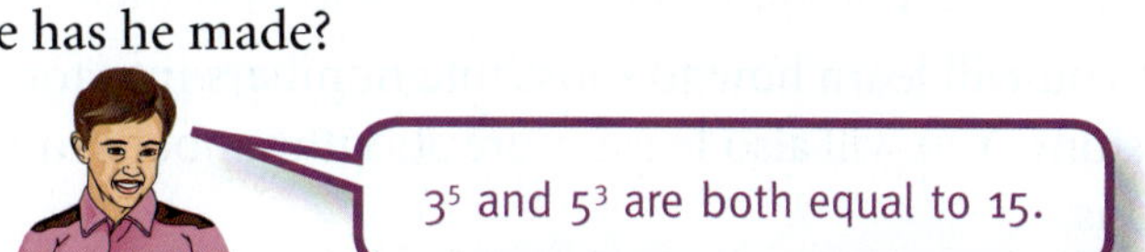

14 The HCF of two numbers is 6. The LCM is 72. One of the numbers is 24.
Find a possible value of the other number.

2 Sequences, expressions and formulae

A formula is a set of instructions for working something out. It is a rule that can be written as letters or in words. The plural of formula is formulae.

People use formulae in everyday life to work out all sorts of things.

An employer may use a formula to work out how much to pay the people who work for them.

They could use a formula such as $P = R \times H$, where P is the pay, R is the amount paid per hour and H is the number of hours worked.

Key words

Make sure you learn and understand these key words:

- linear sequence
- term-to-term rule
- position-to-term rule
- nth term
- function
- function machine
- input
- output
- mapping diagram
- map
- algebraically
- equation
- expression
- variable
- linear expression
- formula (formulae)
- derive

Engineers may use a formula to work out the time it takes for a car to accelerate from one speed to another.

They could use the formula $t = \frac{v-u}{a}$, where t is the time, v is the finishing speed, u is the starting speed and a is the acceleration.

Doctors may use a formula to work out how healthy a person is. They could use the formula for finding the person's body mass index (BMI).

The formula is: $\text{BMI} = \frac{\text{mass}}{\text{height}^2}$, where the person's mass is measured in kilograms and their height is measured in metres.

If a person's BMI is too high or too low the doctor may ask them to lose some weight, or put some on, to make them healthier.

In this unit you will learn how to substitute numbers into formulae and expressions. You will also learn more about number sequences and functions.

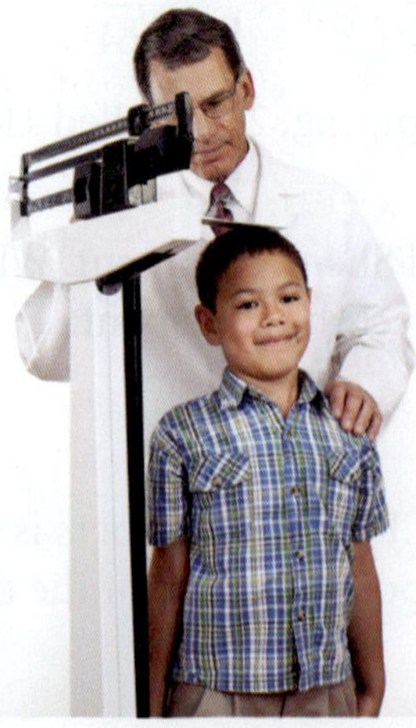

2.1 Generating sequences

This is a sequence of numbers. 5 7 9 11 13 … …

This is a **linear sequence** because the terms in the sequence increase by the same amount each time. Each term is 2 more than the term before, so the **term-to-term rule** is 'add 2'.

In a linear sequence the terms in the sequence can increase **or** decrease by the same amount each time.

You can also use a **position-to-term rule** to describe a sequence.

Position number	1	2	3	4	5
Term	5	7	9	11	13

This table shows the position number of each term in the sequence. The position-to-term rule for this sequence is:
term = 2 × position number + 3

Examples: 3rd term = 2 × 3 + 3 = 6 + 3 = 9 ✓
5th term = 2 × 5 + 3 = 10 + 3 = 13 ✓

Check that this rule works by substituting numbers into the rule.

Worked example 2.1

a The first term of a sequence is 4. The term-to-term rule of the sequence is 'subtract 3'. Write down the first three terms of the sequence.

b The position-to-term rule of a sequence is: term = 4 × position number + 1. Work out the first three terms of the sequence.

a First three terms are 4, 1, −2. Write down the first term, which is 4, then use the term-to-term rule to work out the second and third terms.
2nd term = 4 − 3 = 1, 3rd term = 1 − 3 = −2.

b First three terms are 5, 9, 13. Use the position-to-term rule to work out each term.
1st term = 4 × 1 + 1 = 5, 2nd term = 4 × 2 + 1 = 9,
3rd term = 4 × 3 + 1 = 13.

Exercise 2.1

1 Write down the first three terms of each sequence.
- **a** first term: 1 term-to-term rule: 'add 5'
- **b** first term: 20 term-to-term rule: 'subtract 4'
- **c** first term: 2 term-to-term rule: 'add 12'
- **d** first term: 6 term-to-term rule: 'subtract 5'
- **e** first term: −5 term-to-term rule: 'add 2'
- **f** first term: −3 term-to-term rule: 'subtract 6'

2 The first term of a sequence is 15. The term-to-term rule is add 7.
What is the fifth term of the sequence? Explain how you worked out your answer.

3 This is part of Zalika's homework.

a Is Zalika's answer correct?

b Explain how her method works.

c The first term of a sequence is 5.
The term-to-term rule is 'add 8'.
Use Zalika's method to work out:

i the 10th term **ii** the 20th term

iii the 50th term of the sequence.

> *Question* The first term of a sequence is 3.
> The term-to-term rule is 'add 12'.
> Work out the 10th term of the sequence.
>
> *Answer* $10 - 1 = 9$, $9 \times 12 = 108$
> $3 + 108 = 111$ 10th term = 111

4 Ahmad is trying to solve this problem.
Work out the answer to the problem.
Explain how you solved the problem.

> The fourth term of a sequence is 39.
> The term-to-term rule is 'add 7'.
> Work out the first term of the sequence.

5 Mia is trying to solve this problem.
Work out the answer to the problem.
Explain how you solved the problem.

> The 12th term of a sequence is 16.
> The term-to-term rule is 'subtract 3'.
> Work out the third term of the sequence.

6 The table shows two of the terms in a sequence.
Position-to-term rule: term = position number + 7
Copy the table. Use the position-to-term rule to work out the missing numbers.

Position number	1	2	3	4	5	10	20
Term		9				17	

7 Use the position-to-term rule to work out the first four terms of each sequence.

a term = 6 × position number **b** term = position number − 4

c term = 2 × position number + 1 **d** term = 3 × position number − 1

8 Use the position-to-term rules to work out:

i the 10th term **ii** the 20th term **iii** the 100th term of each sequence.

a term = position number + 5 **b** term = 2 × position number

c term = 4 × position number + 8 **d** term = 5 × position number − 25

9 The fourth term of a sequence is 11. The seventh term of the sequence is 20.
Which of these position-to-term rules is the correct one for the sequence?

A term = position number + 7 **B** term = 2 × position number + 3

C term = 3 × position number − 1 **D** term = 4 × position number − 5

Show how you worked out your answer.

10 This is part of Razi's homework.

> *Question* The position-to-term rule of a sequence is:
> term = 3 × position number + 2
> Work out the first three terms of the sequence.
>
> *Answer* 1st term = $3 \times 1 + 2 = 5$ 2nd term = $3 \times 5 + 2 = 17$
> 3rd term = $3 \times 17 + 2 = 53$

Is Razi's homework correct? Explain your answer.

2.2 Finding rules for sequences

This sequence of patterns is made from dots.

The numbers of dots used to make the patterns form the sequence 5, 7, 9, …, …

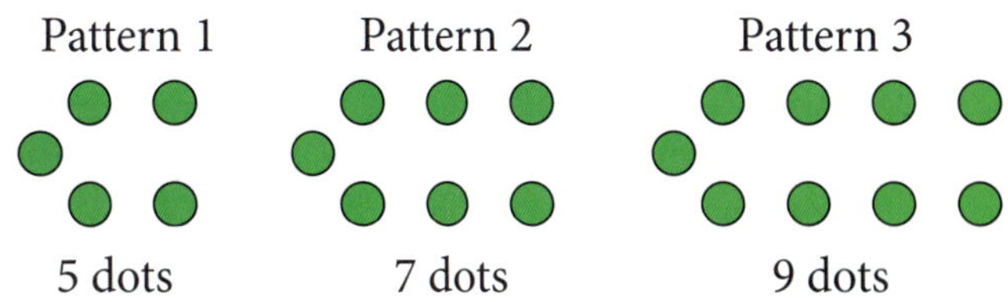

As you go from one pattern to the next, two more dots are added each time. The term-to-term rule is 'add 2'.

You can use the term-to-term rule to work out the position-to-term rule.

The term-to-term rule for this sequence is 'add 2', so start by listing the first three multiples of 2 and compare them with the patterns of dots.

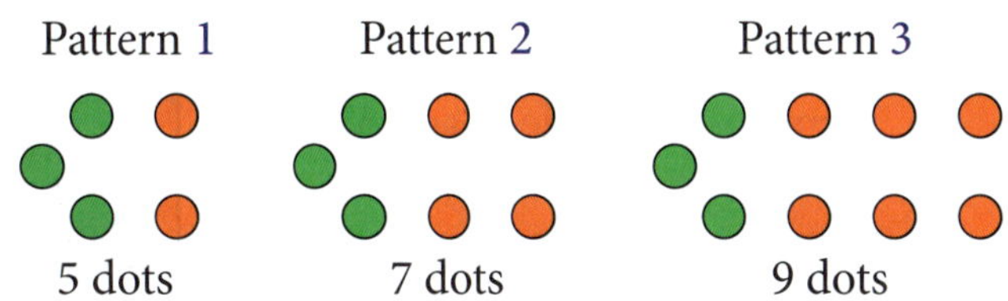

Multiples of 2: $1 \times 2 = 2$ $2 \times 2 = 4$ $3 \times 2 = 6$
Number of dots: $2 + 3 = 5$ $4 + 3 = 7$ $6 + 3 = 9$

The pattern is formed by adding multiples of 2, shown as red dots, to the three green dots at the start of each pattern.

The position-to-term rule for this sequence is:

term = 2 × position number + 3

Draw the next pattern, to check.

Pattern 4: term = $2 \times 4 + 3 = 11$ ✓

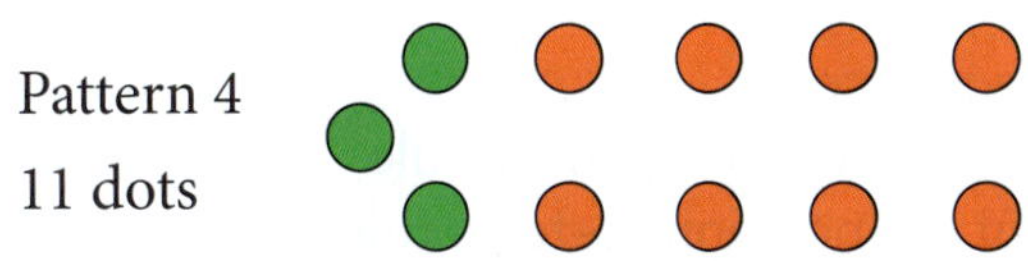

Worked example 2.2

For each sequence: **i** write down the term-to-term rule **ii** work out the position-to-term rule.

a 3, 6, 9, 12, …, … **b** 5, 9, 13, 17, …, …

a **i** Term-to-term rule is 'add 3'.

The numbers in the sequence are increasing by 3 each time.

ii

Position number	1	2	3	4
Term	3	6	9	12
Multiples of 3	3	6	9	12

Start by writing the sequence of numbers in a table. The term-to-term rule is 'add 3', so write down the first four multiples of 3. The sequence matches exactly the multiples of 3.

Position-to-term rule is:
term = 3 × position number.

Check that the rule works for the first few terms:
1st term = $3 \times 1 = 3$, 2nd term = $3 \times 2 = 6$, 3rd term = $3 \times 3 = 9$.

b **i** Term-to-term rule is 'add 4'.

The numbers in the sequence are increasing by 4 each time.

ii

Position number	1	2	3	4
Term	5	9	13	17
Multiples of 4	4	8	12	16

Start by writing the sequence of numbers in a table. The term-to-term rule is 'add 4', so write down the first four multiples of 4. Each term in the sequence is one more than a multiple of 4.

Position-to-term rule is:
term = 4 × position number + 1.

Check that your rule works for the first few terms:
1st term = $4 \times 1 + 1 = 5$, 2nd term = $4 \times 2 + 1 = 9$,
3rd term = $4 \times 3 + 1 = 13$.

Exercise 2.2

1 Copy and complete the working to find the position-to-term rule for each sequence.

a 6, 7, 8, 9, …, …
Term-to-term rule is 'add 1'.
Position-to-term rule is:
term = position number + □

Position number	1	2	3	4
Term	6	7	8	9
Multiples of 1	1	2	□	□

term = 1 × position number + □
can be written as:
term = position number + □

b 1, 4, 7, 10, …, …
Term-to-term rule is 'add 3'.
Position-to-term rule is:
term = 3 × position number − □

Position number	1	2	3	4
Term	1	4	7	10
Multiples of 3	3	6	□	□

2 For each sequence of numbers:
i write down the term-to-term rule
ii write the sequence of numbers in a table
iii work out the position-to-term rule
iv check your rule works for the first three terms.

a 2, 4, 6, 8, …, … **b** 5, 10, 15, 20, …, … **c** 5, 8, 11, 14, …, …
d 6, 8, 10, 12, …, … **e** 7, 11, 15, 19, …, … **f** 7, 12, 17, 22, …, …

3 For each sequence:
i write down the term-to-term rule
ii write the sequence of numbers in a table
iii work out the position-to-term rule
iv check your rule works for the first three terms.

a 4, 5, 6, 7, …, … **b** 10, 11, 12, 13, …, … **c** 24, 25, 26, 27, …, …
d 1, 3, 5, 7, …, … **e** 2, 6, 10, 14, …, … **f** 2, 7, 12, 17, …, …

4 This pattern is made from blue squares.

Pattern 1 Pattern 2 Pattern 3 Pattern 4

a Write down the sequence of the numbers of blue squares.
b Write down the term-to-term rule.
c Explain how the sequence is formed.
d Work out the position-to-term rule.

5 This is part of Harsha's homework.
a Explain the mistake that she has made.
b Work out the correct answer.

Question Work out the position-to-term rule for this sequence of triangles.

Pattern 1 Pattern 2 Pattern 3

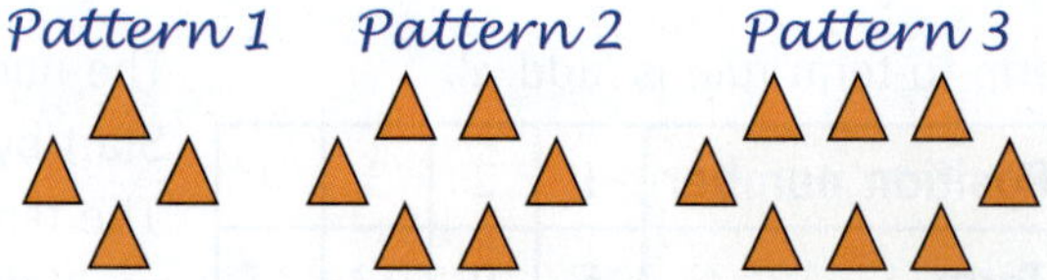

Answer The sequence starts with 4 and increases by 2 every time, so the position-to-term rule is:
term = 4 × position number + 2

2.3 Using the *n*th term

You already know how to work out the position-to-term rule of a linear sequence.

Example: The sequence $5, 7, 9, 11, \ldots, \ldots$
has position-to-term rule: term = $2 \times$ position number + 3

You can also write the position-to-term rule called the **nth term**.

To do this, you replace the words 'position number' with the letter n.

n stands for the term number.

So, in the example above,
instead of writing term = $2 \times$ position number + 3
you write: nth term is $2 \times n + 3$
or simply: nth term is $2n + 3$

$2 \times n$ is usually written as $2n$.

Worked example 2.3

The nth term of a sequence is $2n - 1$. Work out the first three terms and the ninth term of the sequence.

1st term = $2 \times 1 - 1 = 1$	To find the first term, substitute $n = 1$ into the expression.
2nd term = $2 \times 2 - 1 = 3$	To find the second term, substitute $n = 2$ into the expression.
3rd term = $2 \times 3 - 1 = 5$	To find the third term, substitute $n = 3$ into the expression.
9th term = $2 \times 9 - 1 = 17$	To find the ninth term, substitute $n = 9$ into the expression.

Exercise 2.3

1 Work out the first three terms and the 10th term of the sequences with the given nth term.

a $n + 6$ **b** $n - 3$ **c** $4n$ **d** $6n$
e $2n + 5$ **f** $3n - 1$ **g** $5n + 3$ **h** $4n - 3$

2 This pattern is made from pink squares.

Pattern 1 Pattern 2 Pattern 3 Pattern 4

a Write down the sequence of the numbers of pink squares.
b Write down the term-to-term rule.
c Explain how the sequence is formed.
d Work out the position-to-term rule.
e Copy and complete the working to show that the nth term is $3n + 1$.

first term = $3 \times 1 + 1 = 4$ second term = $3 \times \square + 1 = \square$
third term = $3 \times \square + 1 = \square$ fourth term = $3 \times \square + 1 = \square$

3 This pattern is made from dots.

Pattern 1 Pattern 2 Pattern 3 Pattern 4

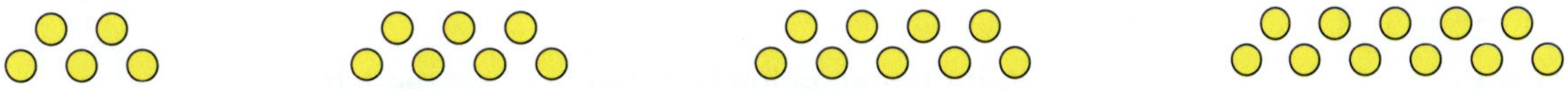

Hassan thinks that the nth term for the sequence of numbers of dots is $2n + 3$.
Is Hassan correct? Explain how you worked out your answer.

2.4 Using functions and mappings

A **function** is a relationship between two sets of numbers.

You can draw a function as a **function machine**, like this.

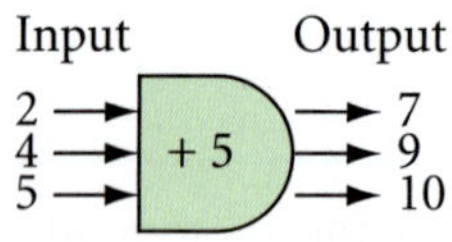

The numbers that go into the function machine are called the **input**.

The numbers that come out of the function machine are called the **output**.

You can also draw a function as a **mapping diagram**, like this.

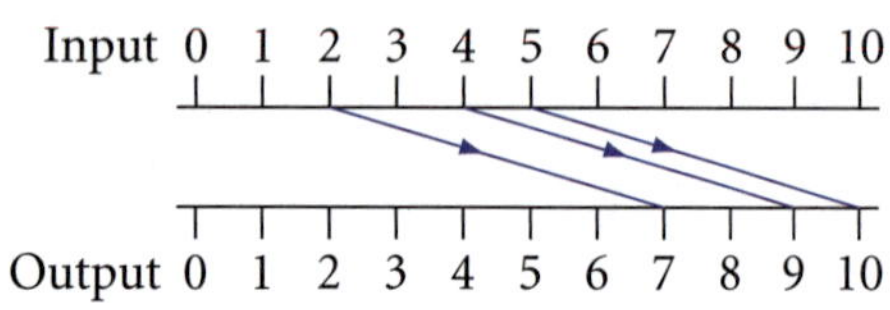

The input numbers **map** to the output numbers.

You can write a function **algebraically** as an **equation**.
Use the letter x to represent the input numbers.
Use the letter y to represent the output numbers.
You can then show the function machine above like this.

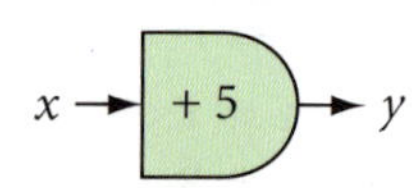

You can write the input (x) and output (y) numbers in a table.

x	2	4	5
y	7	9	10

You can also write the function as an equation like this: $x + 5 = y$

but it is more common to write the equation like this: $y = x + 5$

You usually write a function equation starting with $y = ...$

Worked example 2.4

a Copy and complete the table of values for this function machine.

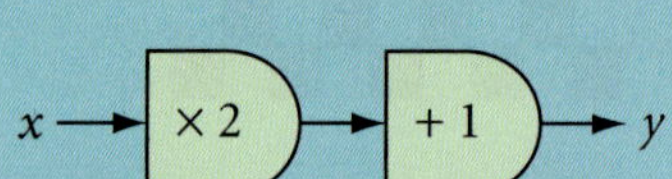

x	1	2	3	4
y				

b Draw a mapping diagram to show the function in part **a**.

c Write the function in part **a** as an equation.

a

x	1	2	3	4
y	3	5	7	9

To work out the y-values, <u>multiply</u> the x-values by 2 then <u>add</u> 1.
$1 \times 2 + 1 = 3$, $2 \times 2 + 1 = 5$, $3 \times 2 + 1 = 7$, $4 \times 2 + 1 = 9$

b

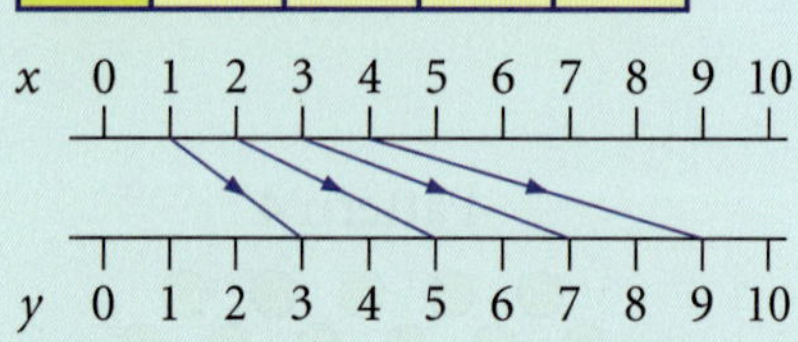

Draw a line connecting each x-value to its y-value.
Draw an arrow on each line to show that 1 maps to 3, 2 maps to 5, 3 maps to 7 and 4 maps to 9.

c $y = 2x + 1$

Write the equation with the '$y =$' on the left.
Remember that you can write $2 \times x + 1$ simply as $2x + 1$.

Exercise 2.4

1 **a** Copy and complete the table of values for each function machine.

i $x \rightarrow$ [+ 3] $\rightarrow y$

x	1	2	3	4
y				

ii $x \rightarrow$ [− 3] $\rightarrow y$

x	4	5	6	7
y				

b Draw a mapping diagram for each function in part **a**.

c Write each function in part **a** as an equation.

2 **a** Copy and complete the table of values for each function machine.

i $x \rightarrow$ [× 2] $\rightarrow$ [+ 3] $\rightarrow y$

x	1	2	4	
y				15

ii $x \rightarrow$ [× 3] $\rightarrow$ [− 1] $\rightarrow y$

x	3	5		12
y			26	

iii $x \rightarrow$ [÷ 2] $\rightarrow$ [+ 5] $\rightarrow y$

x	4		10	
y		9		15

iv $x \rightarrow$ [÷ 2] $\rightarrow$ [− 3] $\rightarrow y$

x	2		8	
y		−1		4

b Write each function in part **a** as an equation.

When you are given a y-value and need to work out the x-value you must work backwards through the function machine. For example, in part 2(a)(i) we are given $y = 15$ and a function machine that tells us to multiply x by 2, then add 3. So, working backwards we would subtract 3 from 15 to give 12. Then divide 12 by 2.

3 **a** Work out the rule for each function machine.

i x: 2, 6, 10 $\rightarrow$ [...] $\rightarrow$ y: 10, 14, 18

ii x: 3, 5, 8 $\rightarrow$ [...] $\rightarrow$ y: 15, 25, 40

b Write each function in part **a** as an equation.

4 Mia and Razi are looking at this function machine.

x: 4, 6, 9 $\rightarrow$ [...] $\rightarrow$ [...] $\rightarrow$ y: 13, 21, 33

I think the equation for this function is $y = 3x + 1$.

I think the equation for this function is $y = 4x - 3$.

Which of them is correct? Explain your answer.

5 Work out the equation for this function machine.

x: 1, 2, 3 $\rightarrow$ [...] $\rightarrow$ [...] $\rightarrow$ y: 5, 8, 11

Explain how you worked out your answer.

2.5 Constructing linear expressions

You can write an algebraic **expression** by using a letter to represent an unknown number.
The letter is called the **variable**.

Example: Let n represent a mystery number.
You write the number that is five more than the mystery number as $n + 5$ or $5 + n$.
You write the number that is three times the mystery number as $3 \times n$ or simply $3n$.
You write the mystery number multiplied by itself as $n \times n$ or simply n^2.

$n + 5$ and $3n$ are called **linear expressions** because the variable is only multiplied by a number.

> $n + 5$ is the same as $1 \times n + 5$.

n^2 is not a linear expression because the variable is being multiplied by itself.

Worked example 2.5

Tyler thinks of a number, x. Write down an expression for the number Tyler gets when he:

a subtracts 5 from the number
b doubles the number and adds 3
c divides the number by 3 and adds 2
d adds 2 to the number then multiplies by 4.

a $x - 5$ Subtract 5 from x.
b $2x + 3$ Multiply x by 2, then add 3. Write $2 \times x$ as $2x$.
c $\frac{x}{3} + 2$ Divide x by 3 then add 2. Write $x \div 3$ as $\frac{x}{3}$.
d $4(x + 2)$ Add 2 to x, then multiply the answer by 4. Write $x + 2$ in brackets to show this must be done before multiplying by 4.

Exercise 2.5

1 Tanesha has a box that contains x DVDs.
Write an expression for the total number of DVDs she has in the box when:

> In each part of the question she starts with x DVDs.

a she takes 7 out
b she puts in 8 more
c she takes out half of them
d she doubles the number in the box and adds an extra 1.

2 Jake thinks of a number, n.
Write an expression for the number Jake gets when he:
a multiplies the number by 6 then adds 1
b divides the number by 4 then adds 5
c multiplies the number by 2 then subtracts 3
d divides the number by 10 then adds 7.

3 The price of one bag of cement is $\$c$.
The price of one bag of gravel is $\$g$.
The price of one bag of sand is $\$s$.
Write an expression for the total cost of:
a one bag of cement and three bags of sand
b three bags of cement, four bags of gravel and 6 bags of sand.

4 Alicia thinks of a number, n. She subtracts 3 then multiplies the result by 2.
Which of these expressions is the correct expression for Alicia's number? Explain your answer.

A $n - 3 \times 2$ **B** $n - 6$ **C** $2(n - 3)$ **D** $3 - n \times 2$ **E** $2(3 - n)$

2.6 Deriving and using formulae

A **formula** is a mathematical rule that shows the relationship between two or more quantities (variables). It is a rule that can be written in letters or words. The plural of formula is **formulae**.

You can write, or **derive**, your own formulae to help you solve problems.

When you substitute numbers into formulae and expressions, remember the order of operations, BIDMAS. Brackets and Indices must be worked out before Divisions and Multiplications. Additions and Subtractions are always worked out last.

> Examples of indices are 2^2, 5^2, 4^3 and 7^3.

Worked example 2.6

a Work out the value of the expression $2x + 4y$ when $x = 5$ and $y = -2$.
b Work out the value of the expression $3x^2 + 4$ when $x = 10$.
c Write a formula for the number of hours in any number of days, using: **i** words **ii** letters.
d Use the formula in part **c** to work out the number of hours in 7 days.

a $2 \times 5 + 4 \times -2$	Substitute $x = 5$ and $y = -2$ into the expression.
$= 10 + -8$	Work out 2×5 and 4×-2.
$= 10 - 8 = 2$	Adding -8 is the same as subtracting 8.
b $3 \times 10^2 + 4$	Substitute $x = 10$ into the expression.
$= 3 \times 100 + 4$	Work out 10^2 first.
$= 300 + 4 = 304$	Work out the multiplication before the addition.
c **i** hours = 24 × days	There are 24 hours in every day.
ii $h = 24d$	Use h for hours and d for days.
d $h = 24 \times 7 = 168$	Substitute $d = 7$ into the formula and work out the value of h.

Exercise 2.6

1 Work out the value of each expression for the given values.

a $p + 5$ when $p = -3$
b $q - 6$ when $q = 4$
c $6h$ when $h = -3$
d $\frac{j}{4}$ when $j = -20$
e $a + b$ when $a = 6$ and $b = -3$
f $c - d$ when $c = 25$ and $d = 32$
g $8m - 5$ when $m = -2$
h $3z + v$ when $z = 8$ and $v = -20$
i $2x + 3y$ when $x = 4$ and $y = 5$
j $20 - 3n$ when $n = 9$
k $\frac{u}{2} - 5$ when $u = 4$
l $\frac{p}{5} + \frac{q}{2}$ when $p = 30$ and $q = -8$

2 Work out the value of each expression.

a $x^2 + 5$ when $x = 4$
b $10 - y^2$ when $y = 5$
c $g^2 + h^2$ when $g = 3$ and $h = 6$
d $m^2 - n^2$ when $m = 7$ and $n = 8$
e $4k^2$ when $k = 2$
f $2d^2 + 1$ when $d = 5$
g r^3 when $r = 1$
h $2y^3$ when $y = 3$
i $x^3 - 5$ when $x = 2$
j $20 - w^3$ when $w = 4$
k $\frac{y^2}{2}$ when $y = 4$
l $\frac{p^3}{5}$ when $p = 10$

> Remember that r^3 means $r \times r \times r$.

3 This is part of Dakarai's homework.
He has made a mistake in his working.

a Explain the mistake that he has made.
b Work out the correct answer for him.
c Work out the value of $y^2 + 4$ when $y = -5$.

Question: Work out the value of $x^2 - 8$ when $x = -3$.

Answer: $x^2 - 8 = (-3)^2 - 8$
$= -3 \times -3 - 8$
$= -9 - 8$
$= -17$

4 This is part of Oditi's homework. She has made a mistake in her working.

a Explain the mistake that she has made.
b Work out the correct answer.
c Work out the value of $2y^3$ when $y = -3$.

Question: Work out the value of $5x^3$ when $x = -2$.

Answer: $5x^3 = 5 \times (-2)^3$
$= (-10)^3$
$= -10 \times -10 \times -10$
$= -1000$

5 **a** Write a formula for the number of months in any number of years, in:
i words **ii** letters.
b Use your formula in part **a** to work out the number of months in 8 years.

6 Use the formula $v = u + 10t$ to work out the value of v when:
a $u = 5$ and $t = 12$ **b** $u = 8$ and $t = 15$ **c** $u = 0$ and $t = 20$.

7 Use the formula $F = ma$ to work out F when:
a $m = 6$ and $a = 2$ **b** $m = 18$ and $a = 3$ **c** $m = 8$ and $a = -4$

8 In the UK the height of a horse is measured in hands (H) and inches (I).
Sasha has a horse with a height of 16 hands and 1 inch. She uses the formula to work out the height of her horse, in centimetres.

$C = 2.5(4H + I)$ where: C is the number of centimetres
H is the number of hands
I is the number of inches.

$C = 2.5(4 \times 16 + 1)$
$= 2.5(64 + 1)$
$= 2.5 \times 65$
$= 162.5$ cm

Work out the height, in centimetres, of a horse with height:
a 14 hands and 2 inches **b** 15 hands and 3 inches
c 13 hands and 1 inch **d** 17 hands and 2 inches
e 16 hands **f** 12 hands.

16 hands exactly means 16 hands and 0 inches.

9 Xavier uses this formula to work out the volume of a triangular prism.

$V = \frac{bhl}{2}$ where: V is the volume
b is the base
h is the height
l is the length.

Remember that bhl means $b \times h \times l$.

Xavier compares two prisms. Prism A has a base of 8 cm, height of 5 cm and length of 18 cm.
Prism B has a base of 9 cm, height of 14 cm and length of 6 cm.

Which prism has the larger volume? How much larger is it?

10 a Shen uses this formula to convert temperatures in degrees Celsius (°C) to degrees Fahrenheit (°F).

$C = 0.6F - 17.8$	where: C is the temperature in °C F is the temperature in °F.

Use the formula to work out the temperature in °C when the temperature in °F is:
i 20°F **ii** 45°F **iii** 82°F.

b Anders knows this relationship between temperatures in °F and temperatures in °C.

$9C = 5F - 160$	where: F is the temperature in °F C is the temperature in °C.

Anders wants to know the temperature in °F when the temperature is 4°C.
This is what he writes.

9C = 5F - 160
Substitute C = 4: *9 × 4 = 5F - 160*
Simplify: *36 = 5F - 160*

Anders now has to solve the equation $36 = 5F - 160$.
Work out the equation that Anders needs to solve when the temperature in °C is:
i 6°C **ii** 18°C **iii** 30°C.

Summary

You should now know that:

★ In a linear sequence the terms increase or decrease by the same amount each time.

★ A sequence can be described using a term-to-term rule and a position-to-term rule.

★ The position-to-term rule of a sequence can be written as an expression called the nth term.

★ A function can be shown as a function machine, as a mapping diagram or written algebraically as an equation.

★ When you write a function as an equation, you usually use the letter x to represent the input numbers and the letter y to represent the output numbers.

★ In algebra you use a letter to stand for an unknown number. The letter is called the variable.

★ A linear expression is where the variable is multiplied by a number only. If the variable is multiplied by itself, it is not a linear expression.

★ You can write or derive a formula to help you solve problems.

You should be able to:

★ Generate terms of a linear sequence using term-to-term and position-to-term rules.

★ Find term-to-term and position-to-term rules of sequences, including patterns.

★ Use a linear expression to describe the nth term of a simple sequence.

★ Express simple functions algebraically and represent them in mappings.

★ Know that letters play different roles in equations, formulae and functions.

★ Construct linear expressions.

★ Derive and use simple formulae.

★ Substitute positive and negative integers into expressions and formulae.

★ Use the order of operations (BIDMAS), including brackets, with more complex calculations.

★ Manipulate numbers and algebraic expressions, and apply routine algorithms.

★ Use logical argument to establish the truth of a statement.

End-of-unit review

1 Write down the first three terms of each of the sequences described.
- **a** first term is 7, term-to-term rule is 'add 3'
- **b** first term is 11, term-to-term rule is 'subtract 5'
- **c** position-to-term rule is term = 8 × position number
- **d** position-to-term rule is term = 4 × position number − 3

2 The third term of a sequence is 9. The eighth term of the sequence is 19.
Which of these position-to-term rules is the correct one for the sequence?
Show how you worked out your answer.

A term = position number + 9	**B** term = 2 × position number + 3
C term = 3 × position number	**D** term = 4 × position number − 3

3 For each sequence of numbers:
- **i** write down the term-to-term rule
- **ii** write the sequence of numbers in a table
- **iii** work out the position-to-term rule
- **iv** check your rule works for the first three terms.

a 6, 12, 18, 24, … … **b** 6, 11, 16, 21, … … **c** 8, 9, 10, 11, … …

4 This pattern is made from dots.

Pattern 1 Pattern 2 Pattern 3 Pattern 4

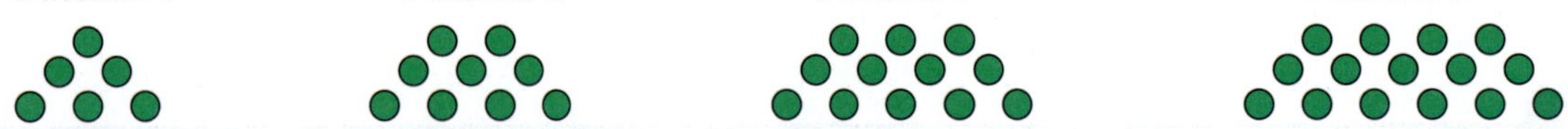

Alicia thinks that the nth term for the sequence of numbers of dots is $3n + 3$.
Is Alicia correct? Explain how you worked out your answer.

5 **a** Copy and complete the table of values for each function machine.

i

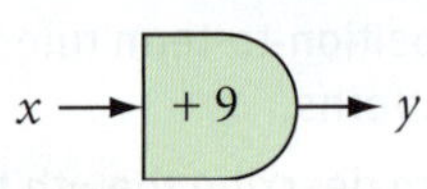

x	1	2		8
y			14	

ii

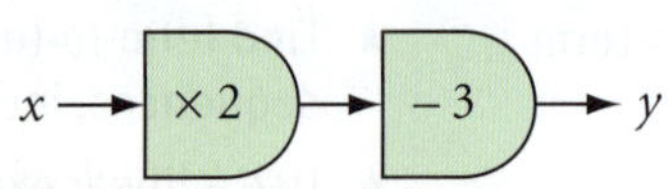

x	1	2		
y			7	19

b Write each of the functions in part **a** as an equation.

6 Ahmad thinks of a number, x. Write an expression for the number Ahmad gets when he:
- **a** multiplies the number by 4
- **b** multiplies the number by 2 then adds 7
- **c** divides the number by 3 then subtracts 10
- **d** adds 4 to the number then multiplies by 5.

7 Work out the value of each expression.
- **a** $x + 7$ when $x = -12$
- **b** $3x - 4y$ when $x = 2$ and $y = 7$
- **c** $3n + 1$ when $n = -6$
- **d** $30 - 5k$ when $k = -2$
- **e** $x^2 - 10$ when $x = 3$
- **f** $4y^3$ when $y = 2$

8 Use the formula $P = mgh$ to work out P when $m = 5$, $g = 10$ and $h = 3$.

9 Zalika uses the formula $v^2 = u^2 + 2as$.
When she substitutes $v = 4$, $u = 3$ and $a = 7$ into the formula she gets the equation $8 = 6 + 14s$.
Is Zalika correct? Show how you worked out your answer.

3 Place value, ordering and rounding

We use numbers every day, but we do not always need them to be exact. Numbers are often rounded. This is because it is easier to work with rounded numbers and compare them.

You can usually round numbers when exact accuracy isn't important. For example, look at these two newspaper articles.

Key words

Make sure you learn and understand these key words:

- powers of 10
- power
- index
- round
- degree of accuracy
- equivalent calculation
- approximate

Real Madrid take the top spot!

On Saturday afternoon 74 836 football fans saw Real Madrid beat FC Barcelona by 2 goals to take the top spot in La Liga (Spain's top football league).

Real Madrid take the top spot!

On Saturday afternoon 75 000 football fans saw Real Madrid beat FC Barcelona by 2 goals to take the top spot in La Liga (Spain's top football league).

The first article gives the accurate number of football fans, 74 836. The second article rounds the number to 75 000. This means the second article is easier to read, and it really isn't important to the story whether 74 836 or 75 000 football fans were there to watch the game.

For market research, companies usually use accurate numbers in their calculations. They will generally round their answers to give final figures that are easier to compare.

For example, a mobile phone company may look at the population figures of different countries and the numbers of mobile phones used in those countries. They may use these figures to help them decide how to increase sales of mobile phones or to decide whether more network coverage is needed.

Look at this information about Bangladesh and Hong Kong.

Bangladesh
Population: 158 570 535
Number of mobile phones: 74 192 350
Number of mobile phones per person: 0.467 882...

Hong Kong
Population: 7 122 508
Number of mobile phones: 13 264 896
Number of mobile phones per person: 1.862 391...

Even though Bangladesh has a much bigger population than Hong Kong, when you compare the number of mobile phones per person, you can see that there are more mobile phones per person in Hong Kong than Bangladesh.

You can round both the decimal numbers that have been calculated and say that there are approximately 0.5 mobile phones per person in Bangladesh compared with about 2 mobile phones per person in Hong Kong.

In this unit you will learn more about rounding. You will also learn about calculating with decimal numbers, as well as estimating and approximating.

3.1 Multiplying and dividing by 0.1 and 0.01

The numbers 10, 100, 1000, 10 000, … can all be written as **powers of 10**.

The **power** of 10 is written as an **index**. This is the number of 10s that you multiply together to get the number. It is also the same as the number of zeros that follow the digit 1.

Look at this pattern of numbers.

$10 = 10^1$	10 is ten to the power of 1, or simply 10.
$100 = 10 \times 10 = 10^2$	100 is ten to the power of 2, or 10 squared.
$1000 = 10 \times 10 \times 10 = 10^3$	1000 is ten to the power of 3, or 10 cubed.
$10\,000 = 10 \times 10 \times 10 \times 10 = 10^4$	10 000 is ten to the power of 4.

This pattern carries on as the numbers get bigger and bigger.

Worked example 3.1a

a Write 10^6 in: **i** numbers **ii** words.
b Write the number 100 000 as a power of 10.

a	**i** 1 000 000	$10^6 = 10 \times 10 \times 10 \times 10 \times 10 \times 10$ which you write as a 1 followed by six zeros.
	ii one million	1 000 000 in words is one million.
b	10^5	There are five zeros after the 1 in 100 000, so $100\,000 = 10^5$.

The decimal number 0.1 is the same as $\frac{1}{10}$. The decimal number 0.01 is the same as $\frac{1}{100}$.

Multiplying a number by 0.1 has the same effect as dividing the number by 10.

Example: $8 \times 0.1 = 8 \times \frac{1}{10}$, and $8 \times \frac{1}{10} = 8 \div 10$

Multiplying a number by 0.01 has the same effect as dividing the number by 100.

Example: $8 \times 0.01 = 8 \times \frac{1}{100}$, and $8 \times \frac{1}{100} = 8 \div 100$

Dividing a number by 0.1 has the same effect as multiplying the number by 10.

Example: $8 \div 0.1 = 8 \div \frac{1}{10}$, and $8 \div \frac{1}{10} = 8 \times 10$

Dividing a number by 0.01 has the same effect as multiplying the number by 100.

Example: $8 \div 0.01 = 8 \div \frac{1}{100}$, and $8 \div \frac{1}{100} = 8 \times 100$

Worked example 3.1b

Work out the answer to each of these.

a 32×0.1 **b** 4.2×0.01 **c** $6 \div 0.1$ **d** $4.156 \div 0.01$

a	$32 \times 0.1 = 3.2$	Multiplying by 0.1 is the same as dividing by 10, and $32 \div 10 = 3.2$.
b	$4.2 \times 0.01 = 0.042$	Multiplying by 0.01 is the same as dividing by 100, and $4.2 \div 100 = 0.042$.
c	$6 \div 0.1 = 60$	Dividing by 0.1 is the same as multiplying by 10, and $6 \times 10 = 60$.
d	$4.156 \div 0.01 = 415.6$	Dividing by 0.01 is the same as multiplying by 100, and $4.156 \times 100 = 415.6$.

Exercise 3.1

1 Write the following in: **i** numbers **ii** words.
a 10^3 **b** 10^5 **c** 10^7 **d** 10^1

2 Write each number as a power of 10.
a 100 **b** 10 000 000 **c** 10 000 **d** 10 000 000 000

3 Work these out.
a 62×0.1 **b** 50×0.1 **c** 125×0.1 **d** 3.2×0.1
e 37×0.01 **f** 600×0.01 **g** 750×0.01 **h** 4×0.01

4 Work these out.
a $7 \div 0.1$ **b** $4.5 \div 0.1$ **c** $52.2 \div 0.1$ **d** $0.67 \div 0.1$
e $2 \div 0.01$ **f** $8.5 \div 0.01$ **g** $0.32 \div 0.01$ **h** $7.225 \div 0.01$

5 Jake works out 23×0.1 and $8.3 \div 0.01$.
He checks his answers by using an inverse operation.

1. $23 \times 0.1 = 23 \div 10 = 2.3$
Check: $2.3 \times 10 = 23$ ✓
2. $8.3 \div 0.01 = 8.3 \times 100 = 8300$
Check: $8300 \div 100 = 83$ ✗
Correct answer: 830

Work out the answers to these questions.
Check your answers by using inverse operations.
a 18×0.1 **b** 23.6×0.01
c $0.6 \div 0.1$ **d** $4.5 \div 0.01$

6 Which symbol, × or ÷, goes in each box?
a $6.7 \square 0.1 = 67$ **b** $4.5 \square 0.01 = 0.045$ **c** $0.9 \square 0.1 = 0.09$
d $550 \square 0.01 = 5.5$ **e** $0.23 \square 0.1 = 2.3$ **f** $12 \square 0.01 = 1200$

7 Which of 0.1 or 0.01 goes in each box?
a $26 \times \square = 0.26$ **b** $3.4 \div \square = 34$ **c** $0.06 \times \square = 0.0006$
d $7 \div \square = 70$ **e** $8.99 \times \square = 0.899$ **f** $52 \div \square = 520$

8 Which calculation, **A**, **B**, **C** or **D**, gives a different answer from the others? Show your working.

A 5.2×0.1	**B** $52 \div 0.01$	**C** $0.052 \div 0.1$	**D** 52×0.01

9 Razi thinks of a number. He multiplies his number by 0.1, and then divides the answer by 0.01. He then divides this answer by 0.1 and gets a final answer of 12 500. What number does Razi think of first?

10 This is part of Harsha's homework.

Question Write down one example to show that this statement is not true. 'When you multiply a number with one decimal place by 0.01 you will always get an answer that is smaller than zero.'
Answer $345.8 \times 0.01 = 3.458$ and 3.458 is not smaller than zero so the statement is not true.

Write down one example to show that each of these statements is not true.
a When you multiply a number other than zero by 0.1 you will always get an answer that is greater than zero.
b When you divide a number with one decimal place by 0.01 you will always get an answer that is greater than 100.

3.2 Ordering decimals

To order decimal numbers, compare the whole-number part first.

When the numbers that you are ordering have the same whole-number part, compare the tenths, then the hundredths, and so on.

> The number of digits after the decimal point is the number of decimal places (d.p.) in the number.

Look at the three decimal numbers on the right. 8.56, 7.4, 8.518

1 Highlight the whole numbers. 8.56, 7.4, 8.518

You can see that 7.4 is the smallest number, so 7.4 goes first.

2 The other two both have 8 units, so highlight the tenths. 7.4, 8.56, 8.518

3 They both have the same number of tenths, so highlight the hundredths. 7.4, 8.56, 8.518

You can see that 8.518 is smaller than 8.56, so in order of size the numbers are: 7.4, 8.518, 8.56

When you order decimal measurements, you must make sure they are all in the same units. You need to remember these conversion factors.

Length	Mass	Capacity
10 mm = 1 cm	1000 g = 1 kg	1000 ml = 1 l
100 cm = 1 m	1000 kg = 1 t	
1000 m = 1 km		

> When you compare decimal numbers you can use these symbols.
>
> = means 'is equal to' ≠ means 'is not equal to'
>
> > means 'is bigger than' < means 'is smaller than'

Worked example 3.2

a Write these decimal numbers in order of size. 5.682, 5.61, 0.95, 5.68.

b Write the correct symbol, = or ≠, between these measures. 7.5 m □ 75 cm

c Write the correct symbol, > or <, between these measures. 4.5 kg □ 450 g

a 0.95, 5.61, 5.68, 5.682 — The smallest number is 0.95 as it has the smallest whole-number part. The other three numbers have the same whole-number part and the same tenths, so compare the hundredths. 1 is smaller than 8 so 5.61 comes next. Finally, compare the thousandths: 5.68 is the same as 5.680 and 0 is smaller than 2, so 5.68 is smaller than 5.682.

b 7.5 m ≠ 75 cm — There are 100 cm in 1 metre. 7.5 m × 100 = 750 cm, so '≠' goes between the two measures.

c 4.5 kg > 450 g — There are 1000 g in 1 kg. 4.5 kg × 1000 = 4500 g, so '>' goes between the two measures.

Exercise 3.2

1 Write these decimal numbers in order of size, starting with the smallest.

a 5.49, 2.06, 7.99, 5.91
b 3.09, 2.87, 3.11, 2.55
c 12.1, 11.88, 12.01, 11.82
d 9.09, 8.9, 9.53, 9.4
e 23.661, 23.592, 23.659, 23.665
f 0.107, 0.084, 0.102, 0.009
g 6.725, 6.178, 6.71, 6.17
h 11.302, 11.032, 11.02, 11.1

2 Write these measures in order of size, starting with the smallest.

a 2.3 kg, 780 g, 2.18 kg, 1950 g
b 5.4 cm, 12 mm, 0.8 cm, 9 mm
c 12 m, 650 cm, 0.5 m, 53 cm
d 0.55 l, 95 ml, 0.9 l, 450 ml
e 6.55 km, 780 m, 6.4 km, 1450 m
f 0.08 t, 920 kg, 0.15 t, 50 kg
g 95 000 cm, 920 m, 9800 mm, 0.85 km, 0.009 km

3 Write the correct sign, < or >, between each pair.

a 4.23 □ 4.54
b 6.71 □ 6.03
c 0.27 □ 0.03
d 27.9 □ 27.85
e 8.55 □ 8.508
f 5.055 □ 5.505
g 4.5 l □ 2700 ml
h 0.45 t □ 547 kg
i 3.5 cm □ 345 mm
j 0.06 kg □ 550 g
k 7800 m □ 0.8 km
l 0.065 m □ 6.7 cm

4 Write the correct sign, = or ≠, between each pair.

a 6.7 l □ 670 ml
b 4.05 t □ 4500 kg
c 0.85 km □ 850 m
d 0.985 m □ 985 cm
e 14.5 cm □ 145 mm
f 2300 g □ 0.23 kg
g 0.072 l □ 720 ml
h 0.52 m □ 520 mm
i 0.85 kg □ 850 g

5 Shen and Mia swim every day. They keep a record of the distances they swim each day for 10 days.

These are the distances that Shen swims each day.

250 m   1.25 km   0.5 km   2500 m   2 km   1.75 km   750 m   1500 m   25 km   0.75 km

a Shen has written down one distance incorrectly. Which one? Explain your answer.

These are the distances that Mia swims each day.

1.2 km   240 m   0.4 km   1.64 km   820 m   640 m   0.2 km   1.42 km   960 m   0.88 km

b Mia says that the longest distance she swam is more than eight times the shortest distance she swam. Is Mia correct? Explain your answer.

Shen and Mia swim in different swimming pools. One of the swimming pools is 25 m long. The other swimming pool is 20 m long. Shen and Mia always swim a whole number of lengths.

c Who do you think swims in the 25 m swimming pool? Explain how you made your decision.

6 Each of the cards describes a sequence of decimal numbers.

A First term: 0.5   Term-to-term rule: 'add 0.5'

B First term: 0.15   Term-to-term rule: 'multiply by 2'

C First term: −1.7   Term-to-term rule: 'add 1'

D First term: 33.6   Term-to-term rule: 'divide by 2'

E First term: 1.25   Term-to-term rule: 'add 0.25'

F First term: 10.45   Term-to-term rule: 'subtract 2'

a Work out the fifth term of each sequence.
b Write the numbers from part **a** in order of size starting with the smallest.

3.3 Rounding

When you are asked to **round** a number you will be told how accurate your answer should be. This is called the **degree of accuracy**.

Whatever the degree of accuracy, the method is always the same.

- Look at the digit in the position of the required degree of accuracy. What you do to this digit depends on the value of the digit to the right of it.
- If the value of the digit to its right is 5 or more, increase the original digit by 1. If the value of the digit to the right is less than 5, leave the original digit as it is.

You may be asked to round a number to the nearest 10, 100, 1000 or even one million. You may also be asked to round a decimal number to the nearest whole number, or to one or two decimal places (1 d.p. or 2 d.p.).

Worked example 3.3

Round each number to the given degree of accuracy.

a 376 to the nearest 100
b 23 252 to the nearest 1000
c 26 580 000 to the nearest million
d 12.67 to the nearest whole number
e 2.706 to 1 d.p.
f 0.4692 to 2 d.p.

a	376 = 400 (nearest 100)	376 to the nearest 100 will be 300 or 400. The digit in the hundreds column is 3. The number to the right of the 3 is 7. 7 is more than 5 so round the 3 up to 4.
b	23 252 = 23 000 (nearest 1000)	The answer will be 23 000 or 24 000. The digit in the thousands column is 3. The number to the right of the 3 is 2. 2 is less than 5, so the 3 stays the same.
c	26 580 000 = 27 000 000 (nearest million)	The digit in the millions column is 6. The number to the right of the 6 is 5, so round the 6 up to 7.
d	12.67 = 13 (nearest whole number)	The digit in the units column is 2. The number to the right is 6, so round the 2 round up to 3.
e	2.706 = 2.7 (1 d.p.)	The number in the tenths column is 7. The number to the right is 0, so the 7 stays the same.
f	0.4692 = 0.47 (2 d.p.)	The number in the hundredths column is 6. The number to the right is 9, so round the 6 up to 7.

Exercise 3.3

1 Round each number to the given degree of accuracy.

a 42 (nearest 10) **b** 157 (nearest 10) **c** 232 (nearest 100)
d 476 (nearest 100) **e** 4380 (nearest 1000) **f** 12 575 (nearest 1000)
g 32 479 (nearest 10 000) **h** 125 450 (nearest 10 000) **i** 452 985 (nearest 100 000)
j 1 427 546 (nearest 100 000) **k** 7 856 920 (nearest million) **l** 25 499 500 (nearest million)

2 Round each number to the given degree of accuracy.

a 75.2 (nearest whole number) **b** 9.55 (nearest whole number)
c 19.924 (nearest whole number) **d** 11.45 (1 d.p.)
e 0.929 (1 d.p.) **f** 125.881 (1 d.p.)
g 9.453 (2 d.p.) **h** 12.915 (2 d.p.)
i 0.0759 (2 d.p.) **j** 146.798 (2 d.p.)

3.4 Adding and subtracting decimals

When you are adding or subtracting decimal numbers, always set out the calculation in columns and remember to keep the decimal points in line.

Worked example 3.4

Work these out. **a** 14.7 + 8.56 **b** 13.5 − 1.72

a	$\begin{array}{r} 14.7 \\ +\ 8.56 \\ \hline 23.26 \\ {\scriptstyle 1\ 1} \end{array}$	Start with the hundredths column: 0 + 6 = 6. The blank space means zero. Next add the tenths: 7 + 5 = 12, write down the 2 and carry the 1. Now add the units: 4 + 8 + 1 = 13, write down the 3 and carry the 1. Finally, add the tens: 1 + 1 = 2.
b	$\begin{array}{r} 1\,{}^{2}\!\not{3}.{}^{14}\!\not{5}\,{}^{1}0 \\ -\ 1.72 \\ \hline 11.78 \end{array}$	Start by writing 13.5 as 13.50, then start subtracting with the hundredths column. You can't subtract 0 − 2. 'Borrow' from the 5 and work out 10 − 2. Now subtract the tenths. You can't subtract 4 − 7. 'Borrow' from the 3 and work out 14 − 7. Now subtract the units, and finally the tens.

Exercise 3.4

1 Work these out.

a 6.24 + 8.35 **b** 11.42 + 25.39 **c** 4.78 + 8.43 **d** 19.45 + 9.83
e 23.3 + 5.42 **f** 16.77 + 9.5 **g** 8.72 + 14.9 **h** 123.8 + 9.37
i 0.48 + 7.8 **j** 67.043 + 5.672 **k** 9.95 + 0.478 **l** 12.376 + 7.8

2 Work these out.

a 4.72 − 2.51 **b** 23.78 − 9.35 **c** 13.73 − 2.44 **d** 19.38 − 6.65
e 48.65 − 12.78 **f** 32.27 − 1.49 **g** 82.77 − 25.93 **h** 45.42 − 7.35
i 74.9 − 3.67 **j** 11.8 − 4.36 **k** 34.9 − 8.77 **l** 1.75 − 0.688

3 Part of Jake's homework is on the right.
Use Jake's method to work these out.

a 23 − 2.65 **b** 46 − 1.76 **c** 87 − 13.45
d 245 − 22.49 **e** 16 − 0.76 **f** 42 − 4.66
g 58 − 9.06 **h** 235 − 18.18

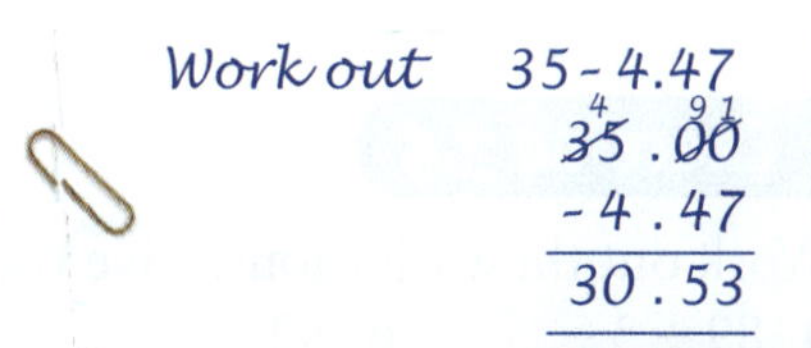

4 Nelson's column in London, UK, is a monument that was built in memory of Admiral Horatio Nelson, who died at the Battle of Trafalgar in 1805.
It has a base, 14.11 m high. On top of this is a column 47.55 m high. At the top, there is a statue 5.18 m high.
What is the total height of Nelson's column?

5 The table shows the results of a javelin competition, in metres.
Is the difference in the distances thrown by the athletes who finished first and second larger than the difference in the distances thrown by the athletes who finished second and third? Show how you worked out your answer.

Position	Distance thrown (m)
1	70.20
2	67.51
3	64.84

3.5 Dividing decimals

When you divide an integer or a decimal number by a single-digit number, it may not divide exactly. Then you will need to continue the division to a given number of decimal places. When you do this make sure that you work out the answer to one decimal place more than you are asked for, then round your answer to the appropriate degree of accuracy.

Worked example 3.5

a Work out 68 ÷ 7. Give your answer correct to one decimal place.
b Work out 2.35 ÷ 4. Give your answer correct to two decimal places.

a

$7\overline{)68.00}$

You are asked to give your answer to one decimal place, so you need to work out the answer to two decimal places first. Write 68 as 68.00.

$7\overline{)68.{}^{5}00}$ with 9. above

6 ÷ 7 can't be done, so work out 68 ÷ 7 = 9 remainder 5. Write down the 9 and carry the 5.

$7\overline{)68.{}^{5}0{}^{1}0}$ with 9.71 above

Now work out 50 ÷ 7 = 7 remainder 1. Write down the 7 and carry the 1. Now work out 10 ÷ 7 = 1 remainder 3. Write down the 1 and stop.

68 ÷ 7 = 9.7 (1 d.p.)

In the answer 9.71, the number after the 7 is a 1, so the 7 stays the same. The answer is 9.7 correct to one decimal place (1 d.p.).

b

$4\overline{)2.350}$

You are asked to give your answer to two decimal places, so you need to work out the answer to three decimal places first. Write 2.35 as 2.350.

$4\overline{)2.3{}^{3}50}$ with 0.5 above

2 ÷ 4 can't be done, so write 0 above the 2 then work out 23 ÷ 4 = 5 remainder 3. Write down the 5 and carry the 3.

$4\overline{)2.3{}^{3}5{}^{3}0}$ with 0.587 above

Now work out 35 ÷ 4 = 8 remainder 3. Write down the 8 and carry the 3. Now work out 30 ÷ 4 = 7 remainder 2. Write down the 7 and stop.

2.35 ÷ 4 = 0.59 (2 d.p.)

The number after the 8 in the answer 0.587 is a 7, so round the 8 up to 9. The answer is 0.59 correct to two decimal places (2 d.p.).

Exercise 3.5

1 Work out these divisions. Give your answers correct to one decimal place.

a 89 ÷ 3 **b** 92 ÷ 7 **c** 56 ÷ 6 **d** 65 ÷ 8
e 879 ÷ 7 **f** 592 ÷ 3 **g** 145 ÷ 9 **h** 275 ÷ 3

2 Work out these divisions. Give your answers correct to two decimal places.

a 5.65 ÷ 3 **b** 7.29 ÷ 4 **c** 1.98 ÷ 8 **d** 0.95 ÷ 7
e 7.6 ÷ 6 **f** 4.3 ÷ 3 **g** 1.9 ÷ 7 **h** 0.7 ÷ 3

3 In an experiment a scientist mixes together three substances. She mixes 18.42 g of substance A, 5.8 g of substance B and 0.75 g of substance C. Then she divides the mixture equally into four containers.
What is the mass of the mixture in each container?
Give your answer correct to two decimal places.

3.6 Multiplying by decimals

When you multiply a number by a decimal, use the decimal place-value table to help you.

Units	•	tenths	hundredths	thousandths
1	•	$\frac{1}{10}$	$\frac{1}{100}$	$\frac{1}{1000}$

If you know the value of the decimal, you can work out an **equivalent calculation** to complete (where one calculation can be replaced by another that gives an identical outcome).

Worked example 3.6

Work these out. **a** 4.37 × 0.3 **b** 24 × 0.08

a (4.37 × 3) ÷ 10 — $0.3 = \frac{3}{10}$, so multiplying by 0.3 is the same as multiplying by 3 and dividing by 10.

$$\begin{array}{r} 4\;3\;7 \\ \times \quad 3 \\ \hline 1\;3\;1\;1 \\ \hline {\scriptstyle 1\;2} \end{array}$$

Start by working out 4.37 × 3.
First of all, ignore the decimal point and work out 437 × 3.

4.37 × 3 = 13.11 — Put the decimal point back into the answer. There are two digits after the decimal point in the question, so there must be two digits after the decimal point in the answer.

4.37 × 0.3 = 1.311 — The final step is to divide 13.11 by 10, so move all the digits in the number one place to the right.

b (24 × 8) ÷ 100 — $0.08 = \frac{8}{100}$, so multiplying by 0.08 is the same as multiplying by 8 and dividing by 100.
Start by working out 24 × 8.

$$\begin{array}{r} 2\;4 \\ \times \quad 8 \\ \hline 1\;9\;2 \\ \hline {\scriptstyle 3} \end{array}$$

24 × 8 = 192
24 × 0.08 = 1.92 — The final step is to divide 192 by 100, so move all the digits two places to the right.

Exercise 3.6

1 Use equivalent calculations to work these out.

a 2.48 × 0.2 **b** 1.76 × 0.3 **c** 5.22 × 0.4 **d** 9.27 × 0.5 **e** 4.18 × 0.06
f 2.9 × 0.07 **g** 14.6 × 0.08 **h** 15.1 × 0.09 **i** 76 × 0.04 **j** 358 × 0.03

2 This is part of Tanesha's homework.

Question Work out 24.3 × 0.06.

Answer 24.3 × 0.06 = (24.3 ÷ 100) × 6
24.3 ÷ 100 = 0.243
0.243 × 6 = 1.458

$$\begin{array}{r} 2\;4\;3 \\ \times \quad 6 \\ \hline 1\;4\;5\;8 \\ \hline {\scriptstyle 2\;1\;\;} \end{array}$$

a Explain why Tanesha's method gives the correct answer.

b Use Tanesha's method to work these out.

i 12.2 × 0.07 **ii** 23.8 × 0.09 **iii** 1.74 × 0.4 **iv** 0.67 × 0.8

3 Mia worked out the multiplication 144 × 6 = 864.
Work these out mentally.

a 144 × 0.6 **b** 1.44 × 0.6 **c** 14.4 × 0.06 **d** 0.144 × 0.06

4 Show that 0.6 × 6839.5 kg is approximately 4.1 t.

Remind yourself of conversion factors using page 34.

3.7 Dividing by decimals

When you divide a number by a decimal, use the place values of the decimal to work out an equivalent calculation.

You already know that dividing a number by 0.1 has the same effect as multiplying the number by 10. When you divide a number by 0.01 it has the same effect as multiplying the number by 100.

Examples: When you divide a number by 0.3, multiply the number by 10 and then divide by 3.

When you divide a number by 0.08, multiply the number by 100 and then divide by 8.

Worked example 3.7

Work these out. **a** 28 ÷ 0.4 **b** 92.4 ÷ 0.06

a (28 × 10) ÷ 4	Dividing by 0.4 is the same as multiplying by 10 and then dividing by 4.
28 × 10 = 280	Start by multiplying by 10.
$\begin{array}{r} 7\ 0 \\ 4\,\overline{)2\ 8\ 0} \end{array}$	Now divide by 4.
28 ÷ 0.4 = 70	Write down the final answer.
b (92.4 × 100) ÷ 6	Dividing by 0.06 is the same as multiplying by 100 and then dividing by 6.
92.4 × 100 = 9240	Start by multiplying by 100.
$\begin{array}{r} 1\ 5\ 4\ 0 \\ 6\,\overline{)9\ {}^{3}2\ {}^{2}4\ 0} \end{array}$	Now divide by 6.
92.4 ÷ 0.06 = 1540	Write down the final answer.

Exercise 3.7

1 Use equivalent calculations to work these out.

a 32 ÷ 0.2 **b** 75 ÷ 0.5 **c** 15 ÷ 0.6 **d** 23.4 ÷ 0.3 **e** 612 ÷ 0.8
f 35 ÷ 0.07 **g** 32 ÷ 0.04 **h** 56 ÷ 0.08 **i** 21 ÷ 0.03 **j** 34 ÷ 0.04
k 81 ÷ 0.06 **l** 8.7 ÷ 0.02 **m** 34.8 ÷ 0.04 **n** 2.1 ÷ 0.05 **o** 156.8 ÷ 0.07

2 This is part of Anders' homework. Use Anders' method to work these out.

Question Work out 28.9 ÷ 0.7.
Give your answer to 1 d.p.

Answer 28.9 ÷ 0.7 = (28.9 × 10) ÷ 7
28.9 × 10 = 289
289 ÷ 7 = 41.3 (1 d.p.)

$\begin{array}{r} 4\ 1\ .\ 2\ 8 \\ 7\,\overline{)2\ 8\ 9\ .\ {}^{2}0\ {}^{6}0} \end{array}$

a 32.5 ÷ 0.3 correct to 1 d.p.
b 7.8 ÷ 0.9 correct to 1 d.p.
c 145 ÷ 0.7 correct to 1 d.p.
d 6.45 ÷ 0.07 correct to 2 d.p.
e 0.79 ÷ 0.06 correct to 2 d.p.

3 Anders knows that 42 ÷ 7 = 6.
Work out these mentally:

a 4.2 ÷ 7 **b** 42 ÷ 0.7 **c** 4.2 ÷ 0.7 **d** 420 ÷ 0.7

4 Work out (42.7 − 6.93) ÷ (2 × 0.45). Give your answer correct to two decimal places.

3.8 Estimating and approximating

When you are solving a mathematical problem it is always useful to check your answer by working out a rough estimate first.

To do this, round each number in the question and then work out an **approximate** answer.

If your accurate answer is close to your approximate answer, it is probably correct.

Remember:

- round numbers between 1 and 10 to the nearest 1
- round numbers in the tens to the nearest 10
- round numbers in the hundreds to the nearest 100
- round numbers in the thousands to the nearest 1000, etc.

You can also use inverse operations to check your answers. To do this, work backwards through the problem to check that you finish with the number you first started with.

Finally, remember to present your work clearly and neatly so that it makes sense to anyone who reads it.

Worked example 3.8

a Mr Nicolo goes on a diet. At the start of the diet he weighs 89.2 kg. He wants to weigh 72.5 kg. After one month he has lost 4.6 kg. How much more does he have to lose?

b For breakfast Mr Nicolo eats:

2 slices of toast	59 calories per slice
1 portion of butter	74 calories
1 portion of jam	32 calories
1 pear	68 calories

What is the total number of calories that he has for breakfast?

a	89.2 − 72.5 = 16.7 Mr Nicolo wants to lose 16.7 kg.	Start by working out how much he wants to lose. Explain what it is that you have worked out.
	16.7 − 4.6 = 12.1 He still has to lose 12.1 kg.	Work out how much more he has to lose. Explain what it is that you have worked out and remember to include the units with your answer (kg).
	Check: 12.1 + 4.6 = 16.7 ✓ 16.7 + 72.5 = 89.2 ✓	Use inverse operations to check both your calculations.
b	59 × 2 + 74 + 32 + 68 = 292 Mr Nicolo has 292 calories for breakfast.	Work out the accurate answer. Explain what it is that you have worked out and remember to include the units with your answer (calories).
	Check: 60 × 2 + 70 + 30 + 70 = 290 ✓	Use estimation to check your answer. Round each number to the nearest 10. 290 is close to 292 so the answer is probably right.

Exercise 3.8

In each question in this exercise:

i Work out the answer to the problem.
ii Show all your working and at each step explain what it is that you have worked out.
iii Make sure your working is clearly and neatly presented.
iv Use estimation or inverse operations to check your answer.

1 Mrs Kumal is saving money to go on holiday.
Altogether she needs to save \$350.
So far she has saved these amounts.
How much more money does she need to save?

Money saved so far:
\$38 \$57 \$22 \$45 \$65 \$54 \$24

2 Jian is an electrician. For each job he does he charges \$32 an hour plus a call-out fee of \$35.
 a Jian does a job for Mr Lee. It takes him $2\frac{1}{2}$ hours.
 How much does he charge Mr Lee?
 b Jian charges Mrs Wu a total of \$171.
 How long did the job for Mrs Wu take?
 Give your answer in hours and minutes.

3 Essian is going to buy a television.
He sees the television he wants advertised in a store.
Essian can either buy the television using cash or a payment plan.
How much more will the television cost Essian if he uses the payment plan rather than paying cash?

4 Maha is going to keep six hens. One hen, on average, will produce five eggs every week.
There are 52 weeks in one year.
Maha is going to sell all the eggs her hens produce for \$1.25 for six eggs.
How much money should Maha make from selling the eggs in one year?

Summary

You should now know that:

★ When you multiply a number by 0.1 (or 0.01) it has the same effect as dividing the number by 10 (or 100).

★ When you divide a number by 0.1 (or 0.01) it has the same effect as multiplying the number by 10 (or 100).

★ When you order decimal numbers that involve measurements, you must make sure all your measurements are in the same units.

★ When you multiply or divide a number by a decimal you can use the value of the decimal to work out an equivalent calculation.

★ When you solve problems, make sure your work is set out neatly and answers are explained so that someone else can understand what you have done.

You should be able to:

★ Read and write positive integer powers of 10.

★ Multiply integers and decimals by 0.1 and 0.01.

★ Order decimals, including measurements.

★ Round whole numbers to the nearest 10, 100, 1000, 10 000, etc.

★ Round decimal numbers to the nearest whole number or one or two decimal places.

★ Add and subtract integers and decimals.

★ Divide integers and decimals by a single-digit number to a given number of decimal places.

★ Multiply and divide integers and decimals by a decimal, by considering equivalent calculations.

★ Use estimation and inverse operations to check working.

End-of-unit review

1 Write 10^4 in: **a** numbers **b** words.

2 Write the number 100 000 000 as a power of 10.

3 Work these out.
a 41×0.1 **b** 23×0.01 **c** $7.2 \div 0.1$ **d** $0.24 \div 0.01$

4 Write these in order of size, starting with the smallest.
a 10.9, 10.98, 10.8, 10.09 **b** 7 m, 750 cm, 0.7 m, 77 cm

5 Write the correct sign, < or >, between each pair.
a 3.65 □ 3.56 **b** 9.01 □ 9.1 **c** 42 mm □ 0.5 cm

6 Write the correct sign, = or ≠, between each pair.
a 3.05 kg □ 3005 g **b** 0.67 l □ 670 ml **c** 0.3 km □ 30 m

7 Round each number to the given degree of accuracy.
a 6725 (nearest 100) **b** 235 890 (nearest 10 000) **c** 8 216 899 (nearest million)
d 63.81 (nearest whole number) **e** 12.62 (1 d.p.) **f** 7.566 (2 d.p.)

8 Ashley takes part in a discus competition.
In the first round he throws the discus a distance of 27.29 m.
In the second round he throws the discus a distance of 29.73 m.
Work out:
a the sum of the two distances he has thrown
b the difference in the two distances he has thrown.

9 Work out these divisions. Give your answers correct to one decimal place.
a $96 \div 7$ **b** $278 \div 3$

10 Work out these divisions. Give your answers correct to two decimal places.
a $8.47 \div 6$ **b** $8.7 \div 9$

11 Use equivalent calculations to work these out.
a 3.12×0.2 **b** 23.5×0.06 **c** 72×0.4 **d** 89×0.08

12 Use equivalent calculations to work these out.
a $84 \div 0.2$ **b** $6.3 \div 0.9$ **c** $72 \div 0.08$ **d** $3.5 \div 0.05$

13 Work out $(23.8 - 2.49) \div (4 \times 0.15)$.
Give your answer correct to two decimal places.

14 i Work out the answer to the problem below.
ii Show all your working and at each step explain what it is that you have worked out.
iii Make sure your working is clearly and neatly presented.
iv Use estimation or inverse operations to check your answer.

Jane runs a fun-fair ride.
The prices she charges are shown in the box.
One Thursday Jane has:
18 customers that have 1 ride
12 customers that have 2 rides
5 customers that have 3 rides.
How much money does Jane take on this Thursday?

Thrills and Spills!
1 ride costs \$15
2 rides cost \$28
3 rides cost \$38

4 Length, mass and capacity

There are many situations in everyday life where you have to measure and weigh. If you want a bookshelf on your bedroom wall you will need to measure the length of the shelf and its position on the wall. If you are baking cakes you will need to weigh the ingredients.

It is very important that you measure carefully and accurately.

All the stories below are true. They made the headlines in newspapers and on the television.

Imagine how the people that made these mistakes must have felt!

Key words

Make sure you learn and understand these key words:

units of measurement
metric units
length
mass
capacity
area
volume
miles
kilometres

London 2012 Olympic swimming pool is too short!

An Olympic-standard swimming pool was built in Portsmouth, UK, to the Olympic length of 50 m. However, no room was allowed for the touch-sensitive timing pads that are needed at each end of the pool. The pool may be about 5 cm too short!

Cardiff half-marathon is 193 m too short!

In 2010, a half-marathon took place in Cardiff, UK. The official length of a half-marathon is 21.0975 km and the course had been measured accurately. However, at the last minute, the course had to be changed as there was an obstruction on the route. The length of the new route wasn't checked before the race and it was only found out afterwards that it was too short!

The Hubble Space Telescope's vision is blurred!

The Hubble Space Telescope was put into orbit in 1990. At first everything seemed to be going well. However, the first picture that was taken was blurred. As more pictures were taken, the scientists realised that something was wrong. They found out that the main mirror was the wrong shape and so it could not focus properly. They discovered that when the mirror was being made, a speck of dust had affected a measuring rod and so the measurements were slightly wrong. Astronauts carried out five spacewalks to fix the problem. Since then the pictures sent back from the telescope have been clear, crisp and amazing!

In this unit you will learn how to choose suitable units of measurement to estimate, measure, calculate and solve problems. You will also learn about the connection between kilometres and miles.

4.1 Choosing suitable units

You need to be able to choose appropriate **units of measurement** to estimate, measure, calculate and solve problems. To do this you must know the **metric units** of **length**, **mass** and **capacity**.

The metric units are:

- length – millimetre (mm), centimetre (cm), metre (m) and kilometre (km)
- mass – gram (g), kilogram (kg) and tonne (t)
- capacity (the volume of liquid something can hold) – millilitre (ml) and litre (l).

You must also know the units to measure:

- **area** – use the square units of length, mm^2, cm^2, m^2 or km^2
- **volume** – use the cube units of length, mm^3, cm^3, m^3 or km^3.

Worked example 4.1

a Which metric units would you use to measure:
 i the length of a football pitch **ii** the area of a football pitch?

b Zalika estimates the weight of an elephant to be 150 kg.
Is this a realistic estimate? Give a reason for your answer.

c A man stands next to a tree. He estimates that the height of the tree is 6 times his height.
Work out an estimate of the height of the tree.

a i m	A football pitch is approximately the same length as a 100 m sprint track, so metres are the best units to use.
ii m^2	The length and width of a football pitch are both measured in metres, so use square metres to measure the area of the football pitch.
b No, an average man weighs about 75 kg. An elephant weighs more than two men.	Compare Zalika's estimate with a weight that you know. Then make a decision and give a reason.
c Height of man = 1.7 m	Start by writing down a reasonable estimate of the height of the man.
Height of tree = 6 × 1.7 = 10.2 m	Use your estimate to work out the height of the tree. Remember to include the units (m) in your answer.

Exercise 4.1

1 Which metric units would you use to measure each of the following?
 a the length of a tennis court **b** the length of a postage stamp
 c the mass of an orange **d** the mass of a cat
 e the capacity of a bathtub **f** the capacity of a spoon

2 Which metric units would you use to measure each of the following?
 a the area of a cricket pitch **b** the area of a city
 c the area of the cover of a book **d** the volume of a swimming pool
 e the volume of an ocean **f** the volume of a tea cup

3 Write down whether you think each of these statements is true (T) or false (F).
 a The height of a horse is 2.5 m. **b** The mass of a new-born baby is 3 kg.
 c The length of banana is 20 mm. **d** The capacity of a bottle is 2 l.

4 Mia estimates that the length of her bedroom is 20 m.
Is this a reasonable estimate? Give a reason for your answer.

5 Maha keeps chickens.
She estimates that the weight of one chicken egg is 75 g.
Is this a reasonable estimate?
Give a reason for your answer.

6 It takes Logan 2 hours to drive from his house to his brother's house.
He estimates that the distance from his house to his brother's house is 400 km.
Is this a reasonable estimate? Give a reason for your answer.

7 Lynn has two cats, Polly and Barney.
Lynn knows that Polly has a mass of 3 kg.
She estimates that Barney's mass is 3 times Polly's mass.
Work out an estimate of Barney's mass.

8 Hassan has a jug with a capacity of 800 ml.
He estimates that his bucket holds 20 times that of his jug.
Work out an estimate of the capacity of his bucket.
Give your answer in litres.

9 Alicia has a bag that contains 12 apples.
Estimate the mass of the bag of apples.
Give your answer in kilograms.

10 Look at the notice that is shown in an elevator.
Eight adults get into the elevator.
Do you think that the elevator is overloaded?
Explain your answer.

Warning!

Total mass of people in elevator must NOT exceed 500 kg

In questions **11** and **12** the diagrams are drawn to scale.

11 The diagram shows a car parked in front of a building.
Estimate the length of the building.
Show how you worked out your answer.

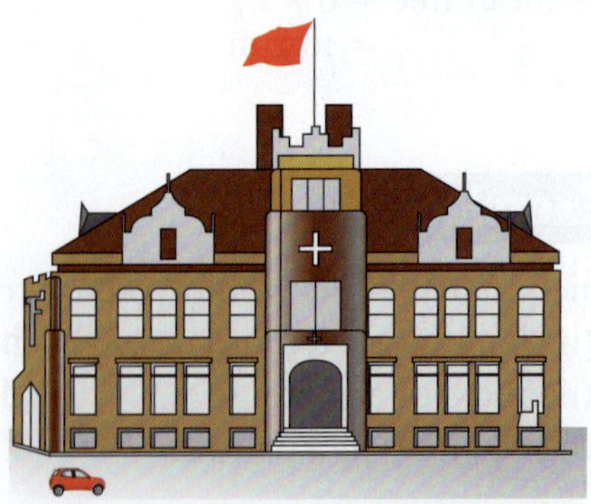

12 The diagram shows a man standing next to a building.
Estimate the height of the building.
Show how you worked out your answer.

4.2 Kilometres and miles

In some countries, such as the USA, Liberia and the UK, distances are measured in **miles** rather than **kilometres**.

A kilometre is a shorter unit of measurement than a mile. One kilometre is about $\frac{5}{8}$ of a mile.

If the blue line below represents a distance of 1 mile, then the red line represents a distance of 1 kilometre.

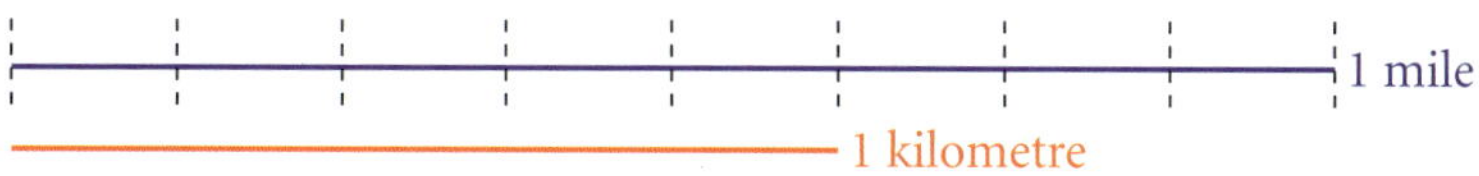

To convert a distance in kilometres to a distance in miles, multiply by $\frac{5}{8}$.

To convert a distance in miles to a distance in kilometres, multiply by $\frac{8}{5}$.

Worked example 4.2

a Which is greater, 20 miles or 20 km?
b Convert 72 kilometres into miles.
c Convert 50 miles into kilometres.
d Which is further, 200 km or 120 miles?

a	20 miles	One mile is greater than one km, so 20 miles is greater than 20 km.
b	$72 \div 8 = 9$	To multiply 72 by $\frac{5}{8}$, first of all divide 72 by 8,
	$9 \times 5 = 45$ miles	then multiply the answer by 5.
c	$50 \div 5 = 10$	To multiply 50 by $\frac{8}{5}$, first of all divide 50 by 5,
	$10 \times 8 = 80$ km	then multiply the answer by 8.
d	$200 \div 8 = 25$	Convert 200 km into miles (or 120 miles into km) so that the units of both
	$25 \times 5 = 125$ miles	distances are the same.
	200 km is further	125 miles is greater than 120 miles, so 200 km is further than 120 miles.

Exercise 4.2

1 Write down true (T) or false (F) for each of these statements.

a 15 miles is further than 15 km.

b 100 km is exactly the same distance as 100 miles.

c 2.5 km is further than 2.5 miles.

d 6 km is not as far as 6 miles.

e In one hour, a car travelling at 70 miles per hour will go a shorter distance than a car travelling at 70 kilometers per hour.

2 Read what Tanesha says.

My brother lives 35 km from my house. My sister lives 35 miles from my house. I live closer to my brother than to my sister.

Is Tanesha correct? Explain your answer.

3 Copy and complete these conversions of kilometres into miles.

a 64 km $64 \div 8 = 8$ $8 \times 5 = \square$ miles
b 40 km $40 \div 8 = \square$ $\square \times 5 = \square$ miles
c 56 km $56 \div \square = \square$ $\square \times \square = \square$ miles

4 Convert these distances into miles.

a 24 km **b** 48 km **c** 96 km **d** 176 km

5 Copy and complete these conversions of miles into kilometres.

a 55 miles $55 \div 5 = 11$ $11 \times 8 = \square$ km
b 20 miles $20 \div 5 = \square$ $\square \times 8 = \square$ km
c 85 miles $85 \div \square = \square$ $\square \times \square = \square$ km

6 Convert these distances into kilometres.

a 10 miles **b** 100 miles **c** 125 miles **d** 180 miles

7 Which is further, 104 km or 70 miles? Show your working.

8 Which is further, 90 miles or 152 km? Show your working.

9 Use only the numbers from the box to complete these statements.

a 120 km = □ miles
b 105 miles = □ km
c □ km = □ miles
d □ miles = □ km

115 140 75 224 184 168

10 Every car in the USA is fitted with a mileometer.
The mileometer shows the total distance that a car has travelled.
Evan is a salesman.

This is the reading on his mileometer at the start of one week. | 1 | 2 | 5 | 4 | 6 | 5 | miles

This is the reading on his mileometer at the end of the week. | 1 | 2 | 6 | 3 | 3 | 5 | miles

a How many kilometres has Evan travelled in this week?
b Evan is paid 20 cents for each kilometre he travels. This is to pay for the petrol he uses. Work out the amount Evan is paid this week for the petrol he uses. Give your answer to the nearest dollar.

Summary

You should now know that:

★ The units you use to measure area are always the square units of length.

★ The units you use to measure volume are always the cube units of length.

★ One kilometre is about $\frac{5}{8}$ of a mile.

★ To convert a distance in kilometres to a distance in miles, multiply by $\frac{5}{8}$.

★ To convert a distance in miles to a distance in kilometres, multiply by $\frac{8}{5}$.

You should be able to:

★ Choose suitable units of measurement, including units of mass, length, area, volume or capacity, to estimate, measure, calculate and solve problems in a range of contexts.

★ Compare distances measured in miles and in kilometres.

★ Convert a distance in kilometres to a distance in miles.

★ Convert a distance in miles to a distance in kilometres.

End-of-unit review

1 Which metric units would you use to measure the following?
- **a** the length of a car park
- **b** the length of an eyelash
- **c** the mass of a motorbike
- **d** the mass of a banana
- **e** the capacity of a egg cup
- **f** the capacity of a refrigerator

2 Which metric units would you use to measure the following?
- **a** the area of a tennis court
- **b** the area of a fingernail
- **c** the volume of a bucket
- **d** the volume of a lake

3 Sharon estimates that the height of her kitchen is 2 m.
Is this a sensible estimate? Give a reason for your answer.

4 Anna is 1.6 m tall. She stands next to a lamppost.
She estimates that the lamppost is $2\frac{1}{2}$ times as tall as she is.

Work out an estimate of the height of the lamppost.

5 Eight adults and six children travel in a cable car.
Estimate the total mass of the people in the cable car.

6 The diagram shows a man standing next to a tree.
Estimate the height of the tree.
Show how you worked out your answer.

The diagram is drawn to scale.

7 Write down true (**T**) or false (**F**) for each of these statements.
- **a** 22 miles is further than 22 km.
- **b** 50 km is exactly the same distance as 50 miles.
- **c** 200 km is not as far as 200 miles.

8 Convert these distances into miles.
- **a** 112 km
- **b** 208 km

9 Convert these distances into kilometres.
- **a** 45 miles
- **b** 205 miles

10 Which is further, 472 km or 300 miles?
Show your working.

11 Caroline is a nurse. She keeps a record of the total number of kilometres she travels to visit her patients each day.
The distances she travels during one week are shown in the box.

Monday	64 km	Tuesday	88 km
Wednesday	52 km	Thursday	72 km
Friday	100 km		

- **a** How many miles has Caroline travelled in this week?
- **b** Caroline is paid 40 cents for each mile she travels.
This is to pay for the fuel she uses.
Work out the amount Caroline is paid this week for the fuel she uses. Give your answer in dollars.

Remember that there are 100 cents in $1.

5 Angles

Do you remember that the angles of a triangle add up to 180°?

How did you find out that this is true?

Did you draw a triangle, tear off the corners and put them together to make a straight line?

Key words

Make sure you learn and understand these key words:

parallel
transversal
corresponding angles
alternate angles
prove
proof
external angle

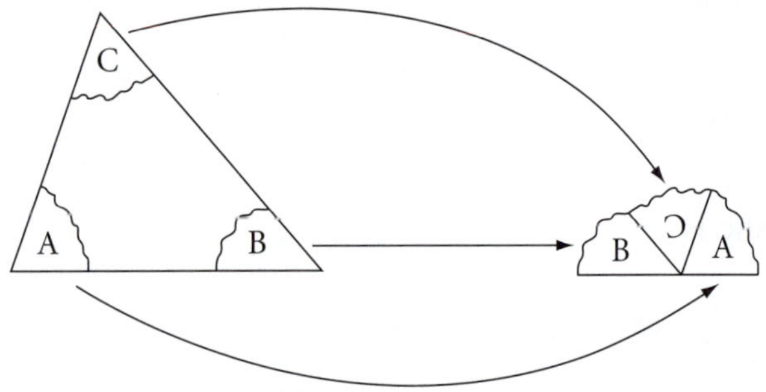

Did you use a protractor to measure the three angles of a triangle, then add them together to get a total close to 180°?

These methods show that the result is reasonable. They do not prove it is true for any triangle.

A proof is a logical argument in which each step is explained or justified by a reason.

Over 2000 years ago the Greek mathematician Euclid wrote a book called *The Elements*. He tried to use logical arguments to prove many facts in geometry and arithmetic. His book was the most successful textbook ever written. It is still in print today.

Euclid started with definitions of basic things such as a point and a straight line. He also had a set of statements which he thought everyone could agree with. These were called axioms.
An example of one of his axioms is:

- Things that are equal to the same thing are equal to one another.

From this simple starting point he proved many complicated results.

In this unit you will learn to understand several proofs. You will also solve geometrical problems and explain your reasons.

5.1 Parallel lines

Here are two **parallel** lines. The arrows show they are parallel.

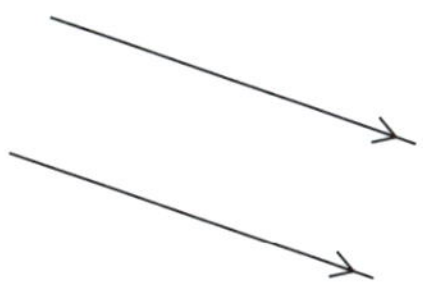

Parallel lines: think of straight train lines or tram lines.

If two lines are parallel the perpendicular distance between them is the same wherever you measure it.

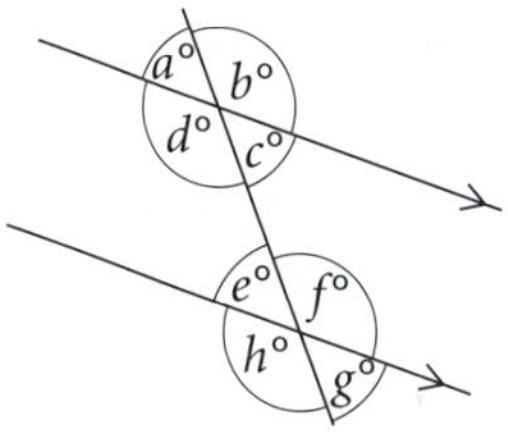

Here is another pair of parallel lines.

A third straight line crosses them. This is called a **transversal**. Angles are formed where the transversal crosses the parallel lines.

The angles marked *a* and *e* are called **corresponding angles**. The angles marked *d* and *h* are also corresponding angles. So are *b* and *f*, and *c* and *g*.

Corresponding angles are equal.

The angles marked *d* and *f* are called **alternate angles**. Angles *c* and *e* are also alternate angles.

Alternate angles are equal.

These are important properties of parallel lines.

To help you remember:

For corresponding angles, think of the letter F.

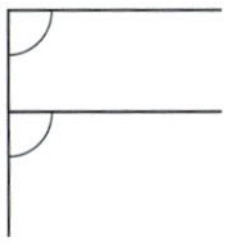

For alternate angles, think of the letter Z.

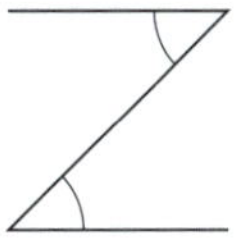

Alternate angles are always between the parallel lines.

Worked example 5.1

The diagram shows two parallel lines and two transversals.
Fill in the missing letters.

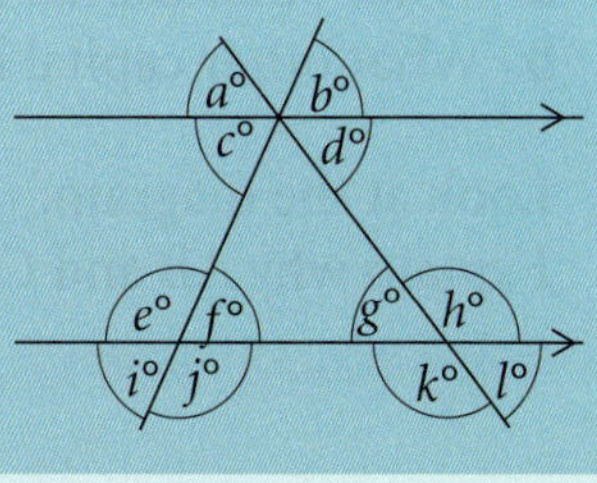

a *c* and ☐ are corresponding angles
b *c* and ☐ are alternate angles
c *d* and ☐ are corresponding angles
d *d* and ☐ are alternate angles

a *i* Look for an angle in the same position on the other parallel line.
b *f* Look for the angles of a Z.
c *l* Using the other transversal to part **a**.
d *g* This time the Z is back to front.

Exercise 5.1

1 Look at the diagram.
  a Write down <u>four</u> pairs of corresponding angles.
  b Write down <u>two</u> pairs of alternate angles.

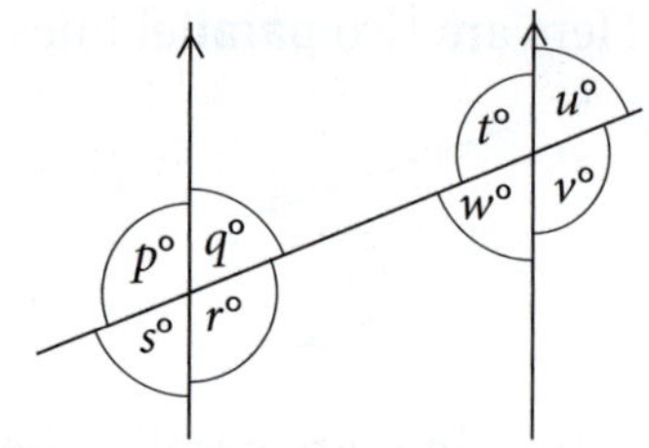

2 In the diagram, the size of one angle is 62°.
  Copy and complete these two sentences.
  a Because corresponding angles are equal, angle ….. = 62°.
  b Because alternate angles are equal, angle ….. = 62°.

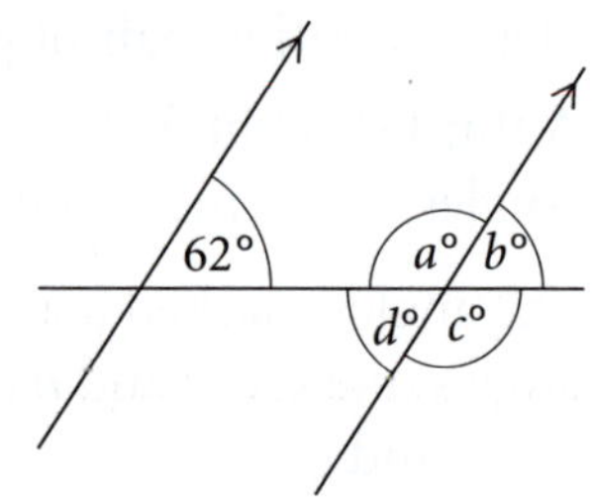

3 In the diagram, the sizes of two angles are marked.
  a What other angles are 105°?
  b What other angles are 75°?

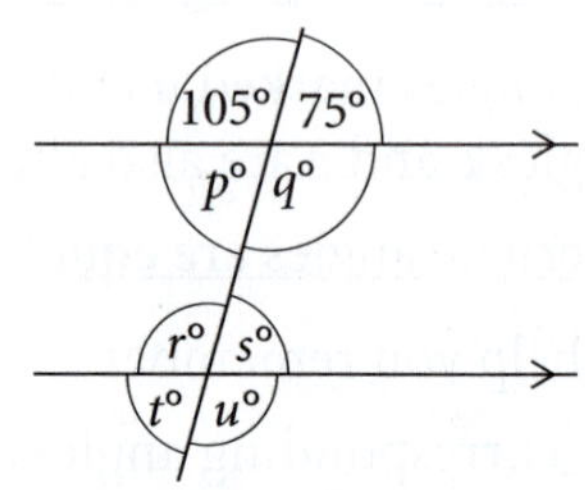

Diagram not drawn accurately

4 Angle APY is marked on the diagram.
  Copy and complete these sentences.
  a APY and CQY are … angles.
  b APY and XQD are … angles.
  c APX and … are corresponding angles.
  d CQX and … are alternate angles.

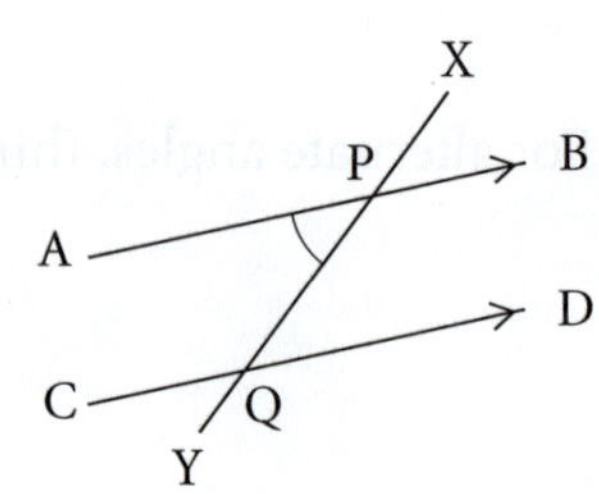

5 The capital letter F has corresponding angles and the letter Z has alternate angles.
  a What other capital letters have corresponding angles?
  b What other capital letters have alternate angles?

6 Look at the diagram.
  Explain why AB and CD cannot be parallel lines.

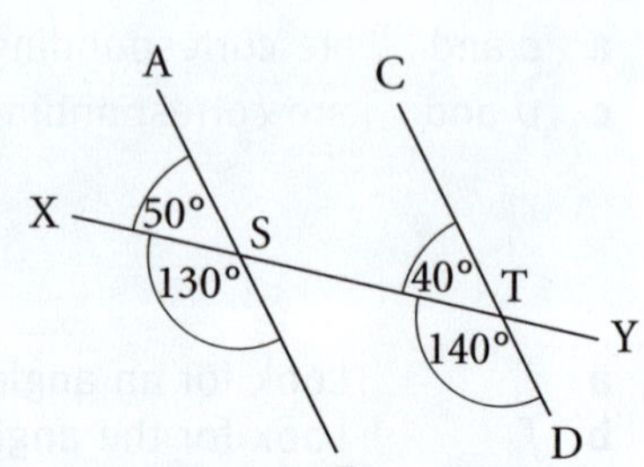

Diagram not drawn accurately

7 Look at the diagram.

a Write down a set of three corresponding angles that includes the angle marked f.

b Write down a pair of alternate angles that includes the angle marked c.

c Write down another pair of alternate angles that includes the angle marked c.

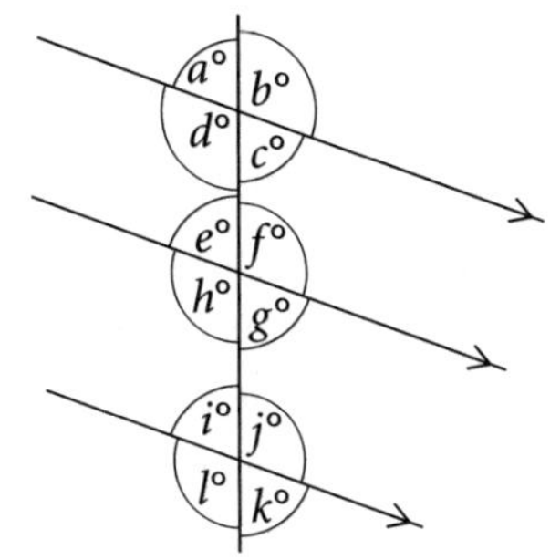

8 In this diagram there are two pairs of parallel lines.

a Write down two pairs of corresponding angles that include the angle marked i.

b Write down two pairs of alternate angles that include the angle marked o.

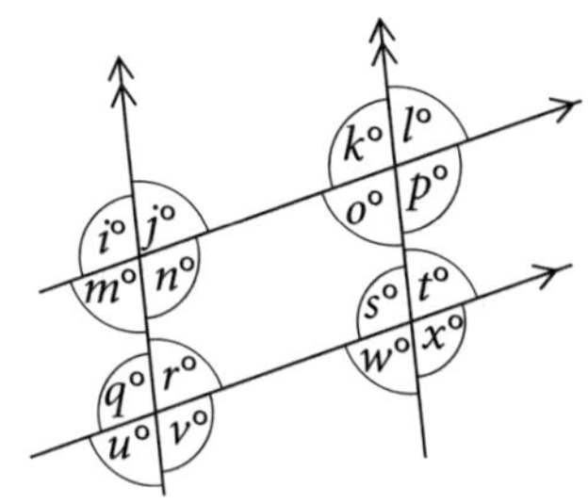

9 Look at the diagram.
Say whether the angles marked with these letters are corresponding angles, alternate angles or neither of these.

a a and d **b** b and f **c** c and g **d** d and e

e a and h

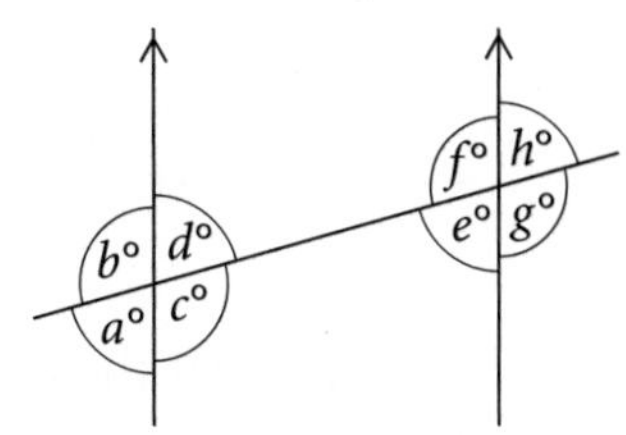

5.2 Explaining angle properties

The angles of a triangle add up to 180°. How do you know that is true?

You can measure the angles of a triangle and add them up. But that will only show it is true for one triangle. How can you show it is true for <u>all</u> triangles?

You can **prove** it by using the properties of parallel lines that you learned in the previous topic.

Proof 1

To prove that the angles of triangle ABC add up to 180°.

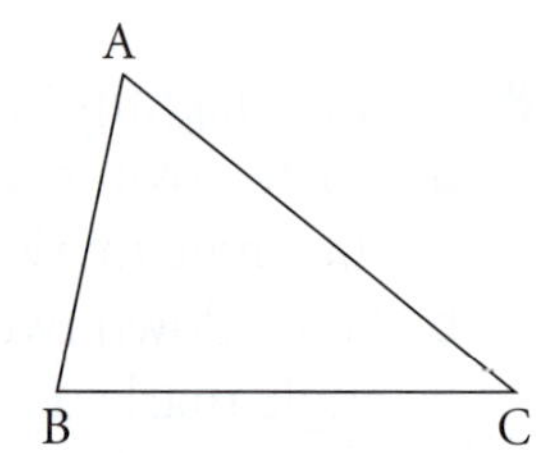

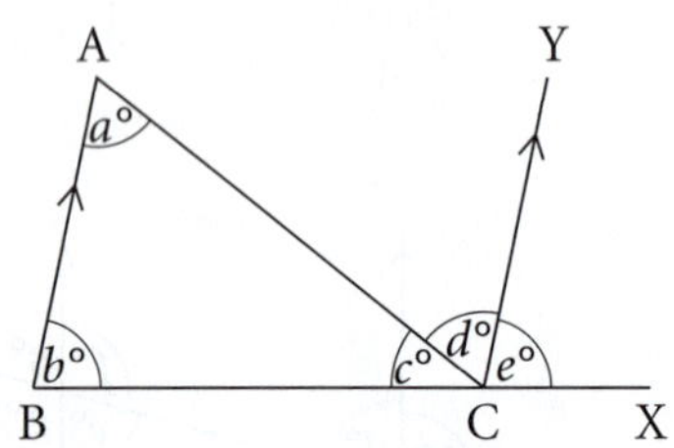

Extend BC to X and draw CY parallel to BA.

Then $a = d$ (alternate angles)

and $b = e$ (corresponding angles)

$c + d + e = 180°$ (angles on a straight line)

$\Rightarrow c + a + b = 180°$.

This is the required result.

⇒ means 'therefore'

This is a **proof** that the angles of any triangle add up to 180°. It gives a reason for each line. You do not need to be able to write proofs in this way, but you should understand them.

The example also proves another important fact.

Angle ACX is called the **external angle** of the triangle at C.

The proof showed that $d + e = a + b$.

This means that the external angle at C is equal to the sum of the interior angles at A and B. This result is true for any triangle.

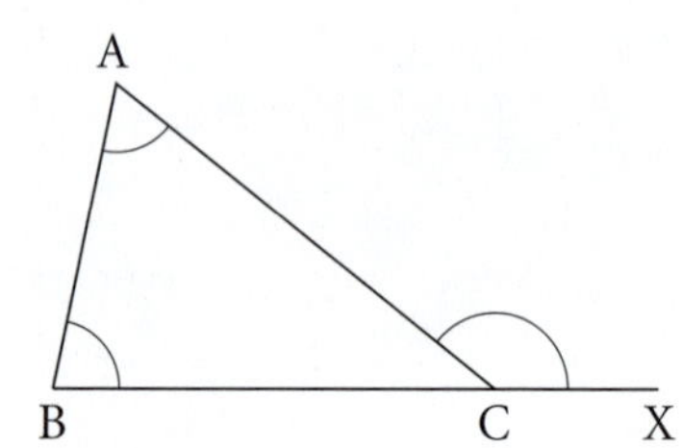

<u>The exterior angle of a triangle is equal to the sum of the two interior opposite angles.</u>

Proof 2

Prove that the angles of this quadrilateral add up to 360°.

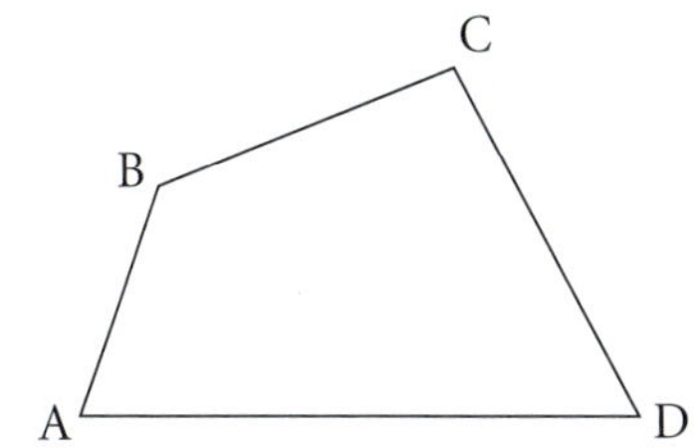

Draw the diagonal BD.

$a + x + y = 180°$ (angle sum of a triangle)

$w + z + c = 180°$ (angle sum of a triangle)

$a + x + y + w + z + c = 360°$

$a + (x + w) + (y + z) + c = 360°$

a and $(x + w)$ and $(y + z)$ and c are the angles of the quadrilateral. This proves the result.

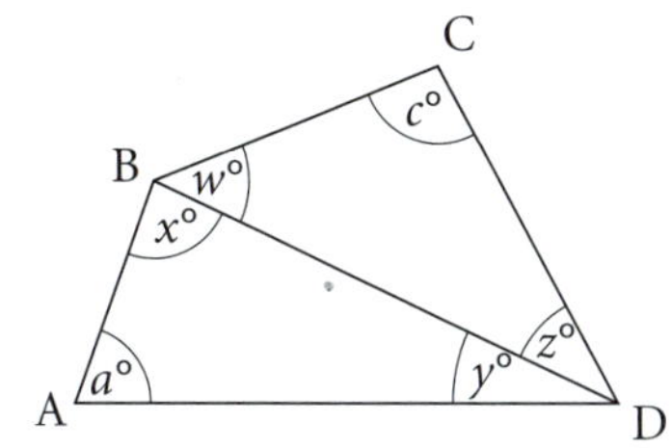

This proof uses the result of the previous proof. You do not need to be able to write proofs. You do need to be able to give reasons for geometrical results.

Exercise 5.2

1 In the triangles, calculate the values of a, b and c.

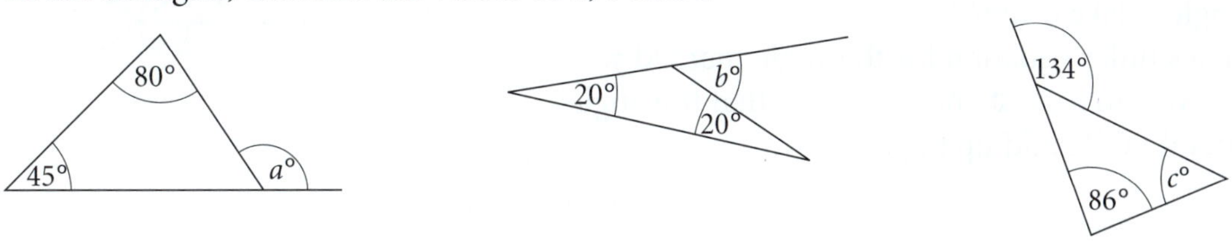

Diagrams not drawn accurately

2 An exterior angle of a triangle is 108°.
One of the interior angles of the triangle is 35°.

a Work out the sizes of the other two interior angles of the triangle.

b Work out the sizes of the other two exterior angles of the triangle.

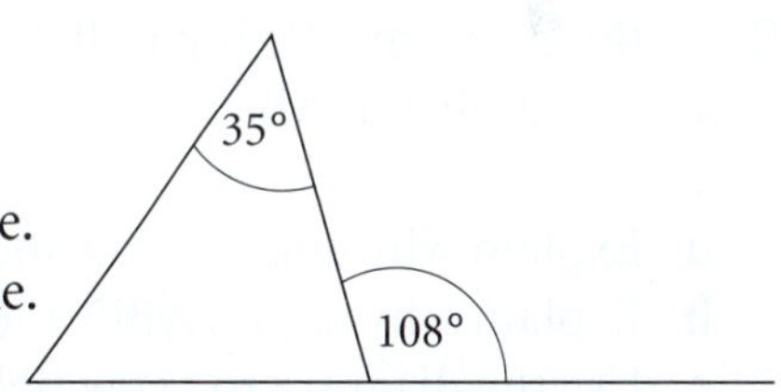

3 PQR is a triangle and PRS is a straight line. RT is parallel to QT.

a

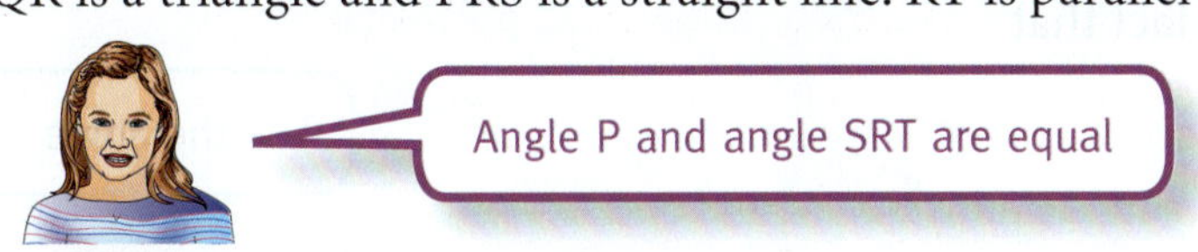

What property of angles is Mia using?

b

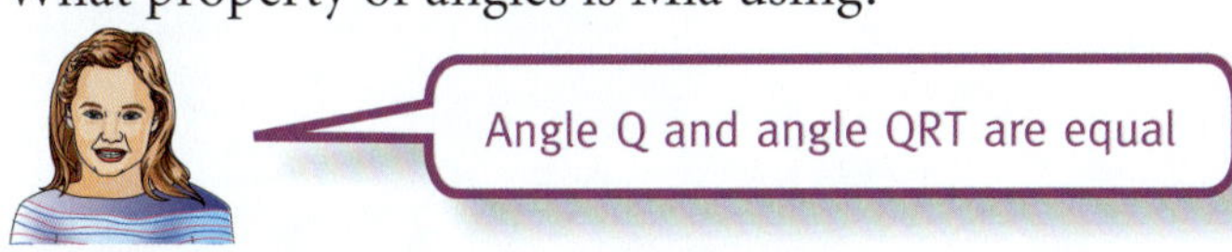

What property of angles is Mia using?

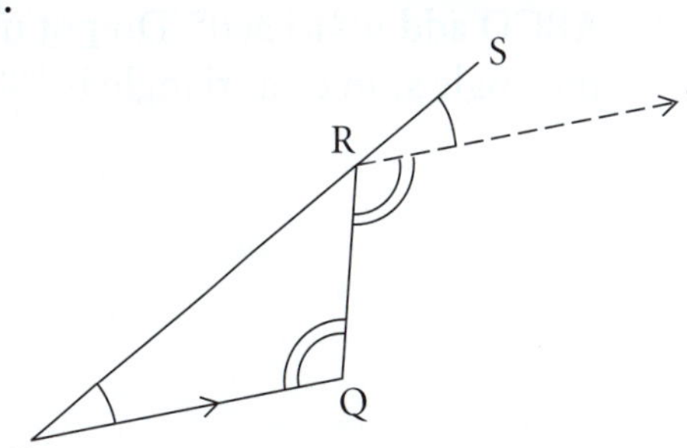

4 In the diagram, XY is parallel to BC.

a Explain why angles XAB and ABC are equal.

b Explain why angles YAC and ACB are equal.

c Explain why the angles of triangle ABC add up to 180°.
Use the results of parts **a** and **b** to help you.

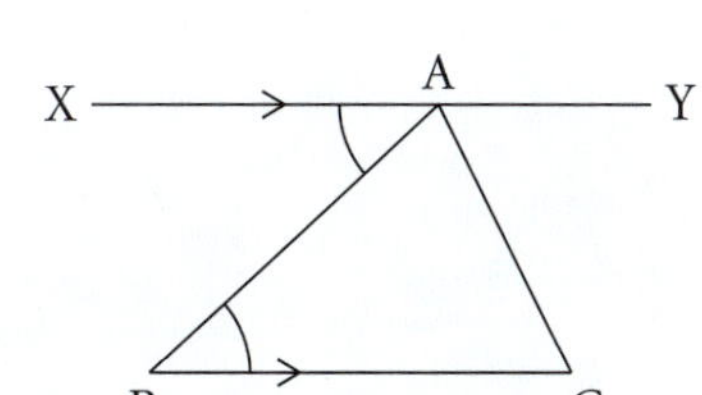

5 The diagram shows a quadrilateral with a reflex angle.
Show that the four angles add up to 360°.

Divide it into two triangles

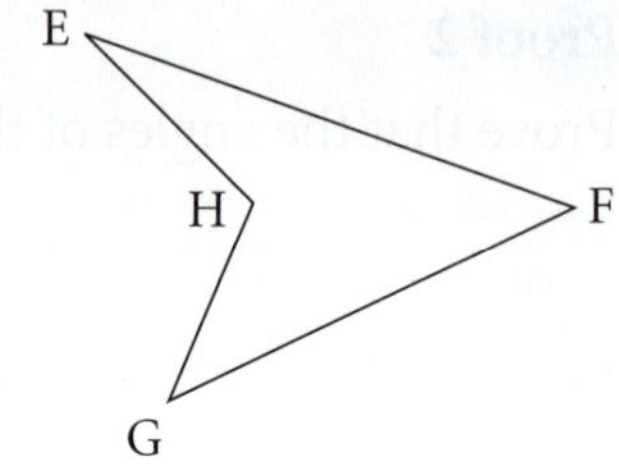

6 In the diagram, PBC is a straight line. AQ is parallel to PC.

a Explain why $y = c$.

b Explain why $x = a + y$.

c Use your answers to parts **a** and **b** to show that, in triangle ABC, the exterior angle at B is equal to the sum of the two interior opposite angles.

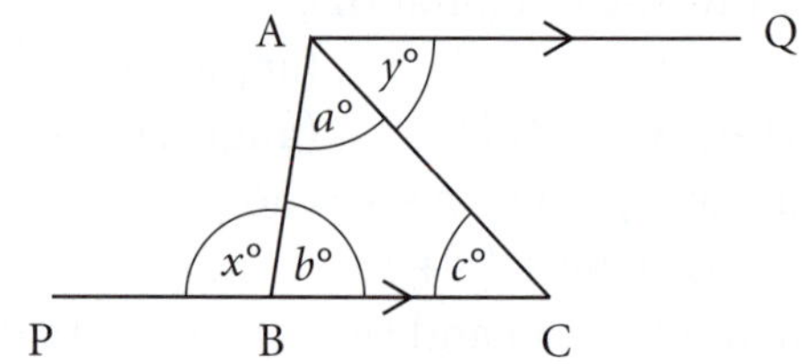

7 In the diagram, PRT is a straight line.

a

x is the exterior angle of a triangle
so $a + b = x$

Which triangle is Jake using?

b Write down a similar equation for the angle marked y.

c Use your answers to parts **a** and **b** to show that the angles of quadrilateral PQRS add up to 360°.

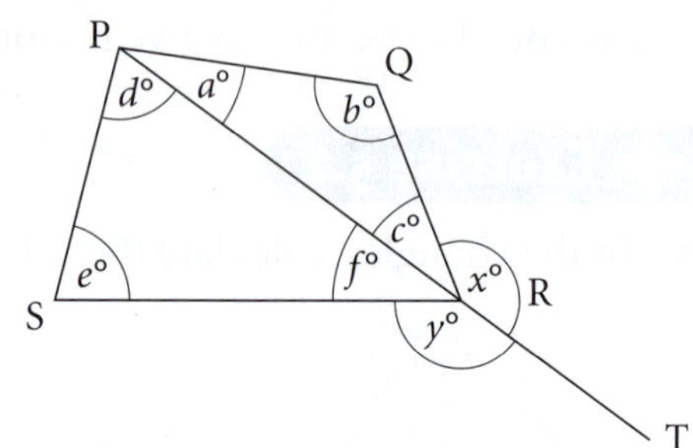

8 In the diagram, DX is parallel to BC.
ZD is parallel to AB.
BDY is a straight line.

a Explain why angles BAD and ADZ are equal.

b Explain why angles ABD and ZDY are equal.

c Use the diagram to show that the angles of quadrilateral ABCD add up to 360°. Do not use the fact that the angle sum of a triangle is 180°.

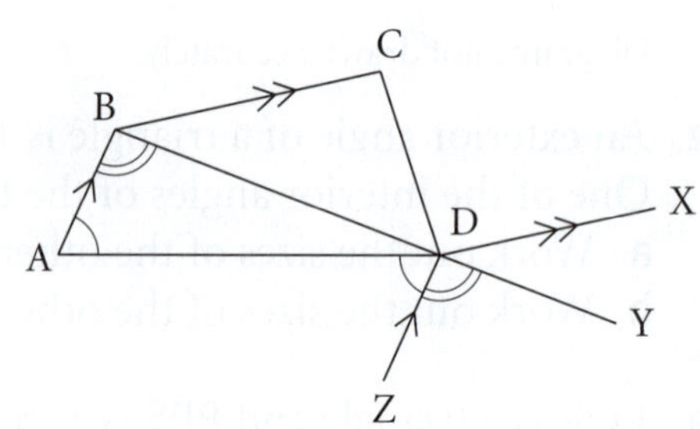

Use the angle at D.

5.3 Solving angle problems

You already know how to calculate angles, but in solving problems you need to give reasons for your answers.

Here are some of the facts you could use.

- The sum of the angles on a straight line is 180°.
- The sum of the angles round a point is 360°.
- Vertically opposite angles are equal.
- Corresponding angles are equal.
- Alternate angles are equal.
- The angle sum of a triangle is 180°.
- The exterior angle of a triangle is the sum of the two opposite interior angles.
- The angle sum of a quadrilateral is 360°.

Worked example 5

Show that the opposite angles of a parallelogram are equal. Give a reason for any statement you make.

Draw a parallelogram with one side extended.	Opposite sides are parallel.
a and x are equal because they are corresponding angles.	Using the sides with two arrows.
c and x are equal because they are alternate angles.	Using the sides with one arrow.
This means a and c must be equal.	This is the first pair.
In the same way, b and d are equal.	This is the second pair.

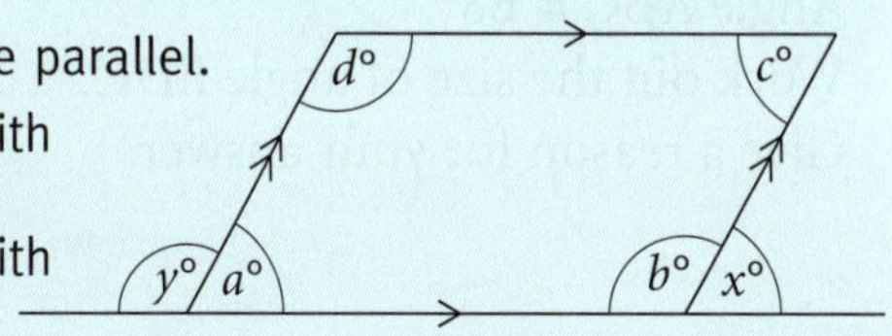

The first step in the worked example was to draw a diagram and label the angles. You often need to do this when you are explaining a geometrical result.

Always give a reason for any statement you make.

Exercise 5.3

1 Maha has made some mistakes in her homework.
Explain why her angles cannot all be correct.

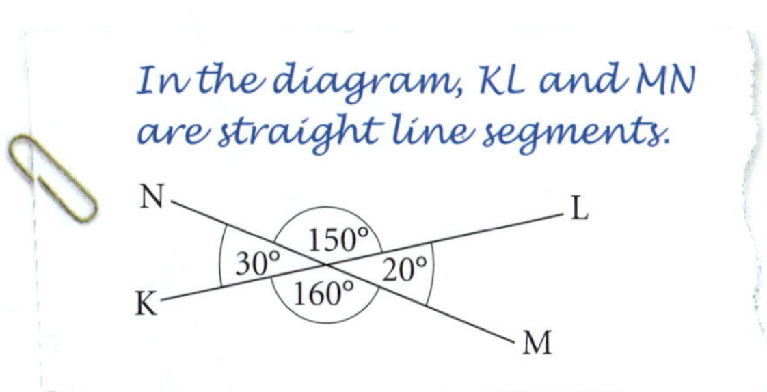

2 In the diagram, KL and MN are parallel.
Find the sizes of the angles marked a, b, c and d.
Give a reason in each case.

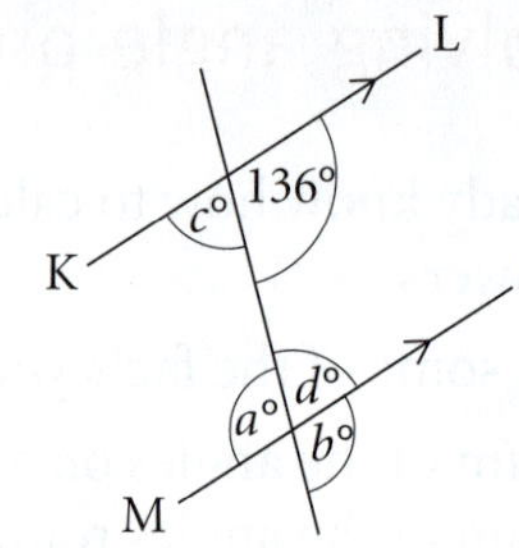

3 In the diagram, the sides of the triangle have been extended, as shown.

a Explain why $d = a + c$.

b Write similar expressions for e and f.

c Show that the sum of the exterior angles of this triangle is 360°.

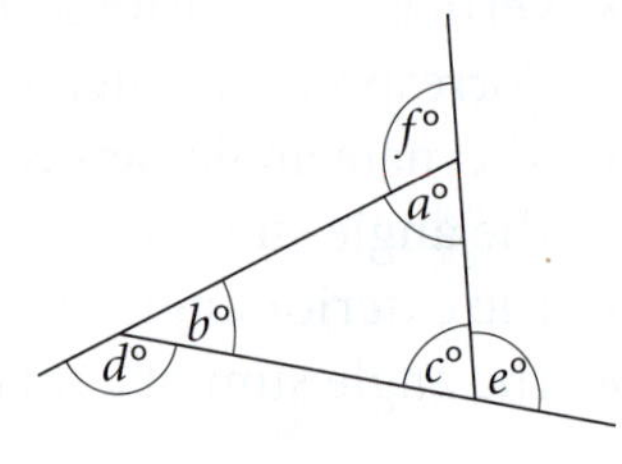

4 In the diagram, ABC is an isosceles triangle.
AB = AC. AB is parallel to DE.
Angle ABC = 68°.
Work out the size of angle EDC.
Give a reason for your answer.

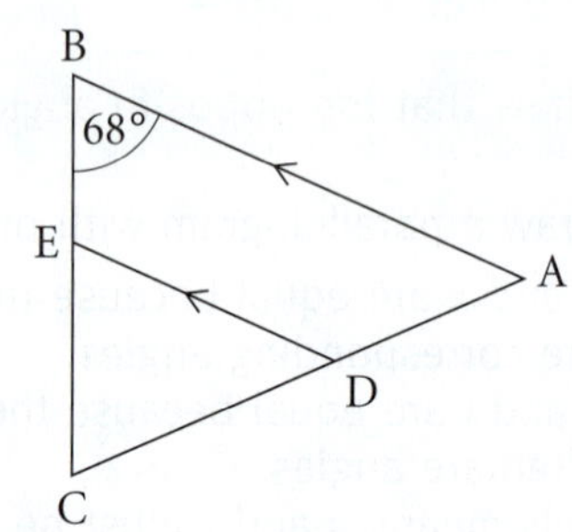

5 This pentagon is divided into a triangle and a quadrilateral.
Show that the angle sum of the pentagon is 540°.

Copy the diagram. Label the angles.

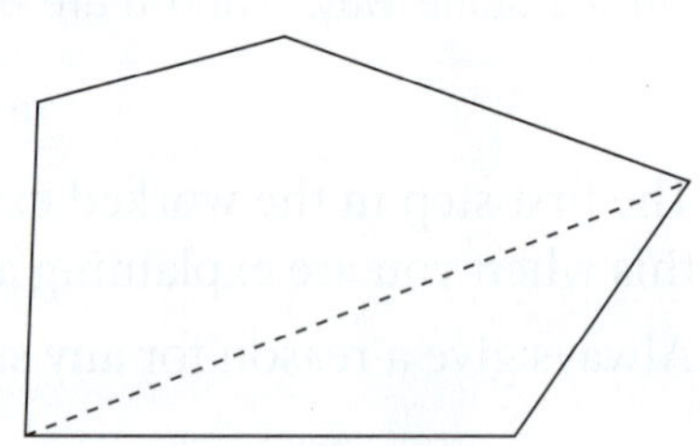

6 In the diagram, AB is parallel to DE.
Show that the angles of triangles ABC and DEC are the same size.

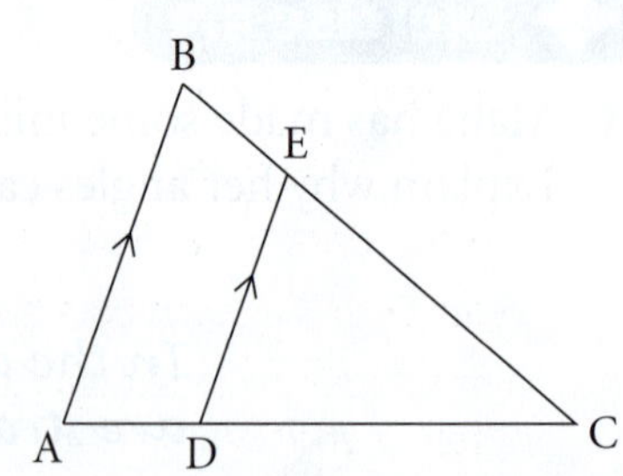

7 In the diagram, ABCD is a parallelogram.
Show that $p + q = r$.

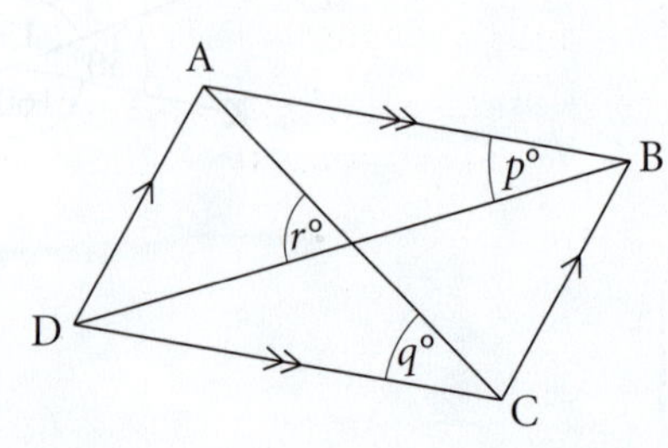

8 In the diagram, two of the sides of the quadrilateral have been extended.

a Show that $w + y = a + b + c + d$.

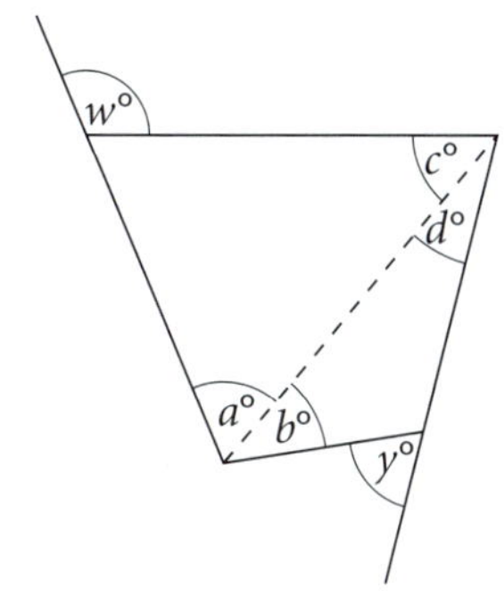

In this diagram, all of the sides of the quadrilateral have been extended.

b Show that $w + x + y + z = 360°$.

> Use the result of part **a**.

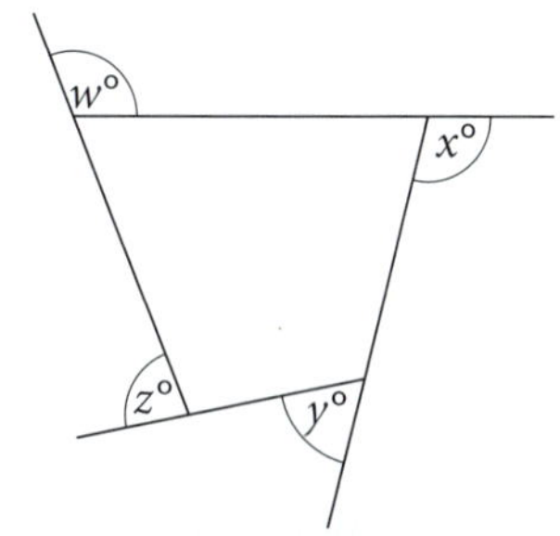

9 Look at the diagram of the irregular five-pointed star.

a Explain why $x = b + d$.

b Explain why $y = c + e$.

c Show that the sum of the angles in the points of the star, $a + b + c + d + e$, is 180°.

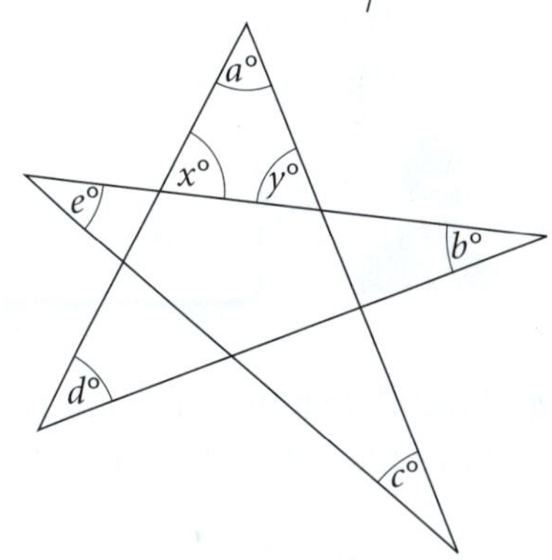

Summary

You should now know that:

- ★ You can identify the special properties of parallel lines and transversals, including corresponding angles and alternate angles.
- ★ Corresponding angles are equal.
- ★ Alternate angles are equal.
- ★ Every vertex of a triangle has an exterior angle.
- ★ A proof using a logical argument is different from a demonstration.
- ★ You can prove the angle sum of a triangle is 180° and the angle sum of a quadrilateral is 360°.
- ★ You can explain your reasoning when you solve a geometric problem.

You should be able to:

- ★ Identify alternate and corresponding angles.
- ★ Understand a proof that the angle sum of a triangle is 180°.
- ★ Understand a proof that the angle sum of a quadrilateral is 360°.
- ★ Understand a proof that the exterior angle of a triangle is equal to the sum of the two interior opposite angles.
- ★ Solve geometrical problems using properties of angles, of parallel and intersecting lines, and of triangles and special quadrilaterals, explaining reasoning with diagrams and text.
- ★ Recognise and use spatial relationships in two dimensions.
- ★ Use logical arguments to interpret the mathematics in a context or to establish the truth of a statement.

End-of-unit review

1 Look at the diagram and complete these sentences.

a Two vertically opposite angles are c and ....
b Two corresponding angles are h and ....
c Two alternate angles are g and ....
d Two angles that add up to 180° are c and ....

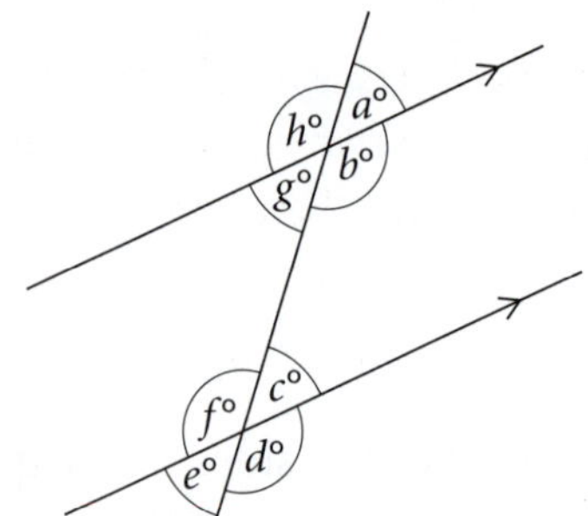

2 Find the values of a, b, c and d.
Give reasons for your answers.

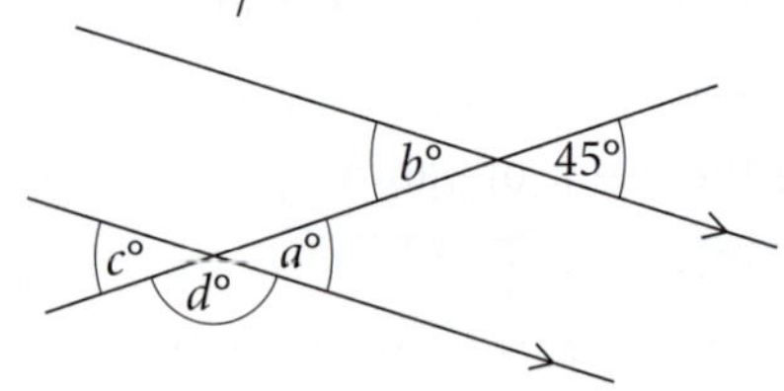

3 Read what Jake says. What are the two angles he is thinking of?

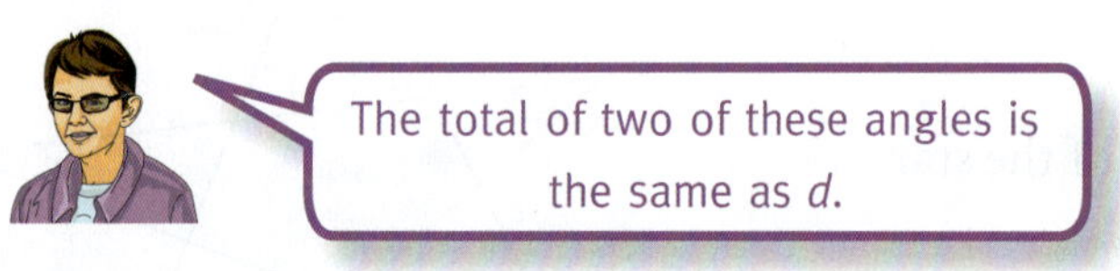

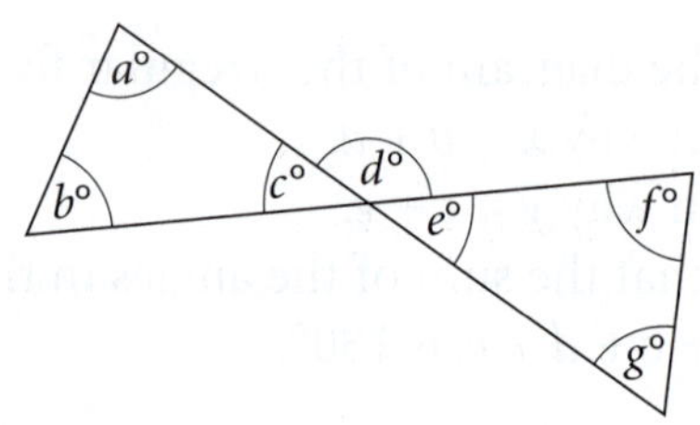

4 Find the values of a and b.
Give reasons for your answers.

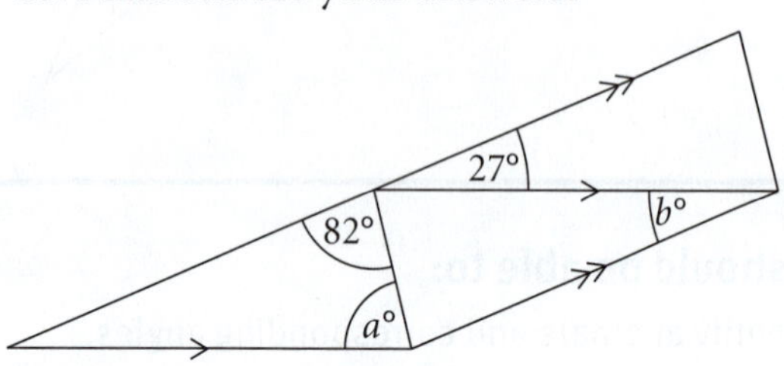

Diagram not drawn accurately

5 Find the sizes of the angles marked a and b.
Give reasons for your answers.

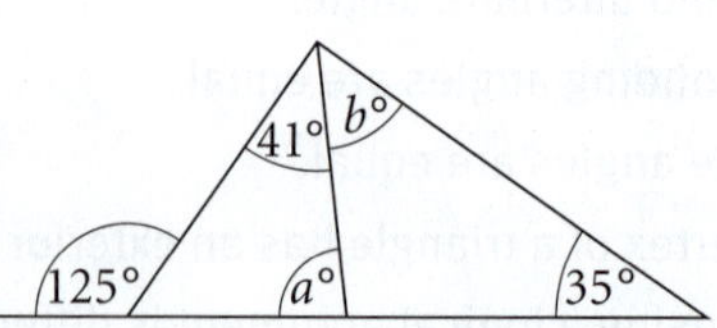

Diagram not drawn accurately

6 Give reasons for each of these statements.

a $a = e$ **b** $b = d$
c $g = c$ **d** $f = d$

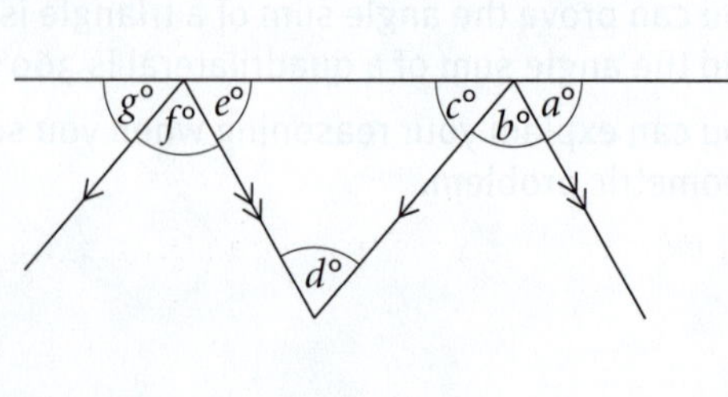

6 Planning and collecting data

In the United States of America elections are held every two years to choose members for the House of Representatives. This is one of the groups of people who run the country.

Each American state chooses representatives. The number they can choose depends on the how many people live in that state. The more people who live in a state, the more representatives they can choose. It is therefore very important that accurate records are kept of the number of people living in each state.

In order to keep accurate records, a census is held every 10 years. A census is a way of collecting data. It is a questionnaire that must be filled in by every household in the USA.

The most recent census was in 2010. The questionnaire had only 10 questions, which people were able to answer in about 10 minutes. The results of the 2010 census showed that there were 308 745 538 people living in the USA. There are 435 representatives in the House of Representatives. This means that there is one representative for roughly every 710 000 people in the USA.

Key words

Make sure you learn and understand these key words:

- method of collection
- survey
- questionnaire
- interview
- experiment
- observations
- population
- sample
- degree of accuracy
- discrete data
- continuous data
- frequency tables
- equal class intervals
- two-way table

The map shows how many representatives there are in each state of the USA. You can see that even though California is not the largest state, it has the largest number of representatives. This is because it has the largest number of people living there, out of all the other states in the USA.

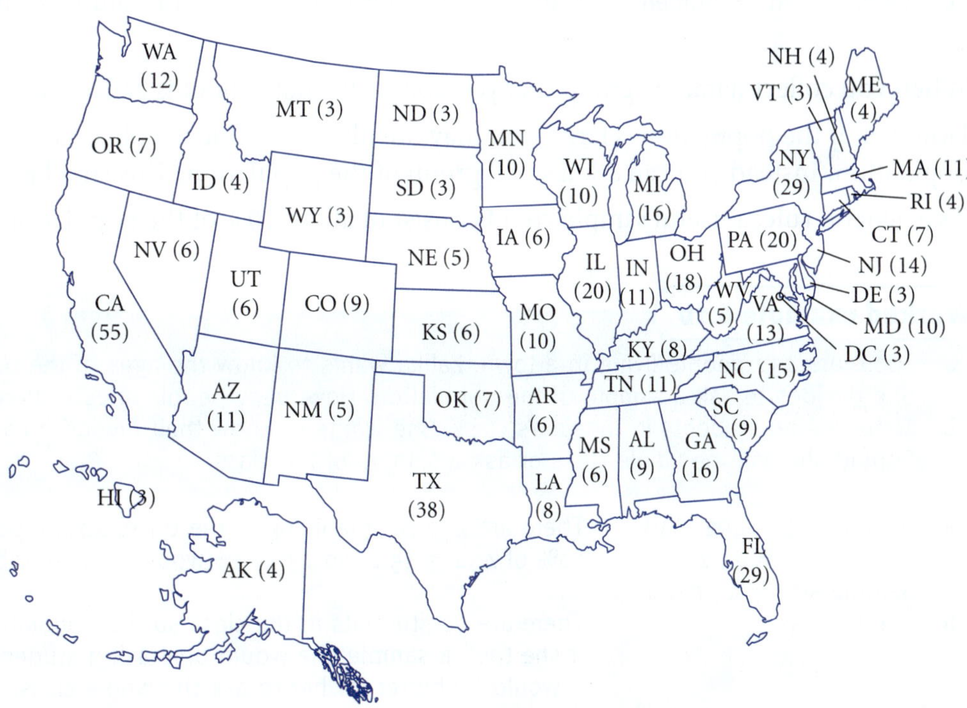

In this unit you will learn more about collecting data, and also about the different types of data.

6.1 Collecting data

When you need to answer a question in statistics, you start by collecting data.

First, you need to decide how to collect the data. You need to decide upon a **method of collection**.

If you need to ask people questions, you can carry out a **survey**. You can do this by:

- giving people a **questionnaire** to fill in
- asking them the questions yourself and carrying out an **interview**.

If you need to record the results of an event happening, you can do this by:

- carrying out an **experiment**
- recording **observations** that you make.

Worked example 6.1a

How would you collect data to answer these questions?

a What is the favourite food and drink of the students in your class?
b How many cars pass your school in one hour?
c How many times will a dice show a 6 when it is rolled 100 times?

a	Carry out a survey.	You could either give the students in your class a questionnaire to fill in, or you could interview each of them and ask them the questions.
b	Record observations.	You could sit outside the school gates and record the number of cars that pass the school in an hour.
c	Carry out an experiment.	You could roll a dice 100 times and record how many times it shows a 6.

When you collect data, the group that you collect the data about is called the **population**.

However, if the population is large, you may not always be able to collect data from everyone in the population. Instead you can ask a small group of the population. This small group is called a **sample**.

As a general rule, a useful sample could consist of about 10% of the population.

Worked example 6.1b

a There are 452 people living in a town. Zalika wants to know the ages of the people living in the town. She decides to ask a sample of the population. How many people should there be in her sample?
b There are 30 students in Tanesha's class. She wants to know their favourite colour. Should she ask the whole class or ask a sample of the class?

a	10% of 452 = 452 ÷ 10 = 45.2 Sample size = 45 people	There are 452 people living in the town, so the population size is 452. 10% of 452 = 45.2, so 45 or 46 would be a suitable sample size.
b	Whole class	There are 30 students in the class so the population is 30. 10% of 30 = 3. If she took a sample she would only ask 3 students. This is too small. It would be better for her to ask the whole class.

When you collect data that involves measurements, you must make sure the data is given to a suitable **degree of accuracy**. For example, if you were recording the heights of the students in your class, you would probably write the measurents to the nearest centimetre. You certainly wouldn't give the measurements to the nearest metre, otherwise they would probably all be the same!

Exercise 6.1

1 Which of the three methods of collection would you use to collect this data?

Experiment	Observation	Survey

a the number of times a drawing pin lands 'point down' when it is dropped 200 times
b the number of people that go into your local grocery shop each hour
c the number of brothers and sisters that students in your class have
d the type and number of pets owned by people living in your street or village
e the number of times the king of hearts is drawn from a pack of playing cards in 100 draws
f the number of people that use your local swimming pool in the morning
g the number of times people in your family travelled by train in the last month

2 Mia runs a rollerskating club. She wants to ask the members of the club if they would like to have training on a Wednesday evening.
There are 38 members in the club.
Should Mia ask all the members of the club, or should she ask a sample of the members?
Explain your answer.

3 A football team has 860 members in their fan club. The secretary of the club wants to know if the fans would like some half-time entertainment during home matches.
a Give two reasons why the secretary should ask a sample of the members.
b How many members of the fan club should there be in the sample?

4 The population of a village is 340. The local nurse wants to know how often the people in the village visit the doctor. She decides to ask a sample of the population. How many people should there be in her sample?

5 There are 948 students in a school. The headteacher wants to know if the students would prefer to have their lunch break at 12.30 pm or 1.30 pm. She decides to ask a sample of the school population. How many students should there be in her sample? Give a reason for your answer.

6 Which of **A**, **B** or **C** would be the most suitable degree of accuracy for measuring:
a the heights of the students in a class
A nearest millimetre **B** nearest centimetre **C** nearest metre
b the weights of the students in a class
A nearest 10 kilograms **B** nearest kilogram **C** nearest 0.1 of a kilogram
c the time it takes students to run 400 m
A nearest minute **B** nearest second **C** nearest 0.01 of a second

7 Ahmad wanted to know how often people in his village go swimming.
He decided to carry out a survey. This is what he wrote.

> *The population of my village is 238.*
> *I interviewed a sample of 15 people and recorded their answers on this data collection sheet.*
>
> *Question* How often do you go swimming?
>
> *Answer*

	Tally	Frequency
Never	|||	3
Sometimes	||	2
Often	𝍸 ||	7
Very often	|||	3

> *Conclusion* My results show me that the people in my village go swimming a lot.

a In groups of two or three, discuss and write down the answers to these questions.
   i What do you think of Ahmad's decision to ask a sample of 15 people?
   ii What do you think of Ahmad's data collection sheet?
   iii What do you think of Ahmad's conclusion?

b Still in your groups, complete this task.
   i Design a better data collection sheet for Ahmad's question.
   ii Use your data collection sheet to collect data from the students in your class.
   iii Write a conclusion based on the data you have collected.

c Compare your data collection sheet and your conclusion with those of other groups.

8 Oditi wanted to know how many pets the people in her village own.
She decided to carry out a survey. This is what she wrote.

> *The population of my village is 576, so I interviewed a sample of 60 people.*
> *I recorded their answers on the data collection sheet below.*
>
> *Question* How many pets do you own?
>
> *Answer*

Number of pets	1-3	3-4	4-6	7-10
Number of people	~~3~~ ~~7~~ ~~9~~ 18	~~2~~ ~~3~~ ~~6~~ 10	~~1~~ ~~4~~ ~~8~~ ~~11~~ 13	~~3~~ ~~9~~ ~~11~~ 12

> *Conclusion* My results show me that the people in my village have lots of pets.

a In groups of two or three, discuss and write down the answers to these questions.
   i What do you think of Oditi's decision to ask a sample of 60 people?
   ii What do you think of Oditi's data collection sheet?
   iii What do you think of Oditi's conclusion?

b Still in your groups, complete this task.
   i Design a better data collection sheet for Oditi's question.
   ii Use your data collection sheet to collect data from the students in your class.
   iii Write a conclusion based on the data you have collected.

c Compare your data collection sheet and your conclusion with those of other groups.

6.2 Types of data

There are two types of data that involve numbers, **discrete data** and **continuous data**.

Discrete data is data that can only have exact values. The values are usually whole numbers, but can include fractions.

> Numbers of goals scored and numbers of people are examples of discrete data.

Continuous data is data that can take any value in a range. All data that is measured is continuous data. If you round the measurements to the nearest whole number, the data is still continuous.

> Heights of trees and masses of babies are examples of continuous data.

Worked example 6.2

Write down whether the data is discrete or continuous.

a the number of cars in a car park.
b the height of trees in a forest.
c the time it takes to run 100 m.

a	Discrete	The number of cars must be a whole number, so it is discrete data.
b	Continuous	Height is measured, so it is continuous data.
c	Continuous	Time is measured, so it is continuous data.

Exercise 6.2

1 Write down whether each type of data is discrete or continuous.

a the number of fence posts in a garden
b the length, in metres, of each car in a car park
c the weights of pineapples in a box
d the number of pineapples in a box
e the number of chairs in a classroom
f the heights of the students in a classroom
g the number of mobile phones sold one day
h the time it takes to complete a crossword puzzle
i the waist sizes of trousers sold in a shop
j the number of pairs of trousers sold in a shop

2 Dakarai is explaining how he carried out a survey.

> I have asked 10 people the size of the shoes they wear. My results are 6, $6\frac{1}{2}$, 8, 9, $9\frac{1}{2}$, $10\frac{1}{2}$, 10, $7\frac{1}{2}$, 8, $6\frac{1}{2}$. This is continuous data as the values aren't whole numbers.

Is he correct? Explain your answer.

3 Harsha is explaining how she carried out a survey.

> I have asked 10 people their ages. My results are 23, 25, 22, 18, 36, 42, 12, 15, 17, 20. This is discrete data as the values are whole numbers.

Is she correct? Explain your answer.

6.3 Using frequency tables

You can use **frequency tables** with **equal class intervals** to gather continuous data.

A frequency table has three columns. The first column lists the class intervals, the second is for recording the tally marks and the third is for the frequency.

When you use a frequency table with tallies, make sure the tally column is wide enough for lots of results.

To describe the class intervals, you can use these symbols:

$<$ which means 'less than'

and $\leqslant$ which means 'less than or equal to'.

Examples: The class 63 kg $< m \leqslant$ 65 kg means any mass (w) from 63 kg, but not including 63 kg, up to and including a mass of 65 kg.

The class 63 kg $\leqslant m <$ 65 kg means any mass (w) from 63 kg, including 63 kg, up to but not including a mass of 65 kg.

Worked example 6.3a

Here are the masses (w kilograms) of 20 teachers, measured to the nearest kilogram. Put these masses into a grouped frequency table.

74	83	79	88	62	76	90	88	91	70
72	77	85	71	95	81	91	66	80	74

Use the class intervals $60 < m \leqslant 70$, $70 < m \leqslant 80$, $80 < m \leqslant 90$ and $90 < m \leqslant 100$.

Mass, m (kg)	Tally	Frequency
$60 < m \leqslant 70$	///	3
$70 < m \leqslant 80$	~~////~~ ///	8
$80 < m \leqslant 90$	~~////~~ /	6
$90 < m \leqslant 100$	///	3
	Total	20

62, 70 and 66 go in this group.
74, 79, 76, 72, 77, 71, 80 and 74 go in this group.
83, 88, 90, 88, 85 and 81 go in this group.
91, 95 and 91 go in this group.
Add the frequencies to check the total is 20.

You can use a **two-way table** to record two or more sets of discrete data. In a two-way table you record different information in the rows and columns in a way that makes it easy to read the information.

Worked example 6.3b

The two-way table shows the results of the games played by a hockey team in one season.

a How many home games did the hockey team lose?
b How many away games did the hockey team win?
c How many games did the hockey team draw altogether?
d What is the total number of games that the hockey team played in this season?

	Win	Draw	Lose	Total
Home games	7	3	2	12
Away games	3	4	5	12
Total	10	7	7	24

a 2 This is the number in the 'Home games' row and 'Lose' column.
b 3 This is the number in the 'Away games' row and 'Win' column.
c 7 This is the number in the 'Total' row and 'Draw' column.
d 24 This is the number in the 'Total' row and 'Total' column.

Exercise 6.3

1 Here are the heights of 20 adults, measured to the nearest centimetre.

161	193	180	167	151	188	170	171	159	179
182	166	177	185	164	175	155	173	180	160

a Copy and complete the grouped frequency table.

b How many of the adults are more than 180 cm tall but less than or equal to 190 cm tall?

c How many of the adults are more than 170 cm tall? Explain how you use the grouped frequency table to work out your answer.

d How many of the adults are less than or equal to 180 cm tall? Explain how you use the grouped frequency table to work out your answer.

Height, h (cm)	Tally	Frequency
$150 < h \leqslant 160$		
$160 < h \leqslant 170$		
$170 < h \leqslant 180$		
$180 < h \leqslant 190$		
$190 < h \leqslant 200$		
	Total	

2 All the students in Mrs Turay's class ran the 200 m race. These are their times, in seconds.

30	33	42	36	32	46	45	34	50
31	49	26	38	44	39	32	40	35
41	38	39	45	40	36	44	37	43

a Copy and complete the grouped frequency table.

b How many students are in Mrs Turay's class?

c How many students ran the 200 m in more than 40 seconds, but less than or equal to 45 seconds?

d How many students took more than 35 seconds to run the 200 m race?

e How many students took 35 seconds or less to run the 200 m race?

Time, t (seconds)	Tally	Frequency
$25 < t \leqslant 30$		
$30 < t \leqslant 35$		
$35 < t \leqslant 40$		
$40 < t \leqslant 45$		
$45 < t \leqslant 50$		
	Total	

3 Here are the heights, in centimetres, of some plants.

10	34	19	10	20	26	17	28	15
41	24	16	18	11	17	25	37	14

a Put these heights into a grouped frequency table.
Use the class intervals $10 \leqslant h < 18$, $18 \leqslant h < 26$, $26 \leqslant h < 34$ and $34 \leqslant h < 42$.

b How many plants are in the survey?

c How many of the plants are greater than or equal to 18 cm high, but less than 26 cm high?

d How many of the plants are less than 34 cm high?

e How many of the plants are at least 26 cm high?

4 The two-way table shows the hair colour and gender of the students in Miss Jebson's class.

	Brown hair	Black hair	Other hair colour	Total
Girls	6	5	3	14
Boys	10	4	2	16
Total	16	9	5	30

a How many of the boys have black hair?
b How many of the girls have brown hair?
c How many students are there altogether in Miss Jebson's class?
d How many of the students do not have brown hair?

5 The two-way table shows the favourite subjects of the students in Mr Hassan's class.

	Maths	Science	English	Other subject	Total
Girls	8	4		1	18
Boys	6		1		
Total		9			32

Use the 'Total' column and 'Total' row to help work out the missing values in the table.

a Copy and complete the table.
b How many of the boys chose science as their favourite subject?
c How many of the students didn't choose maths, science or English as their favourite subject?

6 A school has 42 teachers. All the teachers travel to school by car, bus or bicycle.
20 of the teachers are male. Five of the male teachers and three of the female teachers cycle to school.
17 of the teachers travel to school by bus.
10 of the female teachers travel to school by car.
Copy and complete the two-way table to show the numbers of teachers that travel to school by car, bus and bicycle.

	Car	Bus	Bicycle	Total
Male				
Female				
Total				

Summary

You should now know that:

- ★ You can carry out a survey by either giving people a questionnaire to fill in, or by carrying out an interview.
- ★ You can record the results of an event happening by either carrying out an experiment or by recording observations that you make.
- ★ Discrete data can only have exact values.
- ★ Continuous data can take any value in a range, and it is data that is measured.
- ★ You can use the symbols $<$ and $\leqslant$ to help describe the class intervals in a frequency table.
- ★ In a two-way table you record different information in the rows and columns in a way that makes it easy to read the information.

You should be able to:

- ★ Identify and collect data to answer a question.
- ★ Select the method of data collection.
- ★ Decide on the sample size.
- ★ Decide on the degree of accuracy needed for data that involves measurements.
- ★ Know the difference between discrete and continuous data.
- ★ Construct and use frequency tables, with given equal class intervals, to gather continuous data.
- ★ Construct and use two-way tables to record discrete data.

End-of-unit review

1 Which of the three methods of collection would you use to collect this data?

Experiment | Observation | Survey

a the number of times a coin lands 'face down' when it is dropped 150 times
b the number of people that go into your local hospital each hour
c the number of pairs of shoes owned by students in your class

2 Ros runs a dance class. She wants to ask her students if they would prefer to start the class at 7 pm or 8 pm. There are 46 students in the class.
Should Ros ask all the students in the class, or should she ask a sample of the students?
Explain your answer.

3 The population of a village is 986. Mason wants to know how often the people in the village use the village hall. He decides to ask a sample of the population. How many people should be in his sample?

4 Which of the following, **A**, **B** or **C** would be the most suitable degree of accuracy for measuring:
a the lengths of the longest rivers in the world
A nearest centimetre **B** nearest metre **C** nearest kilometre
b the time it takes students to run 10 km
A nearest hour **B** nearest minute **C** nearest second

5 Write down whether the following data is discrete or continuous.
a the number of eggs in a basket **b** the time it takes to prepare a meal

6 Here are the weights of some kittens, measured to the nearest gram.

155	171	200	195	230	205	208	180
185	198	212	190	205	175	210	224

a Copy and complete the grouped frequency table.
b How many of the kittens weigh more than 170 g but less than or equal to 190 g?
c How many of the kittens weigh more than 190 g?
d How many of the kittens weigh less than or equal to 210 g?
e Altogether, how many kittens were weighed?

Weight, w (g)	**Tally**	**Frequency**
$150 < w \leqslant 170$		
$170 < w \leqslant 190$		
$190 < w \leqslant 210$		
$210 < w \leqslant 230$		
	Total	

7 All the students in Mr Flynn's class took a maths <u>or</u> a science exam. They all scored grade A, B <u>or</u> C.
There are 28 students in the class. 10 of the students took the science exam.
Four of the students scored a grade A for maths, five scored a grade A for science.
Eight students scored a grade C, three of these were in science.

Copy and complete the two-way table to show the numbers of grades A, B and C that were given for maths and science.

	A	**B**	**C**	**Total**
Maths				
Science				
Total				

7 Fractions

Fractions are used in everyday life more often than you think. One important use of fractions is in music.

Here is an example of a few bars of music.

A <u>bar</u> lasts a particular length of time, measured in number of beats. Different types of musical <u>notes</u> last for different numbers of beats. This means that the number of notes that can fit into each bar depends on the type of notes.

Key words

Make sure you learn and understand these key words:

- terminating
- recurring
- common denominator
- improper fraction
- mixed number

Imagine that a bar is like a cake. The number of slices (notes) that it can be cut into depends on how large the slices are (how many beats each note lasts for).

This table to the right shows the names of some of the different types of note. It also shows the length of time (number of beats) that each note must last.

You can see that two minims (half notes) last the same length of time as one semibreve (whole note).

Note	Name	Fraction	Number of beats
	semibreve	whole note (1)	4
	minim	half note $\left(\frac{1}{2}\right)$	2
	crotchet	quarter note $\left(\frac{1}{4}\right)$	1
	quaver	eighth note $\left(\frac{1}{8}\right)$	$\frac{1}{2}$
	semiquaver	sixteenth note $\left(\frac{1}{16}\right)$	$\frac{1}{4}$

The diagram on the right shows how many of each of the different types of note are needed to last four beats.

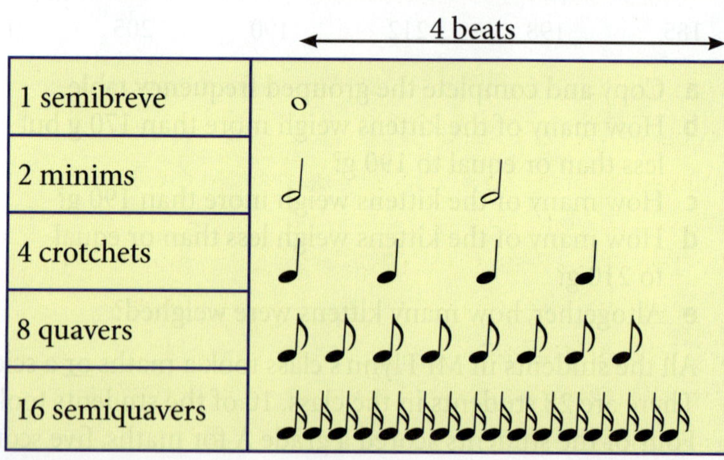

Two or more quavers or semiquavers can be joined together, as shown here:

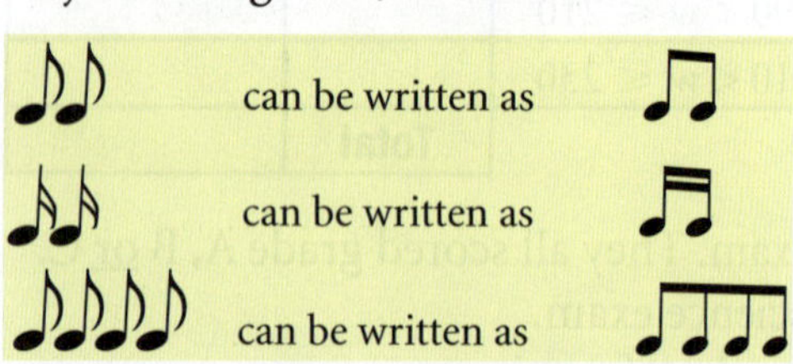

In the piece of music on the right, each bar must contain three beats. Try to think of a combination of notes that would fill the third and fourth bars.

In this chapter you will learn more about fractions. You will learn how to convert between fractions, decimals and percentages. You will also learn how to find fractions of quantities and integers as well as how to add and subtract mixed numbers.

7.1 Finding equivalent fractions, decimals and percentages

Some common equivalent fractions, decimals and percentages are shown below.

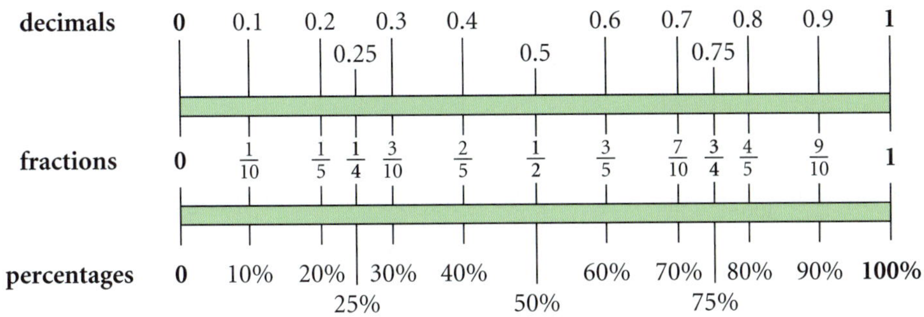

The numerator is the number on top of a fraction; the denominator is the number at the bottom.

Worked example 7.1a

Write **a** 40% as a fraction **b** 0.75 as a percentage.

a $40\% = \frac{2}{5}$ — 40% is a commonly used percentage. 40% as a fraction is $\frac{40}{100} = \frac{2}{5}$.

b $0.75 = 75\%$ — 0.75 is a commonly used decimal. 0.75 as a percentage is 75%.

You can convert between fractions, decimals and percentages. Just follow these steps.

Fraction to decimal

① Write the fraction as an equivalent fraction with a denominator of 10 or 100 or 1000 or …

② Write this equivalent fraction as a decimal. Use a decimal place-value table.

Example: $\frac{3}{5} = \frac{6}{10}$, $\frac{6}{10} = 0.6$

Decimal to percentage

Multiply the decimal by 100 to turn it into a percentage.

Example: $0.6 \times 100 = 60\%$

Fraction to percentage

Follow the 'Fraction to decimal' steps, then the 'Decimal to percentage' step.

Or if you can, write the fraction with a denominator of 100, then the numerator is the same as the percentage.

Example: $\frac{2}{50} = \frac{4}{100}, \frac{4}{100} = 4\%$

Decimal to fraction

① Write the decimal as a fraction. Use a decimal place-value table.

② Cancel this fraction to its lowest terms.

Example: $0.22 = \frac{22}{100}$, $\frac{22}{100} = \frac{11}{50}$

Percentage to decimal

Divide the percentage by 100 to turn it into a decimal.

Example: $5\% \div 100 = 0.05$

Percentage to fraction

① Write the percentage as a fraction with a denominator of 100.

② Cancel this fraction to its lowest terms.

Example: $64\% = \frac{64}{100}$, $\frac{64}{100} = \frac{16}{25}$

Worked example 7.1b

Write: **a** 32% as a fraction **b** $\frac{3}{20}$ as a percentage.

a $32\% = \frac{32}{100}$ First, write 32% as a fraction with a denominator of 100.

$\frac{32 \div 4}{100 \div 4} = \frac{8}{25}$ Cancel the fraction to its lowest terms.

b $\frac{3 \times 5}{20 \times 5} = \frac{15}{100}$ First, write $\frac{3}{20}$ as an equivalent fraction with a denominator of 100.

$\frac{15}{100} = 15\%$ You can either say that $\frac{15}{100}$ is '15 out of 100' so is 15%, or you can change $\frac{15}{100}$ into the decimal 0.15, then multiply by 100 to get 15%.

Exercise 7.1

1 Use the numbers from the box to complete these sentences.
You can only use each number once.

0.6	0.4	$\frac{7}{10}$	75%	$\frac{1}{4}$	80%	$\frac{1}{5}$	0.75	$\frac{1}{2}$

a $0.25 = \square$ **b** $40\% = \square$ **c** $\frac{4}{5} = \square$ **d** $50\% = \square$

e $60\% = \square$ **f** $0.2 = \square$ **g** $0.7 = \square$ **h** $\square = \square$

2 Write each percentage as: **i** a decimal **ii** a fraction.

a 14% **b** 74% **c** 24% **d** 8%

3 Write each decimal as: **i** a percentage **ii** a fraction.

a 0.34 **b** 0.06 **c** 0.68 **d** 0.81

4 Write each fraction as: **i** a decimal **ii** a percentage.

a $\frac{9}{25}$ **b** $\frac{7}{20}$ **c** $\frac{1}{25}$ **d** $\frac{19}{20}$

5 This is part of Harsha's homework.
Use Harsha's method to write these fractions as percentages.

a $\frac{1}{8}$ **b** $\frac{7}{8}$ **c** $\frac{3}{40}$

d $\frac{19}{40}$ **e** $\frac{4}{125}$ **f** $\frac{67}{125}$

g $\frac{51}{200}$ **h** $\frac{3}{200}$ **i** $\frac{133}{200}$

j $\frac{471}{500}$ **k** $\frac{17}{500}$ **l** $\frac{9}{500}$

Question Write these fractions as percentages.
a $\frac{3}{8}$ b $\frac{7}{40}$

Answer a $\frac{3 \times 125}{8 \times 125} = \frac{375}{1000}, \frac{375}{1000} = 0.375$

$0.375 \times 100 = 37.5\%$

b $\frac{7 \times 25}{40 \times 25} = \frac{175}{1000}, \frac{175}{1000} = 0.175$

$0.175 \times 100 = 17.5\%$

7.2 Converting fractions to decimals

You already know how to convert a fraction to a decimal using equivalent fractions. You can also use division to convert a fraction to a decimal.

The fraction $\frac{6}{25}$ is 'six twenty-fifths', 'six out of twenty-five' or 'six divided by twenty-five'.

To work out the fraction as a decimal, divide 6 by 25: $6 \div 25 = 0.24$

> Use a calculator to do this.

The decimal 0.24 is a **terminating** decimal because it comes to an end.

When you convert the fraction $\frac{71}{99}$ to a decimal you get: $71 \div 99 = 0.71717171\ldots$

The number 0.71717171… is a **recurring** decimal as the digits 7 and 1 carry on repeating forever. You can write 0.71717171… with the three dots at the end to show that the number goes on forever. You can also write the number as $0.\dot{7}\dot{1}$, with dots above the 7 and the 1, to show that the 7 and 1 carry on repeating forever.

> A recurring decimal can always be written as a fraction.

Worked example 7.2

Use division to convert each fraction to a decimal. In part **c** give your answer correct to 3 d.p.

a $\frac{3}{8}$ **b** $\frac{5}{11}$ **c** $\frac{3}{7}$

a $3 \div 8 = 0.375$ This answer is a terminating decimal, so write down all the digits.

b $5 \div 11 = 0.\dot{4}\dot{5}$ This answer is a recurring decimal, so write it as $0.\dot{4}\dot{5}$ or 0.4545….

c $3 \div 7 = 0.428571428\ldots$
$= 0.429$ (3 d.p.) This answer is a recurring decimal as the digits 428571 are repeated, but this time you are asked to round the number to three decimal places.

Exercise 7.2

1 Use division to convert each of these fractions to a terminating decimal.

a $\frac{17}{25}$ **b** $\frac{11}{20}$ **c** $\frac{1}{8}$ **d** $\frac{5}{16}$ **e** $\frac{29}{32}$

2 Use division to convert each of these fractions to a recurring decimal.

a $\frac{2}{3}$ **b** $\frac{1}{9}$ **c** $\frac{7}{11}$ **d** $\frac{13}{33}$ **e** $\frac{41}{333}$

3 Use division to convert each of these fractions to a decimal, correct to three decimal places.

a $\frac{5}{13}$ **b** $\frac{6}{7}$ **c** $\frac{16}{21}$ **d** $\frac{18}{35}$ **e** $\frac{126}{289}$

4 Sasha is told that $\frac{1}{15} = 0.0\dot{6}$ and that $\frac{1}{22} = 0.0\dot{4}\dot{5}$.

Without using a calculator, she must match each red fraction card with its correct blue decimal card.

$\frac{4}{15}$ $\frac{7}{22}$ $0.2\dot{6}$ $0.3\dot{1}\dot{8}$

Sasha thinks that $\frac{4}{15} = 0.2\dot{6}$ and that $\frac{7}{22} = 0.3\dot{1}\dot{8}$.

Do you think she is correct? Explain your answer.

7.3 Ordering fractions

To write fractions in order of size, you need to compare the fractions.

One way to do this is to write all the fractions as equivalent fractions with the same denominator. This denominator is called the **common denominator**.

Another way is to use division and write each fraction as a decimal number. You may need to write these numbers to one, two, three or more decimal places to put them in order.

Worked example 7.3

a Use equivalent fractions to write these fractions in order of size, smallest first. $\frac{2}{3}, \frac{8}{15}, \frac{3}{5}$

b Use division to write these fractions in order of size, largest first. $\frac{8}{11}, \frac{7}{8}, \frac{4}{5}$

a $\frac{2}{3} = \frac{2 \times 5}{3 \times 5} = \frac{10}{15}$ The smallest number that 3, 5 and 15 all go into is 15, so use 15 as the common

$\frac{3}{5} = \frac{3 \times 3}{5 \times 3} = \frac{9}{15}$ denominator. $\frac{8}{15}$ doesn't need changing, but $\frac{2}{3}$ and $\frac{3}{5}$ do.

$\frac{8}{15}, \frac{9}{15}, \frac{10}{15}$ The fractions in order of size are $\frac{8}{15}, \frac{9}{15}, \frac{10}{15}$.

$\frac{8}{15}, \frac{3}{5}, \frac{2}{3}$ Write your final answer using the fractions you were given in the question.

b $8 \div 11 = 0.7272...$ This is a recurring decimal, so write down the first few decimal places.

$7 \div 8 = 0.875$ This is a terminating decimal, so write down all the decimal places.

$4 \div 5 = 0.8$ This is also a terminating decimal, so write down all the decimal places.

0.875, 0.8, 0.7272... 0.875 is the largest, followed by 0.8 then 0.7272...

$\frac{7}{8}, \frac{4}{5}, \frac{8}{11}$ Write your final answer using the fractions you were given in the question.

Exercise 7.3

1 Use equivalent fractions to write these fractions in order of size, smallest first.

a $\frac{11}{12}, \frac{5}{6}, \frac{3}{4}$ **b** $\frac{4}{7}, \frac{1}{2}, \frac{9}{14}$ **c** $\frac{2}{3}, \frac{5}{9}, \frac{11}{18}$ **d** $\frac{9}{10}, \frac{3}{4}, \frac{4}{5}$ **e** $\frac{5}{6}, \frac{3}{4}, \frac{5}{8}$ **f** $\frac{7}{10}, \frac{4}{15}, \frac{1}{6}$

2 Use division to write these fractions in order of size, largest first.

a $\frac{1}{3}, \frac{3}{10}, \frac{4}{11}$ **b** $\frac{8}{15}, \frac{11}{20}, \frac{4}{7}$ **c** $\frac{5}{18}, \frac{2}{9}, \frac{18}{61}$ **d** $\frac{12}{21}, \frac{11}{16}, \frac{3}{5}$ **e** $\frac{19}{25}, \frac{17}{20}, \frac{9}{11}$ **f** $\frac{32}{35}, \frac{17}{18}, \frac{11}{12}$

3 Write these fractions in order of size, smallest first. Show your working.

$\frac{5}{12}, \frac{1}{3}, \frac{4}{9}, \frac{11}{27}$

4 Jake arranges these fraction cards in order of size, largest first.

$\frac{5}{6}$ $\frac{4}{5}$ $\frac{3}{4}$ $\frac{2}{3}$ $\frac{1}{2}$

Without doing any calculations, explain how you can tell that Jake has arranged the cards in the correct order.

7.4 Adding and subtracting fractions

You already know that you can only add or subtract fractions when the denominators are the same.

If the denominators are different, you must write the fractions as equivalent fractions with a common denominator, then add or subtract the numerators.

Worked example 7.4a

Work out $\frac{2}{3}+\frac{1}{6}$.

$\frac{2}{3}+\frac{1}{6}=\frac{4}{6}+\frac{1}{6}$ The denominators are not the same so change the $\frac{2}{3}$ into $\frac{4}{6}$.

$\frac{4}{6}+\frac{1}{6}=\frac{5}{6}$ The denominators are now the same so add the numerators.

Remember that the LCM of 3 and 6 is 6.

In an **improper fraction** the numerator is bigger than the denominator.

$\frac{3}{2}, \frac{14}{3}$ and $\frac{53}{34}$ are improper fractions.

A **mixed number** contains a whole-number part and a fractional part.

$1\frac{1}{2}, 2\frac{3}{4}$ and $14\frac{11}{12}$ are mixed numbers.

When you add mixed numbers, follow these steps.

① Add the whole-number parts.

② Add the fractional parts and cancel this answer to its simplest form. If this answer is an improper fraction, write it as a mixed number.

③ Add your answers to steps ① and ②.

When you subtract mixed numbers, follow these steps.

① Change both mixed numbers into improper fractions.

② Subtract the improper fractions and cancel this answer to its simplest form.

③ If the answer is an improper fraction, change it back to a mixed number.

Worked example 7.4b

Work these out. **a** $2\frac{1}{4}+3\frac{5}{6}$ **b** $3\frac{1}{2}-1\frac{3}{5}$

a ① $2+3=5$ Add the whole-number parts.

② $\frac{1}{4}+\frac{5}{6}=\frac{3}{12}+\frac{10}{12}=\frac{13}{12}$ Add the fractional parts using a common denominator of 12.

$\frac{13}{12}=1\frac{1}{12}$ Check that this fraction is in its simplest form and write as a mixed number.

③ $5+1\frac{1}{12}=6\frac{1}{12}$ Add the two parts together to get the final answer.

b ① $3\frac{1}{2}=\frac{7}{2}$ and $1\frac{3}{5}=\frac{8}{5}$ Change both the mixed numbers into improper fractions.

② $\frac{7}{2}-\frac{8}{5}=\frac{35}{10}-\frac{16}{10}=\frac{19}{10}$ Subtract the fractions using a common denominator of 10.

③ $\frac{19}{10}=1\frac{9}{10}$ The answer is an improper fraction so change it back to a mixed number.

Exercise 7.4

1 Work out these additions and subtractions.
Write each answer in its simplest form.

a $\frac{1}{2}+\frac{3}{8}$ **b** $\frac{3}{5}+\frac{1}{10}$ **c** $\frac{2}{9}+\frac{5}{18}$ **d** $\frac{1}{3}+\frac{2}{5}$ **e** $\frac{3}{4}+\frac{1}{6}$ **f** $\frac{2}{9}+\frac{4}{11}$

g $\frac{7}{8}-\frac{1}{4}$ **h** $\frac{4}{5}-\frac{7}{15}$ **i** $\frac{11}{12}-\frac{2}{3}$ **j** $\frac{8}{9}-\frac{1}{2}$ **k** $\frac{4}{5}-\frac{1}{3}$ **l** $\frac{7}{8}-\frac{2}{3}$

2 Work out these additions and subtractions.
Write each answer in its simplest form.
Write it as a mixed number when appropriate.

a $\frac{2}{3}+\frac{7}{9}$ **b** $\frac{3}{4}+\frac{7}{12}$ **c** $\frac{5}{6}+\frac{5}{18}$ **d** $\frac{4}{5}+\frac{5}{9}$ **e** $\frac{2}{3}+\frac{5}{7}$ **f** $\frac{8}{9}+\frac{5}{12}$

g $\frac{3}{2}-\frac{1}{4}$ **h** $\frac{7}{5}-\frac{1}{10}$ **i** $\frac{10}{3}-\frac{5}{6}$ **j** $\frac{8}{3}-\frac{2}{5}$ **k** $\frac{5}{4}-\frac{1}{6}$ **l** $\frac{9}{2}-\frac{8}{3}$

3 Copy and complete these additions.

a $4\frac{1}{3}+2\frac{5}{7}$ ① $4+2=6$ ② $\frac{1}{3}+\frac{5}{7}=\frac{\square}{21}+\frac{\square}{21}=\frac{\square}{21},\ \frac{\square}{21}=1\frac{\square}{21}$ ③ $6+1\frac{\square}{21}=7\frac{\square}{21}$

b $8\frac{4}{15}+5\frac{9}{10}$ ① $8+5=13$ ② $\frac{4}{15}+\frac{9}{10}=\frac{\square}{30}+\frac{\square}{30}=\frac{\square}{30},\ \frac{\square}{30}=\frac{\square}{6}=1\frac{\square}{6}$ ③ $13+1\frac{\square}{6}=14\frac{\square}{6}$

4 Copy and complete these subtractions.

a $4\frac{1}{4}-1\frac{3}{5}$ ① $\frac{17}{4}-\frac{8}{5}$ ② $\frac{17}{4}-\frac{8}{5}=\frac{\square}{20}-\frac{\square}{20}=\frac{\square}{20}$ ③ $\frac{\square}{20}=2\frac{\square}{20}$

b $9\frac{1}{6}-3\frac{5}{12}$ ① $\frac{\square}{6}-\frac{41}{12}$ ② $\frac{\square}{6}-\frac{41}{12}=\frac{\square}{12}-\frac{41}{12}=\frac{\square}{12}$ ③ $\frac{\square}{12}=\frac{\square}{4}=5\frac{\square}{4}$

5 Work out these additions and subtractions. Show all the steps in your working.

a $3\frac{1}{4}+\frac{5}{8}$ **b** $7\frac{4}{5}+1\frac{1}{15}$ **c** $6\frac{5}{9}+3\frac{25}{36}$ **d** $2\frac{3}{4}+\frac{6}{7}$ **e** $12\frac{5}{8}+4\frac{9}{10}$ **f** $6\frac{5}{6}+3\frac{4}{5}$

g $2\frac{3}{5}-\frac{7}{10}$ **h** $3\frac{1}{6}-\frac{11}{18}$ **i** $4\frac{1}{14}-1\frac{5}{7}$ **j** $4\frac{2}{3}-1\frac{11}{12}$ **k** $5\frac{2}{3}-3\frac{1}{4}$ **l** $7\frac{5}{12}-6\frac{11}{18}$

6 Zalika has two pieces of fabric.

One of the pieces is $1\frac{3}{4}$ m long. The other is $2\frac{3}{8}$ m long.

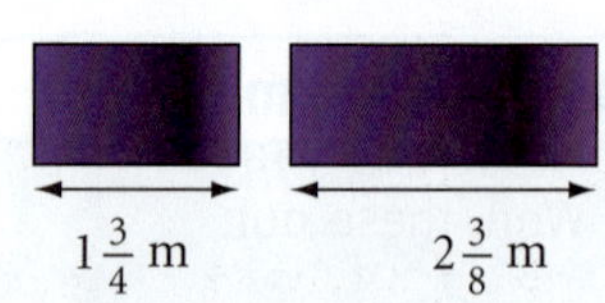

a What is the difference in the lengths of the two pieces of fabric?

b Zalika lays out the pieces end to end.
What is the total length of fabric?

7 Xavier has a length of wood that is $5\frac{1}{4}$ m long.
First of all Xavier cuts a piece of wood $1\frac{3}{5}$ m long from the length of wood.
Then he cuts a piece of wood $2\frac{9}{10}$ m long from the piece of wood he has left.
How long is the piece of wood that Xavier has left over?

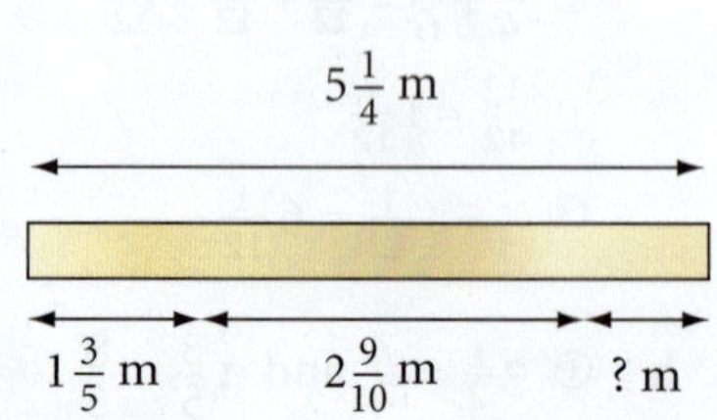

7.5 Finding fractions of a quantity

To work out a fraction of a quantity, divide the quantity by the denominator of the fraction, then multiply your answer by the numerator.

> You can use the multiplication facts that you know to work out simple fractions of quantities mentally.

Worked example 7.5a

Work out $\frac{3}{5}$ of 30 kg.

$30 \div 5 = 6$	First, find $\frac{1}{5}$ of 30 kg by dividing 30 by 5.
$6 \times 3 = 18$ kg	Then multiply your answer of 6 by 3 to find $\frac{3}{5}$ of 30 kg. Remember to include the units (kg) in your answer.

When you find a fraction of a quantity, you do not always get a whole-number answer. You know this is going to happen when the denominator doesn't divide into the quantity exactly.

When this happens, the best method is to multiply the quantity by the numerator first. Then divide the answer by the denominator and write your final answer as a mixed number.

Worked example 7.5b

Work out $\frac{2}{3}$ of 20 km.

$2 \times 20 = 40$	3 does not divide exactly into 20, so multiply 20 by 2 instead.
$40 \div 3 = 13\frac{1}{3}$ km	Now divide 40 by 3. This gives 13, with a remainder of 1, so the answer is $13\frac{1}{3}$. Remember to include the units (km) in your answer.

Exercise 7.5

1 Work these out mentally.

a $\frac{3}{4}$ of \$12 **b** $\frac{2}{5}$ of 10 m **c** $\frac{4}{7}$ of 21 kg **d** $\frac{5}{8}$ of 40 cm **e** $\frac{6}{11}$ of 33 ml

2 Work out these fractions of quantities. Give each answer as a mixed number.

a $\frac{3}{5}$ of 16 kg **b** $\frac{2}{3}$ of 23 t **c** $\frac{3}{8}$ of \$33 **d** $\frac{4}{9}$ of 47 mg **e** $\frac{5}{6}$ of 25 mm

3 Wyn has six blue question cards and five yellow answer cards.

Yellow cards: 14 m; 10 m; $11\frac{2}{3}$ m; $13\frac{1}{3}$ m; $12\frac{2}{3}$ m

Blue cards: $\frac{4}{9}$ of 30 m; $\frac{7}{12}$ of 24 m; $\frac{5}{9}$ of 18 m; $\frac{5}{6}$ of 14 m; $\frac{2}{3}$ of 19 m; $\frac{3}{14}$ of 56 m

a Match each blue card with the correct yellow card.

b What is the answer on the missing yellow card?

7.6 Multiplying an integer by a fraction

You have learned how to find a fraction of a quantity, with whole-number or mixed-number answers. When you multiply an integer by a fraction, you use exactly the same methods as you used previously.

> The word 'of' means 'multiply', so $\frac{2}{3}$ of 15 means the same as $\frac{2}{3} \times 15$.

Worked example 7.6

Work these out. **a** $\frac{2}{3} \times 15$ **b** $26 \times \frac{3}{8}$

a	$15 \div 3 = 5$	You can work this out mentally as 3 will divide exactly into 15 to give you 5.
	$5 \times 2 = 10$	Now multiply the 5 by 2 to give an answer of 10.
b	$26 \times 3 = 78$	8 does not divide exactly into 26, so <u>multiply</u> 26 by 3 instead.
	$78 \div 8 = 9\frac{6}{8}$	Now divide 78 by 8. This gives 9 with a remainder of 6, so the answer is $9\frac{6}{8}$.
	$9\frac{6}{8} = 9\frac{3}{4}$	Cancel $\frac{6}{8}$ to $\frac{3}{4}$, giving $9\frac{3}{4}$ as the final answer in its lowest terms.

Notice that the fraction at the end of the solution to part **b** can be cancelled. It is often easier and quicker to cancel, when possible, <u>before</u> doing any of the calculations.

> Look again at the solution to part **b**. Here is a quicker way to work out the answer.

Looking again at $26 \times \frac{3}{8}$, start by dividing 26 and 8 by 2: $\overset{13}{\cancel{26}} \times \frac{3}{\underset{4}{\cancel{8}}}$

This has simplified the numbers, so now you have to work out $13 \times \frac{3}{4}$.

You cannot cancel any further, so carry on as normal: $13 \times 3 = 39$, $39 \div 4 = 9\frac{3}{4}$

Exercise 7.6

1 Work these out mentally.

a $\frac{3}{4} \times 20$ **b** $\frac{4}{5} \times 30$ **c** $72 \times \frac{3}{8}$ **d** $27 \times \frac{2}{3}$ **e** $81 \times \frac{7}{9}$ **f** $\frac{5}{12} \times 60$

2 Work out the following.
Give each answer as a mixed number in its lowest terms.

a $\frac{3}{8} \times 33$ **b** $\frac{2}{9} \times 20$ **c** $41 \times \frac{3}{5}$

d $14 \times \frac{5}{6}$ **e** $21 \times \frac{7}{12}$ **f** $\frac{3}{20} \times 50$

> In parts **d**, **e** and **f** cancel before you do any calculations.

3 This is part of Dakarai's homework.
Has he worked out the answer correctly?
Explain your answer.

> *Question* Work out $\frac{4}{15} \times 78$.
>
> *Answer* $\frac{4}{\underset{3}{\cancel{15}}} \times \overset{26}{\cancel{78}}$, $4 \times 26 = 104$
>
> $104 \div 3 = 34\frac{2}{3}$

7.7 Dividing an integer by a fraction

To divide an integer by a fraction, turn the fraction upside down then multiply by the integer. Then use the same method that you have used previously.

> Remember to cancel, if possible, before you do any calculations.

Worked example 7.7

Work these out. **a** $12 \div \frac{3}{8}$ **b** $25 \div \frac{10}{13}$

a	$12 \times \frac{8}{3}$	Turn the fraction upside down and multiply.
	$12 \div 3 = 4$	Work out 12 ÷ 3 mentally, as 3 will divide exactly into 12 to give 4.
	$4 \times 8 = 32$	Now multiply the 4 by 8 to give an answer of 32.
b	$25 \times \frac{13}{10}$	Turn the fraction upside down and multiply.
	$\overset{5}{\cancel{25}} \times \frac{13}{\cancel{10}\,_2}$	You can divide 25 and 10 by 5, so cancel first. The question is now $5 \times \frac{13}{2}$.
	$5 \times 13 = 65$	You cannot cancel any further, so multiply the 5 by the 13.
	$65 \div 2 = 32\frac{1}{2}$	Finally work out 65 ÷ 2 and write the answer as a mixed number.

Exercise 7.7

1 Work these out.

a $21 \div \frac{3}{4}$ **b** $15 \div \frac{5}{6}$ **c** $24 \div \frac{6}{7}$ **d** $18 \div \frac{9}{10}$ **e** $30 \div \frac{10}{13}$ **f** $20 \div \frac{4}{11}$

2 Work these out. Give each answer as a mixed number in its lowest terms.
In all parts, cancel before you do any calculations.

a $16 \div \frac{6}{7}$ **b** $12 \div \frac{8}{11}$ **c** $22 \div \frac{4}{9}$ **d** $34 \div \frac{4}{5}$ **e** $45 \div \frac{18}{23}$ **f** $21 \div \frac{14}{15}$

3 Which of these cards gives an answer that is different from the other two?
Show all your working.

A $45 \div \frac{5}{8}$ **B** $51 \div \frac{17}{25}$ **C** $10 \div \frac{2}{15}$

4 This is part of Anders's homework.
Use Anders's method to work these out.

a $4 \div \frac{8}{9}$ **b** $7 \div \frac{14}{19}$

c $3 \div \frac{9}{11}$ **d** $8 \div \frac{24}{29}$

e $6 \div \frac{18}{25}$ **f** $9 \div \frac{36}{41}$

Question Work out $5 \div \frac{10}{17}$

Answer $5 \div \frac{10}{17} = \overset{1}{\cancel{5}} \times \frac{17}{\cancel{10}^{2}}$

$= 1 \times \frac{17}{2}$

$17 \div 2 = 8\frac{1}{2}$

7.8 Multiplying and dividing fractions

When you need to multiply and divide simple fractions mentally, follow these rules.

When you multiply fractions, multiply the numerators together and multiply the denominators together.

Example: $\frac{1}{3} \times \frac{5}{7} = \frac{1 \times 5}{3 \times 7} = \frac{5}{21}$

When you divide fractions, start by turning the second fraction upside down, then multiply the fractions as usual.

Example: $\frac{2}{3} \div \frac{5}{11} = \frac{2}{3} \times \frac{11}{5} = \frac{2 \times 11}{3 \times 5} = \frac{22}{15} = 1\frac{7}{15}$

This is quite a lot of work to do mentally. It is simpler to think of it as multiplying the diagonal pairs of numbers together like this.

$$\frac{2}{3} \div \frac{5}{11} = \frac{2 \times 11}{3 \times 5} = \frac{22}{15}$$

The answer, $\frac{22}{15}$, is an improper fraction, so change it to a mixed number. $\frac{22}{15} = 1\frac{7}{15}$

Whether you are multiplying or dividing, once you have worked out the answer, cancel it to its simplest form when possible. If the answer is an improper fraction, turn it into a mixed number.

Worked example 7.8

Work these out. **a** $\frac{5}{6} \times \frac{2}{3}$ **b** $\frac{3}{4} \div \frac{5}{12}$

a $\frac{5 \times 2}{6 \times 3} = \frac{10}{18}$ Multiply the numerators together and multiply the denominators together.

$\frac{10}{18} = \frac{5}{9}$ 10 and 18 can both be divided by 2, so cancel the answer to its simplest form.

b $\frac{3 \times 12}{4 \times 5} = \frac{36}{20}$ Multiply the diagonal pairs of numbers.

$\frac{36}{20} = 1\frac{16}{20}$ The answer is an improper fraction, so changed to a mixed number.

$1\frac{16}{20} = 1\frac{4}{5}$ 16 and 20 can both be divided by 4, so cancel the answer to its simplest form.

Exercise 7.8

1 Work these out mentally.

a $\frac{1}{4} \times \frac{1}{2}$ **b** $\frac{3}{4} \times \frac{1}{4}$ **c** $\frac{2}{3} \times \frac{1}{5}$ **d** $\frac{4}{5} \times \frac{2}{5}$ **e** $\frac{3}{7} \times \frac{3}{4}$ **f** $\frac{7}{9} \times \frac{2}{3}$

2 Work out mentally.
Cancel each answer to its simplest form.

a $\frac{3}{4} \times \frac{2}{5}$ **b** $\frac{2}{3} \times \frac{3}{4}$ **c** $\frac{4}{5} \times \frac{3}{8}$ **d** $\frac{1}{6} \times \frac{8}{9}$ **e** $\frac{3}{10} \times \frac{5}{6}$ **f** $\frac{6}{11} \times \frac{1}{3}$

3 Work these out mentally.

a $\frac{1}{4} \div \frac{2}{3}$ **b** $\frac{1}{2} \div \frac{3}{5}$ **c** $\frac{3}{8} \div \frac{4}{7}$

d $\frac{4}{5} \div \frac{1}{9}$ **e** $\frac{3}{5} \div \frac{2}{11}$ **f** $\frac{9}{10} \div \frac{1}{3}$

In parts **d, e** and **f** write your answer as a mixed number.

4 Work these out mentally.
Cancel each answer to its simplest form.

a $\frac{3}{4} \div \frac{1}{2}$ **b** $\frac{4}{5} \div \frac{3}{10}$ **c** $\frac{5}{6} \div \frac{2}{3}$ **d** $\frac{4}{9} \div \frac{1}{3}$ **e** $\frac{6}{7} \div \frac{3}{7}$ **f** $\frac{7}{8} \div \frac{3}{4}$

5 Copy this secret code box.

_	E	_	_	_	_	_	_	_	_	_	_	_	_	_	_
$1\frac{1}{9}$	$\frac{1}{6}$	$\frac{4}{7}$	$1\frac{1}{14}$	3	$\frac{8}{9}$	$1\frac{1}{9}$	3	$1\frac{1}{14}$	$\frac{9}{22}$	$\frac{5}{18}$	$\frac{7}{10}$	$\frac{5}{18}$	$\frac{9}{10}$	$\frac{1}{35}$	$\frac{4}{7}$

Work out the answer to each of the questions in the box on the right.
Find the answer in the secret code box, then write the letter from the question box above the answer.

For example, the first question is $\frac{1}{4} \times \frac{2}{3}$.

$\frac{1}{4} \times \frac{2}{3} = \frac{2}{12} = \frac{1}{6}$, so E goes above $\frac{1}{6}$ in the table.

What is the secret message?

E	$\frac{1}{4} \times \frac{2}{3}$	U	$\frac{1}{5} \times \frac{1}{7}$
L	$\frac{2}{3} \div \frac{3}{4}$	I	$\frac{1}{5} \div \frac{2}{7}$
H	$\frac{3}{4} \times \frac{6}{11}$	S	$\frac{4}{9} \times \frac{5}{8}$
F	$\frac{4}{5} \div \frac{8}{9}$	A	$\frac{3}{5} \div \frac{2}{10}$
N	$\frac{6}{7} \times \frac{2}{3}$	T	$\frac{5}{7} \div \frac{2}{3}$
M	$\frac{8}{9} \div \frac{4}{5}$		

Summary

You should now know that:

- ★ You can use division to convert a fraction to a decimal by dividing the numerator by the denominator.
- ★ To work out a fraction of a quantity, when you expect the answer to be a fraction, multiply the quantity by the numerator then divide by the denominator.
- ★ To multiply an integer by a fraction, use the same method as for finding a fraction of a quantity.
- ★ To divide an integer by a fraction, turn the fraction upside down and multiply.
- ★ To multiply one fraction by another, multiply the numerators together and multiply the denominators together.
- ★ To divide one fraction by another, turn the second fraction upside down and multiply.

You should be able to:

- ★ Find equivalent fractions, decimals and percentages by converting between them.
- ★ Convert a fraction to a decimal using division.
- ★ Know that a recurring decimal is a fraction.
- ★ Order fractions by writing with common denominators or dividing and converting to decimals.
- ★ Add and subtract fractions and mixed numbers.
- ★ Calculate fractions of quantities with fraction answers.
- ★ Multiply and divide an integer by a fraction.
- ★ Use the laws of arithmetic to simplify calculations with integers and fractions (cancel).
- ★ Use known facts to multiply and divide simple fractions.

End-of-unit review

1 The table below lists some common fractions, decimals and percentages. Copy and complete the table.

Fraction	$\frac{3}{4}$				$\frac{2}{5}$	
Decimal		0.8		0.3		
Percentage			20%			50%

2 Write 32% as: **a** a decimal **b** a fraction.

3 Write 0.06 as: **a** a percentage **b** a fraction.

4 Write $\frac{4}{25}$ as: **a** a decimal **b** a percentage.

5 Use division to convert each of these fractions to a decimal.
Give your answer to part **c** correct to three decimal places.

a $\frac{3}{8}$ **b** $\frac{4}{11}$ **c** $\frac{17}{41}$

6 Write these fractions in order of size, <u>smallest</u> first.
Show your working.

$\frac{11}{20}$ $\frac{5}{8}$ $\frac{3}{5}$ $\frac{1}{2}$

7 Work out these additions and subtractions.
Write each answer in its simplest form.

a $\frac{1}{4}+\frac{5}{8}$ **b** $\frac{9}{10}-\frac{2}{5}$ **c** $\frac{5}{7}+\frac{2}{3}$ **d** $\frac{2}{3}-\frac{1}{4}$ **e** $2\frac{5}{6}+3\frac{1}{4}$ **f** $4\frac{1}{2}-2\frac{5}{9}$

8 Simon has two pieces of carpet.
One of the pieces is $3\frac{1}{2}$ m long. The other is $4\frac{3}{5}$ m long.

a What is the difference in the lengths of the two pieces of carpet?

b Simon lays the two pieces of carpet together, end to end.
What is the total length of the carpet?

9 Work these out mentally.

a $\frac{3}{4}$ of \$24 **b** $\frac{3}{5}\times 35$ **c** $\frac{1}{3}\times\frac{1}{8}$ **d** $\frac{3}{5}\times\frac{4}{7}$ **e** $\frac{1}{3}\div\frac{2}{5}$ **f** $\frac{4}{7}\div\frac{3}{8}$

10 Work these out. Give each answer as a mixed number in its lowest terms.

a $\frac{2}{3}$ of 14 kg **b** $\frac{3}{5}\times 18$ **c** $\frac{7}{8}\times 22$ **d** $14\div\frac{4}{5}$ **e** $24\div\frac{12}{19}$

In parts **c**, **d** and **e** cancel before you do any calculations.

11 Which of these cards gives an answer that is different from the other two?
Show all your working.

A	**B**	**C**
$32\times\frac{3}{5}$	$81\div\frac{9}{2}$	$42\times\frac{3}{7}$

8 Shapes and geometric reasoning

Wherever you look, you will see objects of different shapes and sizes. Many are natural, but many have been designed by someone.

An architect is a person who plans and designs buildings. Architects make scale drawings, and often scale models, of the buildings they plan. They make sure their designs follow local rules and regulations and they make sure the people who build their buildings follow the plans correctly.

Key words

Make sure you learn and understand these key words:

- hypotenuse
- congruent
- corresponding sides
- corresponding angles
- line symmetry
- rotational symmetry
- diagonal
- bisect
- net
- scale drawing
- scale

Towns and cities all over the world have buildings designed to meet the needs of people who live and work there.

The Burj Khalifa in Dubai is the tallest building in the world (as of 2012). It is over 828 metres tall and contains 163 floors. It holds the record for having an elevator with the longest travel distance in the world. Construction began in September 2004 and the building was officially opened in January 2010. The Burj Khalifa cost $1.5 billion to construct.

In the 1970s Piet Blom designed the Cubic Houses, in Rotterdam, the Netherlands. Each house is a cube, tilted at a 45° angle. Each house is supposed to represent a tree, with the village forming a 'forest'.

In this unit you will learn how to interpret and make scale drawings. You will look at the symmetry of 2D shapes as well as other properties of quadrilaterals.

8.1 Recognising congruent shapes

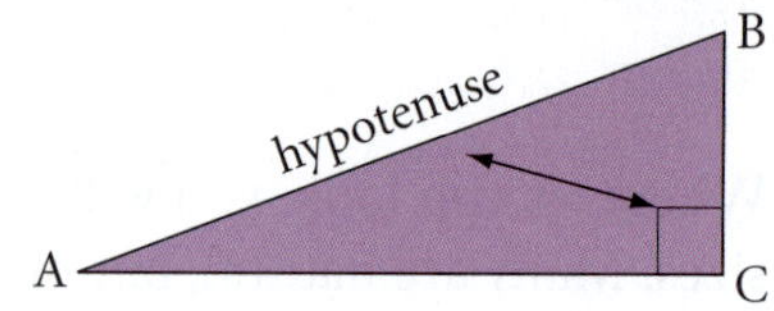

The diagram shows the right-angled triangle, ABC.

The longest side of the triangle, AB, is called the **hypotenuse**.
The hypotenuse is always the side opposite the right angle.

Worked example 8.1a

In each triangle, which side is the hypotenuse?

a

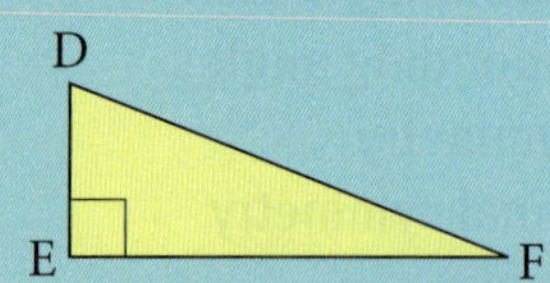

b

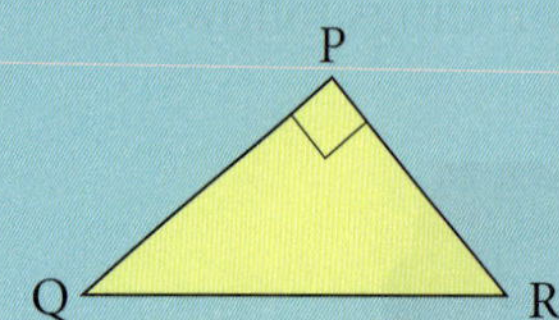

a DF The side DF is the longest side and it is the side opposite the right angle at E.

b QR The side QR is the longest side and it is the side opposite the right angle at P.

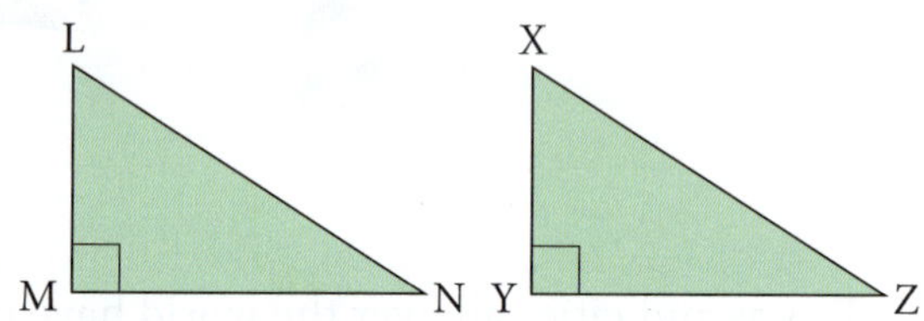

On the right are two right-angled triangles, LMN and XYZ.

Can you see that the triangles are identical in shape and size?
Shapes that are identical in shape and size are **congruent**.

The side LM is equal in length to the side XY. So sides LM and XY are **corresponding sides**.

Angle MLN is equal in size to angle YXZ. So ∠MLN and ∠YXZ are **corresponding angles**.

In congruent shapes, corresponding sides are equal and corresponding angles are equal.

In triangles LMN and XYZ, LM = XY, MN = YZ and LN = XZ and ∠MLN = ∠YXZ, ∠LNM = ∠XZY and ∠NML = ∠ZYX.

> ∠MLN is a mathematical way of writing 'angle MLN'.

Worked example 8.1b

a Which of these shapes are congruent to shape A?

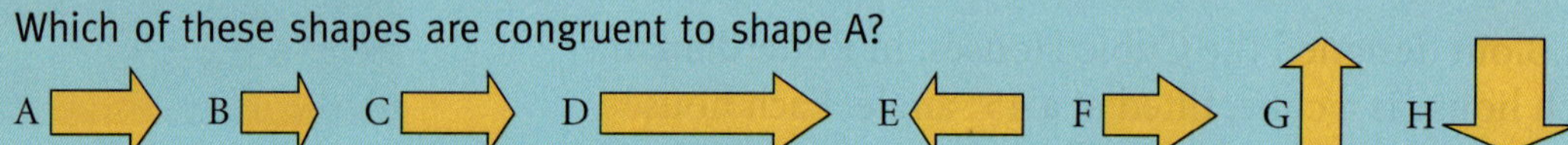

b These two triangles are congruent.

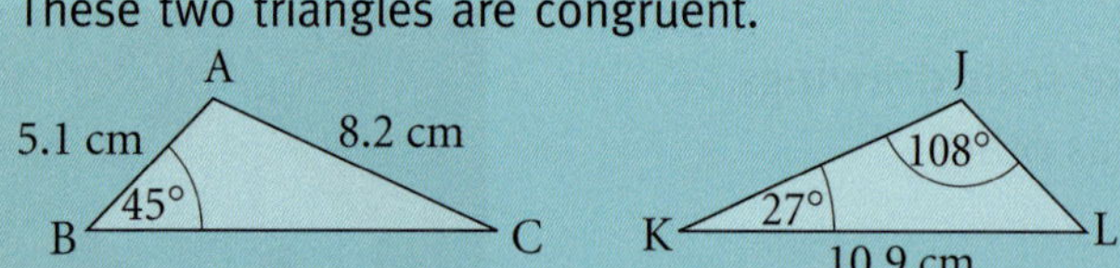

i Write down the lengths of the sides BC and JL.
ii What size are ∠BAC and ∠KLJ?

a C, E and G — Even though E and G are pointing in different directions to A, they are still identical in shape and size, so are congruent to it. B, D, F and H aren't congruent to A because B is shorter than A, D is longer than A, F has a longer arrow head than A, H is wider than A.

b i BC = 10.9 cm — BC and LK are corresponding sides so BC = KL.
JL = 5.1 cm — JL and AB are corresponding sides so JL = AB.

ii ∠BAC = 108° — ∠BAC and ∠LJK are corresponding angles so ∠BAC = ∠LJK.
∠KLJ = 45° — ∠KLJ and ∠CBA are corresponding angles so ∠KLJ = ∠CBA.

Exercise 8.1

1 Which side is the hypotenuse in each right-angled triangle?

a
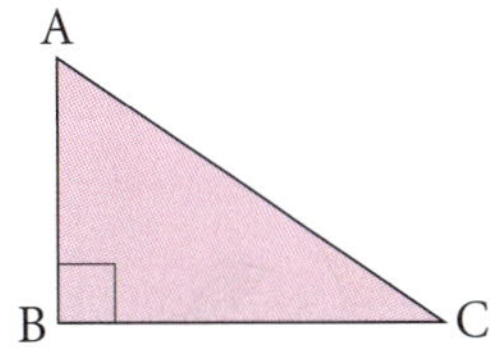

b
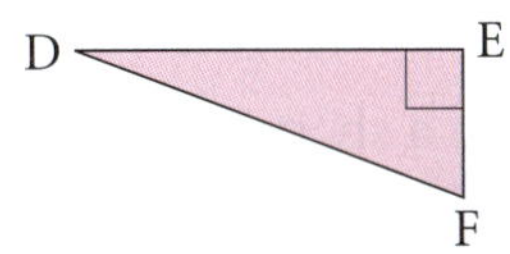

c
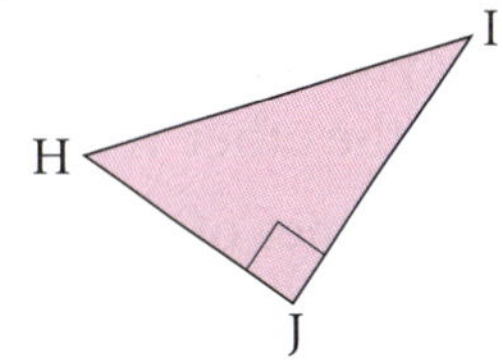

d
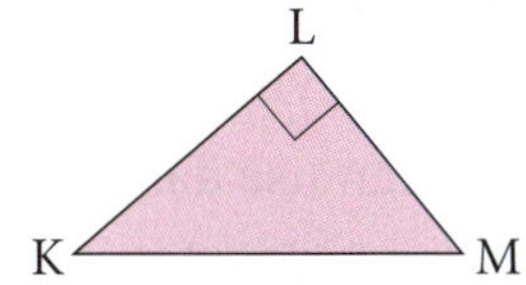

2 Which of these shapes are congruent to shape A?

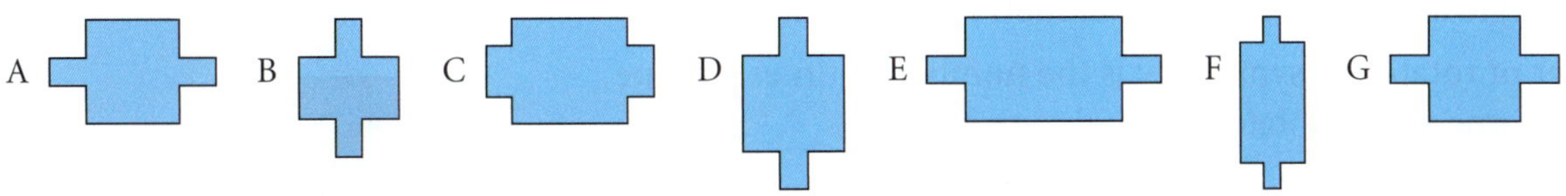

3 These two triangles are congruent.

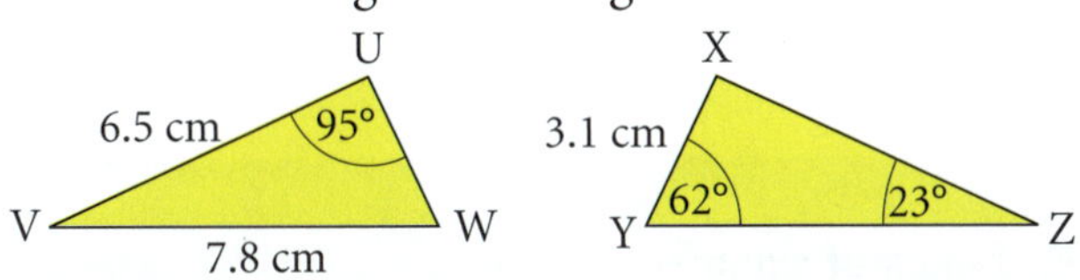

a Write down the length of the side: **i** UW **ii** XZ **iii** YZ.

b Write down the size of: **i** ∠UVW **ii** ∠UWV **iii** ∠YXZ

4 These two shapes are drawn accurately.
They are congruent.

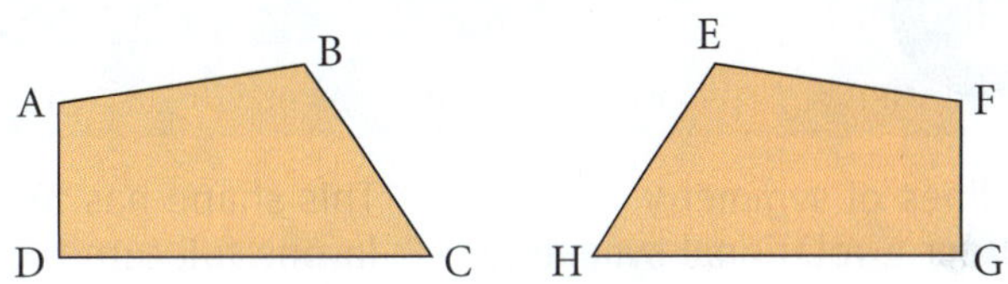

a Which side corresponds to: **i** AD **ii** BC **iii** EF **iv** GH?

b Which angle corresponds to: **i** ∠ADC **ii** ∠BAD **iii** ∠FEH **iv** ∠EHG?

5 This is part of Razi's homework.

Question Here are two accurately drawn congruent shapes.
a Write down one pair of corresponding angles.
b Explain why these angles are corresponding.

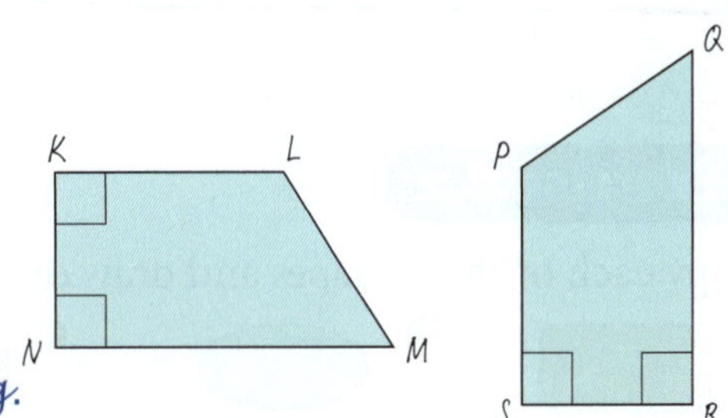

Answer **a** ∠LKN and ∠SRQ are corresponding.
b They are corresponding because they are both 90°.

Has Razi got his homework correct? Explain your answer.

6 Read what Harsha says. Is she correct? Explain your answer.

In an equilateral triangle all the angles are 60°. This means that all equilateral triangles must be congruent as all the angles are the same size.

8.2 Identifying symmetry of 2D shapes

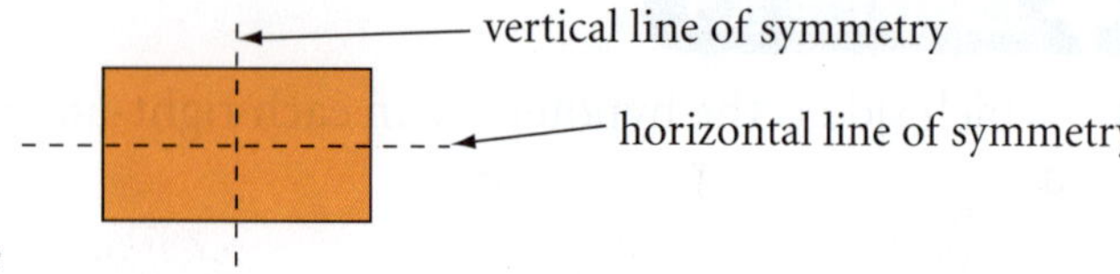

A 2D shape may have **line symmetry** and it may have **rotational symmetry**.

This rectangle has two lines of symmetry. One of the lines of symmetry is horizontal, the other vertical.

You can use dashed lines to show lines of symmetry on a shape.

If you fold a shape along its lines of symmetry, one half of the shape will fit exactly on top of the other half.

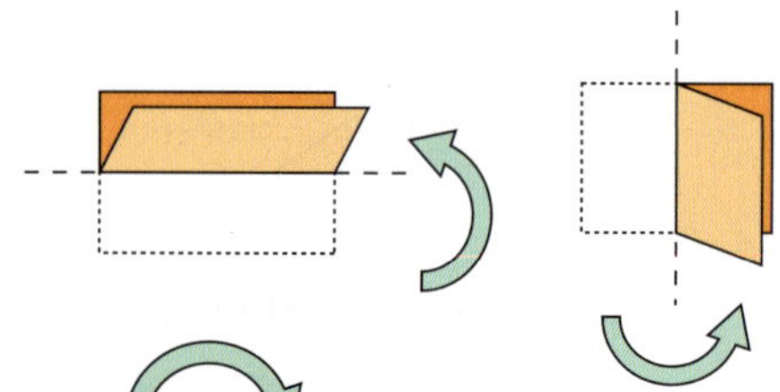

This rectangle also has rotational symmetry of order 2.

The order of rotational symmetry is the number of times a shape looks the same as it is rotated through one full turn.

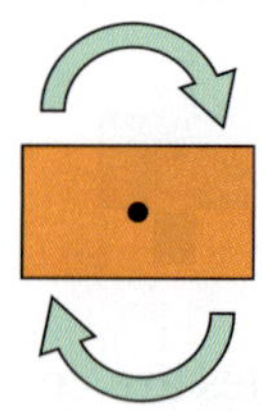

Worked example 8.2

For each of these shapes write down: **i** the number of lines of symmetry
ii the order of rotational symmetry.

a

b

a **i** 2 lines of symmetry
ii Order 2 rotational symmetry

This shape has two diagonal lines of symmetry.
In one full turn the shape will look exactly the same twice, once after rotating it 180° and again after 360°.

b **i** No lines of symmetry

It is not possible to draw any lines of symmetry onto this parallelogram.

ii Order 2 rotational symmetry

In one full turn the parallelogram will look exactly the same twice, once after rotating it 180° and again after 360°.

Exercise 8.2

1 Copy each of these shapes and draw on the lines of symmetry.

a  **b** 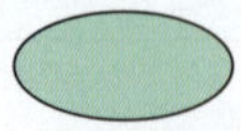 **c**  **d** 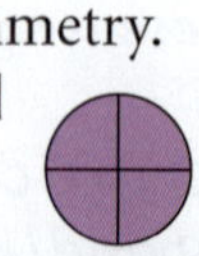

e  **f** 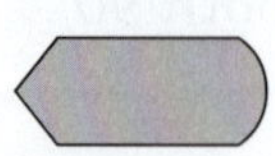 **g**  **h** 

i  **j**  **k**  **l** 

2 For each of the shapes in question **1**, write down the order of rotational symmetry.

3 Write down the number of lines of symmetry for each shape.

a 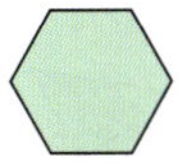 **b** 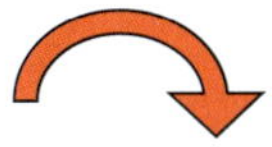 **c** 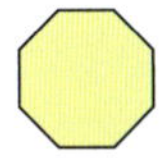 **d** 

e  **f**  **g**  **h** 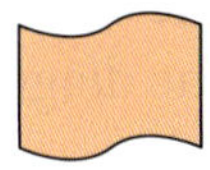

4 For each of the shapes in question **3**, write down the order of rotational symmetry.

5 Copy and complete the table to show the symmetry properties of some quadrilaterals.

Shape	**Square**	**Rectangle**	**Rhombus**	**Parallelogram**	**Kite**	**Trapezium**	**Isosceles trapezium**
Number of lines of symmetry							
Order of rotational symmetry							

6 For each triangle, write down: **i** the number of lines of symmetry
ii the order of rotational symmetry.

a 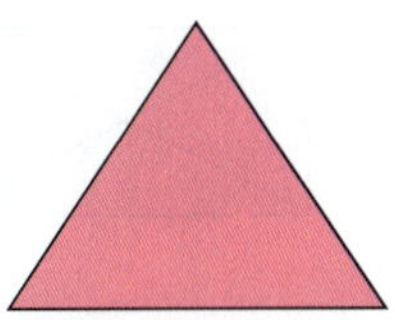
equilateral triangle

b 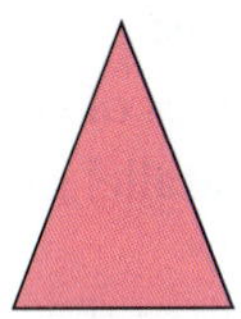
isosceles triangle

c 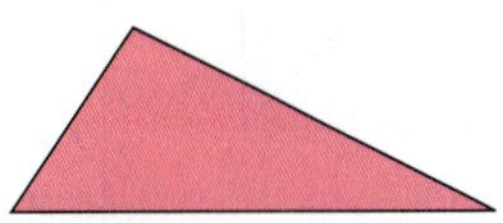
scalene triangle

d 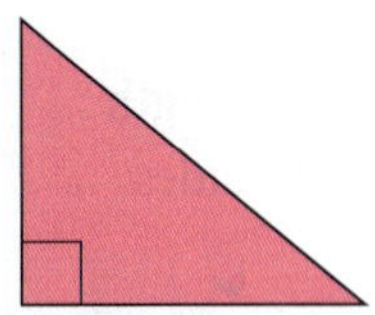
right-angled isosceles triangle

7 In each diagram the blue lines are lines of symmetry. Copy and complete each diagram.

a 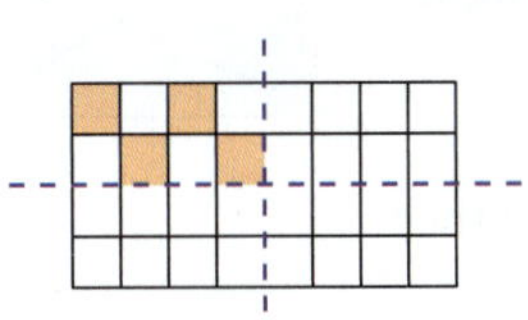

b 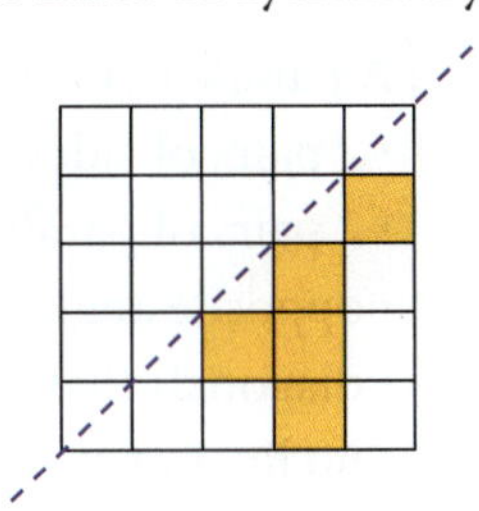

c 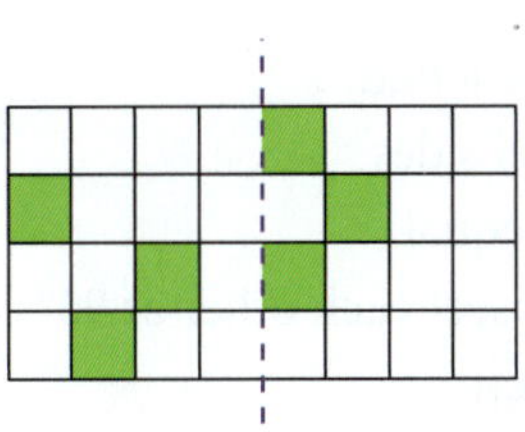

8 Shen has made this pattern from yellow and blue tiles. He also has two spare blue tiles.

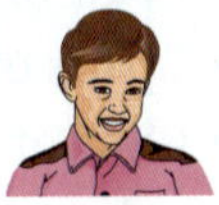

> There are eight different ways I can add the two blue tiles to the pattern to make a pattern with only one line of symmetry.
> There are two different ways I can add the two blue tiles to the pattern to make a pattern with two lines of symmetry.
> There is only one way I can add the two blue tiles to the pattern to make a pattern with four lines of symmetry.

Show that Shen's statements are correct. You can join the tiles side to side 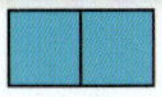 or corner to corner 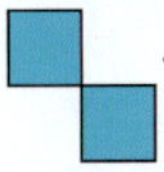.

8.3 Classifying quadrilaterals

A quadrilateral is a 2D shape with four straight sides.

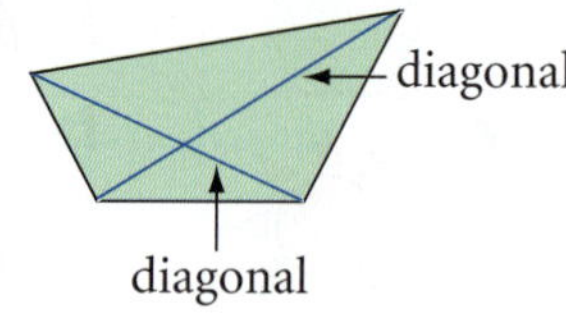

A **diagonal** is a line that joins two opposite corners of a quadrilateral. Every quadrilateral has two diagonals. The diagonals always cut (cross) each other.

In some quadrilaterals the diagonals **bisect** each other. The word 'bisect' means to cut in half.

In a rectangle the diagonals bisect each other.

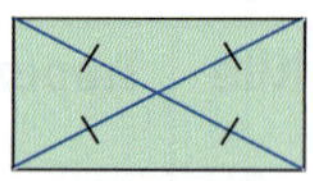

In a kite only one diagonal bisects the other.

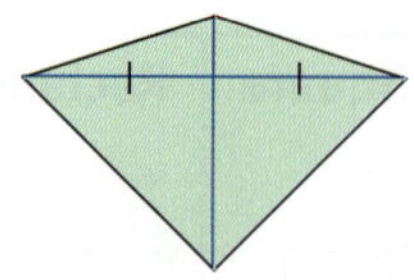

In some quadrilaterals the diagonals cut or bisect each other at 90° (right angles).

In a square the diagonals bisect each other at right angles.

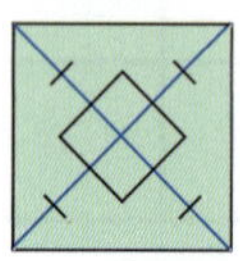

In a parallelogram the diagonals bisect each other, but not at right angles.

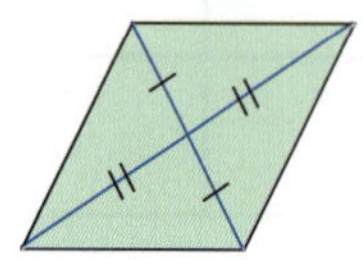

Here is a summary of the properties of the special quadrilaterals that you should know.

A square has:
- all sides the same length
- 2 pairs of parallel sides
- all angles 90°
- diagonals that bisect each other at 90°
- 4 lines of symmetry
- order 4 rotational symmetry.

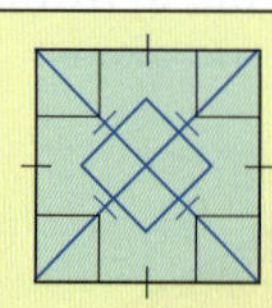

A rectangle has:
- 2 pairs of sides of equal length
- 2 pairs of parallel sides
- all angles 90°
- diagonals that bisect each other
- 2 lines of symmetry
- order 2 rotational symmetry.

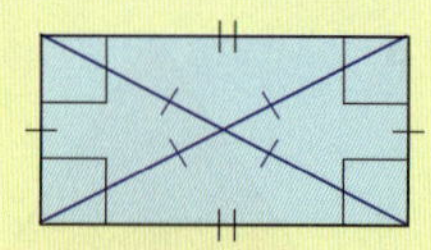

A rhombus has:
- all sides the same length
- 2 pairs of parallel sides
- opposite angles equal
- diagonals that bisect each other at 90°
- 2 lines of symmetry
- order 2 rotational symmetry.

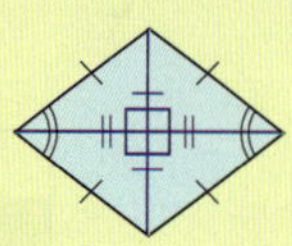

A parallelogram has:
- 2 pairs of sides of equal length
- 2 pairs of parallel sides
- opposite angles equal
- diagonals that bisect each other
- no lines of symmetry
- order 2 rotational symmetry.

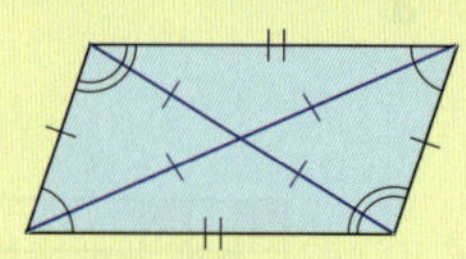

A kite has:
- 2 pairs of equal sides
- no parallel sides
- 1 pair of equal angles
- 1 diagonal that bisects the other
- diagonals that cross at 90°
- 1 line of symmetry
- order 1 rotational symmetry.

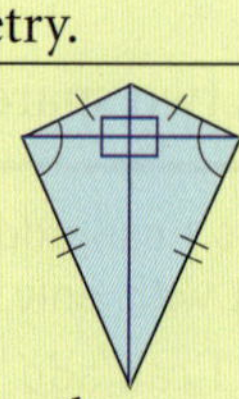

A trapezium has:
- sides of different lengths
- 1 pair of parallel sides
- angles of different sizes
- no lines of symmetry
- order 1 rotational symmetry.

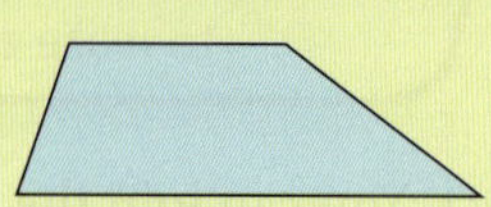

An isosceles trapezium has:
- 2 sides the same length
- 1 pair of parallel sides
- 2 pairs of equal angles
- 1 line of symmetry
- order 1 rotational symmetry.

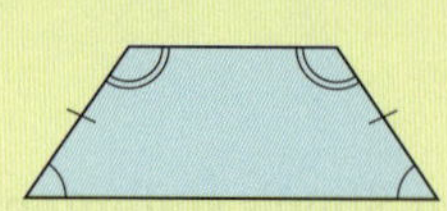

Worked example 8.3

I am a quadrilateral with no lines of symmetry.
My diagonals cross, but not at 90°, and they do not bisect each other.
What shape am I?

Trapezium — No lines of symmetry means the shape could be a parallelogram or a trapezium. The diagonals don't bisect each other means it is a trapezium.

Exercise 8.3

1 Name each special quadrilateral being described.

- **a** All my sides are the same length. My diagonals bisect each other at 90°. I have 4 lines of symmetry.
- **b** I have order 2 rotational symmetry, but no lines of symmetry.
- **c** I have two pairs of equal sides, but only one pair of equal angles.
- **d** I have diagonals that bisect each other, but not at 90°.
- **e** I have one pair of parallel sides. I have order 1 rotational symmetry. I also have one line of symmetry.

2 Check each quadrilateral against this classification flow chart.
Write down the letter where each shape comes out.

- **a** square
- **b** rhombus
- **c** kite
- **d** parallelogram
- **e** trapezium
- **f** isosceles trapezium
- **g** rectangle

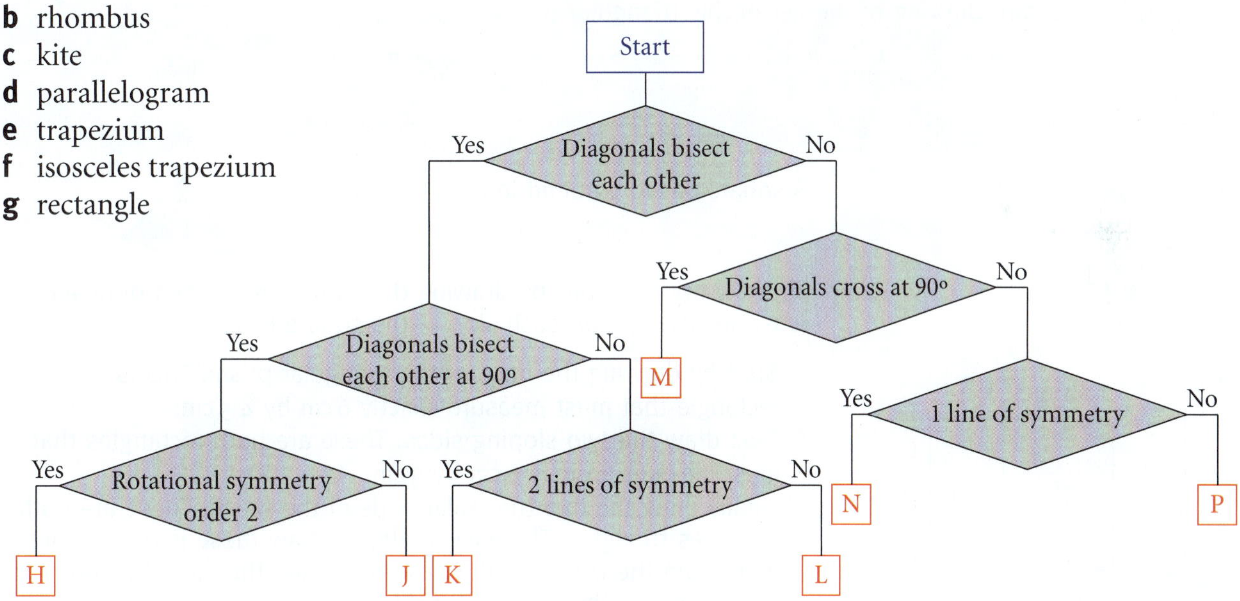

3 Plot these points on a coordinate grid.
A(2, 5), B(4, 5), C(4, 3), D(2, 3), E(1, 3), F(3, 5), G(7, 3), H(3, 1), I(5, 3), J(7, 1)
Join up points to make the following shapes.
Write down the coordinates of the point where the diagonals cross.

a ABCD **b** EFGH **c** EIJH

8.4 Drawing nets of solids

A **net** shows the 2D layout of a 3D solid. The net will fold up to make the solid.

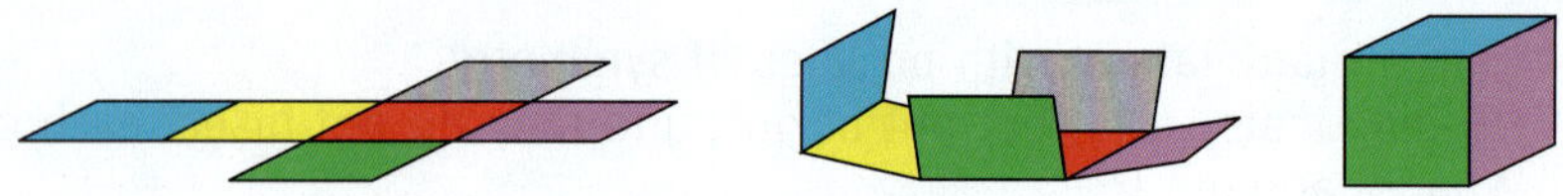

To work out the net of a 3D object, imagine cutting it along its edges and unfolding it.

You need to be able to make a <u>sketch</u> of the net of a 3D solid. You also need to be able to make an <u>accurate drawing</u> of the net of a 3D solid. In an accurate drawing all the lengths must be exactly the correct measurements.

> A sketch is an approximate drawing – the lengths don't need to be accurate.

There are often different ways to draw the net of a 3D solid. For example, here are three of the ways you could draw a net of the cube above.

Worked example 8.4

a Draw a sketch of the net of a square-based pyramid.
b Draw an accurate drawing of the net of this triangular prism.

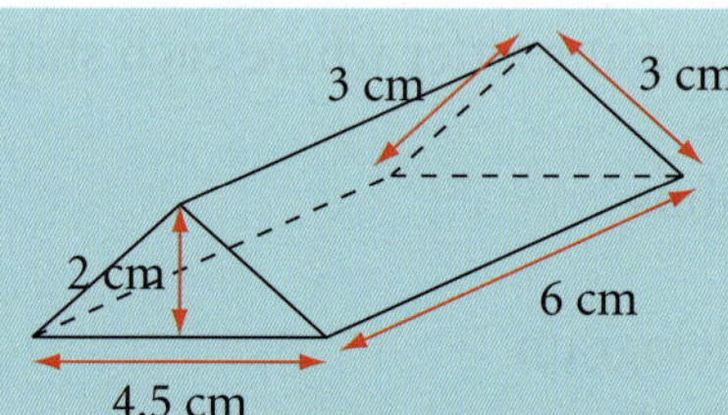

a

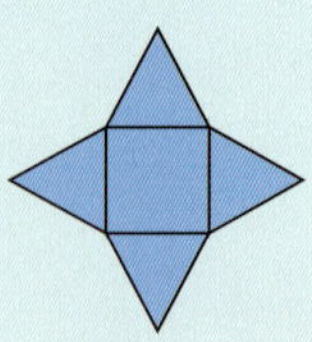

A square-based pyramid looks like this.

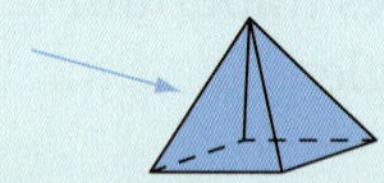

To draw the net, start by drawing the square base, then draw an isosceles triangle on each side of the square base.

b

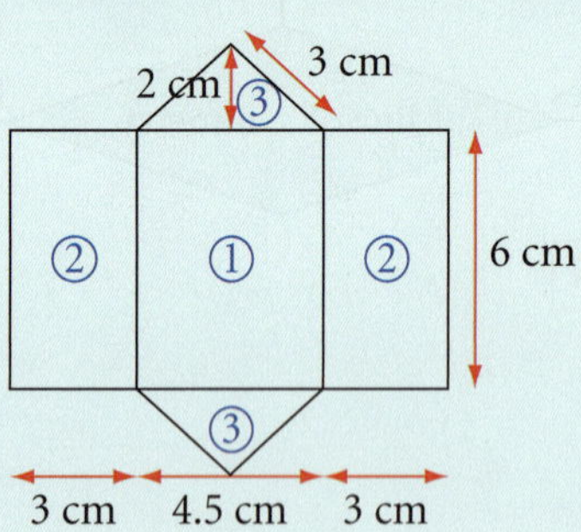

① Start by drawing the base of the triangular prism. This is a rectangle that must measure exactly 6 cm by 4.5 cm.
② Next draw the two sloping sides. These are both rectangles that must measure exactly 6 cm by 3 cm.
③ Finally draw the two triangular ends of the prism. These are both isosceles triangles. The easiest way to draw these is to measure 2 cm from the centre of the base rectangle, then join this point to the corners of the base rectangle.

Exercise 8.4

1 Sketch a net of each cuboid.

a

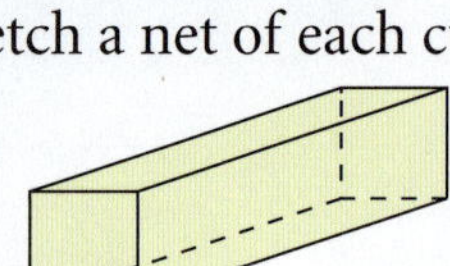

b

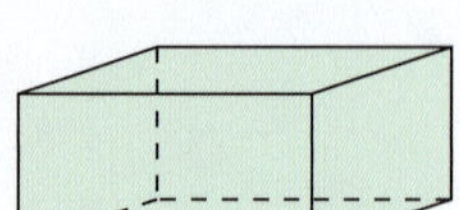

2 Which of the following could be the net of a cube?

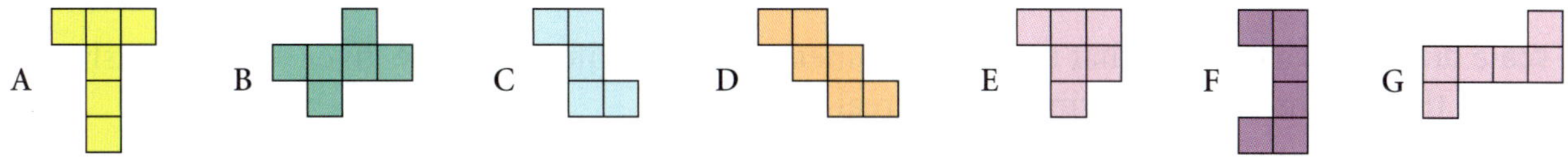

3 Draw a sketch of a net of this tetrahedron (triangular-based pyramid).

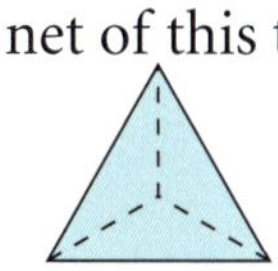

4 Draw an accurate net for each of these 3D solids.

a cube

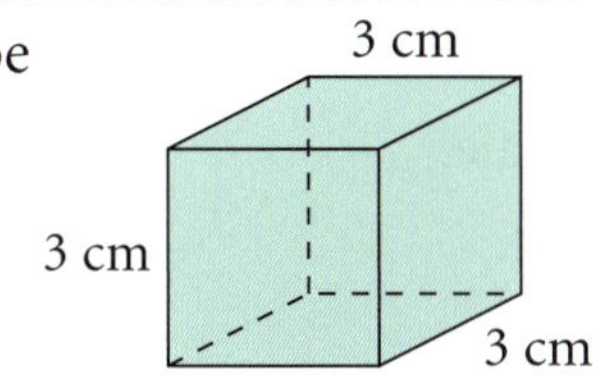

b cuboid

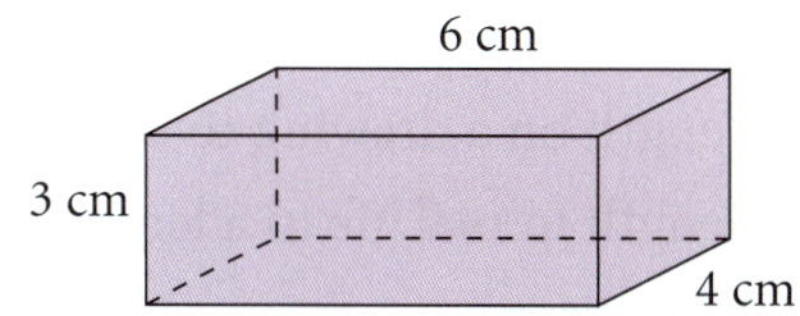

c triangular prism (isosceles triangle)

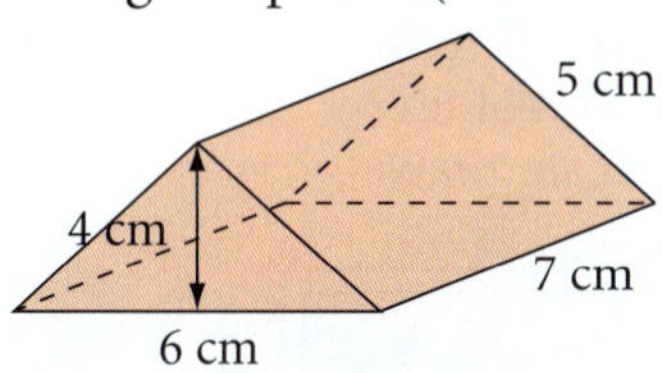

d triangular prism (right-angled triangle)

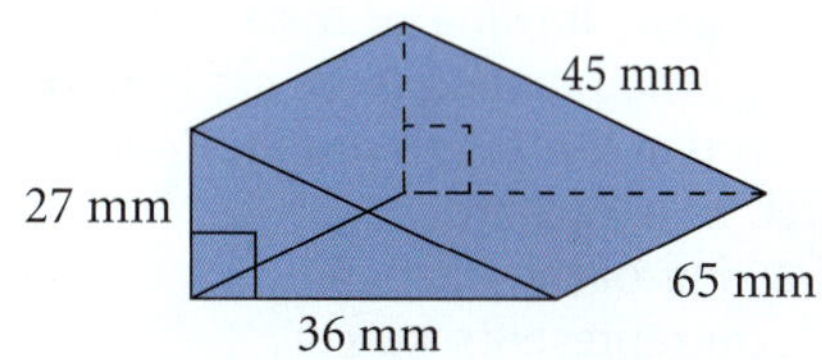

5 Here is the net of a cuboid.
When the net is folded to make the cuboid, side B meets with side D.
Which side meets with:

a side C **b** side K **c** side G
d side A **e** side N **f** side M?

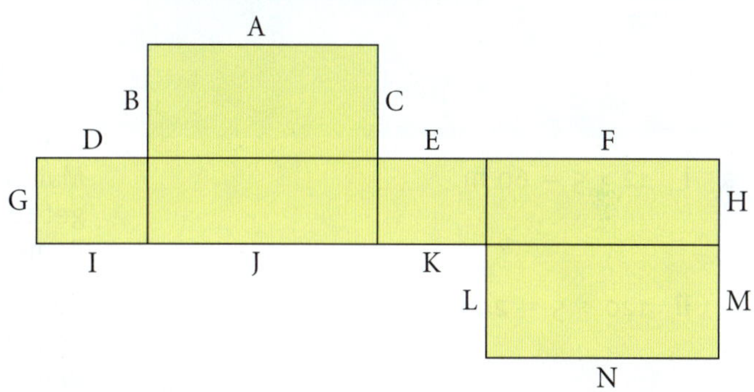

6 Dakarai has a cuboid that measures 8 cm by 5 cm, by 4 cm.
He labels the vertices (corners) A, B, C, D, E, F, G and H, as shown.

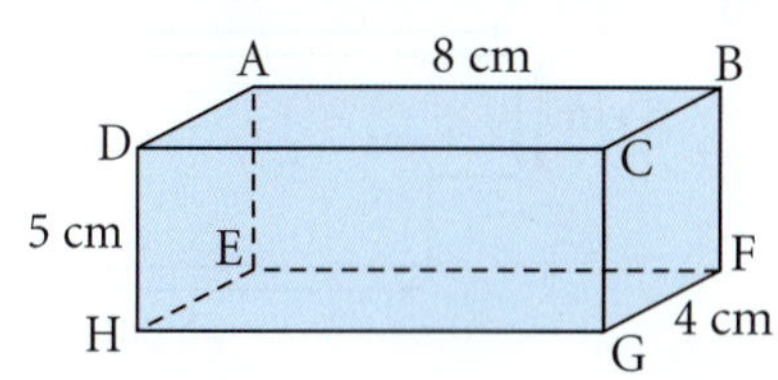

He draws a line from A to H to C to A.

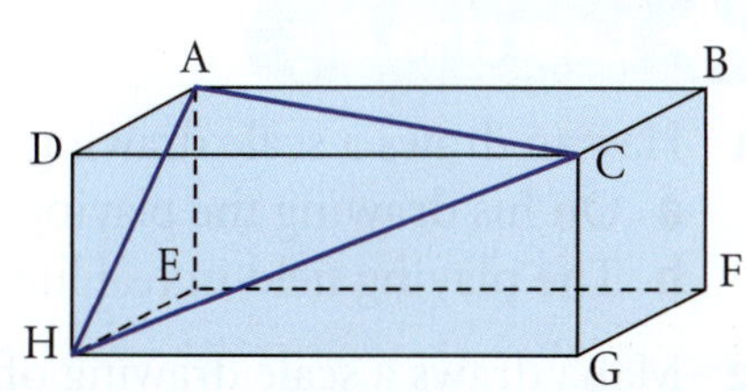

a Draw an accurate net of Dakarai's cuboid.
b Measure the total length of the line that Dakarai draws.
Give your answer to the nearest millimetre.

8.5 Making scale drawings

A **scale drawing** is a drawing that represents something in real life. The **scale** gives the relationship between the lengths on the drawing and the real-life lengths.

You can write a scale in three ways:

- using the word 'represents', for example, '1 cm represents 100 cm'
- using the word 'to', for example, '1 to 100'
- using a ratio sign, for example, '1 : 100'.

When you write a scale using 'to' or the ratio sign, the numbers you use must be in the same units. So you must write the scale '1 cm represents 10 m' as either '1 to 1000' or '1 : 1000'. The scale '1 to 10' or '1 : 10' means that every centimetre on the drawing represents 10 centimetres in real life.

1 m = 100 cm

10 m = 1000 cm

To change a length on a drawing to a length in real life, multiply by the scale.

To change a length in real life to a length on a drawing, divide by the scale.

Worked example 8.5

a Tanesha makes a scale drawing of the front of a building. She uses a scale of '1 cm represents 5 m'.
  i On her drawing, the building is 12 cm long. How long is the building in real life?
  ii The building in real life is 120 m tall. How tall is the building on the scale drawing?

b This is the sketch of a kitchen.
Draw a scale drawing of the kitchen.
Use a scale of '1 cm represents 50 cm'.

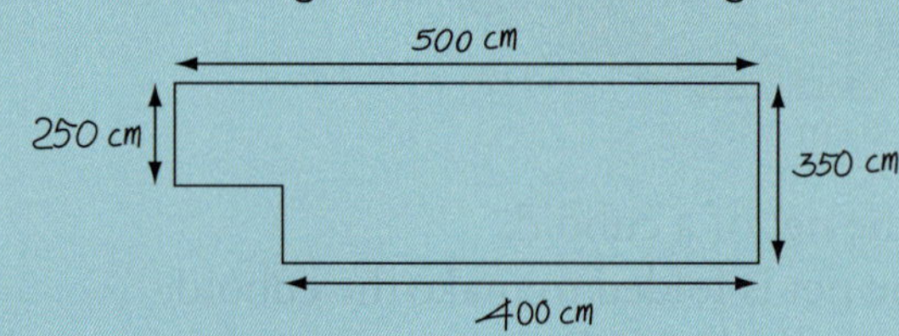

a **i** 12 × 5 = 60 m

Multiply the length on the drawing by the scale of 5 to get to the real-life length.
Remember to include the units (m) with your answer.

ii 120 ÷ 5 = 24 cm

Divide the height in real life by the scale of 5 to get the height of the drawing.
Remember to include the units (cm) with your answer.

b

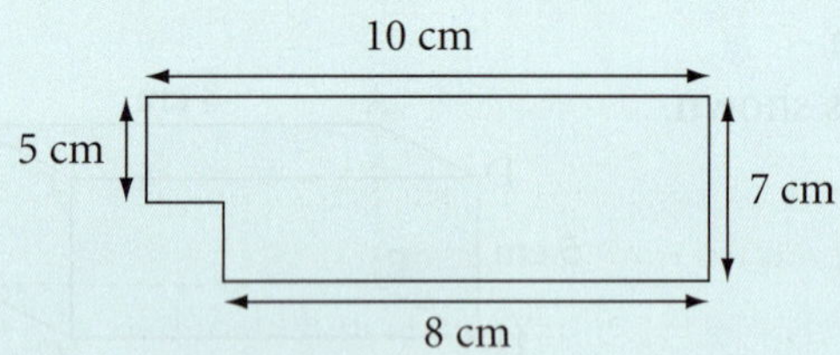

Start by working out all of the lengths on the drawing, by dividing the real-life lengths by the scale of 50.

500 ÷ 50 = 10 cm 350 ÷ 50 = 7 cm
400 ÷ 50 = 8 cm 250 ÷ 50 = 5 cm

Now draw the diagram. Take care to measure all of the lengths accurately.

Exercise 8.5

1 Hassan draws a scale drawing of a playing field. He uses a scale of '1 cm represents 10 m'.
  a On his drawing the playing field is 18 cm long. How long is the playing field in real life?
  b The playing field in real life is 80 m wide. How wide is the playing field on the scale drawing?

2 Maha draws a scale drawing of a room. She uses a scale of '1 cm represents 50 cm'.
  a On her drawing the room is 13 cm long. How long is the room in real life?
  Give your answer in metres.
  b The room in real life is 5 m wide. How wide is the room on the scale drawing?
  Give your answer in centimetres.

3 This scale drawing of Oditi's bedroom is drawn on centimetre squared paper.
The scale is 1 to 25.

a What is the length in real life of the wall:

i AB **ii** BC **iii** CD
iv DE **v** EF **vi** AF?

Give your answers to part **a** in metres.

b The wardrobe in Oditi's room is 50 cm deep.
How deep will it be on the scale drawing?

c The bed in Oditi's room is 1.75 m long.
How long will it be on the scale drawing?
Give your answer in centimetres.

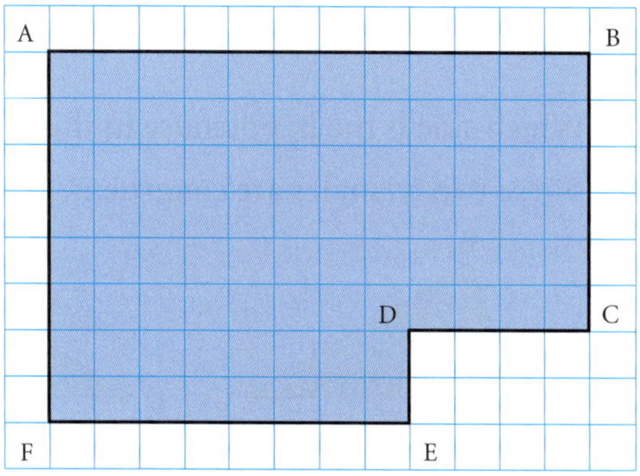

4 This is a sketch of a garden.
Draw a scale drawing of the garden.
Use a scale of '1 cm represents 2 m'.

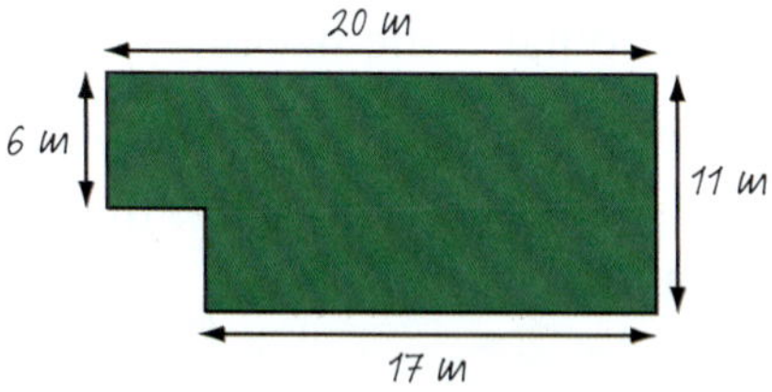

5 This is a sketch of a triangular flowerbed.

a Make a scale drawing of the flowerbed.
Use a scale of 1 : 20.

b What is the real-life length of the hypotenuse of the flowerbed?
Give your answer to the nearest centimetre.

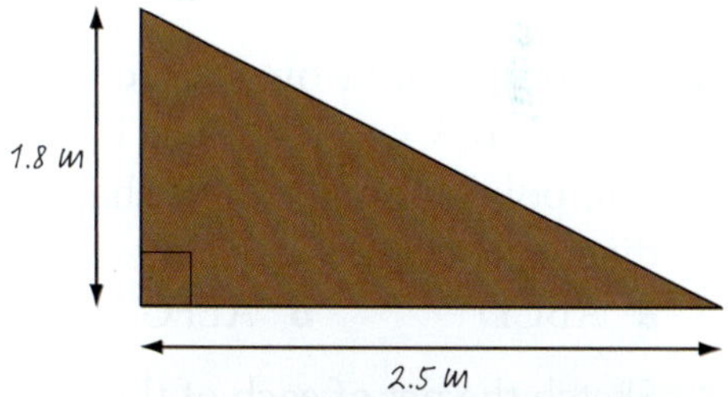

6 A rectangular tennis court has a length of 24 m and a width of 11 m.
What is the length of a diagonal of the court?
Explain how you worked out your answer.
Show all your working.

Summary

You should now know that:

★ If two 2D shapes are congruent their corresponding sides are equal and corresponding angles are equal.

★ There are two types of symmetry that 2D shapes may have: line symmetry and rotational symmetry.

★ A diagonal is a line that joins two opposite corners of a quadrilateral. When diagonals bisect each other they cut each other in half.

★ A net shows the 2D layout of a 3D object.

★ A scale drawing is a drawing that represents something in real life.

You should be able to:

★ Identify the hypotenuse (the longest side) in a right-angled triangle.

★ Identify corresponding sides and angles in congruent shapes, and know that they are equal.

★ Identify all the symmetries of 2D shapes.

★ Classify quadrilaterals according to their properties, including diagonal properties.

★ Draw simple nets of solids such as cuboids, regular tetrahedrons, square-based pyramids, triangular prisms.

★ Interpret and make simple scale drawings.

End-of-unit review

1 Which side is the hypotenuse in this right-angled triangle?

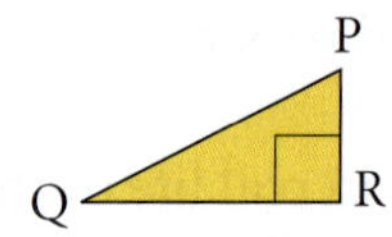

2 These two triangles are congruent.

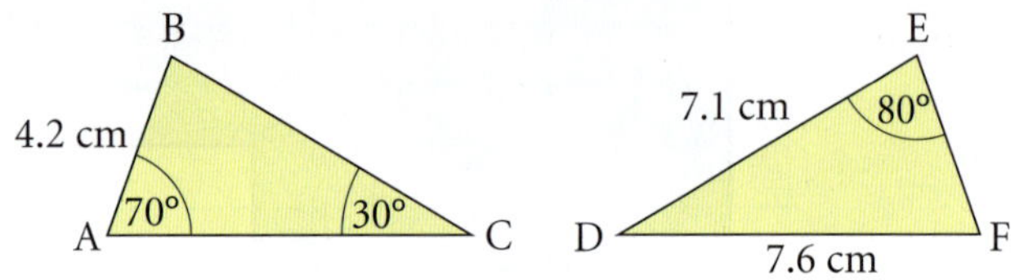

a Write down the length of: **i** EF **ii** BC **iii** AC.
b What is the size of: **i** ∠ABC **ii** ∠EDF **iii** ∠EFD?

3 Write down **i** the number of lines of symmetry
ii the order of rotational symmetry of each of these shapes.

a  **b** 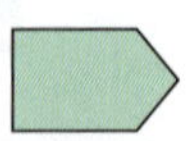 **c** 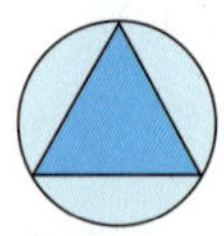 **d** 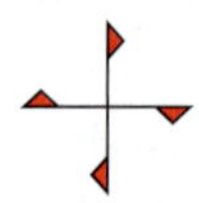

4 Plot these points on a coordinate grid.
A(1, 4), B(3, 4), C(3, 2), D(1, 2), E(4, 6), F(7, 4), G(4, 0), H(6, 4)
Join points to make these shapes and write down the coordinates of the point where the diagonals cross.
a ABCD **b** AEFG **c** AEHC

5 Sketch the net of each of these shapes.
a square-based pyramid **b** triangular prism

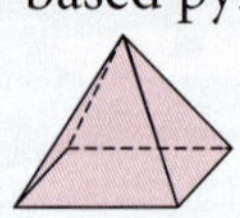 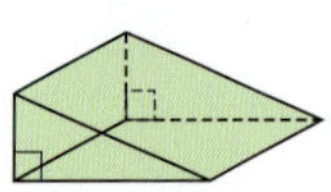

6 Here is the net of a cube.
When the net is folded to make the cube, which side meets with:
a side B **b** side C **c** side H
d side I **e** side A **f** side N?

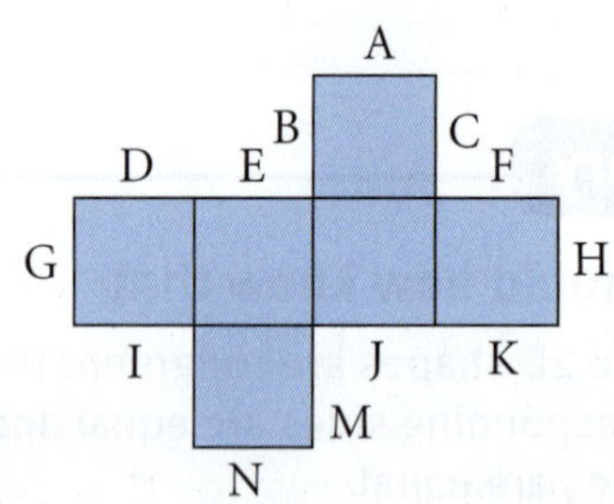

7 Ahmad makes a scale drawing of a car. He uses a scale of '1 cm represents 25 cm'.
a On his drawing the car is 18 cm long. How long is the car, in metres, in real life?
b The car in real life is 1.75 m high. How high is the car, in centimetres, on the scale drawing?

8 This is a sketch of an office.
a Make a scale drawing of the office.
Use a scale of 1 to 100.
b What is the real-life length of the red line AB?
Give your answer in metres.

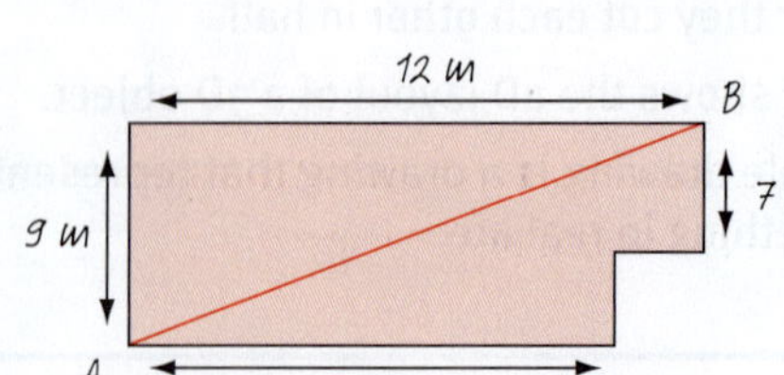

9 Simplifying expressions and solving equations

You won't be surprised to hear that computer programmers, scientists, engineers and statisticians all use algebra in their jobs. But you may be surprised at some other jobs that also need algebra.

Cooks and chefs prepare food for other people. They work in all sorts of places, from cafés and restaurants to international business headquarters. They need to plan menus and adapt recipes for the number of people they are feeding. They must work out quantities of ingredients, their cost and the price their customers will pay for the food. They use algebra when they deal with ingredients and prices.

Key words

Make sure you learn and understand these key words:

simplify
collect like terms
expand
construct

Senior chefs may have to work out earnings, pension and tax payments and sickness benefits for their staff. They use algebra when they work out how many people they need to employ for different catering events and how long each person will work each week. They may also work out how much overtime they can ask their workers to do. They may need to plan to employ extra people.

Farm and ranch managers deal with the day-to-day activities of the ranch or farm. They use algebra when they deal with the farm accounts and write yearly business plans. If they grow crops they need to plan how much fertiliser to apply and when to put it on the crops. They may use quite complicated algebra, as lots of different things have to be taken into account such as soil type, crop to be grown, type of fertiliser, cost of fertiliser, etc. If they have livestock they may use algebra to work out how much food to give to the animals.

Actuaries work for insurance companies. They design insurance plans that will help their company make a profit. They study data and work out probabilities for events such as a person becoming ill, injured or disabled. They work out how much the insurance company might pay out for this event. Then they calculate how much people have to pay for insurance. Actuaries need to be very good at maths, even though they use computers. They use algebra all the time to help calculate probabilities and estimate the company's profits.

In this unit you will use algebra in a variety of ways. You will learn how to simplify expressions and expand brackets, and also how to construct and solve equations.

9.1 Collecting like terms

Do you remember how to construct, or write, linear expressions?

$2n + 3$	$2 \times n + 3$
$3 + 2n$	$3 + 2 \times n$

You can write the same linear expression in different ways. The expressions in the boxes all mean the same thing, although the first expression is the way you would normally write it.

You often need to **simplify** or transform an expression by writing it in a different way. This is usually to make it easier to work with. When you do this to an expression, make sure you don't change the value.

The expression $5n - 3$ is not the same as $3 - 5n$, but it is the same as $-3 + 5n$.

There are some rules you can follow when you write an expression in algebra. These are not strict rules, but are guidelines to make the work easier.

- Write products without the multiplication sign, so write $2 \times n$ as $2n$.
- Write the number before the letter, so write $2x$ not $x2$.
- Generally, write terms with letters before number terms, so write $3y + 4$ rather than $4 + 3y$.
- Generally, write terms in alphabetical order, so write $4a + 5b$ not $5b + 4a$.
- When a term has more than one letter, write them in alphabetical order, so write $6cd$ rather than $6dc$.
- Write negative terms after positive terms, so write $5 - 4z$ not $-4z + 5$ (unless all the terms are negative, in which case follow the other rules, so write $-3x - 8y$, not $-8y - 3x$).

Worked example 9.1a

Use the guidelines above to rewrite these expressions.

a $3 + 5 \times n$ **b** $d \times 5 + 2 \times c$ **c** $-8ba + 9$

a $5n + 3$ Don't write the multiplication sign. Write the term with the letter before the number term.

b $2c + 5d$ Don't write the multiplication signs. Write the letter terms in alphabetical order.

c $9 - 8ab$ The term with letters is negative, so write the number term before the term with letters. Write the term with the letters in alphabetical order.

You can also simplify expressions by **collecting like terms**. Like terms are terms that contain the same letter or letters. You cannot add together terms that contain different letters.

$3n^2$ and $4n^2$ are like terms.
$2xy$ and $7yx$ are like terms.
$2xy$ and $7yz$ are not like terms.

Worked example 9.1b

Simplify these expressions.

a $4 + 2x + 3x$ **b** $2ab + ab - 5ba$ **c** $2y + 6y^2 - 3y^2 - 10y$

a $5x + 4$ $2x$ and $3x$ are like terms, so add them to get $5x$. $5x$ and 4 are not like terms, so you cannot simplify any further. Write the $5x$ before the 4.

b $-2ab$ $5ba$ is the same as $5ab$, so $2ab$, ab and $5ab$ are all like terms. ab is the same as $1ab$, so $2ab + 1ab = 3ab$, $3ab - 5ab = -2ab$.

c $3y^2 - 8y$ $2y$ and $10y$ are like terms, $2y - 10y = -8y$. $6y^2$ and $3y^2$ are like terms, $6y^2 - 3y^2 = 3y^2$. Write the positive term first, then the negative term.

Exercise 9.1

1 Use the guidelines opposite to rewrite these expressions.

a $8 \times n$ **b** $4 + m$ **c** $h8$ **d** $5fe$ **e** $2b + 5a$ **f** $-3d + 5$

g $4 + 2 \times v$ **h** $6 \times k \times j$ **i** $p \times 2 + m6$ **j** $-2a + 5c$ **k** $-4qp + 3$ **l** $-3yx - 8ba$

2 Look at this set of cards.

$2 \times n + m2$ | $2 + n2$ | $-2 + 2n$ | $2 \times n \times n$

$n^2 \times 2$ | $n \times 2 + 2$ | $-2 + 2 \times n \times m$ | $2 \times n - 2 \times 1$

$2n + 2$ | $2m + 2n$ | $2n^2$ | $n2 - 2$

a Put the cards into groups of expressions that have the same meaning.

b **i** Write down the expression on the card that is left over.

ii Simplify the expression on the card that is left over.

3 Simplify each expression.

a $6x + 4x + 3x$ **b** $8y - 2y + 5y$ **c** $7z - z - 9z$

d $2a + 4b + 6a - 3b$ **e** $8c - 4d - 3c + d$ **f** $2ab + 4ba - 3ba$

g $3cd + 4de + 7dc - 2ed$ **h** $4 + 9v - 6v - 11$ **i** $5t - 3u - 8t + 10u$

j $4x^2 + 3x^2 + 8x - 2x$ **k** $11y^2 - 3y - 5y^2$ **l** $a^2 + 2a + 2 - a^2 + 5a$

4 In an algebraic pyramid you find the expression in each block by adding the expressions in the two blocks below it. Copy and complete this pyramid.

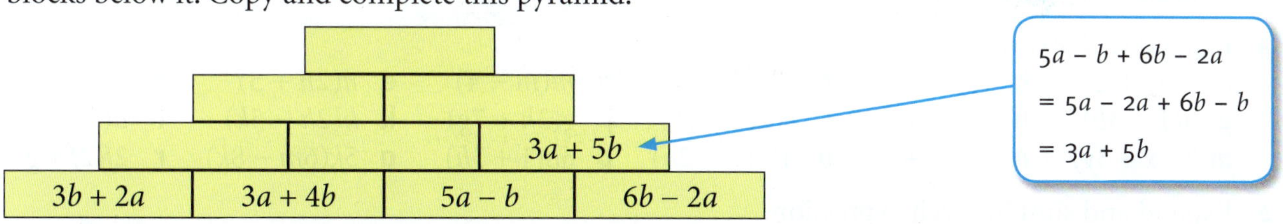

5 Copy and complete this algebraic pyramid.

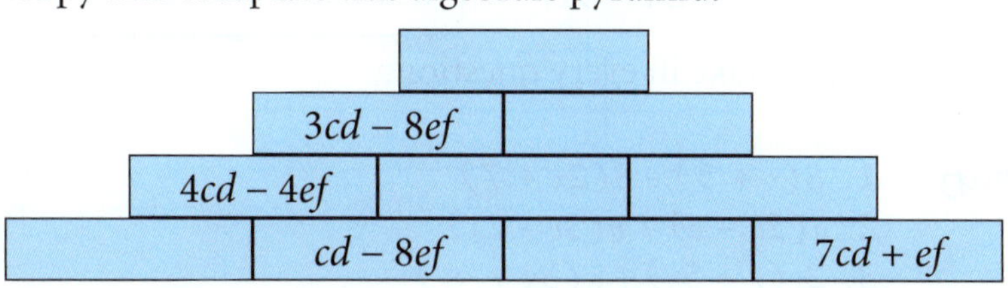

6 This is part of Zalika's homework. She has made several mistakes.

a Explain what she has done wrong.

b Work out the correct answers.

Question Simplify: 1. $8ab - ab + 2ac$
2. $3x^2 + 4xy - 2x^2 - yx$

Answer 1. $8ab - ab + 2ac = 7ab + 2ac = 9a^2bc$
2. $3x^2 + 4xy - 2x^2 - yx = x^2 + 4xy - yx$

9.2 Expanding brackets

To **expand** brackets, multiply each term inside the brackets by the term outside the brackets.

Expanding brackets is sometimes called multiplying out brackets.

Worked example 9.2

a Expand these expressions. **i** $3(b + 5)$ **ii** $a(a - 3)$
b Expand and simplify this expression. $4(2x + 3x^2) - x(6 + x)$

a **i** $3(b + 5) = 3 \times b + 3 \times 5$ — Multiply 3 by b then 3 by 5.
$= 3b + 15$ — Simplify $3 \times b$ to $3b$ and 3×5 to 15.
ii $a(a - 3) = a \times a - a \times 3$ — Multiply a by a then a by 3.
$= a^2 - 3a$ — Simplify $a \times a$ to a^2 and $a \times 3$ to $3a$.
b $4(2x + 3x^2) - x(6 + x)$ — Start by multiplying out both brackets and simplify each term.
$= 8x + 12x^2 - 6x - x^2$ — So, $4 \times 2x = 8x$, $4 \times 3x^2 = 12x^2$, $-x \times 6 = -6x$, $-x \times x = -x^2$.
$= 2x + 11x^2$ — Collect like terms, so $8x - 6x = 2x$ and $12x^2 - x^2 = 11x^2$.

Exercise 9.2

1 Expand each expression.
a $4(x + 6)$ **b** $3(y + 7)$ **c** $7(z - 2)$ **d** $2(w - 4)$ **e** $2(5 + a)$ **f** $8(9 + g)$
g $5(8 - b)$ **h** $6(6 - d)$ **i** $3(2a + 8)$ **j** $12(3 + 4b)$ **k** $5(2c - 1)$ **l** $6(3 - 4e)$
m $2(2p + 3q)$ **n** $4(5c + 4d)$ **o** $9(6t - 2s)$ **p** $3(2ab + 3c)$ **q** $7(6xy - 2z)$ **r** $5(2x + y + 4)$

2 Expand and simplify each expression.
a $2(x + 3) + 3(x + 4)$ **b** $4(y + 5) + 2(2y + 2)$ **c** $8(z + 3) + 5(4 + 3z)$
d $5(2w + 3) - 6(w + 2)$ **e** $6(5 + 4v) - 4(3v + 7)$ **f** $3(5a + 3b) - 2(3a - 5b)$

3 Expand each expression.
a $x(3y + 2)$ **b** $y(y + 8)$ **c** $z(2w - 1)$ **d** $m(m - 4)$ **e** $n(2n + 5)$ **f** $n(9 - 8n)$
g $a(1 - 3b)$ **h** $c(5 - d)$ **i** $e(2e + 7f)$ **j** $g(3h + 7g)$ **k** $h(2h - 5k)$ **l** $d(3c - 5e)$
m $2x(x + 3y)$ **n** $3y(5y + 6)$ **o** $4b(6b - 2a)$ **p** $6h(1 + 3h)$ **q** $5k(6m - 8k)$ **r** $2f(2f + g - 3)$

4 Expand and simplify each expression.
a $x(x + 2) + x(x + 5)$ **b** $z(2z + 1) + z(4z + 5)$
c $u(2u + 5) - u(u + 3)$ **d** $w(6w + 2x) - 2w(2w - 9x)$

Remember that $-2 \times -9 = +18$

5 This is part of Shen's homework. He has made a mistake in every question.

Question Expand and simplify: 1. $8(x + 5) - 3(2x + 7)$
2. $a(2b + c) + b(3c - 2a)$
3. $2y(y + 5x) + x(3x + 4y)$
Answer 1. $8(x + 5) - 3(2x + 7) = 8x + 40 - 6x + 21 = 2x + 61$
2. $a(2b + c) + b(3c - 2a) = 2ab + ac + 3bc - 2ab = ac + 3bc = 3abc^2$
3. $2y(y + 5x) + x(3x + 4y) = 2y^2 + 10xy + 9x^2 + 4xy = 9x^2 + 2y^2 + 14xy$

a Explain what he has done wrong.
b Work out the correct answers.

9.3 Constructing and solving equations

When you are given a problem to solve, you may need to **construct**, or write, an equation to help you solve the problem.

Worked example 9.3

The diagram shows a rectangle.
Work out the values of x and y.

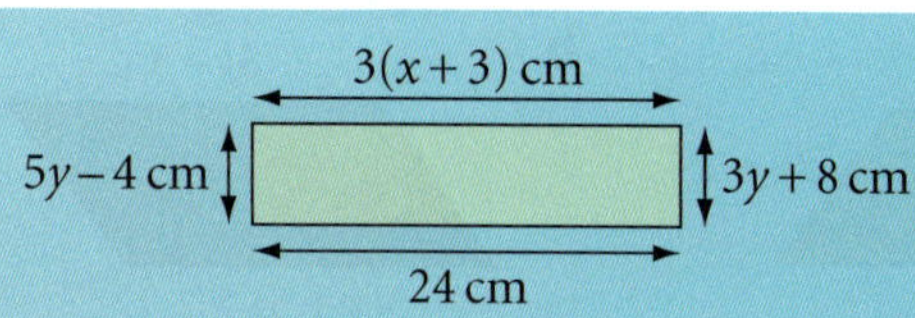

$3(x + 3) = 24$	The two lengths must be equal, so construct an equation by writing one length equal to the other.
$3x + 9 = 24$	The first step is to multiply out the brackets.
$3x + 9 - 9 = 24 - 9$	Use inverse operations to solve the equation. Start by subtracting 9 from both sides.
$3x = 15$	Simplify both sides of the equation.
$x = \frac{15}{3}$,	Divide 15 by 3 to work out the value of x.
$x = 5$	
$5y - 4 = 3y + 8$	The two widths must be equal, so write one width equal to the other.
$5y - 4 - 3y = 3y + 8 - 3y$	Rewrite the equation by subtracting $3y$ from both sides.
$2y - 4 = 8$	Simplify.
$2y - 4 + 4 = 8 + 4$	Use inverse operations to solve the equation. Start by adding 4 to both sides.
$2y = 12$	Simplify both sides of the equation.
$y = \frac{12}{2}$,	Divide 12 by 2 to work out the value of y.
$y = 6$	

Exercise 9.3

1 Work out the value of x and y in each of these diagrams. All measurements are in centimetres.

a
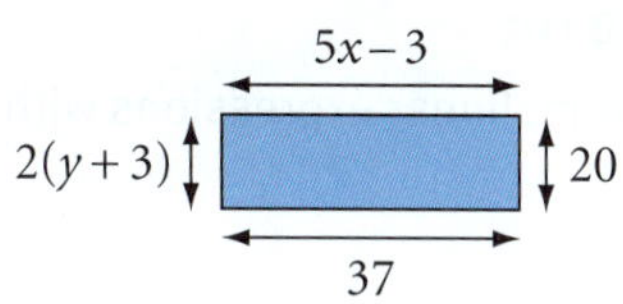

b
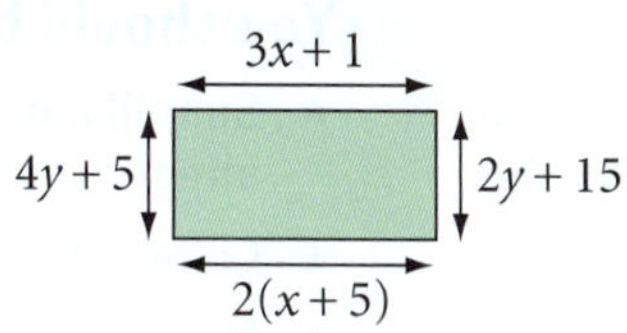

c
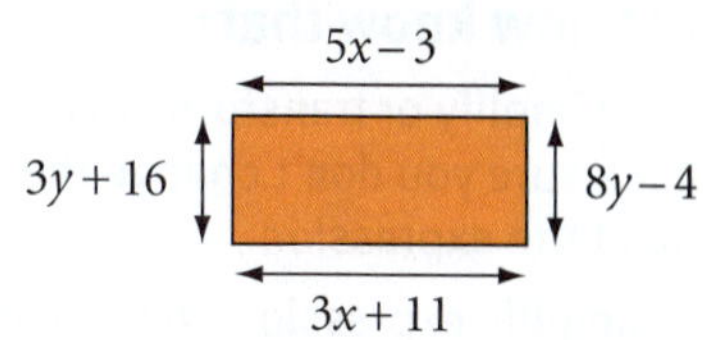

d
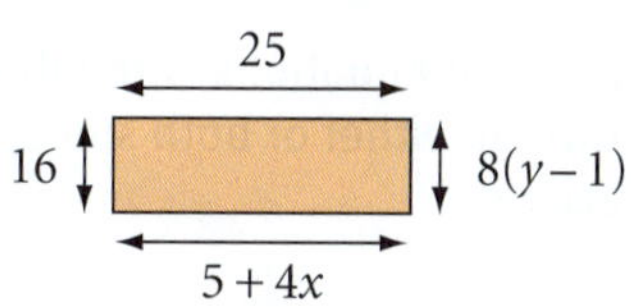

e
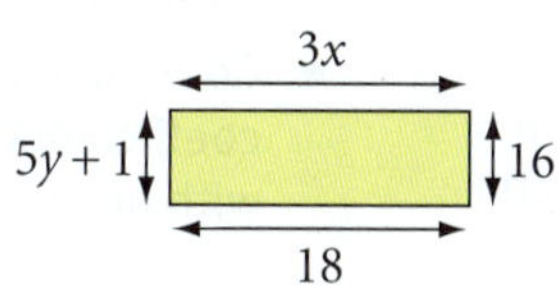

f
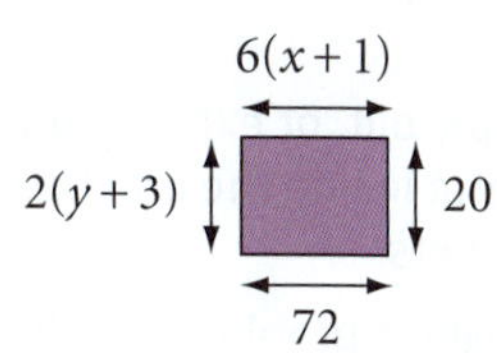

2 Work out the value of x in each of these isosceles triangles. All measurements are in centimetres.

a

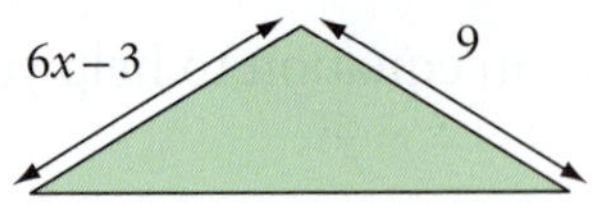

b

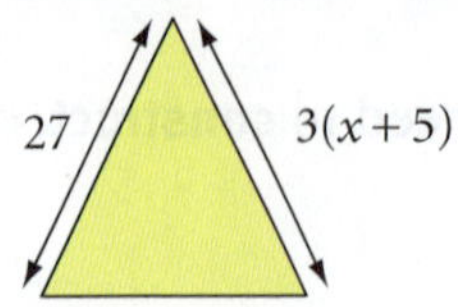

c

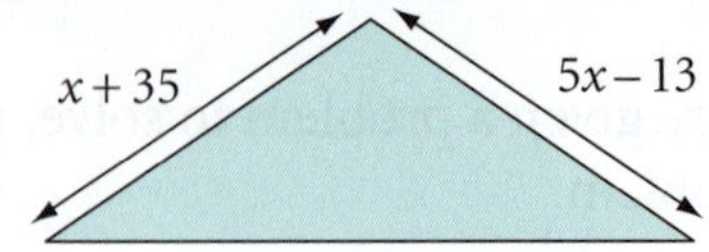

3 Work out the value of y in each of these shapes. All measurements are in centimetres.

a

b

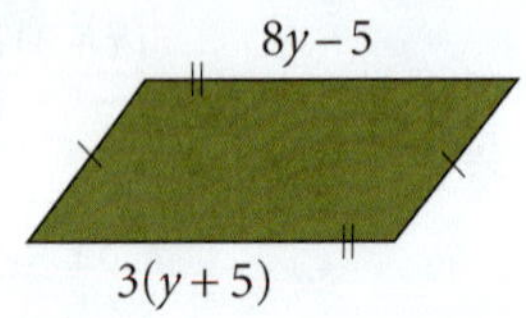

c

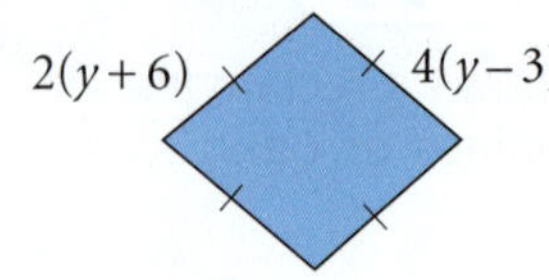

4 Work in a group of three or four. For each part of this question:

i write down an equation to represent the problem

ii compare the equation you have written with the equations written by the other members of your group and decide who has written the correct equation in the easiest way

iii solve the equation that you chose in part **ii**.

a Xavier thinks of a number. He multiplies it by 3 then adds 8. The answer is 23. What number did he think of?

b Anders thinks of a number. He divides it by 4 then subtracts 8. The answer is 5. What number did he think of?

c Sasha thinks of a number. She multiplies it by 5 then subtracts 4. The answer is the same as 2 times the number plus 20. What number did Sasha think of?

d Alicia thinks of a number. She multiplies it by 3 then adds 7. The answer is the same as 4 times the number. What number did Alicia think of?

e Jake thinks of a number. He adds 5 then multiplies the result by 2. The answer is the same as 5 times the number take away 14. What number did Jake think of?

f Harsha thinks of a number. She subtracts 2 then multiplies the result by 3. The answer is the same as subtracting 6 from the number then multiplying by 7. What number did Harsha think of?

Summary

You should now know that:

★ When you simplify or transform an expression you must make sure you don't change the value or the meaning of the expression.

★ You can simplify expressions by collecting like terms.

★ When you multiply out, or expand, brackets, you multiply each term inside the brackets by the term outside the brackets.

★ When you are given a problem to solve, you may need to construct or write an equation to help you solve the problem.

You should be able to:

★ Simplify, or transform, linear expressions with integer coefficients.

★ Collect like terms.

★ Multiply a single term over brackets.

★ Construct and solve linear equations with integer coefficients (unknown on either or both sides, with or without brackets).

End-of-unit review

1 Use the guidelines at the start of this unit to rewrite these expressions.
a $6 \times p$ **b** $7 + n$ **c** $cb9$ **d** $-6u + 1$ **e** $9 + 5 \times x$ **f** $b \times 3 + a6$

2 Simplify these expressions.
a $3a + 7b + 5a - 2b$ **b** $8 + 6v - 2v - 12$ **c** $3x^2 + 7y + 9 - x^2 + 5y$

3 In an algebraic pyramid the expression in each block is found by adding the expressions in the two blocks below it. Copy and complete this pyramid.

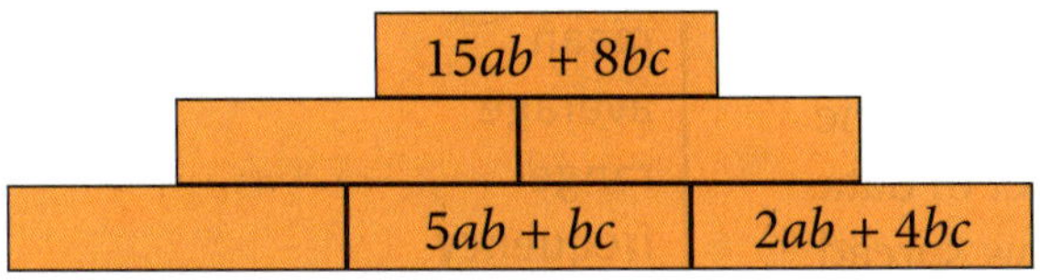

4 Expand these expressions.
a $3(x + 4)$ **b** $8(y - 1)$ **c** $4(3a + 2)$ **d** $5(4 - 7b)$ **e** $3(2c + 6d)$ **f** $8(4xy - 3z)$
g $x(2y + 1)$ **h** $n(4n + 6)$ **i** $e(8 - d)$ **j** $k(2h + 8k)$ **k** $2y(3y + 9)$ **l** $3m(2m + n - 5)$

5 Expand and simplify each expression.
a $3(x + 4) + 5(x + 6)$ **b** $6(3w + 1) - 4(w + 5)$ **c** $2(4a + 7b) - 3(2a - 3b)$
d $x(x + 8) + x(x + 4)$ **e** $u(3u + 4) - u(u + 2)$ **f** $w(10w + 4x) - 3w(3w - 4x)$

6 Work out the value of x and y in each of these diagrams. All measurements are in centimetres.

a

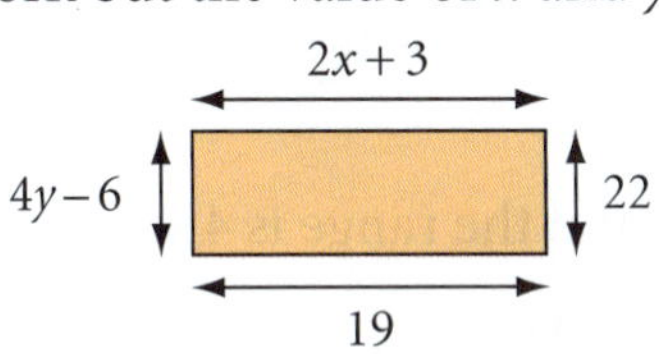

b

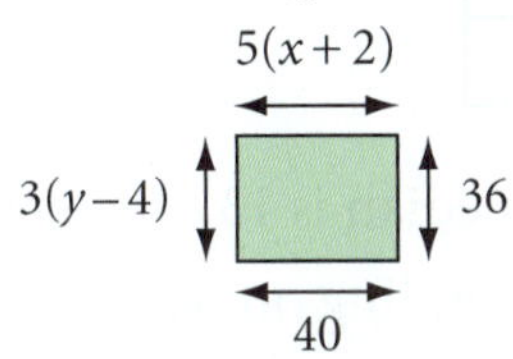

c

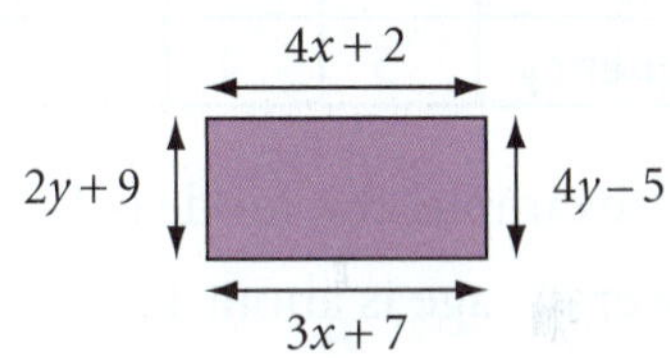

7 Work out the value of x in each of these shapes. All measurements are in centimetres.

a

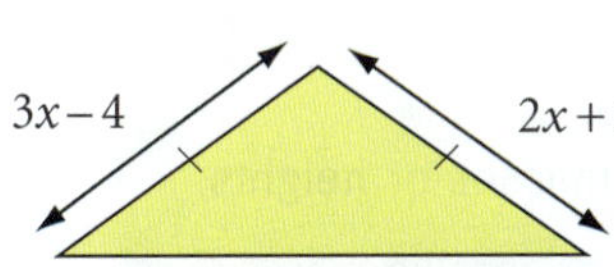

b

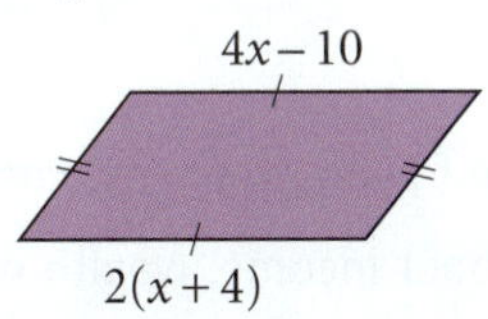

c

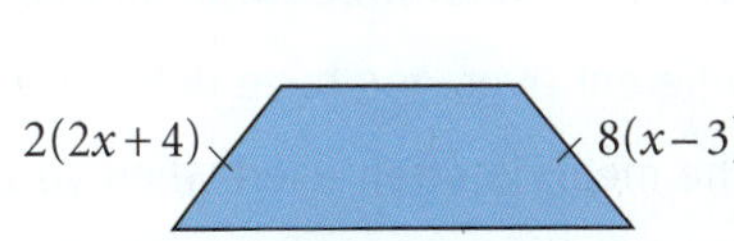

8 For each part of this question:
i write down an equation to represent the problem
ii solve the equation.

a Razi thinks of a number. He multiplies it by 5 then adds 9. The answer is 44.
What number did Razi think of?

b Dakarai thinks of a number. He divides it by 3 then subtracts 7. The answer is 4.
What number did Dakarai think of?

c Mia thinks of a number. She multiplies it by 5 then subtracts 10. The answer is the same as 2 times the number plus 11.
What number did Mia think of?

d Tanesha thinks of a number. She adds 2 then multiplies the result by 3. The answer is the same as adding 5 to the number then multiplying by 2.
What number did Tanesha think of?

10 Processing and presenting data

The internet is full of facts and figures. Data is everywhere. People in almost every profession gather data all the time, so that they can use it to obtain information.

How do they obtain information from data?

Many of them calculate statistics from the data. A statistic is any number that is obtained from a set of data.

You should already be familiar with some simple statistics.

- There are three types of average: the mode, the median and the mean. Each of these uses one number to represent a set of data.
- You should also know about the range. It describes how spread out the data is.

Key words

Make sure you learn and understand these key words:

statistics
mode
median
mean
average
range
frequency
class
modal class

This set of data is the ages of a group of 20 people.

12 11 15 12 13 11 13 14 12 14
11 14 11 14 12 14 14 11 14 14

You could show the ages more neatly in a frequency table.

Age	11	12	13	14	15
Frequency	5	4	2	8	1

In this example, the mode is 14 years, the median is 13, the mean is 12.8 and the range is 4 years. The average age is about 13 or 14 years, depending on which average you use.

Why are there three different averages?

Different averages have different uses.

The mean is often used when you talk about average prices, costs, production, masses or heights.

The median is often used when you talk about income, wealth or qualities such as intelligence.

The mode is often used when you look at clothing sizes, weather forecasting and some applications in biology and business.

In this unit, you will learn more about discrete and continuous data, and find out how to calculate statistical information from both types.

10.1 Calculating statistics from discrete data

In **statistics**, the **mode**, the **median** and the **mean** are **averages**.

The **range** is a measure of how spread out the numbers are. It is not an average.

Use what you know to check the results for this set of 10 masses.

An average is a single value that summarises the whole set of numbers.

12 kg	14 kg	14 kg	14 kg	14 kg
15 kg	17 kg	17 kg	20 kg	22 kg

Mode = 14 kg Median = 14.5 kg
Mean = 15.9 kg Range = 10 kg

Mode = most common value

Median = middle value, when the values are put in order

Mean = sum of all values ÷ total number of values

Range = largest value – smallest value

When you have a large set of numbers they will be given in a **frequency** table. You need to be able to work out averages and range from a frequency table.

Worked example 10.1

The table shows the number of children in 72 families.

Number of children	1	2	3	4	5	6
Frequency	8	26	20	9	4	5

Find: **a** the mode **b** the median
c the mean **d** the range.

a The mode is 2 children. 2 has the largest frequency (26).

b The median is 3 children. $(72 + 1) \div 2 = 36.5$ so the middle number is halfway between 36th and 37th. There are 8 1s, 26 2s, $8 + 26 = 34$ 1s and 2s. The 36th and 37th are both 3.

c The mean is 2.9 children. It is useful to put the calculations in a table. There are 206 children in 72 families. $206 \div 72 = 2.861...$

d The range is 5 children. $6 - 1 = 5$

Children, n	Frequency, f	$n \times f$
1	8	8
2	26	52
3	20	60
4	9	36
5	4	20
6	5	30
Total	72	206

Exercise 10.1

1 The box shows the midday Celsius temperatures, over a two-week period, in a particular town. Find:

7	4	4	5	8	8	8
6	6	4	4	4	–2	0

a the median temperature **b** the modal temperature
c the mean temperature **d** the range.

2 The median of the five numbers in the box is 10. The range is 12.

10	5	15	5	x

a What is the value of x? **b** What is the mean?

3 Hassan recorded the number of people in 60 passing cars.
Here are his results. Find:

a the missing frequency
b the modal number of people in a car
c the median **d** the mean.

People	1	2	3	4	5	6
Frequency	28		3	7	1	1

4 Oditi throws two dice and adds the scores.
She does this 36 times. Here are the results.
Find:

a the mode **b** the median
c the mean **d** the range.

Score	2	3	4	5	6	7	8	9	10	11	12
Frequency	3	0	2	4	5	4	6	8	1	1	2

5 A quiz has 10 questions. 120 students take the quiz.
The table shows their scores.

Questions answered correctly	4	5	6	7	8	9	10
Frequency	3	5	12	13	17	30	40

How many students scored:

a more than the median **b** more than the mode **c** more than the mean?

6 This table shows the results of 60 throws of a biased dice. Read what Ahmad, Harsha and Alicia say.

Score	1	2	3	4	5	6
Frequency	11	9	10	8	19	3

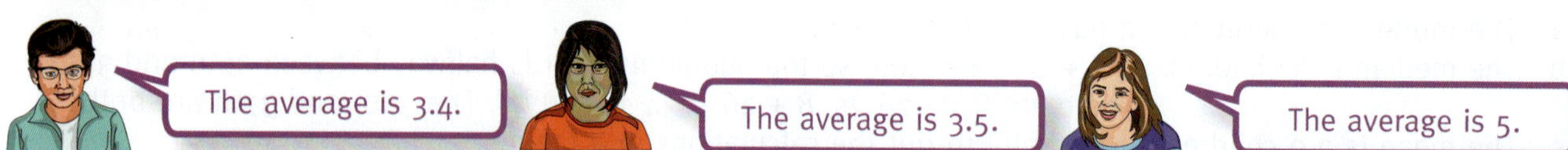

Explain how Ahmad, Harsha and Alicia could all be correct.

7 The table shows the ages of 50 members of a club.

a Find: **i** the mean age **ii** the median age
iii the modal age **iv** the age range

Age	11	12	13	14	15	16
Frequency	10	21	8	5	3	3

b Read what Dakarai says.
Is he correct?

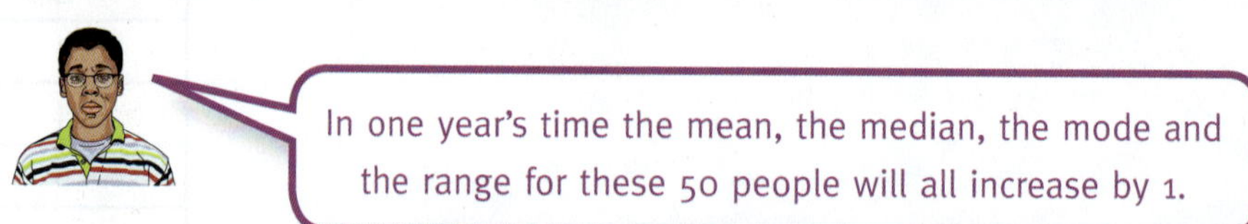

8 This table shows the number of goals scored by a football club in each match in one season.

a Find: **i** the number of games played
ii the mode **iii** the median
iv the mean number of goals.

Goals	0	1	2	3	4	5	6	7	8
Frequency	6	11	5	11	4	0	2	0	1

b Maha asked: 'What is the average number of goals?'
Which would be the best average to use to answer this question? Give a reason for your answer.

9 Twenty people each choose a number, from a choice of 1, 2, 3, 4 or 5.
The mode is larger than the median.
The median is larger than the mean.
Copy the table. Fill in a set of possible frequencies.

Number	1	2	3	4	5
Frequency					

10.2 Calculating statistics from grouped or continuous data

Sets of data with lots of values may be written in grouped frequency tables.This example shows the masses of 100 girls, to the nearest kilogram.

Mass (kg)	16–20	21–25	26–30	31–35	36–40	41–45
Frequency	12	14	20	30	17	7

The masses are divided into six **classes**. This shows the overall shape of the distribution.

You do not know the separate mass of each girl, so you cannot find the mode, the median, the mean or the range. You can estimate the median, the mean and the range. The next worked example shows how to do this.

You cannot find the mode, but you can find the **modal class**. This is the class with the largest frequency.

Mass is a continuous variable. For example, the class 21–25 kg includes girls with mass from 20.5 kg to 25.5 kg.

Worked example 10.2

Look at the table of girls' masses, above.

a Find the modal class. **b** Estimate the median height. **c** Estimate the mean. **d** Estimate the range.

a The modal class is 31–35 kg. This class has the largest frequency (30).

b An estimate of the median is 31 kg. There are 100 girls. The median mass is between the 50th and the 51st, arranged in order. 12 + 14 + 20 = 46 girls have mass up 30.5 kg. 46 + 30 = 76 girls have a mass up to 35.5 kg. A reasonable estimate of the median is in the class 31–35 kg.

c An estimate of the mean is 30.4 kg. Find the midpoint (the halfway point) of each class and multiply by the frequency.

An estimate of the mean is 3035 ÷ 100 = 30.4 kg to 1 d.p.

Mass	Midpoint, m	Frequency, f	$m \times f$
16–20	18	12	216
21–25	23	14	322
26–30	28	20	560
31–35	33	30	990
36–40	38	17	646
41–45	43	7	301
Total		100	3035

d The range is between 20 and 30 kg.
For grouped data we can only find the largest and smallest possible value of the range:
largest range = 45.5 − 15.5 = 30 (largest value from class 41–45 − smallest value from class 16–20)
smallest range = 40.5 − 20.5 = 20 (smallest value from class 41–45 − largest value from class 16–20)

Exercise 10.2

1 These are the marks for 40 students in an examination.

Mark	11–20	21–30	31–40	41–50
Frequency	8	16	9	7

a What is the modal class?
b Explain why the midpoint of the first class is 15.5.
c Estimate the mean mark.

2 These are the times for 50 runners to complete a race.

Time (minutes)	20–	25–	30–	35–	40–	45–
Frequency	5	8	22	12	3	0

20– means '20 minutes or more but less than 25'.

a Write down the modal class.
b Explain why the midpoint of the first class is 22.5.
c Estimate the median time.
d Estimate the mean time.

3 This table shows the heights of 60 young children.

Height (cm)	80–84	85–89	90–94	95–99	100–104	105–109
Frequency	10	20	15	10	3	2

a Estimate the median height.
b What is the largest possible value of the range?
c Estimate the mean height.

4 This table shows the lengths of 50 text messages sent from a mobile phone.

Number of characters	1–10	11–20	21–30	31–40	41–50	51–60
Frequency	10	8	12	16	3	1

a Write down the modal class.
b Explain why the median must be more than 20.
c Explain why the range must be more than 40.
d Estimate the mean length of a text message.

5 A survey of the time people spent travelling to work one morning gave these results.
a How many people were involved in the survey?
b Write down the modal class.
c Estimate the median journey time.
d Estimate the mean journey time.

Journey time	Frequency
Up to 30 minutes	15
30 minutes or more but less than one hour	30
One hour of more but less than $1\frac{1}{2}$ hours	10
$1\frac{1}{2}$ hours or more but less than two hours	2

6 A group of people took part in a test to see how long they could hold their breath.
The results are shown in this frequency diagram.
a Write down the modal class.
b How many people were involved?
c Estmate the median time.
d Estimate the mean.
e Maha asked: 'What is the average time?'
What is the best answer to use?
Give a reason for your answer.

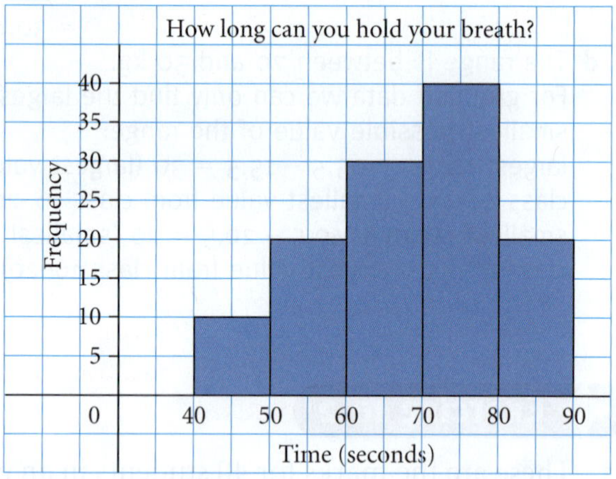

10 people held their breath for 40–50 seconds.

10.3 Using statistics to compare two distributions

Suppose you have two sets of test marks, or the heights of two groups of people. How can you compare the two sets?

One way is to find one or more of the averages, and the range. The range will show which of the two sets of data is more spread out.

The average that is most appropriate will depend on the actual data.

Worked example 10.3

These frequency tables show the masses of a group of girls and a group of boys.

Girls' masses (kg)	16–20	21–25	26–30	31–35	36–40	41–45
Frequency	12	14	20	30	17	7

Boys' masses (kg)	16–20	21–25	26–30	31–35	36–40	41–45	46–50
Frequency	5	18	15	18	29	11	14

Calculate suitable statistics to complare the two distributions.

The median for the girls is 31 kg.
The median for the boys is 35 kg.

This was calculated in Worked example 10.2.
There are 110 boys. The median is between the 55th and 56th values. The table shows that 56 boys have a mass of 35.5 kg or less.

The mean for the girls is 30.4 kg.
The mean for the boys is 34.2 kg.

This was calculated in Worked example 10.2.
Using the midpoints of the classes gives $3765 \div 110 = 34.2$.

The median and the mean both show that on average the mass of a girl is about 4 kg less than the mass of a boy.

The range for the girls is between 20 and 30 kg.
The range for the boys is between 25 and 35 kg.
The range of the boys' masses is estimated to be about 5 kg more than the girls' masses.

This was calculated in Worked Example 10.2.
This is larger because of the 46–50 kg group.

Exercise 10.3

1 These are students' marks in two test papers.
  a Which paper was more difficult?
  b Which paper had a greater variation in marks?
  Give reasons for your answers.

	Paper 1	Paper 2
Number of questions	20	15
Marks available	100	100
Median	46	41
Mean	49.5	42.8
Range	38	27
Lowest mark	20	26

2 The users of two websites were asked to grade them for ease-of-use. They used a scale of 1 to 5. 1 was poor and 5 was excellent. The results are shown in this table.

Grade		1	2	3	4	5
Frequency	Website A	4	10	16	20	10
	Website B	20	35	15	10	20

Use averages to decide which website is better.

3 This table shows the goals scored by Juventus and AC Milan in each match in the Italian Premier League in the 2010–11 season.

Goals scored		0	1	2	3	4	5	6	7
Number of matches	Juventus	5	8	14	6	3	1	0	1
	AC Milan	9	9	9	6	3	0	2	0

Compare the average number of goals per match scored by each team.

4 These are the heights of two groups of children, measured to the nearest centimetre.

Height (cm)	120–124	125–129	130–134	135–139	140–144	145–149
Boys	4	10	10	6	4	2
Girls	4	13	20	22	13	8

What is the difference between the average heights of the boys and the girls?
Give a reason for your answer.

5 This table shows the rainfall in a town in May and November, over a period of 25 years.

Rainfall (cm)		0–	5–	10–	15–	20–	25–
Number of years	May	7	11	4	2	1	0
	November	0	3	4	7	7	4

Compare the rainfall in May and November. Find any statistics that will be useful.

6 A group of people went on a special diet for three months. The table shows their masses before and after the diet.

Mass (nearest kg)		80–84	85–89	90–94	95–99	100–104	105–109	110–114
Number of people	Before diet	0	0	5	6	8	12	14
	After diet	4	5	7	15	8	4	2

a How many people went on the diet?
b Did everyone lose mass? Give a reason for your answer.
c How did the range of masses change?
d What was the average reduction in mass? Give a reason for your answer.

Summary

You should now know that:

★ The mean, median and mode are averages and the range is a measure of spread.

★ The mean, median and range can be found from a simple frequency table where the data is not grouped.

★ The modal class in a grouped frequency table is the class with the largest frequency.

★ The mean cannot be found exactly from a grouped frequency table but it can be estimated by using the midpoint of each class.

★ You can use averages or ranges to compare two distributions.

You should be able to:

★ Calculate statistics for sets of discrete and continuous data.

★ Recognise when to use the range, mean, median, mode and, for grouped data, the modal class.

★ Compare two distributions, using the range and one or more of the mode, median and mean.

★ Record and compare reasoning, solutions and conclusions.

End-of-unit review

1 The table shows the lengths of the passwords used by 30 people on a website.

Length (characters)	8	9	10	11	12	13
Number of people	11	10	4	0	3	2

Find:

a the modal password length

b the median password length

c the mean **d** the range.

2 In some countries trousers are sold by waist size, in centimetres.
The table shows the sizes of 40 pairs of trousers sold in a shop on one day.

Waist size (cm)	80	85	90	95	100	105	110
Number sold	2	3	8	8	14	1	4

a Find: **i** the median size **ii** the mode **iii** the mean **iv** the range.

b Which average would be most useful for the shop manager? Why?

3 The table shows the numbers of words in 50 sentences in a magazine.

Number of words	1–5	6–10	11–15	16–20	21–25	26–30	31–35
Frequency	2	5	10	10	14	6	3

a Write down the modal class.

b Find the mean number of words in a sentence.

c What can you say about the median?

4 The table shows the results of a survey of the waiting time for 80 people at an airport passport control.

Waiting time (minutes)	10–	20–	30–	40–	50–60
Frequency	8	30	25	10	7

a Find the modal class.

b Estimate the median waiting time.

c Estimate the mean.

d Estimate the range.

5 Students were asked to name the capital cities of 12 countries. The table shows their results.

Correct answers		**6**	**7**	**8**	**9**	**10**	**11**	**12**
Number of students	**Boys**	1	0	5	8	6	13	2
	Girls	0	4	0	10	12	5	1

a How many boys and girls took part?

b Use averages to decide whether boys or girls did better.

6 This table shows the number of words in 40 sentences in a newspaper.

Number of words	1–5	6–10	11–15	16–20	21–25
Frequency	2	7	16	10	5

Compare the sentence lengths in the newspaper with the magazine in question **3**.
Find any useful statistics you need.

11 Percentages

Percentages are used, instead of actual numbers, in articles in newspapers and magazines, on television or on the internet.

Percentages are easier to interpret than the actual numbers if you want to:

- describe one number as a fraction of another
- describe an increase or a decrease
- compare two different fractions or two different increases or decreases.

In this unit you will learn how to calculate percentages in realistic situations and begin to appreciate how useful they are.

Key words

Make sure you learn and understand these key words:

percentage
increase
decrease
reduction

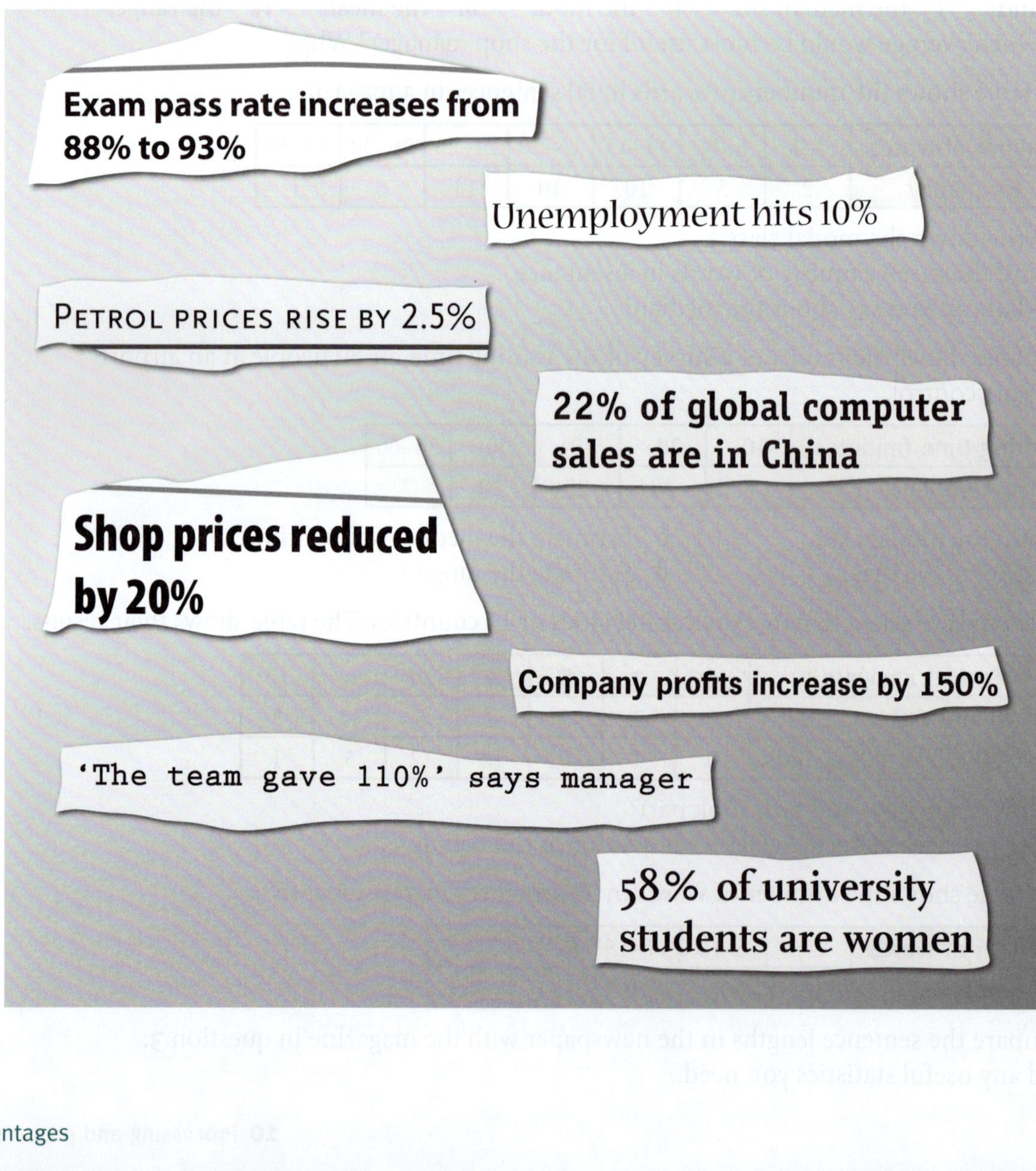

11.1 Calculating percentages

Percentage means 'out of 100', so a percentage is just a fraction with 100 as the denominator.

You need to be able to write percentages as fractions. There are some simple percentages, with the equivalent fractions, in the box.

$50\% = \frac{1}{2}$ $25\% = \frac{1}{4}$ $75\% = \frac{3}{4}$

$10\% = \frac{1}{10}$ $20\% = \frac{1}{5}$

$33\frac{1}{3}\% = \frac{1}{3}$ $66\frac{2}{3}\% = \frac{2}{3}$

Can you work out a percentage of an amount?

If the percentage is a simple fraction you should be able to work it out mentally. For other percentages you could use a calculator.

Worked example 11.1

a Lynn has 600 dollars ($600) and decided to give 40% to charity. How much was that?
b Chris earns $723 and had to pay 27% in tax. How much was that?

a $40\% = \frac{2}{5}$ — $20\% = \frac{1}{5}$ so 40% is $\frac{2}{5}$ because 40 is double 20.

$\frac{2}{5}$ of $600 = $240 — $\frac{1}{5}$ of $600 = 600 \div 5 = 120$, so $\frac{2}{5}$ of 600 is $120 \times 2 = 240$.

b 27% = 0.27 — 27% is not a simple fraction so write it as a decimal.
27% of 723 = 0.27 × 723 — Use a calculator to multiply the decimal by the amount.
= $195.21

Exercise 11.1

1 Here are some decimals and some fractions.
Match each percentage to the corresponding fraction.

5%	30%	$37\frac{1}{2}\%$	45%	50%	60%
$\frac{1}{2}$	$\frac{3}{5}$	$\frac{3}{8}$	$\frac{1}{20}$	$\frac{3}{10}$	$\frac{9}{20}$

2 Write each percentage as a decimal.
a 15% **b** 5% **c** 90% **d** 6.5% **e** 150%

3 Calculate these amounts. Do not use a calculator. Start by changing the percentages to fractions and simplifying them as much as possible.
a 25% of 60 kg **b** 75% of 1000 litres **c** 40% of $300 **d** 70% of 120 g

4 Find the following amounts. Do not use a calculator.
a 10% of 45 cm **b** 60% of 60 people **c** $33\frac{1}{3}\%$ of 2400 **d** $12\frac{1}{2}\%$ of 40

5 Use a calculator to find these amounts.
a 27% of $43 **b** 57% of 280 **c** 93% of 3700 **d** 6% of 9200

6 **a** Which of these would be easy to find without using a calculator?
A $66\frac{2}{3}\%$ of 90 **B** 82% of 200 **C** 60% of 55 **D** 3% of 2100 **E** 23% of 50
b Find the values of each percentage in part **a**.

7 Find:
a 7% of 30 **b** 17% of 30 **c** 107% of 30 **d** 117% of 30.

8 Use the facts in the boxes to find:
a 74% of X **b** 48% of X **c** 61% of X
d 18.5% of X **e** 13% of X.

37% of X is 44.03

24% of X is 28.56

9 When 420 students took an examination, 80% passed.
a How many passed? **b** What percentage failed? **c** How many failed?

10 In an election, 4600 people voted. They had the choice of three parties. The results are shown in the box.
a How many votes did each of those parties get?
b What percentage of the voters did not vote for those three parties?

Red Party: 37%
Blue Party: 28%
Yellow Party: 20%

11 There are 40 000 people at a soccer match. 83% support the home team.
a How many people support the home team?
b How many do not support the home team?
c What percentage do not support the home team?

12 a What amounts of copper and tin are there in 30 grams of bronze?
b What amounts of copper and tin are there in one kilogram of bronze?

The metal bronze is made from 95% copper and 5% tin.

13 a What percentage of stainless steel is iron?
b What amounts of chromium and nickel are there in a stainless steel knife blade with a mass of 140 g?
c The Parliament House of Australia, in Canberra, has a stainless steel flagpole with a mass of about 200 tonnes. How much chromium and nickel does it contain?

Stainless steel is made from 18% chromium, 8% nickel and the rest is iron.

1 tonne = 1000 kilograms

14 The population of Europe is 850 million.
This table gives the percentage of the population of Europe living in some of its countries.

Country	Germany	France	Spain	Sweden
Percentage of European population	9.6%	7.8%	5.5%	1.1%

Estimate the population of each country. Give your answers to the nearest million.

15 There were 5623 people at a music concert.
Work out the numbers of men, women, boys and girls at the concert.

At the concert

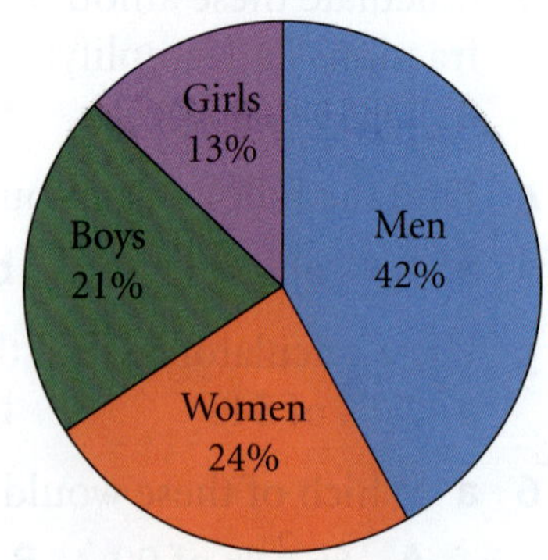

16 The population of a town is 32 600.
About 27% are over 60 years old. About 19% are 16 or under. How many are between 16 and 60?

17 Which of these amounts are different from the others? Give a reason for your answer.

32% of 48	12% of 128	3% of 512
96% of 16	18% of 84	9% of 168
120% of 12.8	24% of 64	1.5% of 1024

11.2 Percentage increases and decreases

Percentages are often used to describe **increases** or **decreases**.

Examples: The population of the town decreased by 13%.
I received a 7% pay rise.
The price was reduced by 30%.
Production rose by 150%.

A decrease is often called a **reduction.**

You can find the result of an increase or decrease in two steps.

① First, calculate the increase or decrease.

② Then add it to or subtract it from the original amount.

Worked example 11.2

Yi-ling bought a car for $15 800. After a year it was worth 20% less. How much was it worth after a year?

$20\% = \frac{1}{5}$ You could also say 20% = 0.2 and multiply by that decimal.

$\frac{1}{5}$ of $15\,800 = 15\,800 \div 5 = 3160$ This is the reduction in value.

$15\,800 - 3160 = 12\,640$ Subtract 20% from the original cost.

The car is worth $12 640.

Exercise 11.2

1 **a** Find 15% of $60. **b** Increase $60 by 15%. **c** Decrease $60 by 15%.

2 **a** Find 70% of 3200 people. **b** Increase 3200 by 70%. **c** Decrease 3200 by 70%.

3 **a** Find 2% of 19.00. **b** Increase 19.00 by 2%. **c** Decrease 19.00 by 2%.

4 Read what Tanesha says. How much will she have if she increases her savings by:
a 10% **b** 50% **c** 70%
d 100% **e** 120%?

5 The population of a town is 45 000.
The population is expected to rise by 15% in the next ten years.
Estimate the population in ten years' time.

6 A metal bar is 1.800 metres long.
It is heated and the length increases by 0.5%.
How long is the bar now?

7 A shop lists its prices in a table.
a In a sale, all the prices are reduced by 30%.
Calculate the sale prices.
b How much would you save if you bought all four items in the sale?

Item	Price in $US
Table	280
Armchair	520
Bed	190
Mattress	430

8 Electricity costs are rising by 8%.
The table shows the costs for one year for four customers. Copy the table and fill in the last column to show their estimated costs for one year after the price rise. Give the prices to the nearest dollar.

Customer	Cost before rise ($)	Estimated cost after rise
A	415	
B	629	
C	390	
D	812	

9 A garage is reducing the prices of new cars. Calculate the new prices.

Model	Old price ($)	Decrease (%)	New price ($)
Ace	15 800	2	
Beta	17 425	3	
Carro	21 280	1.5	
Delta	24 172	1.8	

10 A shop is selling a phone for $80. The shop increases the price by 10%.

a Find the new price.

After two weeks, the shop decreases the new price by 10%.
Read what Shen and Zalika say.

The price will go back down to $80.

The price now will be less than $80.

b Explain why Shen is wrong and Zalika is correct.

c Find the price of the phone after the decrease.

11 The same shop is selling a television for $400.

a The shop increases the price by 20%. Find the new price.

b Find 20% of the new price.

c The shop increases the price by a further 20%. Find the new price.

11.3 Finding percentages

There are times when you need to write one number as a percentage of another.

Here are some examples:

- writing a price increase as a percentage
- finding the percentage of people who are unemployed
- estimating the percentage change in a population.

To write one number as a percentage of another, write the numbers in the form of a fraction and then change the fraction to a percentage.

> To write a fraction as a decimal, divide the numerator by the denominator.
>
> $\frac{7}{8} = 7 \div 8 = 0.875$
>
> To write a decimal as a percentage, multiply by 100.
>
> $0.875 = 87.5\%$

If the numbers are simple, you can do this mentally. For more complicated numbers, use a calculator.

Worked example 11.3

a There are 40 people on a bus and 28 are women. What percentage are women?
b One Monday, the bus carried 364 passengers and 157 were women. What percentage were women?
c On Tuesday there were 427 passengers. What is the percentage increase in the number of passengers?

a The fraction who are women is $\frac{28}{40} = \frac{7}{10}$.
$\frac{7}{10} = 70\%$ are women.

It is easy to cancel the numbers to give a simple fraction.
$\frac{1}{10} = 10\%$ so $\frac{7}{10} = 7 \times 10 = 70\%$.

b The fraction who were women is $\frac{157}{364}$.

This fraction does not cancel to a simple fraction.

$\frac{157}{364} = 0.431...$

Divide to find the equivalent decimal, $157 \div 364 = 0.431...$

$0.431... = 43.1\%$

Multiply the decimal by 100 to get the percentage. Round the answer if necessary.

c The increase is $427 - 364 = 63$.

The percentage increase is $\frac{63}{364} \times 100 = 17.3\%$

Divide by the initial number of passengers, 364, not by 427.

Exercise 11.3

1 a Anders' test marks are shown in the box. Change each of them to a percentage.

Science: 7 out of 10	History: 17 out of 20	Geography: 27 out of 40
English: 37 out of 50	Maths: 67 out of 80	Art: 17 out of 30

b Which subject gave him the best mark?

2 There are 753 students in a college. 419 are female.
a What percentage of the students are female? **b** What percentage of the students are male?

3 Sasha is reading a novel with 427 pages. She has read 276 pages.
a What percentage has she read? **b** What percentage has she still got to read?

4 There are 24 men and 36 women in a choir.
a What percentage of the choir are men? **b** What percentage are women?
c 10 more men and 10 more women join the choir. What are the percentages of men and women now?

5 In a children's club there are 23 girls and 14 of them wear glasses.
There are 42 boys and 12 of them wear glasses.
a What percentage of the girls wear glasses?
b What percentage of the boys wear glasses?
c What percentage of all the children wear glasses?

6 The cost of an aeroplane flight increases from \$250 to \$295.
a What is the increase? **b** What is the percentage increase?

7 Concert tickets cost \$30, \$40 or \$50.
If you buy a ticket online you pay an extra \$3 as a booking fee.
What percentage of each ticket price is the booking fee?

8 This table shows the populations, in millions, of five countries in 1990 and in 2010.
a Calculate the percentage increase in population for each country over the 20-year period.
In the same period the world population increased from 5.3 billion to 6.9 billion.
b What was the percentage increase in the world population from 1990 to 2010?
c In 2010, what percentage of the world's population lived in China?

One billion = 1000 million

Country	Population (millions)	
	1990	**2010**
China	1145	1341
India	874	1225
Indonesia	184	240
Japan	122	127
Nigeria	98	158
United States	253	310

9 The table shows the masses of four people who were on a diet from March to July.
a Calculate the percentage change in mass for each person.
b Who was the most successful dieter? Give a reason for your answer.

Person	Mass in March (kg)	Mass in July (kg)
A	95.2	88.7
B	89.4	79.0
C	84.5	87.3
D	102.5	87.4

10 This table shows a boy's mass at different ages.
Work out the percentage increase in mass:
a from 1 year to 2 years
b from 2 years to 4 years
c from 1 month to 1 year.

Age	1 month	1 year	2 years	4 years
Mass (kg)	4.5	9.6	12.2	16.3

11.4 Using percentages

The price of a scarf increases from \$20 to \$25.

The price of a coat increases from \$100 to \$105.

Both prices have increased by the same amount but they have not increased by the same percentage.

Percentages are a better way than amounts to compare changes of this sort.

Both prices increase by \$5.

The price of the scarf increases by 25%.

The price of the coat increases by 5%.

Worked example 11.4

There are 247 people at a concert. 103 of them are children.
There are 305 children and 527 adults at a football match.
Which had a larger proportion of children?

The fraction of children at the concert is $\frac{103}{247}$.	This is the number of children over the total audience.
The percentage of children is 41.7%.	This is 103 ÷ 247 × 100.
The fraction of children at the match is $\frac{305}{832}$.	The denominator is 305 + 527, the total number of people.
The percentage of children is 36.7%.	This is 305 ÷ 832 × 100.
There is a larger proportion of children at the concert.	Compare the proportions with percentages.

Exercise 11.4

1 **a** Change these fractions to percentages.

b Write the fractions in order from smallest to largest.

$\frac{13}{17}$ $\frac{27}{38}$ $\frac{69}{93}$

2 This table shows the ages of students in three colleges.

School		New College	City College	State College
Age	Under 13	141	183	254
	13 or more	291	208	372

a Find the percentage of students who are under 13 in each college.

b Which college has the greatest proportion of students aged 13 or more?

3 The table shows some price changes in a sale. All prices are in dollars.

a Find the percentage reduction for each item.

b Which item has the best reduction?

Item	Computer	Printer	Game console	Software
Normal price	549	189	135	109
Sale price	449	119	65	85

4 A survey records how many trains arrive at a station on time or late on three separate days.

a Find the percentage of trains that are late on each day.

b Which day had the best record?

Day	Friday	Saturday	Sunday
On time	67	53	35
Late	10	12	9

5 In a music examination candidates can get a distinction, a pass or a fail.
Here are the results.

	Distinction	Pass	Fail
Boys	28	214	35
Girls	23	91	37

a Compare the proportion of boys and girls who gained a distinction.
b Compare the proportion of boys and girls who failed.
c Did boys or girls do better in the examination? Give a reason for your answer.

6 Users gave feedback on three music tracks they had been listening too. They rated them as poor, average, good or excellent. Here are the results.

	Poor	Average	Good	Excellent	Total
Track A	30	24	64	31	149
Track B	9	24	27	23	83
Track C	6	18	22	20	66

a What percentage of the feedback for each track was average?
b Which track had the highest proportion of average ratings?
c Which track had the highest proportion of ratings that were either good or excellent?
d Which track got the best feedback? Give a reason for your answer.

7 The table shows the masses, to the nearest kilogram, of two groups of adults who were recorded as underweight, normal or overweight.
Use percentages to compare the weight distributions of men and women. Comment on the proportions that are underweight and the proportions that are overweight.

	Underweight	Normal	Overweight	Total
Women	245	562	314	1121
Men	85	266	285	636

Summary

You should now know that:

★ A percentage is a fraction out of a hundred.
★ You can find a percentage of a quantity by writing the percentage as a fraction or a decimal and converting.
★ You can find simple percentages mentally. For more complicated questions, you can use written working or a calculator.
★ You can find a new amount after a percentage increase (or decrease) by first calculating the increase (or decrease) and then adding it to (or subtracting it from) the original amount.
★ Percentages are a good way to compare parts of, or changes to, two different quantities.
★ When solving a word problem using percentages, it is important to choose the calculations carefully to avoid errors.

You should be able to:

★ Calculate percentages and solve problems involving them.
★ Calculate percentage increases and decreases and solve problems involving them.
★ Express one given number as a fraction or percentage of another.
★ Use equivalent fractions, decimals and percentages to compare different quantities.
★ Calculate accurately, choosing operations and mental or written methods appropriate to the numbers and context.
★ Solve word problems involving percentages.

End-of-unit review

1 Write these percentages as fractions in their simplest terms.
a 90% **b** 40% **c** 5% **d** 2.5%

2 Calculate these amounts.
a 60% of 120 metres **b** 43% of 15 metres **c** $66\frac{2}{3}$% of 27 kg **d** 9.5% of 5800

3 There were 7200 cars involved in a survey. 17% were driven by women.
a What percentage were driven by men? **b** How many were driven by men?

4 One year, out of 365 days, 29% were sunny and 42% were cloudy.
a How many days were sunny? **b** How many days were cloudy?

5 On Friday 460 people visited a museum.
a There were 20% more people on Saturday. How many visited on Saturday?
b On Sunday there were 15% fewer than on Friday. How many visited on Sunday?

6 812 people made a contribution to a charity.
Read what Ahmad says.

Is he correct? Give a reason for your answer.

7 17% tax is added to the cost of meals sold in a restaurant.
Here are some prices before tax. Work out the price when tax is added.
a \$7.55 **b** \$19.10 **c** \$45.99

8 In a sale, a shop reduces prices by 65%. What will be the reduced prices of items that cost:
a \$50 **b** \$85 **c** \$229?

9 On Thursday morning, a shop had 468 customers. 314 were women and 75 were children.
a What percentage were women? **b** What percentage were not children.

10 The number of students in a school fell from 629 last year to 574 this year.
What is the percentage reduction?

11 This table shows the value of a painting at different times.
Find the percentage increase or decrease in value:

Year	1992	2002	2012
Value (\$)	750	1250	1150

a from 1992 to 2002 **b** from 2002 to 2012 **c** from 1992 to 2012.

12 This table shows the numbers of people who live in two towns. It is separated into age groups.
Which town has a greater proportion of people under 25 years old? Give percentages to justify your answer.

Town	**Under 25 years old**	**25 or more**
X	4825	7362
Y	10 209	23 627

12 Constructions

You will have already used some of the mathematical instruments that you need to draw lines, angles and 2D shapes.

Ruler

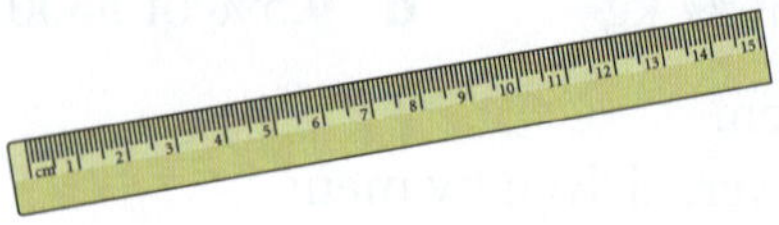

Protractor

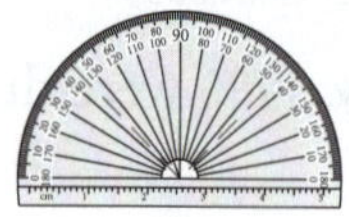

Key words

Make sure you learn and understand these key words:

circumference
radius, radii
diameter
arc
sector
chord
segment
line segment
midpoint
perpendicular bisector
angle bisector
SSS (side, side, side)
RHS (right angle, hypotenuse, side)

You also need to be able to use a pair of compasses to draw circles and arcs. They are usually made of metal or plastic. They have two arms – one holds a pencil and the other has a sharp point on the end. This is to hold the compass in place when you turn it to draw a circle.

Pair of compasses

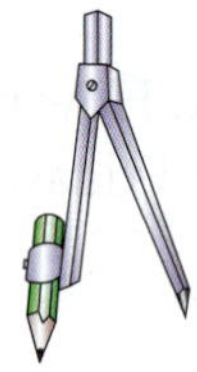

Before you start drawing circles, you need to know the names of the different parts of a circle.

The **circumference** of a circle is a line made up of points that are always the same distance from the centre. It is the perimeter of a circle.

The **radius** of a circle is a line segment that joins the centre of a circle to any point on the circumference.

The **diameter** of a circle is a line segment that passes through the centre and joins two points on the circumference. The diameter is twice the length of the radius.

An **arc** is part of the circumference of a circle.

A **sector** of a circle is the area enclosed between two radii (plural of radius) and an arc.

A **chord** is a line segment that joins two points on the circumference of a circle.

A **segment** is the area enclosed between a chord and an arc.

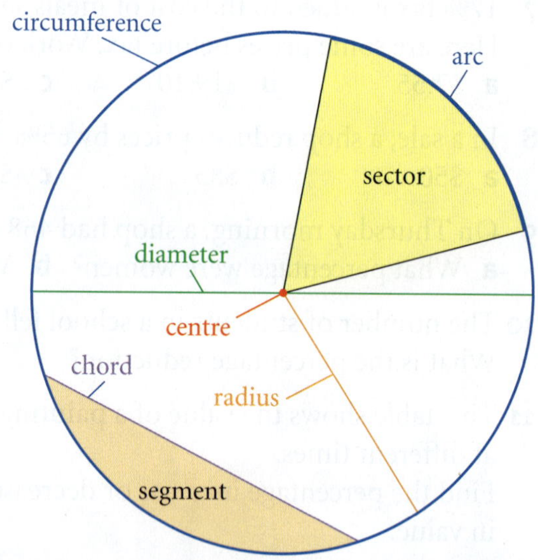

In this unit you will learn how to draw accurate circles and arcs. You will also learn how to use a pair of compasses to make other constructions such as perpendicular bisectors and angle bisectors. At the end of the unit you will use compasses again, to draw triangles when you are given only certain pieces of information.

12.1 Drawing circles and arcs

You must always use a pair of compasses to draw a circle or an arc accurately.

Follow the steps in Worked example **12.1** to draw a circle and an arc.

Worked example 12.1

a Draw a circle with radius 4 cm.
b Draw an arc with radius 5 cm and a centre angle of 45°.

a

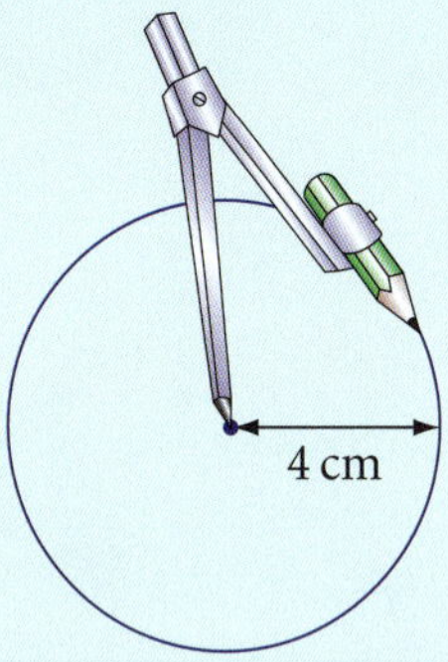

Draw a small dot to represent the centre of the circle.
Open the compasses to a radius of 4 cm.
Put the compass point on the centre of the circle.
Draw the circle carefully. As you draw, make sure you keep the compass point on the centre of the circle, and don't change the 4 cm radius.

> The radius on the compasses is the distance between the tip of the metal point and the tip of the pencil, measured along a ruler.

b

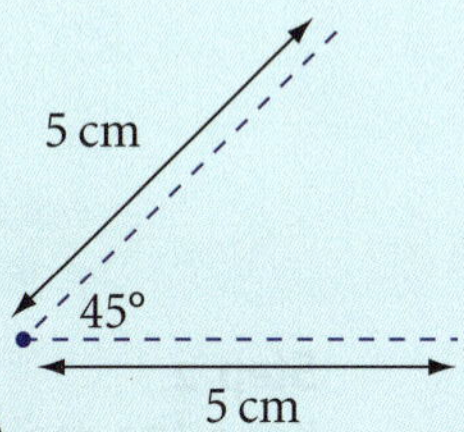

Draw a small dot to represent the centre of the circle.
Draw two dotted lines, from the small dot, at an angle of 45°.
Use a protractor to measure the angle. Make each dotted line 5 cm long.
The dotted lines must meet at the centre of the arc.

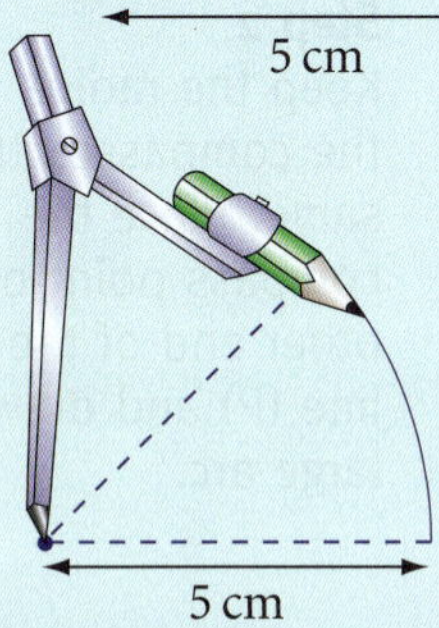

Open the compasses to a radius of 5 cm.
Put the compass point on the dot.
This is the centre of the arc.
Draw the arc carefully from the end of one dotted line to the end of the other.

> Always use a sharp, hard pencil so that the lines you draw are clear.

Exercise 12.1

1 Draw circles with:

a radius 6 cm **b** radius 3.5 cm **c** radius 45 mm
d diameter 8 cm **e** diameter 5 cm **f** diameter 60 mm.

2 The diagram shows a horizontal line AB 8 cm long.
The points C, D and E lie on the line. They are 1 cm, 2 cm and 4 cm from A.

a Make an accurate copy of the diagram.
b Draw the following circles onto the diagram:
  i radius 4 cm, centre at E
  ii radius 2 cm, centre at D
  iii radius 1 cm, centre at C.
c What can you say about point A on the line segment?

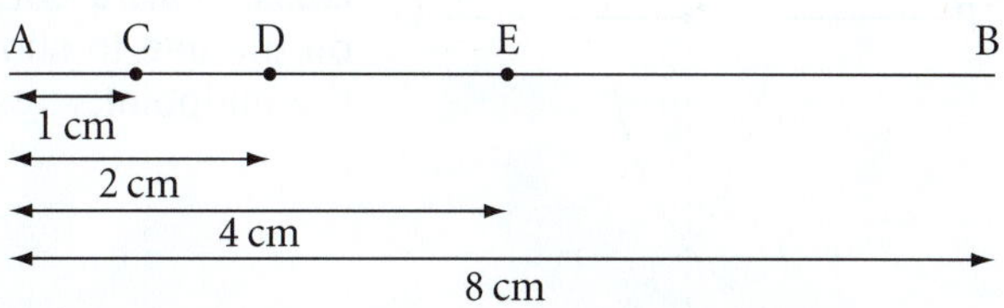

3 Draw arcs with:

a radius 4 cm and angle 50° **b** radius 5 cm and angle 85° **c** radius 35 mm and angle 120°.

12.2 Drawing a perpendicular bisector

AB is a **line segment**.

The **midpoint** of the line segment is the point that is exactly halfway between A and B.

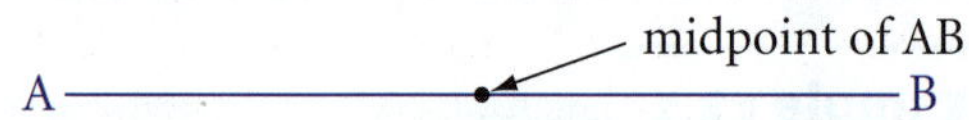

The **perpendicular bisector** of the line segment AB is the line that passes through the midpoint of AB at right angles to AB.

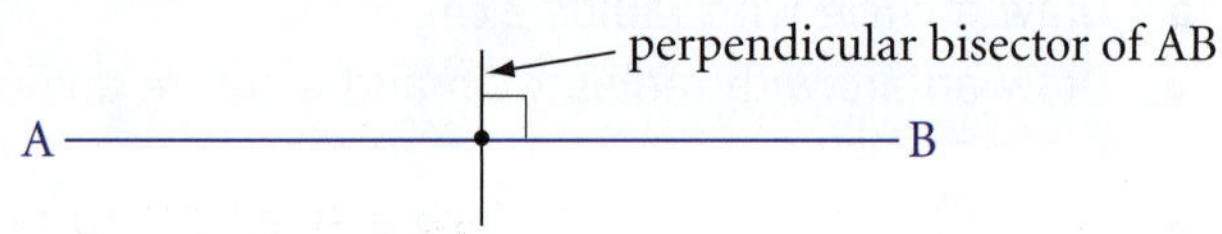

'Perpendicular' means 'at right angles to'. 'Bisect' means 'cut in half'.

Worked example **12.2** shows how to draw the midpoint and perpendicular bisector of a line segment, using only a straight-edge and compasses.

Worked example 12.2

PQ is a line segment.
Draw onto PQ:
a the midpoint **b** the perpendicular bisector.

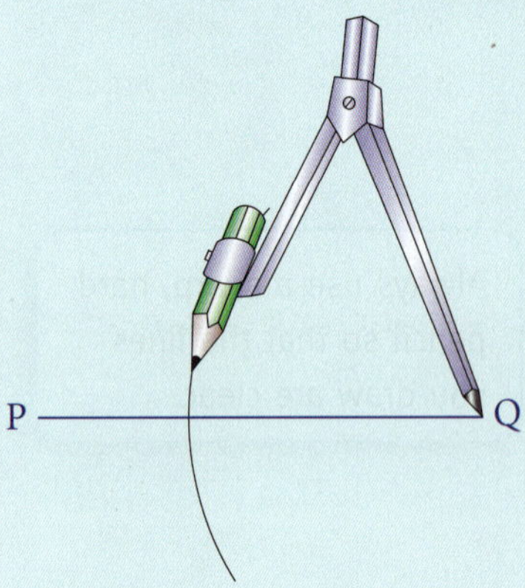

Step 1
Open the compasses to a radius that is more than half the length of the line PQ. Place the compass point on one end of the line (Q) and draw a large arc.

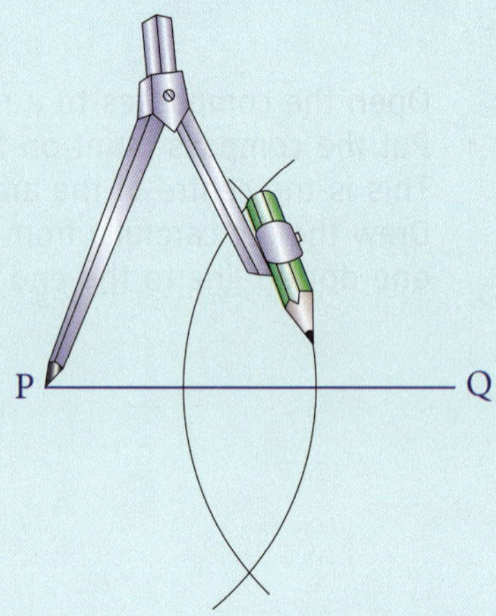

Step 2
Keep the radius of the compasses the same. Place the compass point on other end of the line (P) and draw a large arc.

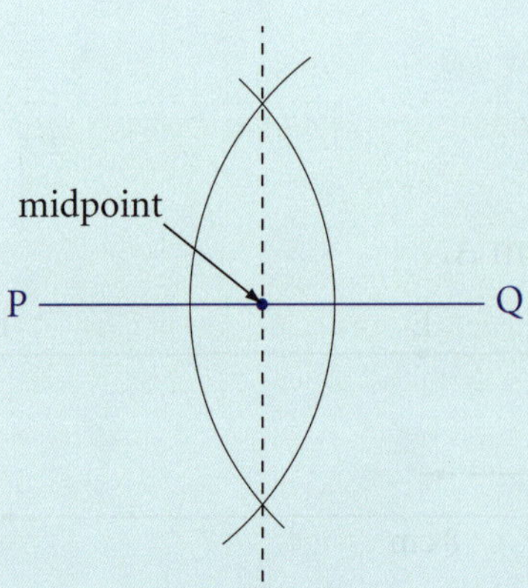

Step 3
Place your straight-edge along the line joining the points where the two arcs cross. Draw a dot on the line to show the midpoint.

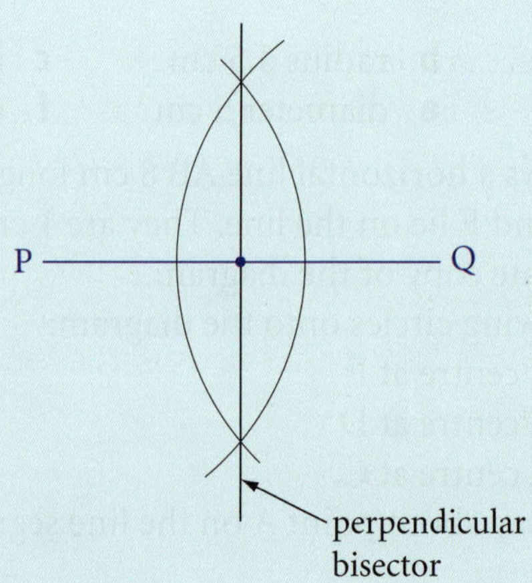

Step 4
Hold the straight-edge still and draw a straight line to join the points where the two arcs cross. This is the perpendicular bisector of PQ.

Exercise 12.2

1 Follow these instructions to draw the perpendicular bisector of a line segment AB.

a Draw a line segment 8 cm long. Label one end A and the other end B.
Make sure you allow 6 cm of space above and below the line for drawing the arcs.

b Open your compasses to a radius that is more than half the length of AB.

c Put the compass point on the end of the line that is marked A. Draw a large arc.

d Put the compass point on the end of the line that is marked B.
Draw a large arc that crosses the other arc in two places.

e Join the points where the two arcs cross. Make sure you draw a straight line.

2 Follow these instructions to draw the midpoint on a line segment CD.

a Draw a line segment 5 cm long. Label one end C and the other end D.
Make sure you allow 4 cm of space above and below the line, for drawing the arcs.

b Open your compasses to a radius that is more than half the length of CD.

c Put the compass point on the end of the line marked C. Draw a large arc.

d Put the compass point on the end of the line marked D. Draw a large arc that crosses the other arc in two places.

e Place your straight-edge along the line joining the points where the two arcs cross.

f Mark a dot where the straight-edge crosses CD.

g Check this is the midpoint. Use a ruler to measure the distance from C to the midpoint, and the distance from D to the midpoint. They should both be 2.5 cm.

3 Work with a partner. You will each need a clean sheet of plain paper.

a Draw a line segment EF. The line segment can be any length between 4 cm and 14 cm long.
Make sure you allow plenty of space above and below the line for drawing arcs.

> You should both draw the line on your own paper.

b Exchange papers with your partner.

c Using only compasses and a straight-edge, draw the perpendicular bisector of EF on the paper you have been given.

d Exchange with your partner again, so you now have your own paper back.

e Now use a ruler to check that your partner has draw the perpendicular bisector <u>exactly</u> through the midpoint of EF.

f Use a protractor to check that your partner has drawn the perpendicular bisector at <u>exactly</u> 90° to EF.

4 A builder buys a rectangular plot of land.
The sketch shows the dimensions of the plot of land ABCD.

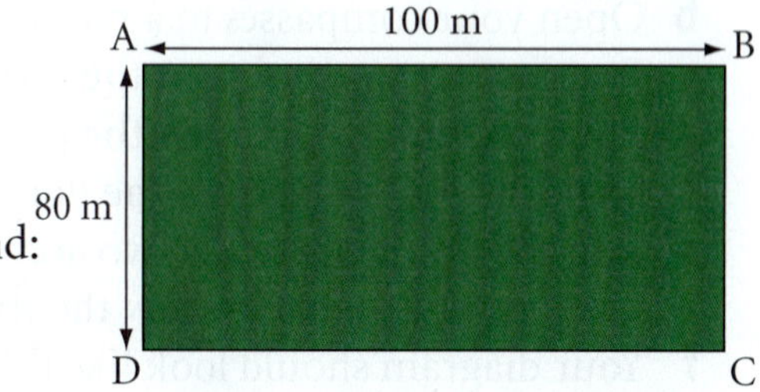

a Using a ruler and protractor, draw an accurate copy of the plot of land. Use a scale of '1 cm represents 10 m'.

b Using compasses and a straight-edge, on your diagram, find:
i the midpoint of AB **ii** the midpoint of BC.

c The builder is going to put a fence from the midpoint of AB to the midpoint of BC.
Draw this fence on your diagram.

12.3 Drawing an angle bisector

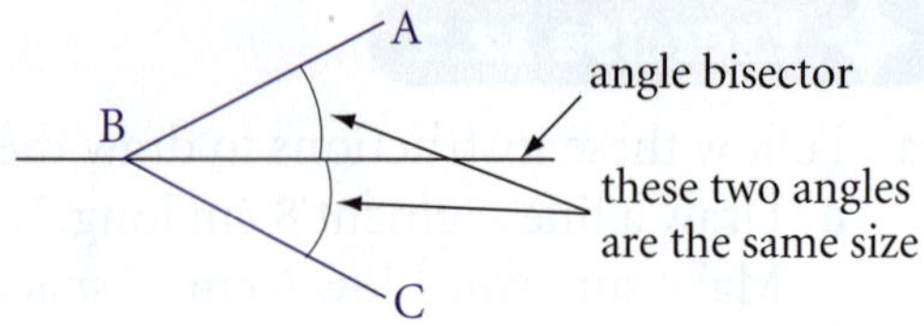

Look at the angle ABC.

There is a line that divides the angle exactly in half.
This is the bisector of angle ABC.

You can draw an **angle bisector** using only a straight-edge and compasses. Worked example **12.3** shows the steps you must follow to do this accurately.

Worked example 12.3

Draw the angle bisector of angle PQR.

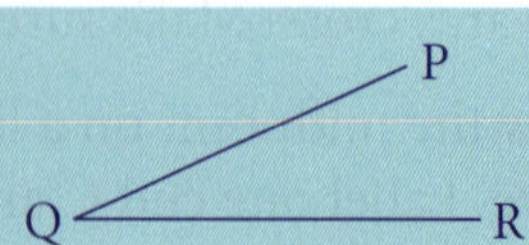

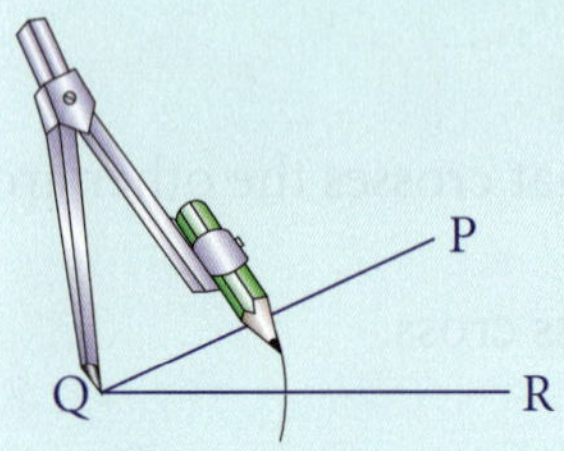

Step 1
Open the compasses to a radius that is about half the length of the line QP. Place the compass point on Q, the vertex of the angle. Draw an arc that crosses QP and QR.

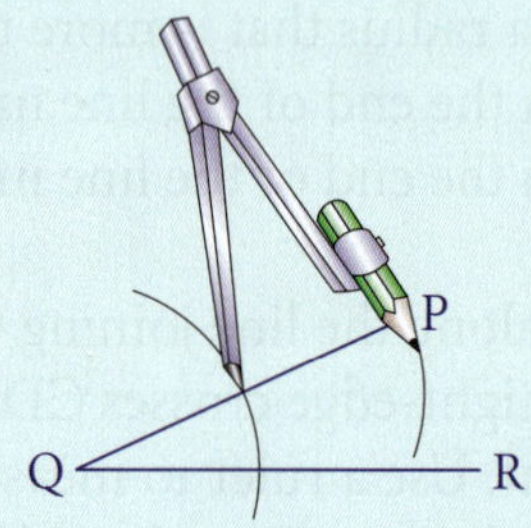

Step 2
Move the compass point to where the arc crosses QP. Draw an arc in the middle of the angle.

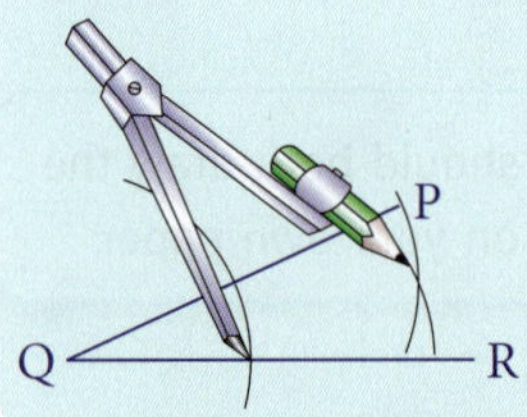

Step 3
Move the compass point to where the arc crosses QR. Draw another arc in the middle of the angle.

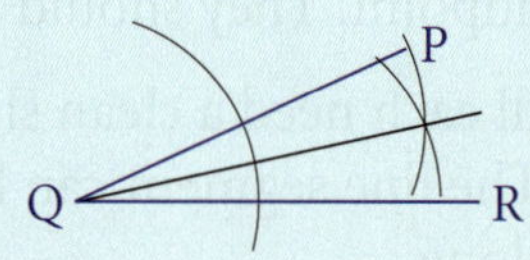

Step 4
Use the straight-edge to draw a straight line, joining the point where the two arcs cross to the point Q. This is the angle bisector.

Exercise 12.3

1 Follow these instructions to draw the angle bisector of angle ABC.

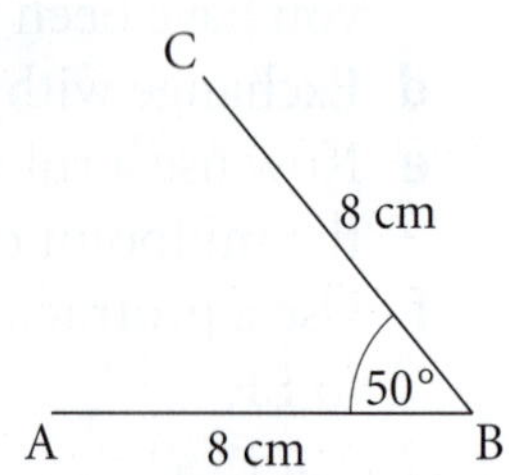

- **a** Draw a line 8 cm long and label it AB.
  Use a protractor to measure an angle of 50° from B.
  Draw another line 8 cm long to complete the angle.
  Label the end of the line C.
- **b** Open your compasses to a radius of about 4 cm.
- **c** Put the compass point on the vertex of angle B and draw an arc that crosses BA and BC.
- **d** Put the compass point on the point where the arc crosses BA and draw an arc in the middle of the angle. Do the same from the point where the arc crosses BC.
- **e** Join the point where the two arcs cross, in the middle of the angle, to point B.
  Use a straight-edge to draw the straight line.
- **f** Your diagram should look like this.
  Use a protractor to check that the angle bisector is accurate.
  Measure the two smaller angles.
  They should both measure 25°.

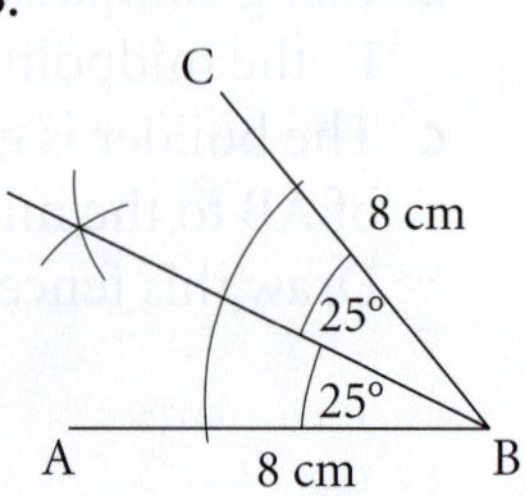

2 Follow these instructions to draw the angle bisector of angle DEF.

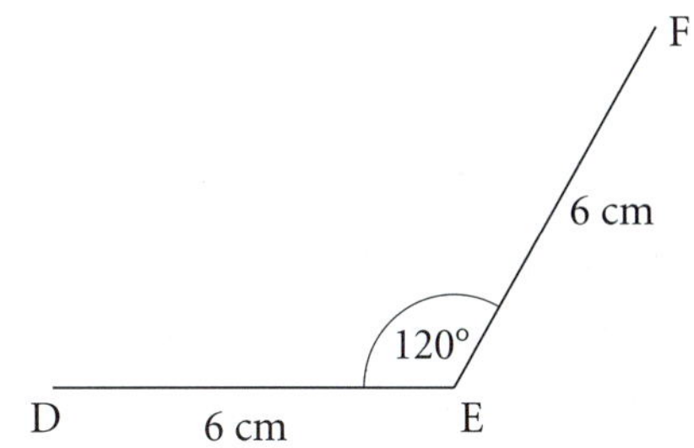

a Draw a line 6 cm long and label it DE.
Use a protractor to measure an angle of 120° at E.
Draw another line 6 cm long to complete the angle.
Label the end of the line F.

b Open your compasses to a radius of about 4 cm.

c Put the compass point on the vertex of the angle at E.
Draw an arc that crosses ED and EF.

d Put the compass point on the point where the arc crosses ED and draw an arc in the middle of the angle. Do the same from the point where the arc crosses EF.

e Join the point where the two arcs cross, in the middle of the angle, to point E. Use a straight-edge to draw the straight line.

f Your diagram should look like this.
Use a protractor to check that the angle bisector is accurate.
Measure the two smaller angles. They should both measure 60°.

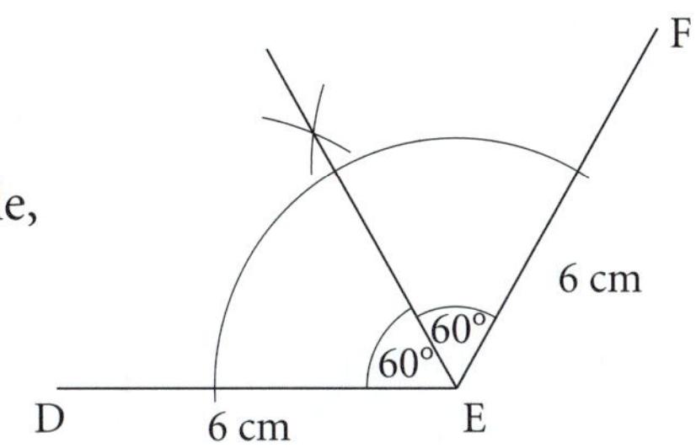

3 Work with a partner. You will each need a clean sheet of plain paper.

a Draw two angles UVW and XYZ.
Angle UVW can be any size between 20° and 90°.
Angle XYZ can be any size between 90° and 160°
Make sure the sides of the angles (UV, VW, XY and YZ) are between about 5 cm and 10 cm long.

b Exchange papers with your partner.

c Using only compasses and a straight-edge, draw the angle bisectors of UVW and XYZ onto the paper you now have.

d Exchange with your partner again, so you now have your own paper back.

e Use a protractor to check that your partner has drawn the angle bisectors to cut your angles exactly in half.

4 Shot put is a sports competition where a person throws a heavy metal ball as far as possible.
The diagram shows a shot put circle on a school athletics field.
The shot must land anywhere outside the circle but between the sides of the landing area (this is shaded yellow in the diagram).
The angle between the sides of the landing area is 35°.

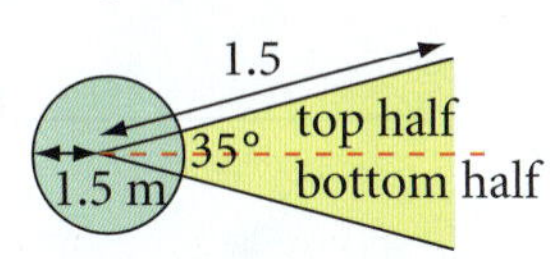

Angharad is practising throwing the shot. She wants to count how many times the shot lands in the top half of the landing area and how often it lands in the bottom half .

a Draw an accurate scale drawing of the shot put circle and landing area.
Use only compasses and a straight-edge.

b Draw on your diagram the angle bisector, shown by the red dotted line.

c Use a protractor to check that you have drawn the angle bisector accurately.

5 At a beach resort, the lifeguards rope a section of sea that is safe to use.
The angle between the ropes of the safe area is 70°.
The lifeguards fix a rope along the angle bisector.
Swimmers can use the area to the left of the rope.
People in boats can use the area to the right of the rope.

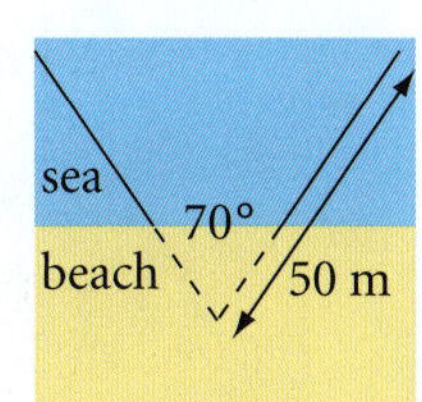

a Draw an accurate scale drawing of the diagram.

b Draw onto the diagram the angle bisector.

c Use a protractor to check that you have drawn the angle bisector accurately.

12.4 Constructing triangles

You already know how to construct some triangles using only a ruler and compasses.

You have used SAS (Side, Angle, Side) and ASA (Angle, Side, Angle).

There are two more types of triangle construction that you still need to learn.

When you know the lengths of all three sides, you can use **SSS** or **Side, Side, Side.**

When you know the lengths of the hypotenuse and one other side, you can use **RHS** or **Right angle, Hypotenuse, Side.**

Worked example **12.4** shows you how to draw these triangles.

> You can use just a ruler and compasses to draw these triangles.

Worked example 12.4

Make accurate drawings of these triangles.

a

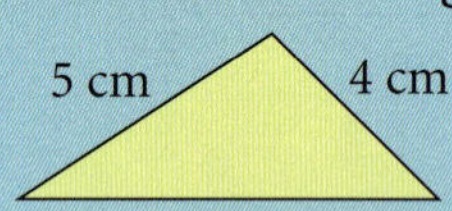

b

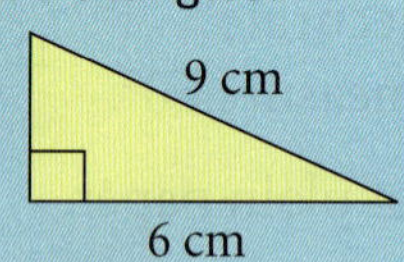

> One is SSS and the other is RHS.

a

Step 1
Draw the base line 8 cm long.

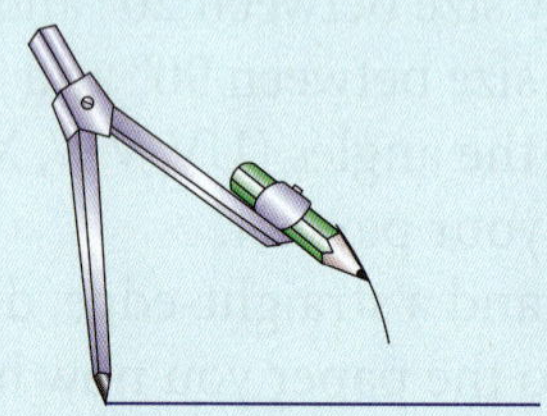

Step 2
Open the compasses to a radius of 5 cm. Put the point on the left end of the base line, and draw an arc above the base line.

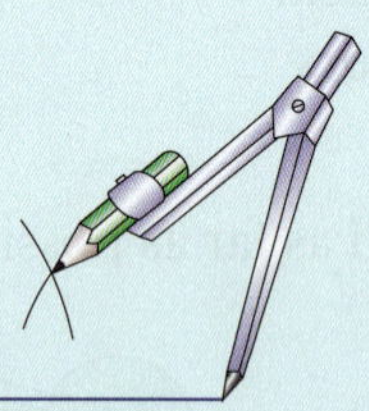

Step 3
Change the compasses to a radius of 4 cm. Put the point on the right end of the base line, and draw an arc above the base line, to cross the first arc.

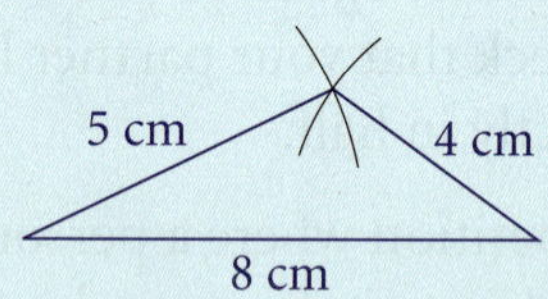

Step 4
Where the two arcs cross is the top of the triangle. Join this point to each end of the base line. Make sure your lines are straight.

b

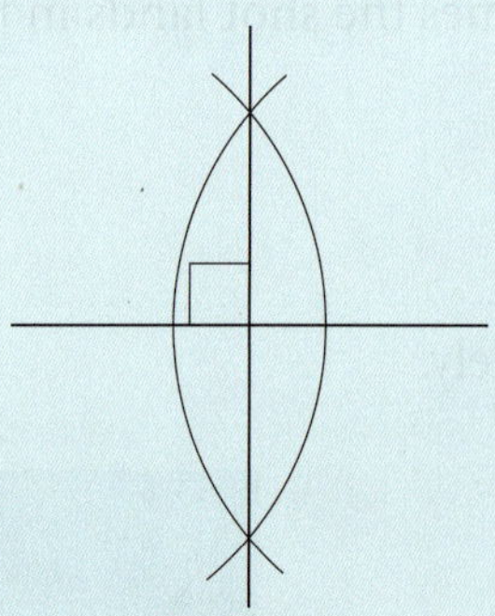

Step 1
Draw a line 12 cm long.
Draw the perpendicular bisector of the line.
Make this vertical line longer than usual.

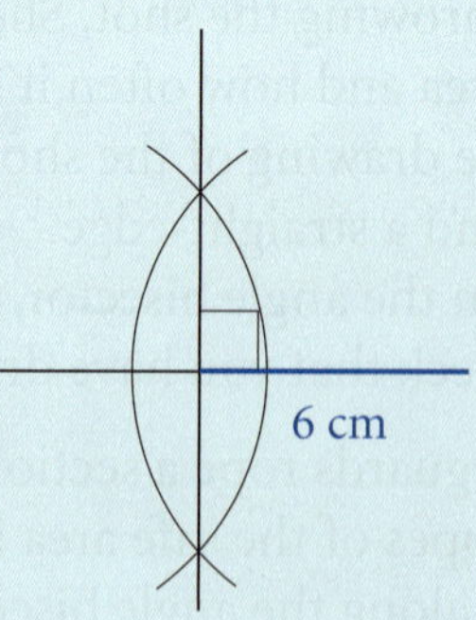

Step 2
Check that the distance from the point of the right angle to the end of the base line is exactly 6 cm.

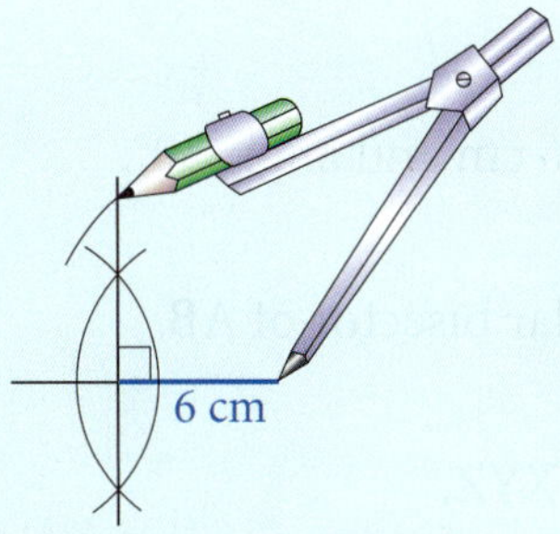

Step 3
Open the compasses to a radius of 9 cm. Put the point on the right-hand end of the base line. Draw an arc that meets the vertical line.

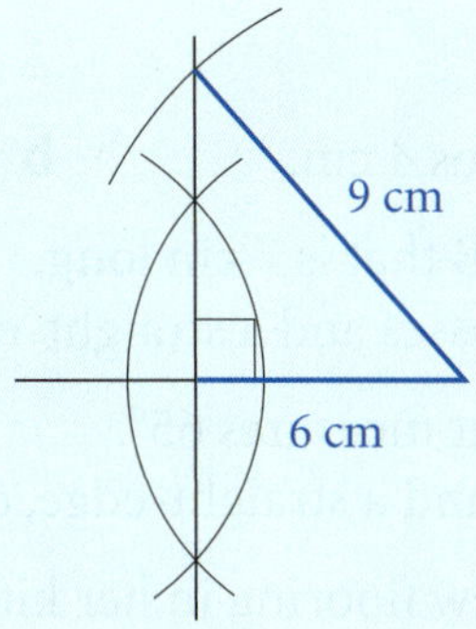

Step 4
Where the arc crosses the vertical line is the top of the triangle. Join this point with a straight line to the right-hand end of the base line.

Exercise 12.4

1 **a** Draw an accurate copy of triangle ABC.
b Measure and write down the size of angle:
i ABC **ii** BAC **iii** ACB.
c Add together the three answers you gave in part **b**.
d Explain how you can use your answer to part **c** to check that you have measured the angles in the triangle accurately.

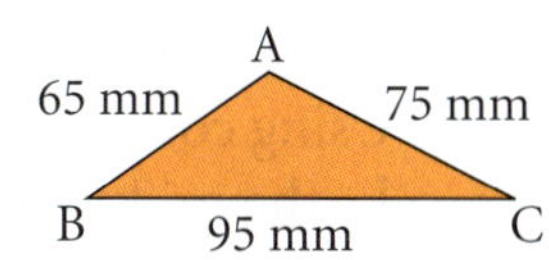

2 **a** Draw an accurate copy of triangle DEF.
b Measure and write down the length of the side DF.
c Measure and write down the size of angle:
i DEF **ii** EDF
d What type of triangle is DEF? Explain your answer.

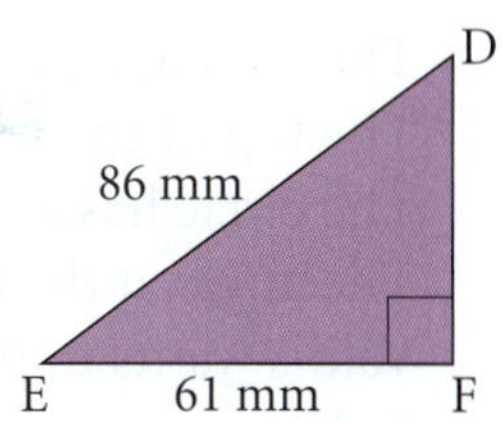

3 Sasha and Dakarai both sketch a triangle XYZ. Read what Sasha says.

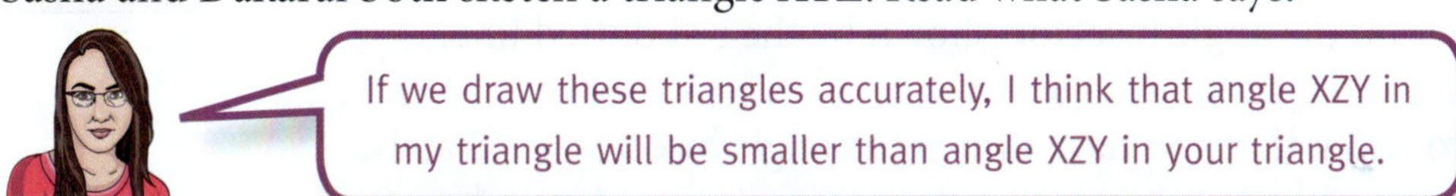

Sasha's sketch

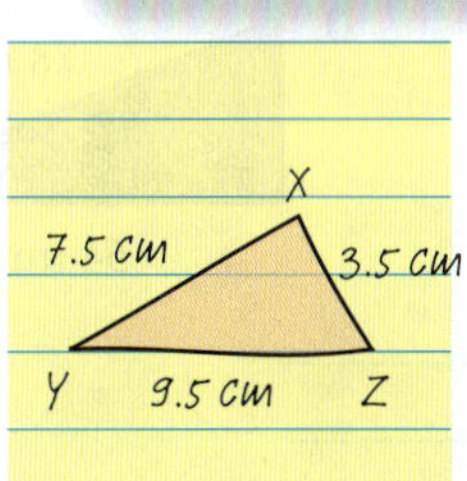

Dakarai's sketch

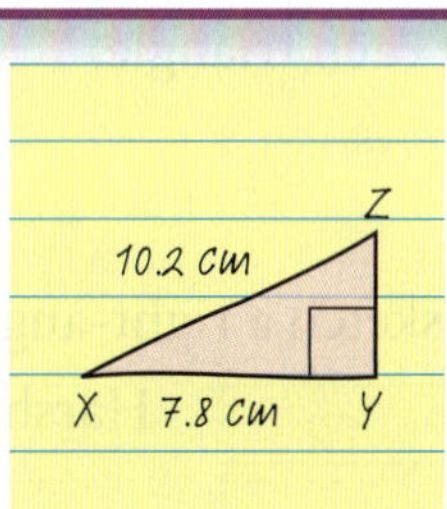

Is Sasha correct? Show how you worked out your answer.

Summary

You should now know that:

★ The midpoint of a line segment AB is the point that is exactly halfway between A and B.

★ The perpendicular bisector of a line segment AB is the line that passes through the midpoint of AB at right angles to AB.

★ The angle bisector of angle ABC is the line that cuts the angle exactly in half.

You should be able to:

★ Use a ruler and compasses to construct circles and arcs.

★ Use a straight-edge and compasses to construct the midpoint and perpendicular bisector of a line segment and the bisector of an angle.

★ Use a ruler and compasses to construct a triangle, given three sides (SSS) and given a right angle, hypotenuse and one side (RHS).

End-of-unit review

1 a Draw a circle with radius 4 cm. b Draw an arc with radius 6 cm and angle 30°.

2 a Draw a line segment AB that is 7 cm long.
  b Using only your compasses and a straight-edge, draw the perpendicular bisector of AB.

3 a Draw an angle XYZ that measures 65°.
  b Using only compasses and a straight-edge, draw the bisector of angle XYZ.

4 Mrs Jones wants to put new flooring in her kitchen.
Her kitchen is in the shape of a rectangle.
The sketch on the right shows the dimensions of her kitchen floor, ABCD.

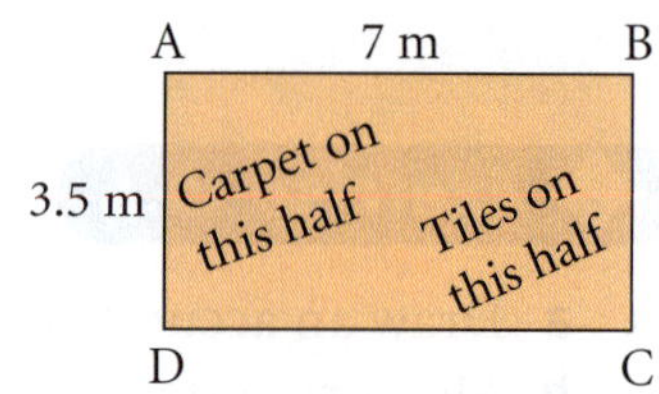

Not to scale

  a Draw an accurate copy of her kitchen floor.
    Use a scale where 1 cm represents 1 m.
  b Using compasses and a straight-edge, draw on your diagram:
    i the midpoint of AB ii the midpoint of CD.
  c Mrs Jones is going to have carpet on half of the floor and tiles on the other half.
    Draw the halfway line on your diagram.

5 Valdis makes jewellery. The diagram shows one of her latest pendant designs.
The pendant is made from an isosceles triangle and a circle.
The top of the triangle is joined to the centre of the circle.
The circle has a radius of 1.5 cm.
The angle at the top of the triangle is 30°. The triangle has a side length of 5 cm.
Valdis wants to paint the left side of the triangle a different colour from the right side.

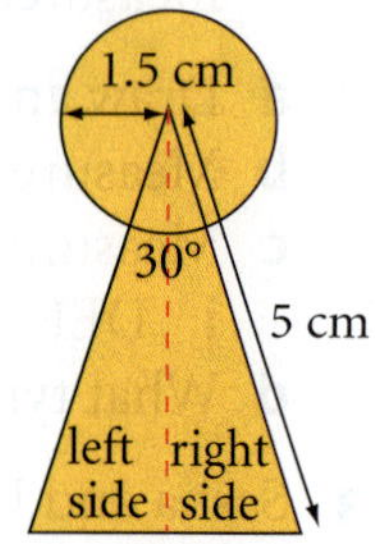

  a Draw an accurate drawing of the pendant.
  b Draw on your diagram the angle bisector, shown by the red dotted line.
    Use only compasses and a straight-edge.
  c Use a protractor to check that you have drawn the angle bisector accurately.

6 Draw an accurate copy of each triangle.

a
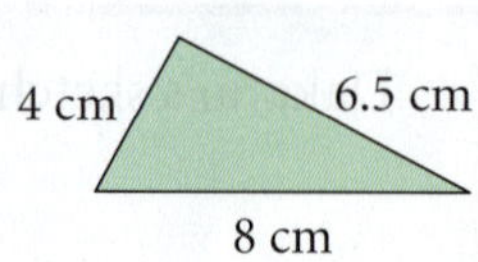

b
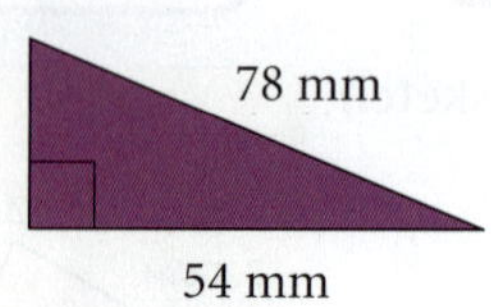

7 Hassan and Harsha both sketch a right-angled triangle.

Hassan's sketch
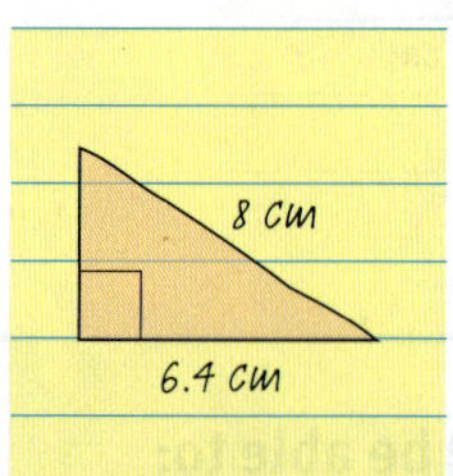

Harsha's sketch
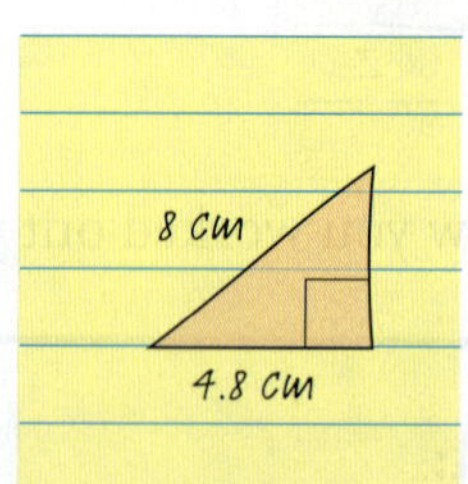

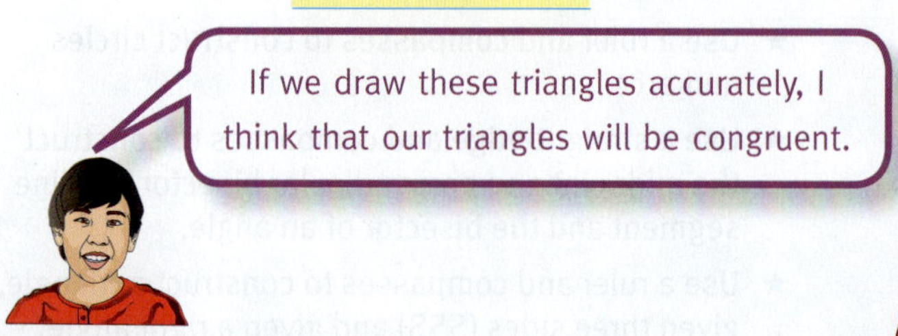

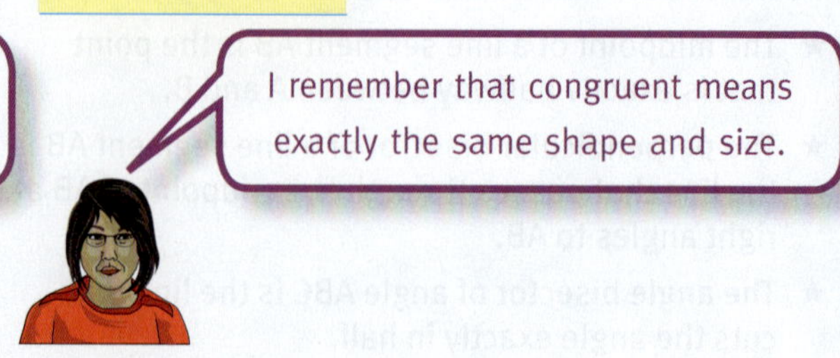

Is Hassan correct? Show how you worked out your answer.

13 Graphs

In the 17th century the Frenchman René Descartes showed how to plot points on a grid and use this to draw lines and curves.

In his honour we still call this method 'Cartesian coordinates'.

You have used positive and negative numbers as coordinates to show points on a Cartesian grid. You know that equations involving x and y can correspond to lines and curves on such a coordinate grid.

Key words

Make sure you learn and understand these key words:

- equation
- line segment
- midpoint

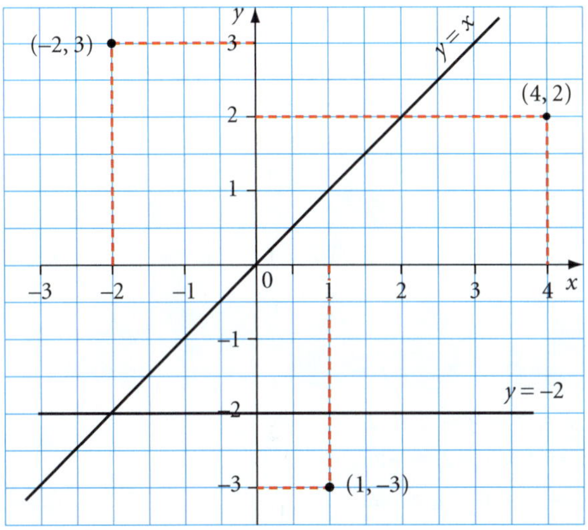

Graphs also have many practical applications in real life. A graph can be easier to read and understand than a table or chart.

This table shows the speed of a car at five-second intervals. The graph shows the same information. Which is easier to understand?

Time (seconds)	0	5	10	15	20	25	30
Speed (km/h)	50	60	70	70	70	50	30

In this unit you will concentrate on straight-line graphs.

Two examples, $y = -2$ and $y = x$, are shown in the diagram at the top of the page.

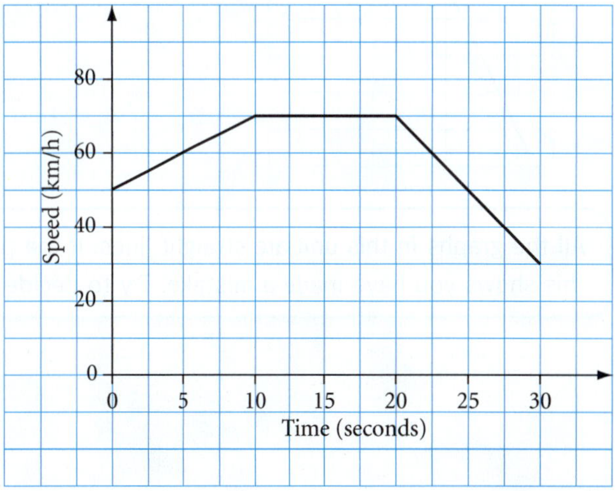

13.1 Drawing graphs of equations

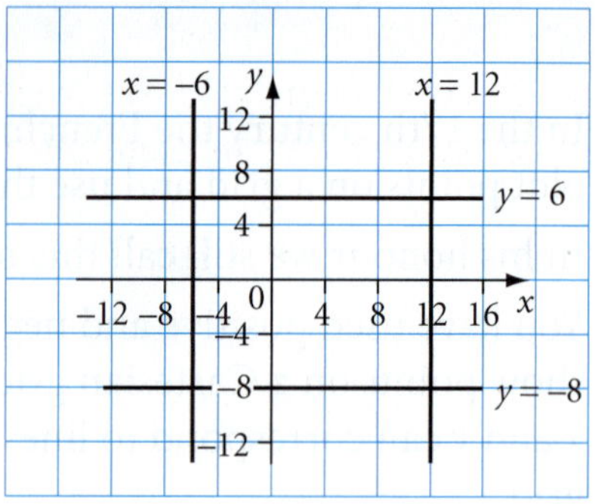

Lines parallel to the x-axis have **equations** of the form y = a number.
Lines parallel to the y-axis have equations of the form x = a number.
This makes them easy to recognise and draw.

In these examples, the number may be referred to as a constant.

For more complicated equations it is helpful to start with a table of values. The table will give the coordinates of points on the line. Then you can plot the points and join them to draw the graph.

The equation of the x-axis is $y = 0$.
The equation of the y-axis is $x = 0$.

Worked example 13.1

a Complete the table of values for $y = 2x - 4$.

x	−2	−1	0	1	2	3	4
y	−8				0		4

b Draw a graph of $y = 2x - 4$.

a

x	−2	−1	0	1	2	3	4
y	−8	−6	−4	−2	0	2	4

If $x = 3$, $y = 2 \times 3 - 4 = 2$
If $x = 1$, $y = 2 \times 1 - 4 = -2$
If $x = 0$, $y = 2 \times 0 - 4 = -4$
If $x = -1$, $y = 2 \times -1 - 4 = -6$

b

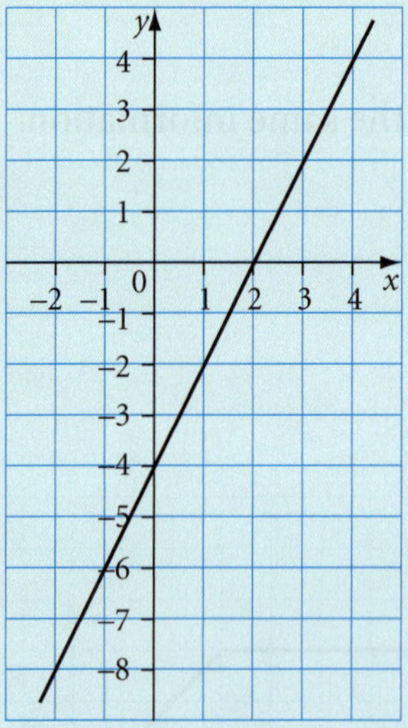

Plot the points and use a ruler to draw a line through them all. It should be a straight line. Extend the line to the end of the grid.

All the graphs in this unit are straight lines. If the points you plot are not in a straight line, this shows you have made a mistake. Try to decide which point is incorrect and correct it.

Exercise 13.1

Use a copy of the grid to the right to draw each graph in questions **1** to **4**.

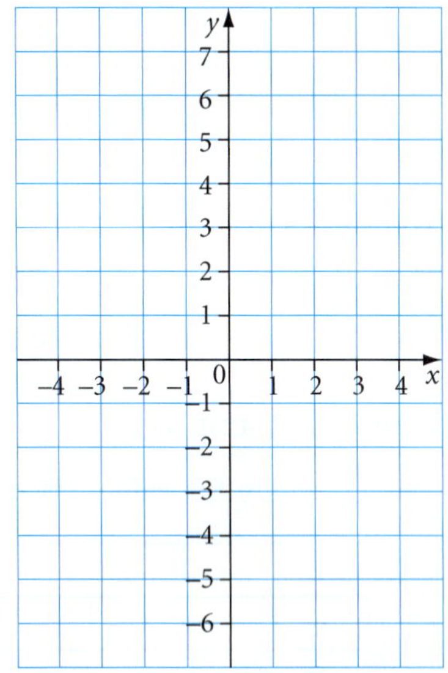

1 **a** Copy and complete this table for $y = x - 2$.

x	−4	−3	−2	−1	0	1	2	3	4
y	−6			−3		−1		1	

b Draw a graph of $y = x - 2$.

2 **a** Copy and complete this table for $y = 2x$.

x	−3	−2	−1	0	1	2	3
y		−4			2		

b Draw a graph of $y = 2x$.

3 **a** Copy and complete this table for $y = 0.5x + 2$.

x	−4	−2	0	1	2	3	4
y		1			3	3.5	

b Draw a graph of $y = 0.5x + 2$.

4 **a** Copy and complete this table for $y = -2x + 1$.

x	−3	−2	−1	0	1	2
y		5		1		

b Draw a graph of $y = -2x + 1$.

5 **a** Copy and complete this table for $y = 2x - 3$.

x	−2	−1	0	1	2	3	4	5
y	−7				1			7

b Draw a graph of $y = 2x - 3$. Include all the points in the table.

6 **a** Copy and complete this table for $y = -0.5x + 2$.

x	−2	−1	0	1	2	3	4	5
y	3			1.5			0	

b Draw a graph of $y = -0.5x + 2$. Include all the points in the table.

7 **a** Copy and complete this table for $y = 3 - x$.

x	−2	−1	0	1	2	3	4	5	6
y			3						−3

b Draw a graph of $y = 3 - x$. Include all the points in the table.

8 **a** Draw up a table of values for $y = 3x + 2$. Values of x should be from −3 to 3.
b Draw a graph of $y = 3x + 2$.

13.2 Equations of the form $y = mx + c$

$y = 2x + 3$ $y = -5x - 4$ $y = 20x - 30$ $y = -0.5x + 10$

All these equations are in the form $y = mx + c$ where m and c are numbers.

The values of m in these examples are 2, −5, 20 and −0.5.

The values of c are 3, −4, −30 and 10.

A graph of an equation like this will always be a straight line.

Worked example 13.2

a Complete the table of values for $y = 5x + 10$.

x	−3	−2	−1	0	1	2	3
y		0			15		25

b Draw a graph of the straight line $y = 5x + 10$.

c Show that (−20, −90) is on the line but (20, 90) is not.

a

x	−3	−2	−1	0	1	2	3
y	−5	0	5	10	15	20	25

If $x = 2$, $y = 5 \times 2 + 10 = 20$

If $x = 0$, $y = 5 \times 0 + 10 = 10$

If $x = -1$, $y = 5 \times -1 + 10 = -5 + 10 = 5$

If $x = -3$, $y = 5 \times -3 + 10 = -15 + 10 = -5$

b

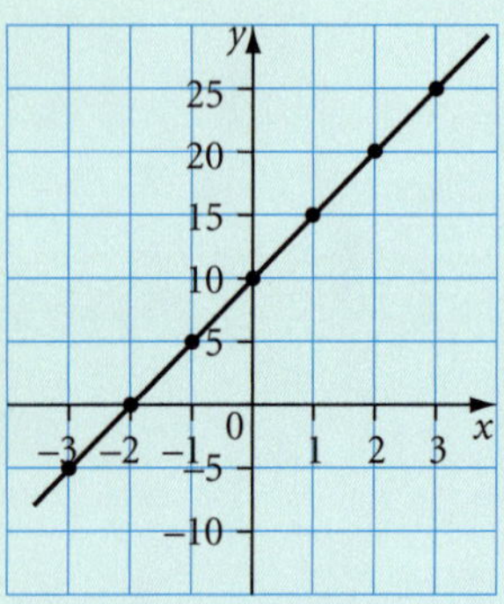

The scales on the two axes are not the same.

They have been chosen so that all the points can be plotted.

Plot the points and draw a line through them all with a ruler.

It should be a straight line.

c If $x = -20$, $y = 5 \times -20 + 10 = -90$
so (−20, −90) is on the line.
If $x = 20$, $y = 5 \times 20 + 10 = 110$
so (20, 90) is not on the line.

This shows (20, 110) is on the line.

Exercise 13.2

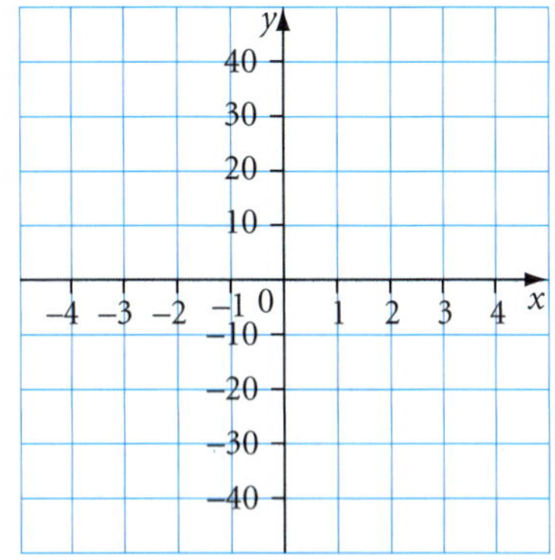

For questions **1** to **4**, draw the graph on a copy of this grid.

1 **a** Copy and complete this table for $y = 10x$.

x	−4	−3	−2	−1	0	1	2	3	4
y	−40			−10		10			40

b Draw a graph of $y = 10x$.

2 **a** Copy and complete this table for $y = 5x - 20$.

x	−4	−2	0	2	4
y	−40		−20		

b Draw a graph of $y = 5x - 20$.
c Show that (20, 80) is on the line $y = 5x - 20$.

3 **a** Copy and complete this table for $y = 15x - 5$.

x	−2	−1	0	1	2	3
y		−20		10		

b Draw a graph of $y = 15x - 5$.
c Is (5, 80) on the line $y = 15x - 5$? Give a reason for your answer.

4 **a** Copy and complete this table for $y = 20 - 10x$.
b Draw a graph of $y = 20 - 10x$.
c $(7, c)$ is on the line $y = 20 - 10x$. Find the value of c.
d $(-4, d)$ is on the line $y = 20 - 10x$. Find the value of d.

x	−2	−1	0	1	2	3	4
y		30		10			−20

5 **a** Copy and complete this table for $y = 0.2x + 3$.
b Draw a graph of $y = 0.2x + 3$. Choose suitable scales for the axes.
c $(3, a)$ is on the line $y = 0.2x + 3$. Find the value of a.

x	−20	−15	−10	−5	0	5	10	15	20
y	−1								7

6 **a** Copy and complete this table for $y = 40x + 20$.

x	−3	−2	−1	0	1	2	3
y			−20		60		140

b Draw a graph of $y = 40x + 20$. Choose suitable scales for the axes.
c Show that Anders is not correct.

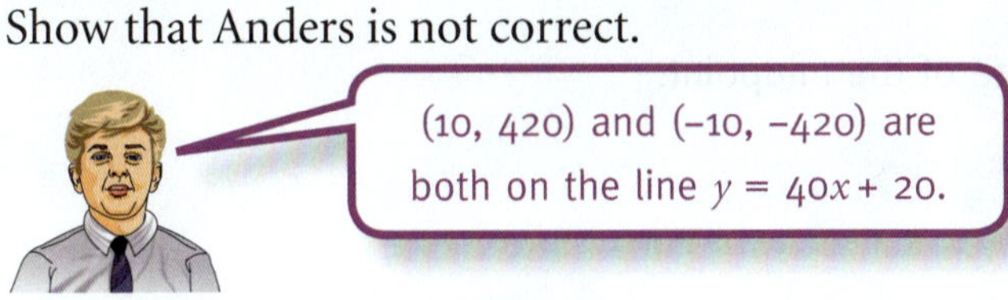

7 The line $y = 0.5x + 8$ passes through $(-10, a)$ and $(-20, b)$. Find the values of a and b.

8 **a** Where does the line $y = 5x - 10$ cross the y-axis?
b Where does the line $y = 5x - 10$ cross the x-axis?

13.3 The midpoint of a line segment

The diagram shows two **line segments**, AB and CD.

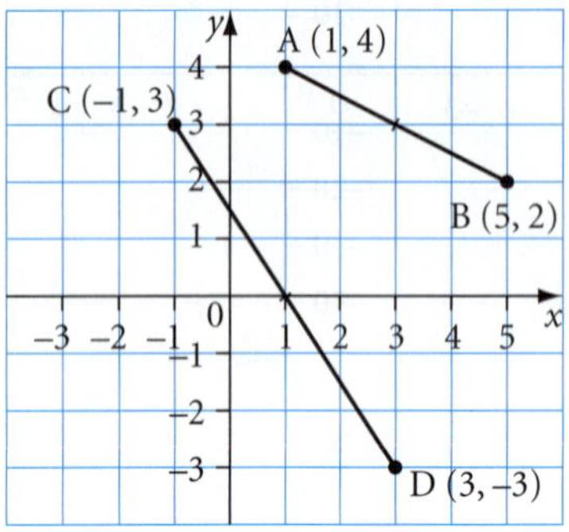

The **midpoint** of AB is halfway between A and B. You can see from the diagram that the midpoint of AB is (3, 3).

The midpoint of CD is (1, 0).

You can find the midpoint of a line segment by finding the means of the x-coordinates and the y-coordinates of the end points.

This gives the midpoint of AB as $\left(\frac{1+5}{2}, \frac{4+2}{2}\right) = (3, 3)$.

The midpoint of CD is $\left(\frac{-1+3}{2}, \frac{3+-3}{2}\right) = (1, 0)$.

The mean of a and b is $\frac{a+b}{2}$.

Worked example 13.3

a The diagram shows points P(10, 4) and Q(−4, −6).

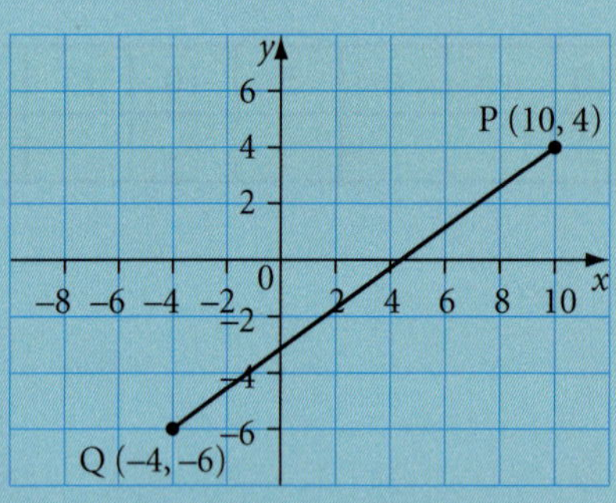

Find the coordinates of the midpoint of PQ.

a $\frac{10+-4}{2} = \frac{6}{2} = 3$ This is the x-coordinate of the midpoint.

$\frac{4+-6}{2} = \frac{-2}{2} = -1$ This is the y-coordinate of the midpoint.

The midpoint of PQ is (3, −1).

Exercise 13.3

1 A is the point (2, 4) and B is the point (6, 0).
  a Mark A and B on a coordinate grid and draw the line segment AB.
  b Find the coordinates of the midpoint of AB.

2 Find the coordinates of the midpoint of each side of this pentagon.

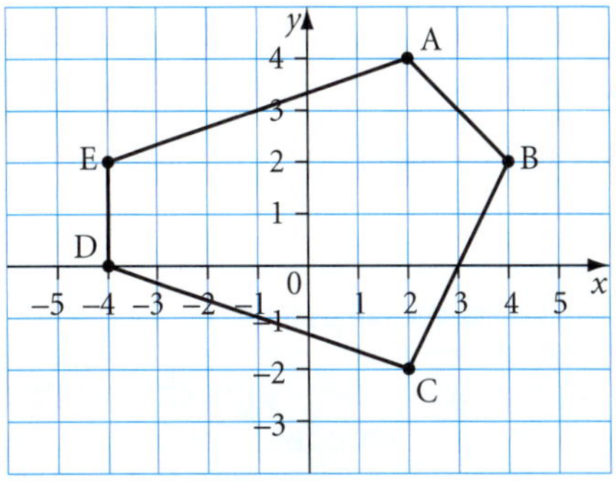

3 A is the point (8, 0), B is the point (0, 6) and C is the point (10, 12).
Find the midpoint of:
  a AB **b** AC **c** BC.

Draw a diagram if you want to.

4 Find the midpoint of the line segment between:
  a (1, −1) and (7, 5) **b** (−4, −3) and (2, 5) **c** (10, −2) and (−2, 10).

5 Find the midpoint of the line segment between:
  a (5, −2) and (2, −6) **b** (−4, 5) and (3, 0) **c** (−7, 5) and (−10, 10).

6 Find the midpoint of the line segment between:
  a (20, 10) and (50, 30) **b** (20, 30) and (−40, −10) **c** (−17, 14) and (19, −20).

7 Find the coordinates of the midpoint of each side of this triangle.

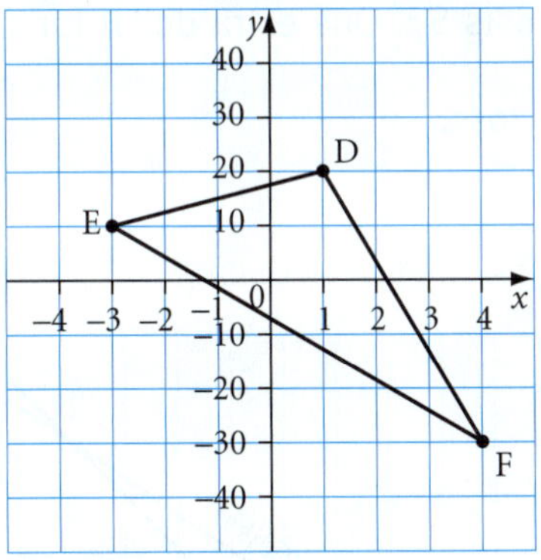

8 A square has vertices at A(2, 3), B(3, −1), C(−1, −2) and D(−2, 2).
  a Draw the square.
  b The diagonals are AC and BD. Show that the diagonals have the same midpoint.

9 A parallelogram has vertices at P(2, 5), Q(−2, 3), R(2, −1) and S(6, 1). The diagonals are PR and QS. Show that the diagonals have the same midpoint.

10 A quadrilateral has vertices at (−2, 1), (0, 4), (5, 2) and (1, −1). Do the diagonals have the same midpoint? Justify your answer.

11 The midpoint of a line segment is (4, 1). One end of the line segment is (2, 5). Find the coordinates of the other end of the line segment.

13.4 Graphs in real-life contexts

Graphs give information in a visual form. Therefore, they are often used in real-life contexts because they can be easier to interpret than a table or chart.

Real-life graphs usually only have positive axes. They may not start at zero.

The numbers on the axes can represent almost anything. You will usually see a different variable on each axis. Often, one of the axes will show time.

Read any labels on the axes and look at the scale carefully to see what the intervals on each axis stand for.

Worked example 13.4

This graph shows fares charged by two different taxis.

a How much does each taxi charge for a journey of 7 km?
b How much does taxi A charge for each kilometre?
c Taxi B has a fixed charge and then charges a certain amount for each kilometre.
  i How much is the fixed charge?
  ii How much is each kilometre?
d What distance will cost the same amount in either taxi?

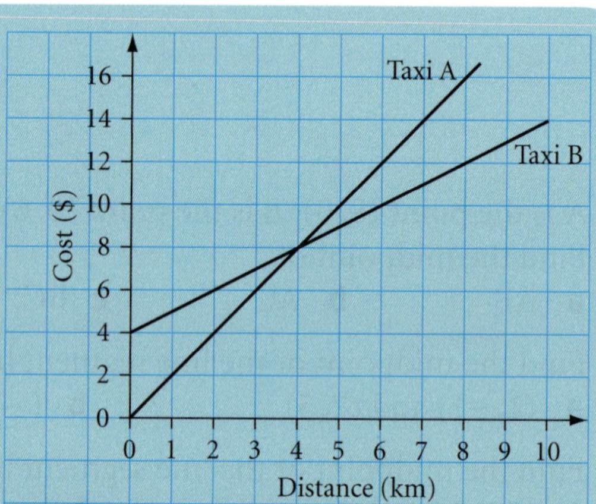

a A charges $14, B charges $11.	Find the cost coordinate when the distance coordinate is 7.
b $2	1 km costs $2, 2 km costs $4, and so on.
c i $4	If the distance is 0, the charge is $4.
ii $1	1 km costs $5, 2 km costs $6, 3 km costs $7. One extra dollar for each extra kilometre.
d 4 km	This is the point where the two lines cross.

Exercise 13.4

1 Zalika and Tanesha are cycling on the same route. The graph shows their journeys.

  a Zalika started at 09 00. What time did Tanesha start?
  b How far did Zalika travel in the first hour?
  c How long was Tanesha cycling before she caught up with Zalika?

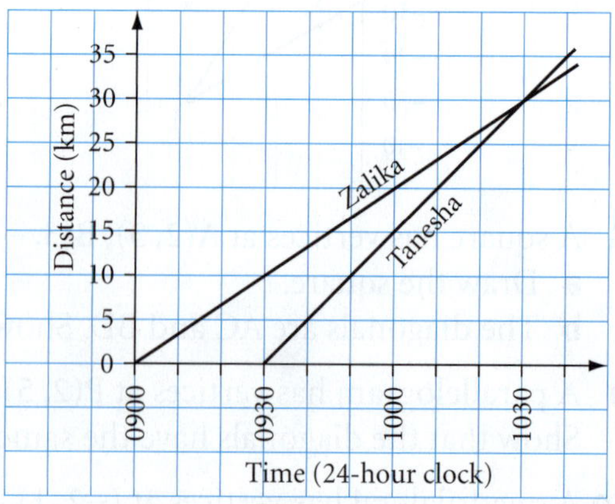

2 Lucas is driving from Ayton to Bibury.
Simone is driving from Bibury to Ayton.

a How long did Lucas take to get to Midley?

b How long did Lucas stop at Midley?

c How long did Simone take to get from Bibury to Ayton?

d How far were the cars from Bibury when they passed one another?

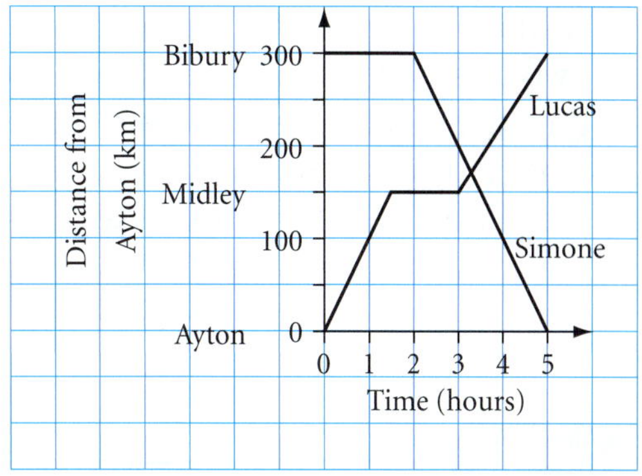

3 Razi and Jake are running laps of a running track.

a How do you know from the graph that Jake is running faster than Razi?

b How long had Razi been running before Jake started?

c Where were the runners 9 minutes after Razi started running?

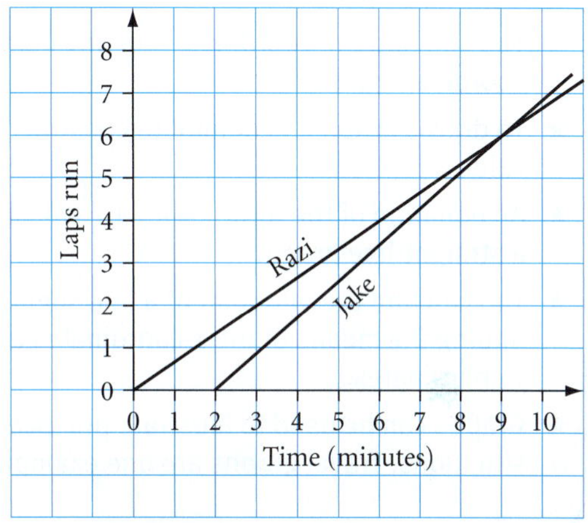

4 **a** A van travels at a constant speed of 15 m/s for 60 seconds.
Show this on a graph. Put time on the horizontal axis and speed on the vertical axis.

b The speed of a car increases steadily from 0 m/s to 30 m/s over 20 seconds. It travels at 30 m/s for 30 seconds. Then the speed steadily decreases from 30 m/s to 0 m/s in 10 seconds.
Show the speed of the car on the same graph.

c For how many seconds is the car travelling faster than the van?

5 At 13 00 Shen leaves home on a cycle ride. By 15 00 he has travelled 35 km.
He stops for $1\frac{1}{2}$ hours and then cycles back. He arrives back home at 18 00.

a Show this journey on a graph. Put time on the horizontal axis and distance from home on the vertical axis.

b At 15 00 Shen's sister leaves home and cycles after him at the same speed. Show this on the graph.

c How far from home will they meet?

6 Xavier is doing some athletics training. He runs for 5 minutes, covering one kilometre, and then he rests for five minutes. He continues in this way until he has run 4 kilometres.

a Show this on a graph with time on the horizontal axis and distance on the vertical axis.

b Ten minutes after Xavier has started, Alicia runs after him. She runs at the same speed but without stopping, for 4 kilometres. Show this on the graph.

c Explain how the graph shows that they are running together for part of the time.

d Who finishes running first?

7 A straight track is 400 metres long.
Two cars drive from one end to the other, in opposite directions. Each goes at a constant speed.
One car takes 30 seconds to get from one end to the other. The other takes 50 seconds. They both reach the end at the same time.
Draw a graph and use it to find how far the cars are from each end of the track when they pass one another.

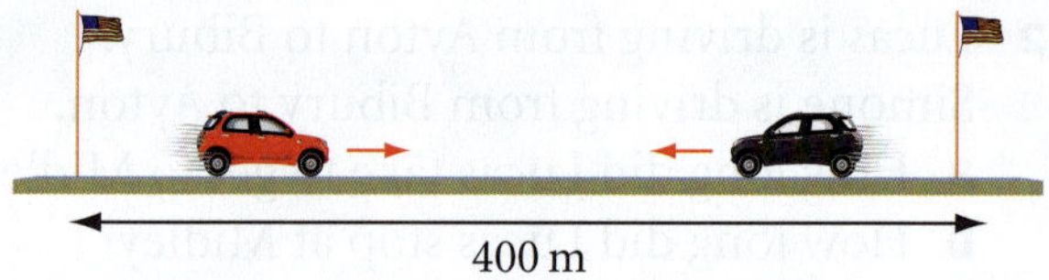

Summary

You should now know that:

- ★ You can find the coordinates for any point on a coordinate grid.
- ★ To draw a graph it is helpful to construct a table of values.
- ★ An equation of the form $y = mx + c$ will always give a straight-line graph.
- ★ You can find the midpoint of a line segment by finding the means of the x-coordinates and the y-coordinates.
- ★ Graphs can be used to illustrate practical situations. Travel graphs are one example.

You should be able to:

- ★ Construct tables of values.
- ★ Use all four quadrants to plot the graphs of straight lines, where y is given explicitly in terms of x.
- ★ Recognise that equations of the form $y = mx + c$ correspond to straight-line graphs.
- ★ Find the midpoint of the line segment AB, given the coordinates of points A and B.
- ★ Draw and interpret graphs in real-life contexts involving more than one component.
- ★ Draw accurate mathematical graphs.

End-of-unit review

1 Write down the equations of the lines on this grid.

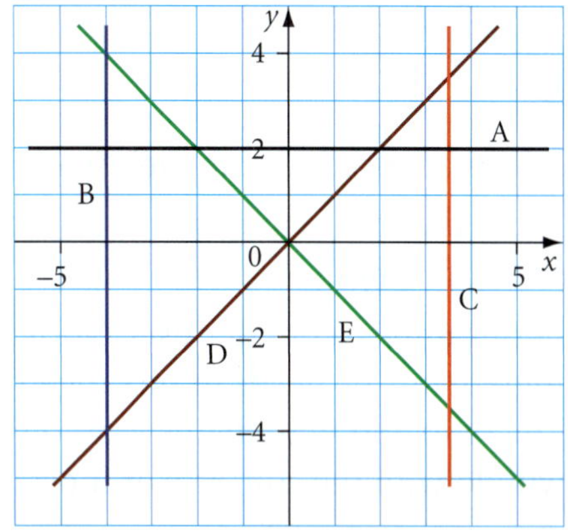

2 **a** Complete this table of values for $y = 2x + 2$.
b Use the values in the table to draw a graph of $y = 2x + 2$.

x	−3	−2	−1	0	1	2	3
y		−2			4		

3 **a** Complete this table of values for $y = 4 - x$.
b Use the values in the table to draw a graph of $y = 4 - x$.
c Show that $(-24, 28)$ is on the line.

x	−2	−1	0	1	2	3	4	5	6
y	6								−2

4 **a** Complete this table of values for $y = 10x + 20$.
b Use the values in the table to draw a graph of $y = 10x + 20$.
c Is $(15, 180)$ on the line? Give a reason for your answer.
d $(-6, a)$ is on the line. Find the value of a.

x	−3	−2	−1	0	1	2	3
y		0				40	

5 Find the midpoints of the line segments joining:
a $(12, 0)$ and $(0, -4)$ **b** $(-3, 6)$ and $(1, -2)$ **c** $(16, -17)$ and $(24, 15)$

6 The graph shows the amount of petrol left in the tanks of two cars, a Nisota and a Toysan, as they make a journey.
a Which car has a more economical fuel consumption?
b How far had they travelled when they both had the same amount of fuel left?
c If they continue to use petrol at the same rate, what will be the total distance travelled by the Toysan when it runs out of petrol?
d How much further than the Toysan will the Nisota travel?

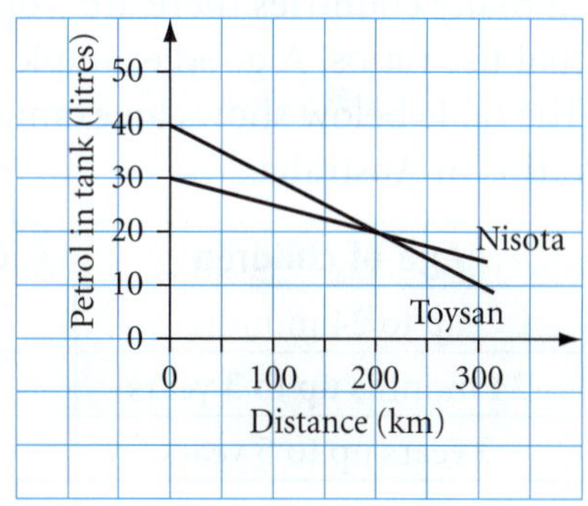

7 A car leaves Newton at 13 00 to travel to Danville. The graph shows the first part of the journey.
a How long did the car take to travel 50 km?
b The driver stopped for 90 minutes and then went on to Danville, arriving at 17 00. Copy the graph and show the rest of the journey.
c A second car leaves Danville at 15 00 and drives straight to Newton, arriving at 18 00. Show this on the graph.
d How far from Newton did the cars pass one another?

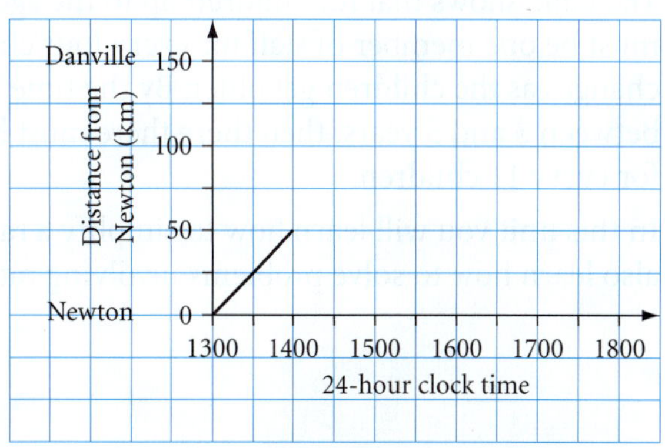

14 Ratio and proportion

Ratios are used to compare two or more numbers or quantities.

Every day, ratios are used in all sorts of ways for working out all sorts of things.

For example, a builder uses ratios to work out the amounts of ingredients he needs to mix together, to make concrete or mortar. The ratio and ingredients vary, depending on what the builder will do with the concrete or mortar.

To make the mortar for laying brickwork or block pavements, a builder would use cement and sand in the ratio 1 : 4. This means that every 1 kg of cement must be mixed with 4 kg of sand.

Builders often use a shovel or bucket to measure their ingredients. For this mortar, they would need one shovel (or bucket) of cement for every four shovels (or buckets) of sand.

To make a medium-strength concrete for a floor, a builder would use three components, cement, sand and gravel, mixed in the ratio 1 : 2 : 4. This means that every 1 kg of cement must be mixed with 2 kg of sand and 4 kg of gravel.

It is important that a builder uses the correct ratio of ingredients for the job, otherwise walls may fall down or floors may crack.

Key words

Make sure you learn and understand these key words:

- ratio
- simplify
- direct proportion
- unitary method

In many countries there are workplace rules and regulations that use ratios. A good example of this is in childcare centres. The table below shows an example of the legal child : staff ratios in Australia.

Age of children	Child : staff ratio
up to 24 months	4 : 1
24 months up to 3 years	5 : 1
3 years up to 5 years	11 : 1

The table shows that for children up to the age of 24 months, there must be one member of staff for every four children. The ratio changes as the children get older. By the time the children are aged between 3 and 5 years, then there there must be one member of staff for every 11 children.

In this unit you will learn how to simplify a ratio and how to share an amount in a given ratio. You will also learn how to solve problems involving ratio and proportion.

14.1 Simplifying ratios

A **ratio** is a way of comparing two or more quantities.

In this pastry recipe, the ratio of flour to butter is 500 : 250.

Pastry recipe
500 g flour
250 g butter
water to mix

You can **simplify** this ratio by dividing the numbers by the highest common factor. In this case the highest common factor is 250.

Divide both numbers by 250 to simplify the ratio to 2 : 1.

500 : 250 → ÷ 250 → 2 : 1

If you cannot work out the highest common factor of the numbers in a ratio, you can simplify the ratio in stages. Divide the numbers in the ratio by common factors until you cannot divide any more.

In the example above you could start by:

- dividing by 10
- then by 5
- then by 5 again
- giving you the same answer of 2 : 1.

500 : 250 → ÷ 10 → 50 : 25 → ÷ 5 → 10 : 5 → ÷ 5 → 2 : 1

When you simplify a ratio you must make sure that all the quantities are in the same units.

Worked example 14.1

Simplify these ratios.

a 12 : 20 **b** 12 : 30 : 24 **c** 2 m : 50 cm

a 12 : 20 → ÷ 4 → 3 : 5

The highest common factor of 12 and 20 is 4, so divide both numbers by 4.

b 12 : 30 : 24 → ÷ 6 → 2 : 5 : 4

The highest common factor of 12, 30 and 24 is 6, so divide all three numbers by 6.

c 2 m : 50 cm
200 : 50 → ÷ 50 → 4 : 1

First, change 2 metres into 200 centimetres.
Once the units are the same you don't need to write them down.
The highest common factor of 200 and 50 is 50, so divide both numbers by 50.

Exercise 14.1

1 Simplify these ratios.

a 2 : 10 **b** 3 : 18 **c** 5 : 25 **d** 30 : 5 **e** 36 : 12 **f** 180 : 20
g 4 : 6 **h** 9 : 15 **i** 10 : 35 **j** 75 : 10 **k** 72 : 20 **l** 140 : 112

2 Simplify these ratios.

a 5 : 10 : 15 **b** 8 : 10 : 12 **c** 20 : 15 : 25
d 18 : 15 : 3 **e** 27 : 9 : 45 **f** 72 : 16 : 32

3 Simplify these ratios.

a 500 m : 1 km **b** 36 seconds : 1 minute **c** 800 ml : 2.4 l
d 1.6 kg : 800 g **e** 3 cm : 6 mm **f** 2 days : 18 hours
g 2 hours : 48 minutes **h** 8 months : 1 year **i** 4 days : 1 week

4 Simplify these ratios.

a 600 m : 1 km : 20 m **b** 75 cm : 1 m : 1.5 m **c** 300 ml : 2.1 l : 900 ml
d 3.2 kg : 1600 g : 0.8 kg **e** \$1.08 : 90 cents : \$9 **f** 4 cm : 8 mm : 0.2 m

5 Sasha uses this recipe for orange preserve.

Orange preserve
750 g oranges
1.5 kg sugar
juice of one lemon

Is Sasha correct? Explain your answer.

6 This is part of Jake's homework.
Use Jake's method to simplify these ratios.

a 0.5 : 2 **b** 1.5 : 3
c 1.2 : 2.4 **d** 0.7 : 2.1
e 3.6 : 0.6 **f** 7.5 : 1.5
g 2.4 : 4 **h** 1.8 : 6.3
i 2.1 : 0.7 : 1.4 **j** 0.03 : 0.15

Question
Simplify these ratios.
a 1.5 : 2 *b* 0.8 : 3.6
Answer
a 1.5 : 2 (× 10) → 15 : 20 (÷ 5) → 3 : 4
b 0.8 : 3.6 (× 10) → 8 : 36 (÷ 4) → 2 : 9

For questions **7** and **8**, work in a group of three or four.

i Work out the answer to each question by yourself.
ii Compare your answers with the answers given by the other members of your group.
iii Decide which member of the group has given the best answers.

7 Razi and Tanesha are mixing paint.
They mix 250 ml of white paint with 750 ml of red paint and 1.2 litres of yellow paint.

Is either of them correct? Explain your answer.

8 Oditi goes for a run three times a week.
Her notebook shows the time she took for each run one week.

Monday	1 hour 40 mins
Wednesday	50 mins
Friday	$2\frac{1}{2}$ hours

a Oditi thinks that the ratio of her times for Monday to Wednesday to Friday is 1 : 2 : 3. Without doing any calculations, explain how you know that Oditi is wrong.

b Oditi's mum uses this method to work out the ratio of Oditi's times.
Explain the mistakes that Oditi's mum has made.

c Work out the correct ratio of Oditi's times.

Monday : Wednesday : Friday
1 hour 40 mins : 50 mins : 2½ hours
1.4 : 0.5 : 2.5
× 10 14 : 5 : 25
÷ 5 14 : 1 : 5

14.2 Sharing in a ratio

Sometimes you need to share an amount in a given ratio.
For example, Alan, Bob and Chris buy a painting for \$600.
Alan pays \$200, Bob pays \$300 and Chris pays \$100.
You can write the amounts they pay as a ratio like this: Alan : Bob : Chris
200 : 300 : 100
Simplify the ratio by dividing by 100 to give: 2 : 3 : 1
You can see that Alan paid twice as much as Chris, and Bob paid three times as much as Chris.
When they sell the painting, they need to share the money fairly between them.
They can do this by using the same ratio of 2 : 3 : 1.
Follow these steps to share an amount in a given ratio.

① Add all the numbers in the ratio to find the total number of parts.
② Divide the amount to be shared by the total number of parts to find the value of one part.
③ Use multiplication to work out the value of each share.
④ Check that the total of their shares is the same as the amount they shared.

Worked example 14.2

Share \$840 between Alan, Bob and Chris in the ratio 2 : 3 : 1.

2 + 3 + 1 = 6	① Add the numbers in the ratio to find the total number of parts.
840 ÷ 6 = 140 1 part = \$140	② Divide the amount to be shared by the total number of parts to find the value of one part.
Alan gets 2 × 140 = \$280 Bob gets 3 × 140 = \$420 Chris gets 1 × 140 = \$140	③ Work out the value of each share using multiplication. Make sure you write the name of the person with each amount.
280 + 420 + 140 = \$840 ✓	④ Check that the total of the shares is the same as the amount to be shared.

Exercise 14.2

1 Share these amounts between Andi, Beth and Charlie in the given ratios.
   a \$90 in the ratio 1 : 2 : 3 **b** \$225 in the ratio 2 : 3 : 4
   c \$432 in the ratio 3 : 5 : 1 **d** \$396 in the ratio 4 : 2 : 5

2 Dave, Ella and Franz share their electricity bills in the ratio 3 : 4 : 5.
How much does each of them pay when their electricity bill is:
   a \$168 **b** \$192 **c** \$234?

3 A choir is made up of men, women and children in the ratio 5 : 7 : 3.
Altogether there are 285 members of the choir.
   a How many members of the choir are:
      i men **ii** women **iii** children?
   b How many more women than men are there in the choir?
   c How many more men than children are there in the choir?

4 A box of chocolates contains milk, white and dark chocolates in the ratio 4 : 2 : 3.
The box contains 72 chocolates altogether.

a How many chocolates in the box are:
i milk **ii** white **iii** dark?

b The ratio of the number of milk, white and dark chocolates is changed to 3 : 1 : 4.
There are still 72 chocolates in the box.
How many chocolates in this box are:
i milk **ii** white **iii** dark?

5 Aden, Eli, Lily and Ziva run their own business. They share the money they earn from a project in the ratio of the number of hours they put into the project.
On the right is the time-sheet for one of their projects.
How much does each of them earn from this project?

Project earnings: $450
Time spent working on project:
Aden: 6 hours *Eli: 4 hours*
Lily: 3 hours *Ziva: 5 hours*

6 A grandmother leaves $2550 in her will to be shared among her grandchildren in the ratio of their ages.
The grandchildren are 6, 12, 15 and 18 years old.
How much does each of them receive?

7 Every year, on his birthday, David shares $300 among his children in the ratio of their ages.
This year the children are aged 4, 9 and 11.
How much less will the oldest child receive in two years' time, than in this year?

8 Van, Willem and Zeeman buy a flat for $180 000.
Van pays $60 000, Willem pays $90 000 and Zeeman pays the rest.
Five years later they sell the flat for $228 000.
They share the money in the same ratio that they bought the flat.
How much profit does Zeeman make on the sale of the flat?

9 Here is a pack of ratio cards.

Share $150 ... | $50 | $84 | Share $120 ... | $75
... in the ratio 2 : 3 : 1 | ... in the ratio 2 : 6 : 1
$25 | $14
... in the ratio 3 : 1 : 4 | $45 | Share $132 ... | $60
$55 | $15 | $11 | $28 | ... in the ratio 1 : 5 : 6
Share $126 ... | $66

Sort the cards into their correct groups.
Each group must have one pink, one yellow and three blue cards.

14.3 Solving problems

If two values are in **direct proportion**, when one increases or decreases then so does the other, in the same ratio.

For example, tickets for a concert cost \$25 each.

Two tickets cost twice as much:	$2 \times 25 = \$50$
Three tickets cost three times as much:	$3 \times 25 = \$75$
Ten tickets cost ten times as much:	$10 \times 25 = \$250$, etc.

Concert tickets
\$25 each
Starts 7 30 pm

As the number of tickets increases, so does the total cost, in the same ratio.

You can use the **unitary method** to solve ratio and proportion problems. The unitary method only works when the values are in direct proportion. When you use the unitary method you need to find the value of one part (unit) first.

Worked example 14.3

a Eight folders cost \$16. Work out the cost of 5 folders mentally.
b A fruit drink contains orange juice and mango juice in the ratio 2 : 3.
There are 500 ml of orange juice in the drink.
i How much mango juice is there in the drink?
ii How much drink is there altogether?

a 1 folder costs $16 \div 8 = \$2$	In your head, use division to work out the cost of 1 folder (1 unit) first.
5 folders costs $5 \times 2 = \$10$	In your head, use multiplication to work out the cost of 5 folders.
b i 1 part is worth $500 \div 2 = 250$ ml	2 parts of the drink are orange juice, so use division to work out the number of millilitres in 1 part (1 unit) first.
mango juice: $3 \times 250 = 750$ ml	3 parts of the drink is mango juice, so use multiplication to work out the number of millilitres in 3 parts.
ii total: $500 + 750 = 1250$ ml	Add together the number of millilitres of orange and mango juice.
$= 1.25$ litres	Change your answer into litres.

Exercise 14.3

1 Four pens cost \$2. Mentally, work out the cost of:
a 1 pen **b** 3 pens **c** 10 pens.

2 The cost of two cups of coffee is \$3. Mentally, work out the cost of:
a 1 cup of coffee **b** 5 cups of coffee **c** 7 cups of coffee.

3 A cleaner is paid \$72 for 8 hours' work.
Mentally, work out how much the cleaner is paid for working 3 hours.

4 Look at the ingredients for honey biscuits.
Mentally, work out how much of each ingredient is needed to make:
a 100 honey biscuits
b 40 honey biscuits.

Honey biscuits (makes 25)
50 g butter 75 g plain flour
75 g icing sugar 100 ml honey

5 A fruit dessert contains raspberries and strawberries in the ratio 1 : 2.
There are 400 g of strawberries in the dessert.
   a How many grams of raspberries are there in the dessert?
   b How much fruit is there altogether in the dessert?

6 Xavier and Alicia share some money in the ratio 3 : 5.
Xavier gets $75.
   a How much does Alicia get?
   b How much money do they share?

7 Kaya and Akiko share their electricity bills in the ratio 4 : 3.
In January Akiko pays $18.
   a How much does Kaya pay?
   b What is their total bill?

8 Three children share some sweets in the ratio of their ages.
The children are 4, 7 and 9 years old.
The oldest child gets 54 sweets.
   a How many sweets do the other children get?
   b How many sweets do they share?

9 When Alicia makes oat biscuits she uses syrup, butter and oats in the ratio 1 : 2 : 4.

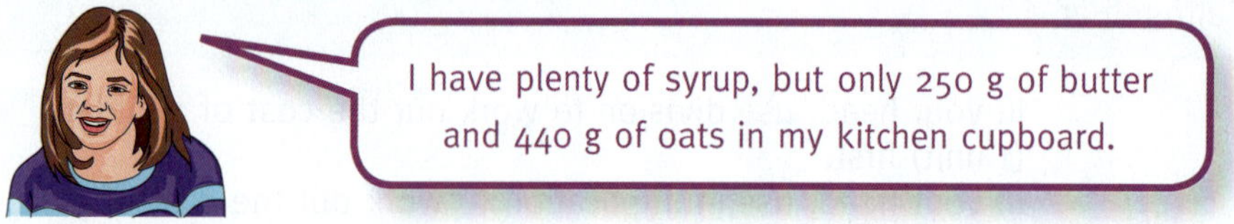

Alicia makes as many oat biscuits as she can with these ingredients.
How much of each ingredient does she use?

10 Xavier makes some green paint.
He mixes yellow, blue and white paint in the ratio 4 : 5 : 1.
He uses 750 ml of blue paint.
How much green paint does he make?

Summary

You should now know that:

★ You can simplify a ratio by dividing the numbers in the ratio by the highest common factor.

★ When you simplify a ratio you must make sure that all the quantities are in the same units.

★ When you share an amount in a given ratio you must divide the amount by the total number of parts to find the value of one part. Then multiply the value of one part by each number in the ratio.

★ Two values are in direct proportion when they increase or decrease in the same ratio.

You should be able to:

★ Simplify ratios, including those expressed in different units.

★ Divide a quantity into more than two parts in a given ratio.

★ Use the unitary method to solve simple problems involving ratio and direct proportion.

★ Mentally solve simple word problems, including direct proportion problems.

End-of-unit review

1 Simplify these ratios.

a 3 : 12 **b** 8 : 10 **c** 35 : 7 **d** 45 : 40 **e** 2 : 10 : 16

f 8 : 24 : 12 **g** 0.4 : 5 **h** 1.2 : 1.8 **i** 2.8 : 0.8

2 Simplify these ratios.

a 250 m : 2 km **b** 9 months : 2 years **c** 600 ml : 3.3 l

3 Share \$360 between Hassan, Mia and Xavier in the ratio 2 : 3 : 5.

4 A tin of biscuits contains shortbread, fruit and chocolate biscuits in the ratio 3 : 1 : 4.
The tin contains 56 biscuits altogether.
How many biscuits in the box are:

a shortbread **b** fruit **c** chocolate?

5 A grandfather gives \$2640 to be shared to his grandchildren in the ratio of their ages.
The grandchildren are 8, 10, 13 and 17 years old.
How much more does the oldest receive than the youngest?

6 Elise, Raine and Avery buy a boat for \$33 000.
Elise pays \$12 000, Raine pays \$6000 and Avery pays the rest.
Six years later they sell the boat for \$25 300.
They share the money in the same ratio that they bought the boat.
How much money does Avery lose on the sale of the boat?

7 Five notebooks cost \$15. Mentally, work out the cost of:

a 1 notebook **b** 4 notebooks **c** 20 notebooks.

8 A waitress is paid \$54 for 6 hours' work.
Mentally, work out how much the waitress is paid for 5 hours' work.

9 A fruit conserve contains blackcurrants and redcurrants in the ratio 5 : 2.
There are 300 g of redcurrants in the conserve.

a How many grams of blackcurrants are there in the conserve?

b How much fruit is there altogether in the conserve?

10 Four children share some strawberries in the ratio of their ages.
The children are 6, 8, 10 and 14 years old.
The youngest child gets 18 strawberries.

a How many strawberries do the other children get?

b How many strawberries do they share?

11 When Anders makes scones he uses sugar, butter and flour in the ratio 1 : 2 : 8.

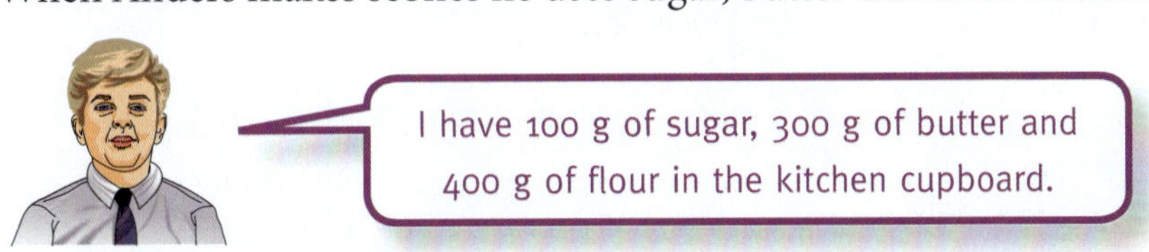

Anders makes as many scones as he can with these ingredients.
How much of each ingredient does he use?

15 Probability

Do you know the game 'rock, paper, scissors'? It is a very old game and is known by other names as well.

Two people simultaneously show either a fist (rock), the first two fingers pointing forwards (scissors) or an open hand (paper).

Scissors beats paper, paper beats rock and rock beats scissors. This is because scissors cut paper, paper wraps rock and rock blunts scissors.

If both players choose the same thing it is a draw (neither wins) and they play again.

Key words

Make sure you learn and understand these key words:

at random
mutually exclusive
experimental probability
theoretical probability

This may seem a trivial game but in 2005 the Maspro Denkoh electronics corporation used it to decide whether to give the contract to auction its $20 million collection of paintings to Sotheby's or to Christie's auction houses.

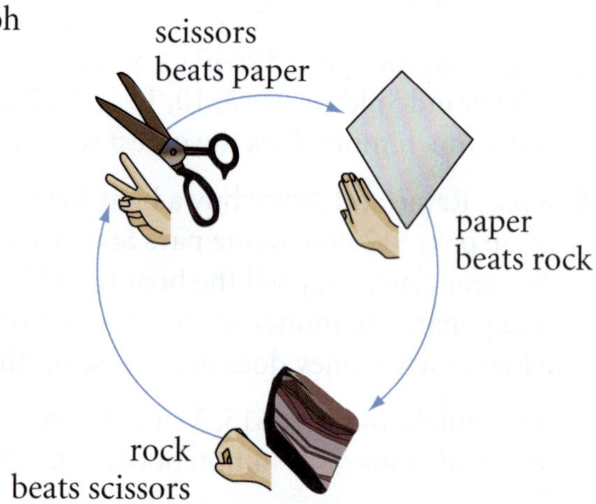

Christie's won with paper, after taking the advice of Flora and Alice, the 11-year-old daughters of one of the directors of the company. Their argument was that for beginners, rock seems strongest, so they tend to start with that. Playing against a beginner, you should start with paper.

This is a good example of when probabilities may not be equally likely although they appear to be at first. It also shows the (financial!) value of a sound logical argument. Auction houses typically take 10% of any money paid in an auction.

This game illustrates two methods of finding probabilities.

One method is to say that each different play – rock, scissors, paper – is equally likely. Because there are three outcomes (results), each one has a probability of $\frac{1}{3}$.

However, this only works if each play is equally likely and the player chooses at random. Flora and Alice realised that, for less experienced players, the probability of starting with rock is more than $\frac{1}{3}$.

To find out what this probability actually is, you could do an experiment. You could teach the game to lots of new players and then make a note of their moves. Then you could look at the fraction of times they started with rock and that would give a value for the probability.

The first method, equally likely outcomes, gives a theoretical probability. The second method, doing an experiment, gives an experimental probability. You will look at both of these in this unit.

15.1 The probability that an outcome does not happen

Here are some outcomes and their probabilities p.

Throwing a four with a dice: $\frac{1}{6}$.   It will rain tomorrow: 0.3.   I shall win a game of chess: 90%.

The probability that an outcome does <u>not</u> happen = 1 – (probability that it <u>does</u> happen). $(1 - p)$

Here are the probabilities of the outcomes listed above <u>not</u> happening.

Not throwing a 4: $\frac{5}{6}$.   It will not rain tomorrow: 0.7.   I shall not win the game: 10%.

Worked example 15.1

Jake estimates that the probability that his bus will be early is 0.05 and the probability that it will be more than five minutes late is 0.3.

a What is the probability that it will not be early?

b What is the probability that it will not be more than 5 minutes late?

a 0.95   That is 1 – 0.95.

b 0.7   That is 1 – 0.3.

Exercise 15.1

1 The probability that it will be warmer today than it was yesterday is 0.1.
The probability that it will be colder today than it was yesterday is 0.7.

a What is the probability that it will not be colder today than it was yesterday?

b What is the probability that it will not be warmer today than it was yesterday?

2 The table shows the age distribution of members of a gym. A member of the gym is chosen at random. What is the probability that the person is:

Age	Under 21	21 to 35	36 to 55	Over 55
Percentage	12%	42%	32%	14%

a 21 or more   **b** 55 or less   **c** not in the 21 to 35 age group?

3 The manager of a football team says the probability that the team win the next match is 0.6 and the probability it will lose is 0.1.
Find the probability that the team will: **a** not win   **b** not lose   **c** not draw.

4 A survey of the makes of cars using a particular road gave these results.

Make	Volksota	Toywagen	Nindai	Hyussan
Percentage	12%	8%	7%	11%

a Harsha says that it must be wrong because the probabilities do not add up to 100%. Explain why she is wrong.

b Find the probablity that the next car to use the road is:

i not a Toywagen   **ii** not a Nindai   **iii** not a Toywagen or a Nindai.

5 If you throw three dice, the probability of getting three sixes is 0.5%. The probability of getting no sixes is 57.9%. Find the probability of getting:

a fewer than 3 sixes   **b** at least one six.

15.2 Equally likely outcomes

When you throw a dice, there are six possible outcomes, the numbers 1, 2, 3, 4, 5 and 6. If the dice is fair and is thrown fairly, all the numbers are equally likely.
Each number has a probability of $\frac{1}{6}$.
What is the probability that the number is less than 5?

The probability the number is less than 5 is $\frac{4}{6}$.

Four numbers less than 5

Six equally likely outcomes

This is equivalent to $\frac{2}{3}$.

For this method to work, all the outcomes must be equally likely.

Suppose someone chooses a month of the year. What is the probability that they choose July?

There are 12 possible months, so the probability is correct <u>if</u> every month is equally likely to be chosen.
'**At random**' means that all months have an equal possibility of being chosen.
If the month is chosen at random, the probability that it is July is $\frac{1}{12}$.

One way to choose the month at random is to write the name of each month on a different piece of paper and then pick one without looking.

Worked example 15.2

All of the letters of the word 'PROBABLY' are written on separate cards. One card is chosen at random. What is the probability that it is <u>not</u> a B?

2 cards out of 8 have a B.

The probability of B is $\frac{2}{8}$ or $\frac{1}{4}$. 'At random' means all cards are equally likely to be chosen.

The probability it is not a B is $\frac{3}{4}$. $1 - \frac{1}{4} = \frac{3}{4}$

Exercise 15.2

It will be easiest to write probabilities as fractions in this exercise.

1 Ahmad throws a dice. Find the probability that it is:
a a 2 **b** not a 2 **c** not a 5
d not a multiple of 3.

2 Maha writes the letters of the word 'MATHEMATICS' on separate cards.
She takes one card at random. Find the probability that the letter on the card is:
a an M **b** not an M **c** S or T **d** B
e before J in the alphabet.

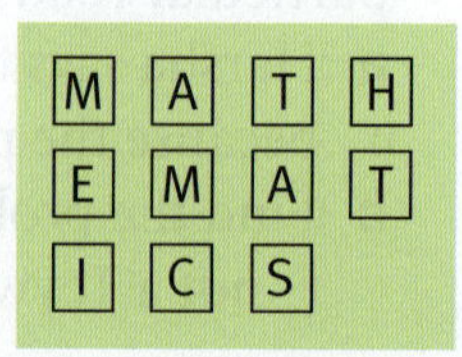

3 In the game of 'Scrabble' there are 100 tiles. Each has one letter or a blank.
The table shows the numbers of tiles with vowels.
One tile is taken at random. Find the probability that it is:
a A **b** U **c** not O
d a vowel **e** not a vowel.

Letter	A	E	I	O	U
Frequency	9	12	9	8	4

4 Harsha chooses a number at random from this grid.
Find the probability that the number she chooses is:

a 27 **b** in the bottom row
c in the first column **d** not in the last two columns.

Harsha chooses another number at random from the top two rows.
Find the probability that her number is:

e less than 10 **f** more than 10
g not 10 **h** more than 20.

1	2	3	4	5	6	7	8
9	10	11	12	13	14	15	16
17	18	19	20	21	22	23	24
25	26	27	28	29	30	31	32
33	34	35	36	37	38	39	40

5 This is a calendar for April in one year.

Monday	Tuesday	Wednesday	Thursday	Friday	Saturday	Sunday
		1	2	3	4	5
6	7	8	9	10	11	12
13	14	15	16	17	18	19
20	21	22	23	24	25	26
27	28	29	30			

Anders chooses a day at random. Find the probability that the day he chooses is:

a a Monday **b** not a Monday **c** 16 April **d** not 16 April **e** a Thursday or a Friday.

6 Zalika chooses one day of the year 2015 at random.

a What is the probability that it is: **i** 5 August **ii** not 5 August **iii** in August **iv** not in August?

b Suppose she chose a day in 2016 instead of 2015. Which probabilities in part **a** would be greater now?

7 A computer generates a single-digit random number. It could be any number from 0 to 9.
Find the probability that it is:

a 0 **b** not 0 **c** a multiple of 3 **d** 3.5 **e** less than 7.

8 A computer generates a two-digit number random number. It can be any number from 00 to 99.
Find the probability that it:

a is 99 **b** is not 99 **c** has no 9s in it **d** has at least one 9 in it.

9 When Razi throws two coins there are four equally likely outcomes.

(H)(H) (H)(T) (T)(H) (T)(T)

H = head
T = tail

a How many of these four outcomes will give:
i two heads **ii** one head and one tail **iii** two tails?

b If two coins are thrown, what is the probability of getting:
i two heads **ii** one head and one tail **iii** two tails?

10 Sasha tosses three coins together.

a Explain why there are eight equally likely outcomes.

b Find the probability that there will be:
i three heads **ii** three tails **iii** two heads and one tail **iv** two tails and one head.

15.3 Listing all possible outcomes

If you throw two dice together, what is the probability of getting a double six?

To find out, you need a list of all the possible outcomes. You could use a table.

Suppose you have a red dice and a blue one.

Draw the table like this.

This shows that there are 36 **mutually exclusive** outcomes.

If the dice are thrown fairly, the outcomes are all equally likely.

The probability of a double six is $\frac{1}{36}$.

blue dice (columns), red dice (rows)

	1	2	3	4	5	6
1	1, 1	1, 2	1, 3	1, 4	1, 5	1, 6
2	2, 1	2, 2	2, 3	2, 4	2, 5	2, 6
3	3, 1	3, 2	3, 3	3, 4	3, 5	3, 6
4	4, 1	4, 2	4, 3	4, 4	4, 5	4, 6
5	5, 1	5, 2	5, 3	5, 4	5, 5	5, 6
6	6, 1	6, 2	6, 3	6, 4	6, 5	6, 6

Outcomes are mutually exclusive if only one of them can happen.

Worked example 15.3

Two fair dice are thrown and the scores are added.
What is the probability of scoring a total of:

a 8 **b** less than 8 **c** 8 or more?

This table shows the possible totals. This table is based on the outcome table above.

	1	2	3	4	5	6
1	2	3	4	5	6	7
2	3	4	5	6	7	(8)
3	4	5	6	7	(8)	9
4	5	6	7	(8)	9	10
5	6	7	(8)	9	10	11
6	7	(8)	9	10	11	12

a $\frac{5}{36}$ The five 8s have been circled in the table.

b $\frac{21}{36} = \frac{7}{12}$ There are 21 numbers in the table less than 8.

c $\frac{15}{36} = \frac{5}{12}$ There are 15 numbers that are 8 or more.

Exercise 15.3

1 Xavier throws two fair dice together. What is the probability of scoring:

a two fours **b** no fours **c** exactly one four?

2 Mia throws two fair dice and adds the scores.

a What is the smallest possible total?

b What is the largest possible total?

c What is wrong with Mia's argument on the right?

There are eleven possible totals so the probability of a total of 3 is $\frac{1}{11}$.

3 Shen throws two dice and adds the numbers together.

a What is the most likely possible total? **b** What is the least likely possible total?

Find the probability that the total will be:

c 2 **d** 7 **e** less than 7 **f** an odd number **g** a prime number.

4 Razi throws two dice. Find the probability that:

a the numbers are the same **b** the difference between the two numbers is 2.

5 Dakarai spins a coin and throws a dice. One possible outcome is a head and a 6.

a Show that there are 12 mutually exclusive outcomes and list them in a table.

b Find the probability of scoring:

i a tail and a 1 **ii** a head and an even number **iii** a tail and a 5 or a 6.

6 Alicia has two three-sided spinners.
One shows the numbers 1, 1, 3.
The other shows the numbers 2, 3, 5.

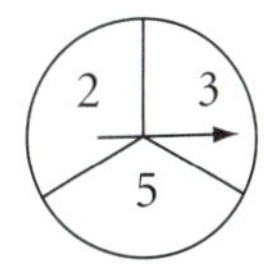

+	2	3	5
1			
1		4	
3			8

a Copy and complete the table to show the total score of the two spinners.

b Find the probability of a total of:

i 3 **ii** 6 **iii** 5 or more **iv** an even number.

7 Oditi throws two dice and multiplies the scores together.

The product is the result of multiplying two numbers.

a Draw a table to show the possible values of the product.

b How many different products are possible?

c Find the probability that the product is:

i 12 **ii** not 12 **iii** less than 12 **iv** more than 17 **v** an even number.

8 Hassan has four blue pens and a red pen in his pocket. He takes out one without looking, and then he takes another.

a Copy and complete the table to show the possible selections.

b Why are there Xs down the diagonal?

c Find the probability that:

i both pens are blue **ii** the first pen is red

iii one of the pens is red.

		Second pen				
		B1	**B2**	**B3**	**B4**	**R**
First pen	**B1**	X	B1, B2			
	B2		X			
	B3			X		
	B4				X	
	R					X

The blue pens are labelled B1, B2, B3 and B4 to distinguish them.
B1, B2 means first B1 then B2.

9 Shen and Tanesha play 'rock, paper, scissors'. They simultaneously make a sign for one of the items.

a Make a table to show the different possible outcomes.

b If each person chooses at random, what is the probability that they will not choose the same thing?

c Rock beats scissors. Scissors beat paper. Paper beats rock. What is the probability Shen beats Tanesha, if they play one game?

15.4 Experimental and theoretical probabilities

One way to find probabilities is to use equally likely outcomes. Another way is to collect data from a survey or an experiment.

If you want to know the probability that a seed will germinate, you cannot use equally likely outcomes. You need to plant seeds and count how many germinate.

Certain computer programs, called spreadsheets, have a random number generator that you can use to simulate throwing a dice.

Here are the results of 20 throws of a dice simulated on a computer.

5 2 5 1 2 6 2 5 3 1 3 3 5 1 1 1 1 3 3 3

Here are the results in a frequency table.

Score	1	2	3	4	5	6
Frequency	6	3	6	0	4	1
Relative frequency	0.3	0.15	0.3	0	0.2	0.05

The relative frequencies (RF) give an **experimental probability** for each number.

The **theoretical probability** for each number, based on equally likely outcomes, is $\frac{1}{6} = 0.167$.

Relative frequency = frequency ÷ total throws

The experimental and theoretical probabilities are not close. This is because 20 is a small number of throws.

What happens if you have more throws? Another set of throws will give different results.

This table shows the results after 20, 50, 100 and 200 throws.

Score	20 throws		50 throws		100 throws		200 throws	
	Frequency	RF	Frequency	RF	Frequency	RF	Frequency	RF
1	6	0.3	11	0.22	19	0.19	36	0.18
2	3	0.15	11	0.22	19	0.19	36	0.18
3	6	0.3	8	0.16	19	0.19	35	0.175
4	0	0	5	0.1	15	0.15	31	0.155
5	4	0.2	7	0.14	13	0.13	29	0.145
6	1	0.05	8	0.16	15	0.15	33	0.165
Total	20	1	50	1	100	1	200	1

As the number of throws increases, the experimental probabilities get closer to the theoretical probabilities. These results illustrate two important results.

1 If you repeat an experiment you get different results. Compare the first 10 throws with the second 10 throws to see this.

2 If you increase the number of times an experiment is repeated you generally get better estimates of probabilities. 200 throws give more reliable results than 20 throws.

In realistic examples, such as the seed planting described above, we do not have theoretical probabilities to compare with the experimental probabilities. That is why you need to do the experiment!

However, it remains true that different experiments will give different estimates, and you can have more confidence in the estimates if the experiment is repeated more often.

Experimental probabilities are usually given as decimals or percentages.

Exercise 15.4

1 Alicia has a biased coin (it has been altered to land on one side more often). She wants to find the experimental probability of getting a head.
She spins the coin 10 times. She gets 6 heads and 4 tails.
  a What is the experimental probability of getting a head based on these 10 throws? Give your answer as a decimal.
  b Explain why this is not a reliable estimate of the probability.
She spins the coin another 10 times. This time she gets 3 heads and 7 tails.
  c Find the experimental probability of getting a head based on the 20 throws so far.
She spins the coin another 30 times and gets 9 heads and 21 tails.
  d Find the experimental probability of getting a head based on all the throws so far.
Another 50 throws give 19 heads and 31 tails.
  e Find the experimental probability of getting a head based on all the throws so far.
  f Explain why the last estimate of the probability of getting a head is the most reliable one.

2 Zalika throws four dice at the same time.
  a What is the smallest possible total? **b** What is the largest possible total?
Zalika wants to find the experimental probability of scoring a total of 15 or more when she throws four dice. She decides to do a simulation on a spreadsheet. Her results are in the table above.

Throws of four dice	25	50	100	150	200
Frequency of a total of 15 or more	7	16	42	68	88

  c Find separate estimates of the probability of a total of 15 or more based on 25 throws, 50 throws, 100 throws, 150 throws and 200 throws.
Mia repeats Zalika's experiment and gets these results.

Throws of four dice	25	50	100	150	200
Frequency of a total of 15 or more	11	24	45	76	94

  d Find Mia's successive estimates of the probability.
  e Compare Zalika's results and Mia's results.
  f Put Zalika's and Mia's results together to get an experimental probability based on all 400 results.

3 Maha spins a coin 10 times. She gets 8 heads and 2 tails.
  a Find the experimental probability of throwing: **i** a head **ii** a tail.
  b Is there evidence that Maha is not throwing the coin fairly?
Hassan spins a coin 100 times. He gets 80 heads and 20 tails.
  c Find the experimental probability of throwing: **i** a head **ii** a tail
  d Is there evidence that Hassan is not throwing the coin fairly?

4 Oditi makes a dice out of card. She tests it by throwing it 30 times. She gets these results.

Score	1	2	3	4	5	6
Frequency	4	4	5	4	9	4

  a Read what Oditi says. Is she correct? Give a reason for your answer.

The dice is biased because 5 appeared much more than the other numbers.

Anders made a dice and threw it 300 times.
He got these results.

Score	1	2	3	4	5	6
Frequency	45	58	48	48	46	55

b Anders is not correct. How could you convince him that the dice may be fair?

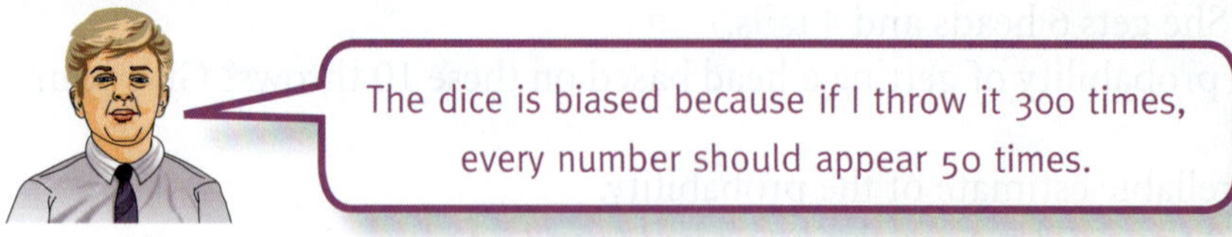

5 A group of five students want to find the experimental probability of getting at least one 6 when throwing six dice. Each of them throws six dice 20 times to produce this data.

Student		A	B	C	D	E
Frequency	At least one 6	12	11	15	11	15
	No 6s	8	9	5	9	5

a Find the experimental probability of at least one 6 from student A's results.

b Find the experimental probability of at least one 6 by combining the results of:
i A and B **ii** A, B and C **iii** A, B, C and D **iv** A, B, C, D and E.

c What is the best estimate of the experimental probability?

The students repeated the experiment with another 20 throws each.
The combined results this time were as shown.

At least one 6	70
No 6s	30

d Calculate a new estimate for the experimental probability of throwing at least one 6.

e In fact the theoretical probability for this outcome is 0.6651. How do the experimental probabilities compare with this?

Summary

You should now know that:

★ If the probability of an outcome of an event occurring is p, then the probability of it not occurring is $1 - p$.

★ Probabilities can be based on equally likely outcomes in practical contexts.

★ A good strategy for calculating probabilities is listing systematically all possible equally likely outcomes.

★ Experimental probabilities can vary from one experiment to the next.

★ Experimental probabilities are usually more reliable if the experiment is repeated more often.

★ A logical argument can be used to establish the truth of a statement.

You should be able to:

★ Use the probability of an outcome of an event occurring to find the probability it will not occur.

★ Find probabilities based on equally likely outcomes in practical contexts.

★ Find and list systematically all possible outcomes for single events and for two successive events.

★ Compare estimated experimental probabilities with theoretical probabilities.

★ Use logical argument to interpret the mathematics in a context or to establish the truth of a statement.

End-of-unit review

1 If ten coins are spun together, the probability of four or more heads is 0.83.
The probability of eight or more heads is 0.05. Find the probability of:
a less than four heads **b** fewer than eight heads.

2 Ahmad plays chess against his father. Ahmad's probability of winning is 0.1. His probability of losing is 0.3.
Find the probability that:
a Ahmad will not win **b** Ahmad's father will not win.

3 The letters of the word 'EXPERIMENT' are placed on ten separate cards. One card is chosen at random.
a How could you make sure the card is chosen at random?
b Find the probability that the card does not show an E.
c Find the probability that the letter on the card is in the word 'EMPIRE'.

4 A number generator produces two digits in boxes like this.
Each digit is generated randomly. It can be any digit from 0 to 9.
Find the probability that:

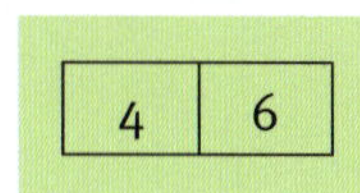

a the first number is 4 **b** the second number is less than 8 **c** there are no 0s.

5 Two four-sided spinners are each numbered 1 to 4.

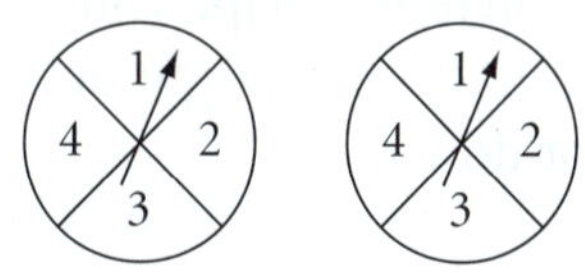

a Construct a table to show the possible totals of the two dice.
b What is the most likely total?
c Find the probability that the total is:
i 3 **ii** more than 3 **iii** 5 or less.
d Construct a table to show the possible products when the two numbers are multiplied.
e Find the probability that the product is:
i 4 **ii** 11 **iii** more than 11 **iv** less than 11 **v** an odd number.

6 Shen wants to find the experimental probability that, when you throw three dice, all three numbers will be the same.
a After 20 throws he has not thrown the same number three times. What is the experimental probability of getting all three numbers the same?
b He continues to throw three dice until he has done it 200 times. Here are his results.

After	20 throws	50 throws	100 throws	200 throws
Frequency of three identical numbers	0	3	4	9

Find the experimental probability of throwing three identical numbers after 50, 100 and 200 throws.
c Explain why more throws may be necessary for Shen to be confident about the experimental probability.
d Shen asks four friends to throw four dice 200 times. Here are their results.

Person	A	B	C	D
Frequency of three identical numbers in 200 throws	5	3	1	7

Find the experimental probability of throwing three identical numbers for each of these four people.
e Combine the results of all five people to find a new experimental probability.
f Why is the answer to part **e** likely to be the most reliable estimate?

16 Position and movement

In earlier work you learned how to **transform** 2D shapes by reflecting, translating or rotating them.

Here is a summary of the key points.

The shape before any transformation is called the **object**.

The shape after the transformation is the **image**.

You need a mirror line to **reflect** a shape.

Key words

Make sure you learn and understand these key words:

- transform
- object
- image
- reflect
- translate
- rotate
- enlargement
- combination of transformations
- scale factor
- centre of enlargement

When you reflect a shape on a coordinate grid, you can give the equation of the mirror line.

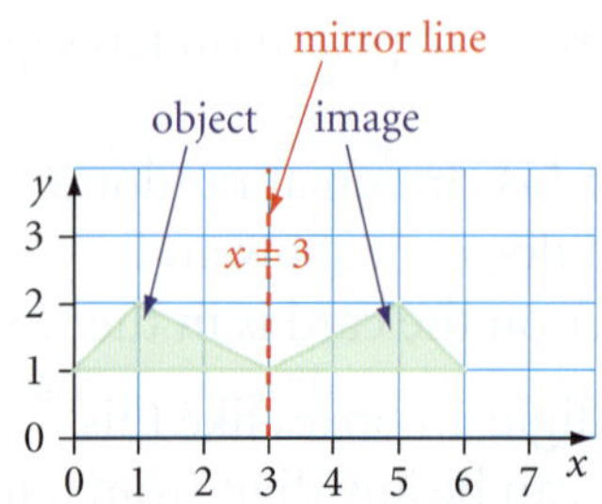

When you **translate** a shape you move it a given distance, right or left and up or down.

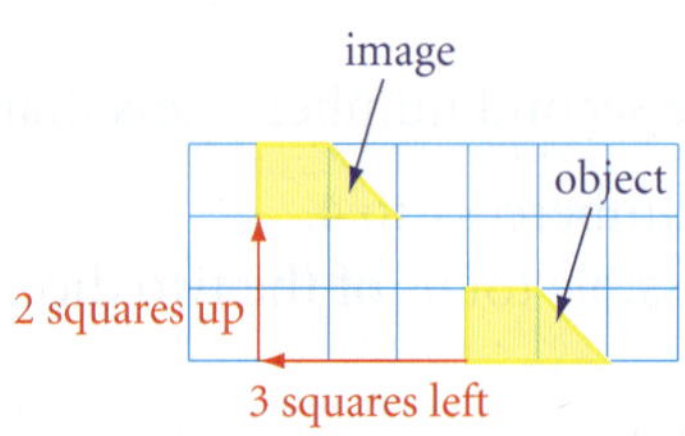

When you **rotate** a shape you turn it through a given number of degrees, or fraction of a whole turn.

You turn it about a fixed point, called the centre of rotation. You turn it either clockwise or anticlockwise.

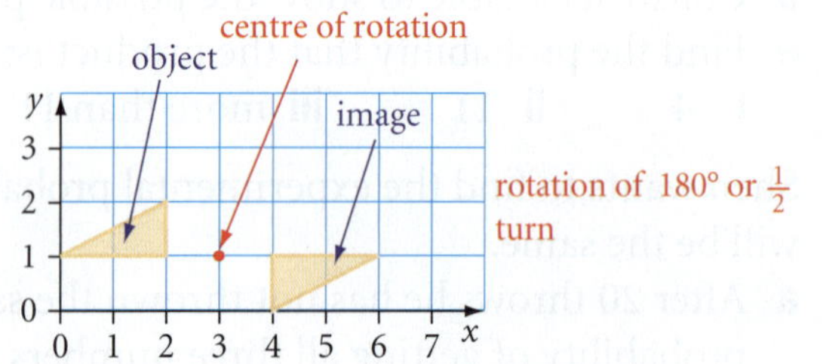

With any of these three transformations the shape only changes its position. It doesn't change its shape and size. An object and its image are always identical. They are congruent.

An **enlargement** of a shape is a copy of the object, but it is bigger.

You can use a microscope to look at enlarged images of very small objects. In this picture you can see a dust mite. These are about 0.04 mm long so they cannot usually be seen without the use of a microscope. A typical mattress on a bed may have from 100 000 to 10 million mites inside it. This is not a very nice thought as you go to bed at night!

In this unit you will look again at using reflections, translations and rotations to transform shapes. You will also learn how to enlarge 2D shapes.

16.1 Transforming shapes

You can already transform 2D shapes by reflecting, translating or rotating them. You can also use a **combination of transformations** to transform a shape.

Worked example 16.1

The diagram shows a triangle A.
Draw the image of triangle A after:

a reflection in the line $y = 4$; label the image B

b translation 3 squares right and 2 squares down; label the image C

c rotation of 180° about the point (4, 5); label the image D

d rotation of 90° clockwise about the centre of rotation at (1, 5), followed by reflection in the line $x = 2$; label the image E.

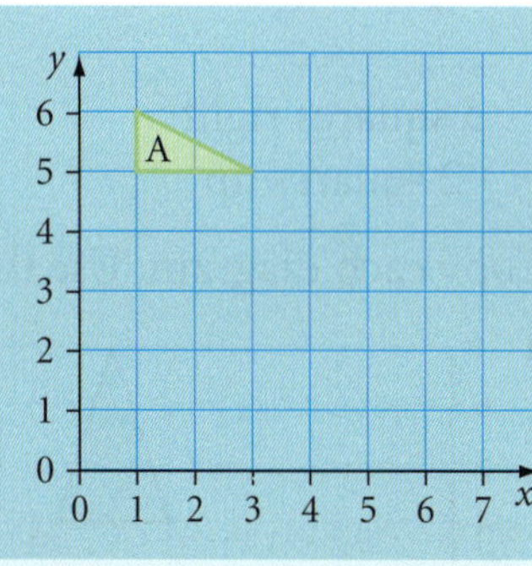

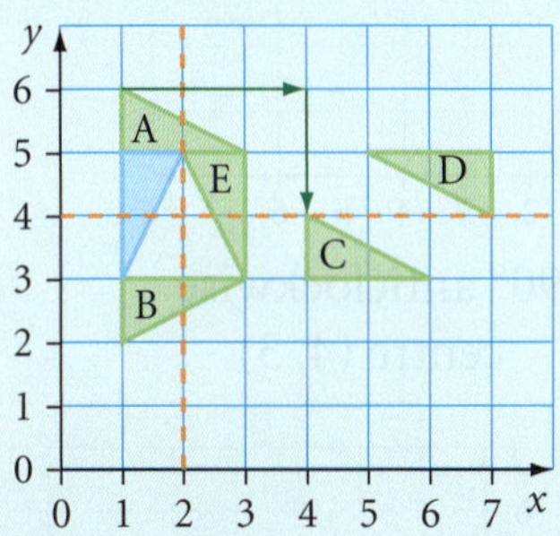

a Draw the line $y = 4$ (shown in red). Draw the reflection of triangle A in the red mirror line. Label the image B.

b Move triangle A three squares right and two squares down (shown by the green arrows). Label the image C.

c Use tracing paper to trace triangle A. Put the point of your pencil on the tracing paper over the point (4, 5) and turn your tracing paper 180°. Draw the image of A and label it D.

d Use tracing paper to trace triangle A. Put the point of your pencil on the tracing paper over the point (1, 5) and turn your tracing paper 90° clockwise. Draw the image (shown in blue). Draw the line $x = 2$ (shown in orange). Draw the reflection of the blue triangle in the orange mirror line. Label the image E.

Exercise 16.1

1 Copy each diagram. Add the mirror line with the given equation. Reflect the shape in the mirror line.

a

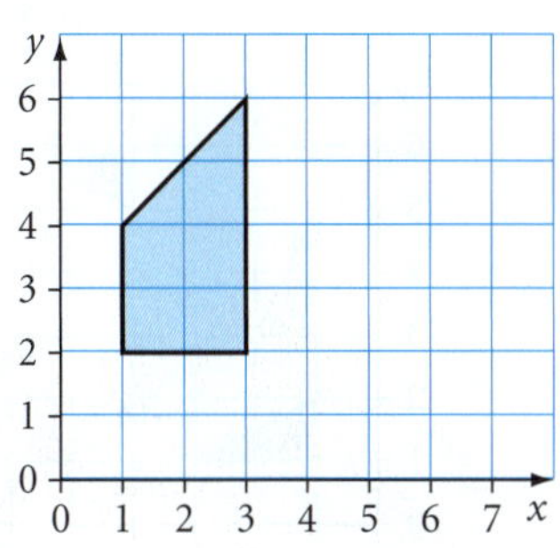

mirror line $x = 4$

b

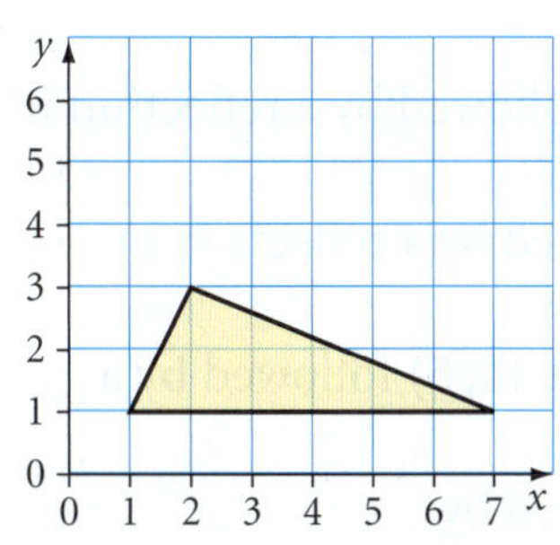

mirror line $y = 3$

c

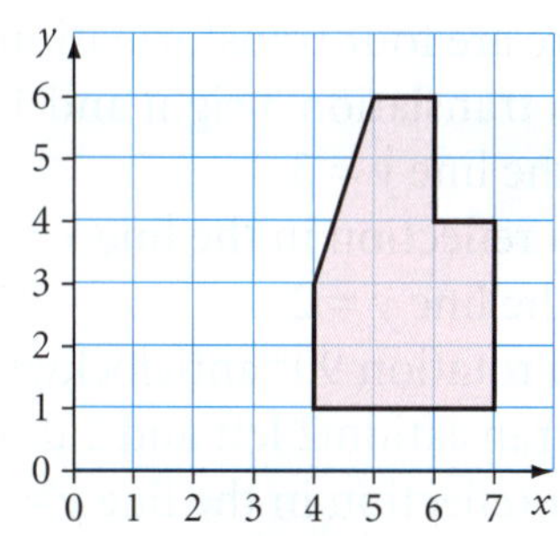

mirror line $x = 3.5$

2 Copy each diagram. Use the translation you are given to draw the image of the object.

a

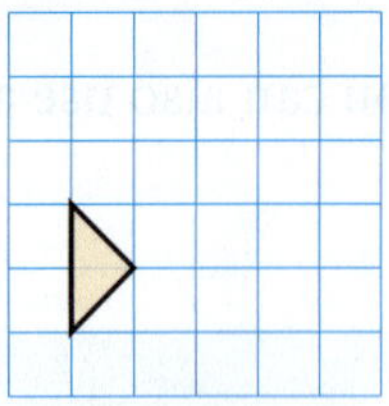

3 squares right
2 squares up

b

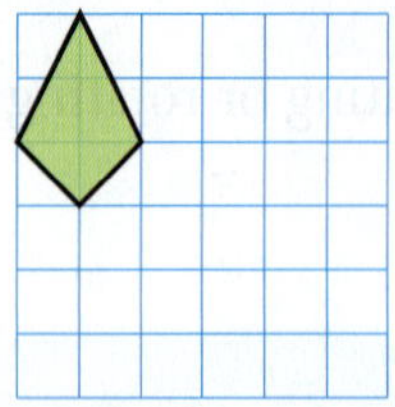

2 squares right
3 squares down

c

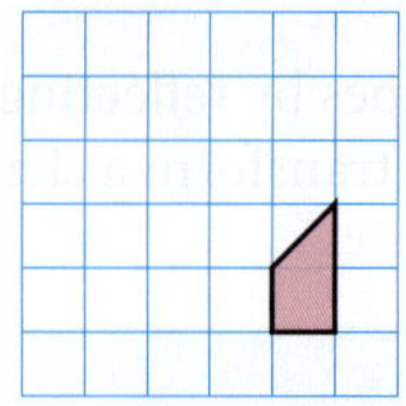

4 squares left
1 square up

d

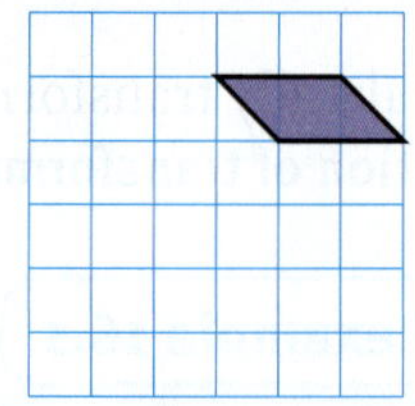

1 square left
3 squares down

3 Copy each diagram. Use the information you are given to rotate the shape.

a

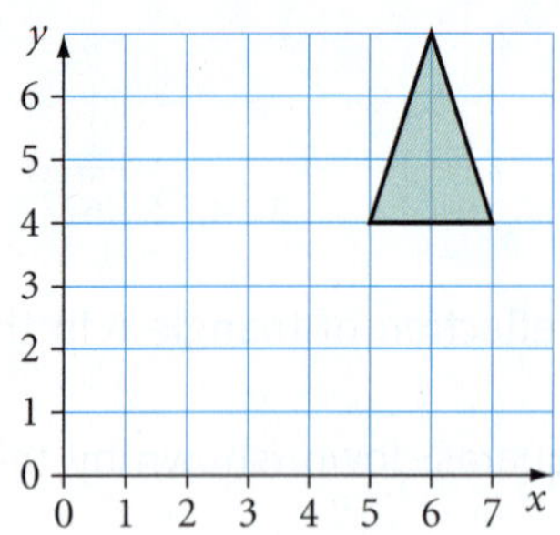

180°
centre (4, 4)

b

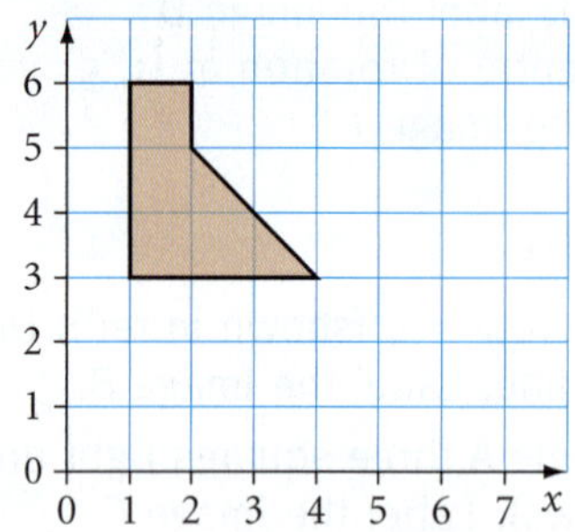

90° clockwise
centre (4, 3)

c

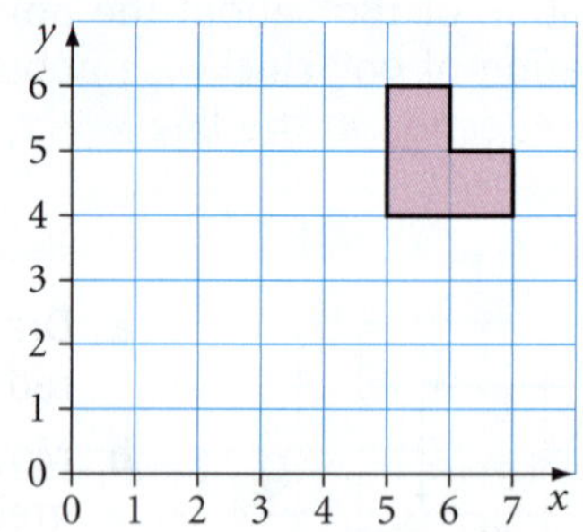

90° anticlockwise
centre (4, 3)

4 The diagram shows triangle A. Make three copies of the diagram.
Draw the image of A after each combination of transformations.
Use a different copy of the diagram for each part.

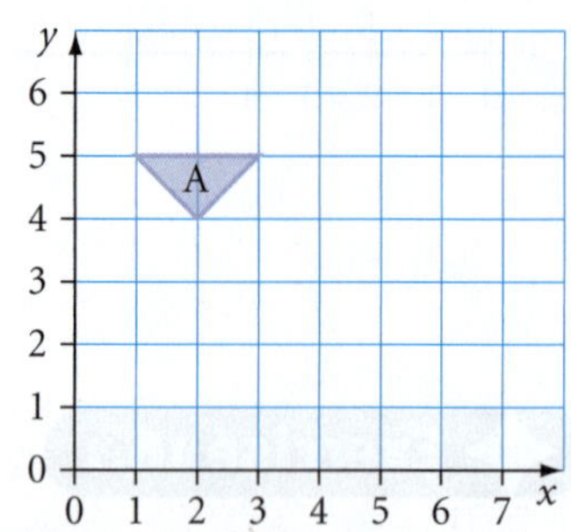

a a translation 4 squares right and 1 square down followed by a reflection in the line $y = 3$

b a rotation of 90° anticlockwise, centre (3, 5) followed by a translation 3 squares right and 2 squares down

c a reflection in the line $x = 4$ followed by a rotation of 180°, centre (6, 4).

5 The diagram shows five triangles, A to E.
Here are four transformations.

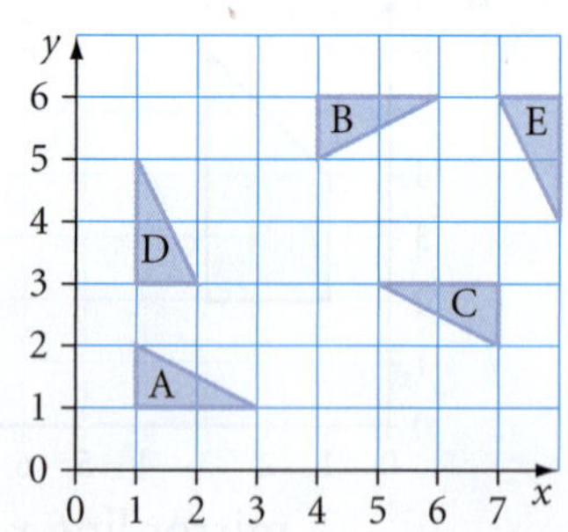

a a translation 3 right and 1 down followed by a reflection in the line $y = 3$

b a reflection in the line $x = 4$ followed by a reflection in the line $y = 2$

c a rotation 90° anticlockwise, centre (4, 5) followed by a translation 2 left and 2 down

d a reflection in the line $y = 4$ followed by a rotation 90° anticlockwise, centre (7, 6)

Work out which triangle is transformed to which other triangle by each of the transformations.

16.2 Enlarging shapes

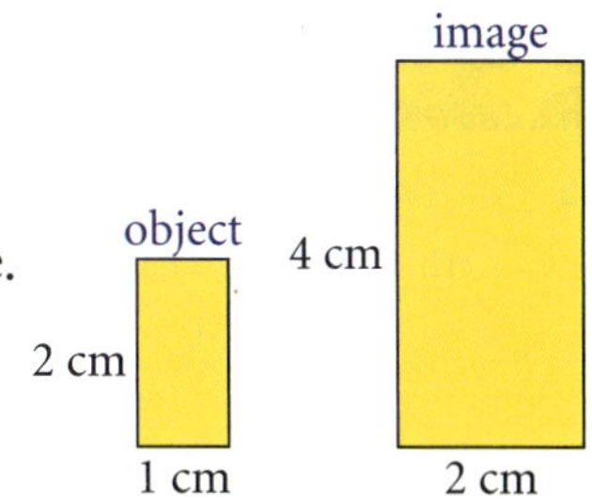

An enlargement of a shape is a copy of the shape that changes the lengths, but keeps the same proportions. In an enlargement all the angles stay the same size.

Look at these two rectangles.

The image is an enlargement of the object. Every length on the image is twice as long as the corresponding length on the object.

The **scale factor** is 2.

The **centre of enlargement** tells you where to draw the image on a grid. In this case, as the scale factor is 2, not only must the image be twice the size of the object, it must be twice the distance from the centre of enlargement.

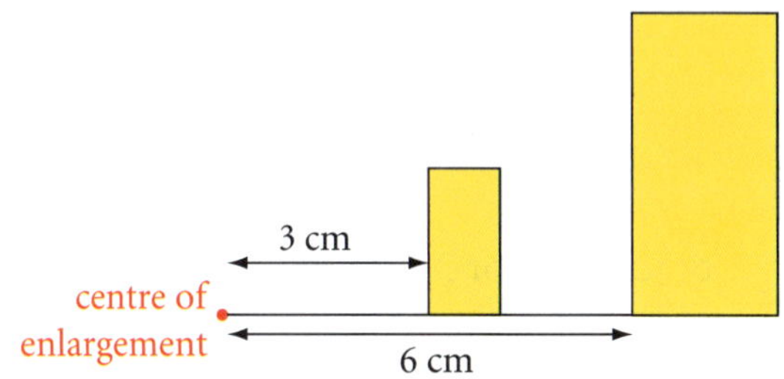

You can check you have drawn an enlargement correctly by drawing lines through the corresponding corners of the object and image.

The lines should all meet at the centre of the enlargement. This is also a useful way to find the centre of enlargement if you are only given the object and the image.

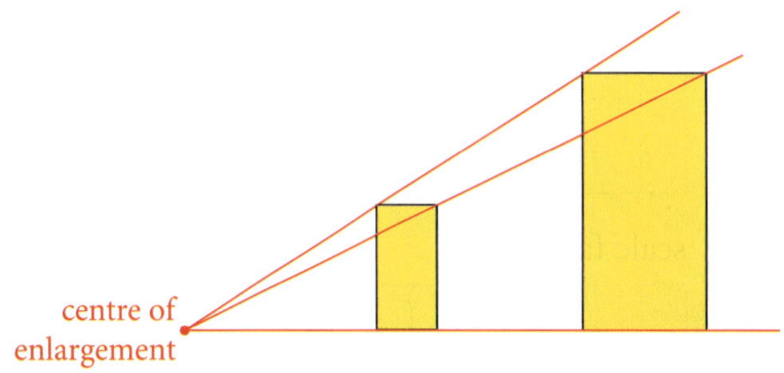

Worked example 16.2

Draw enlargements of the following triangles using the given scale factors and centres of enlargements.

a scale factor 2

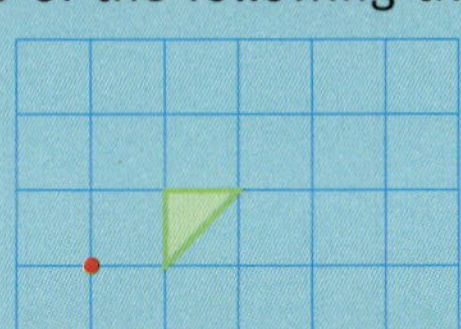

b scale factor 3

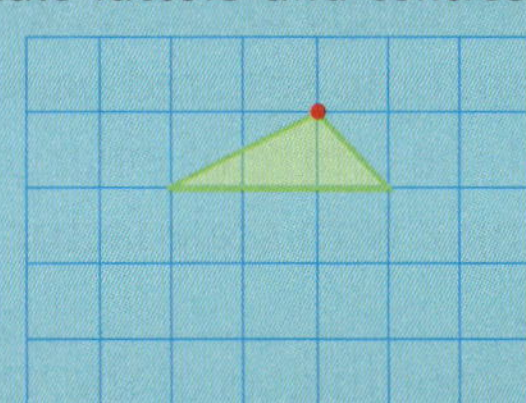

a

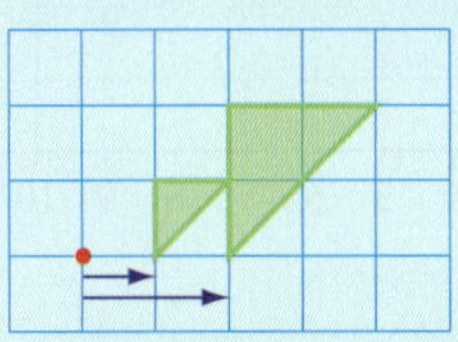

Start by looking at the corner of the triangle that is closest to the centre of enlargement (COE). This corner is 1 square to the right of the COE, so with a scale factor of 2, the image will be 2 squares to the right of the COE. Plot this point on the grid, then complete the triangle, remembering to double all the other lengths.

b

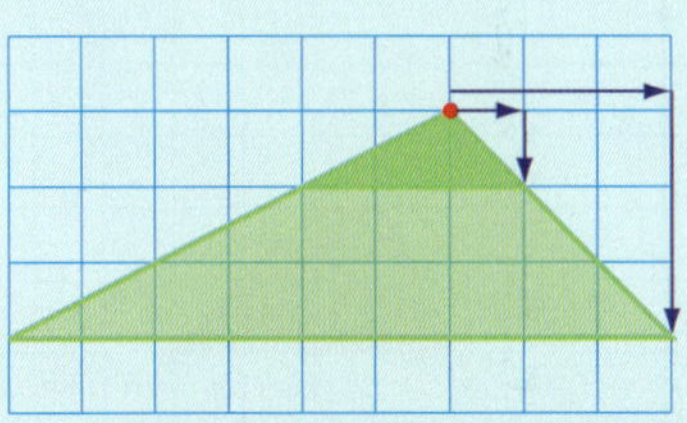

One of the corners of this triangle is on the centre of enlargement, so this corner doesn't move. Look at the bottom right corner of the triangle. This corner is 1 square to the right and 1 square down from the COE. With a scale factor of 3, the image will be 3 squares to the right and 3 squares down from the COE. Plot this point on the grid then complete the triangle, remembering to multiply all the other lengths by 3.

Exercise 16.2

1 Copy each of these shapes onto squared paper.
Enlarge each one using the given scale factors and centres of enlargement.

> Make sure you leave enough space around your shape to complete the enlargement

a scale factor 2

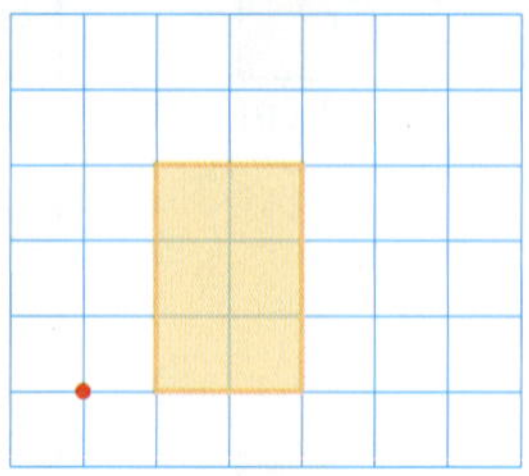

b scale factor 3

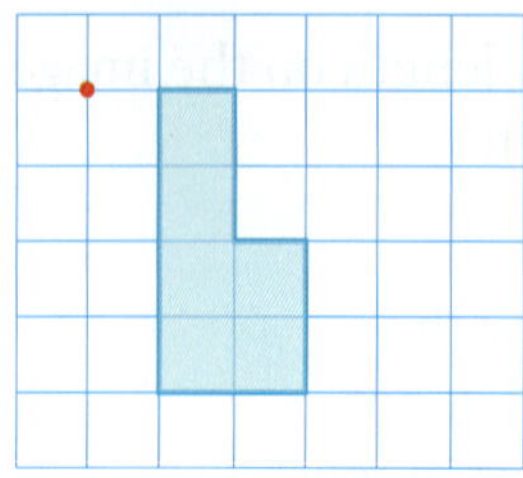

c scale factor 4

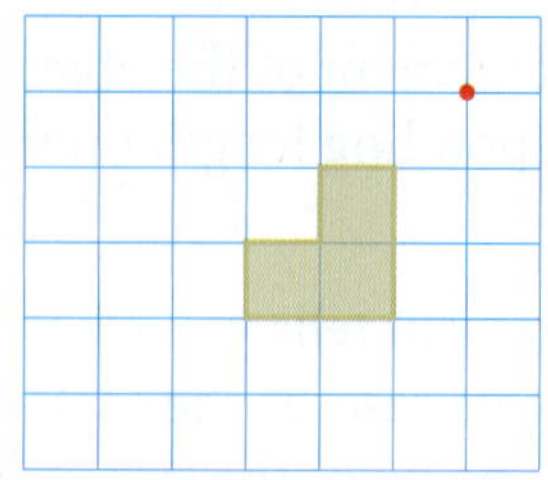

d scale factor 2

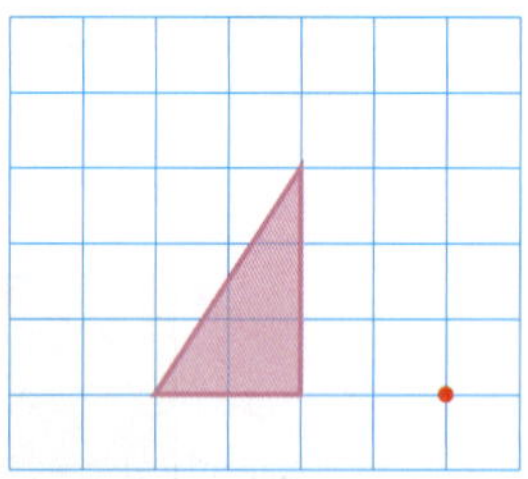

e scale factor 3

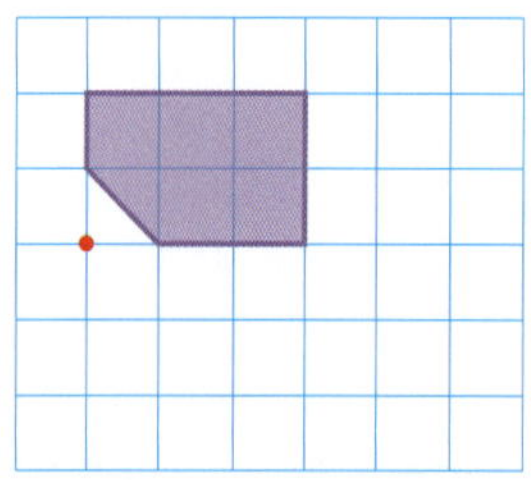

f scale factor 4

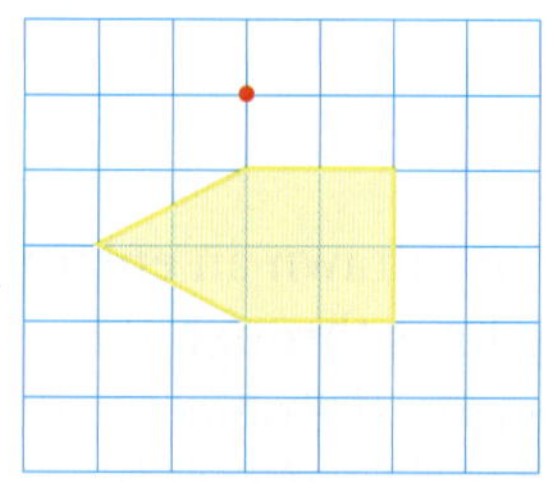

g scale factor 2

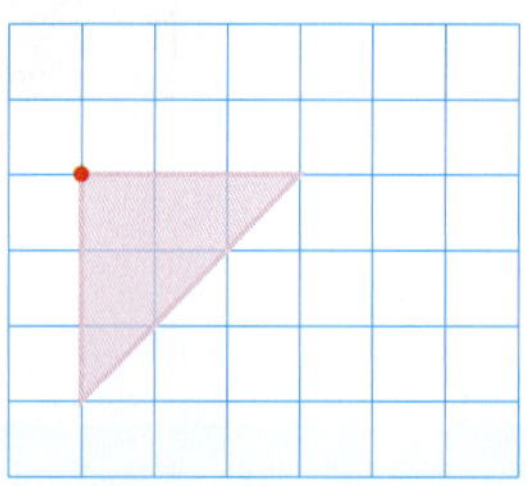

h scale factor 3

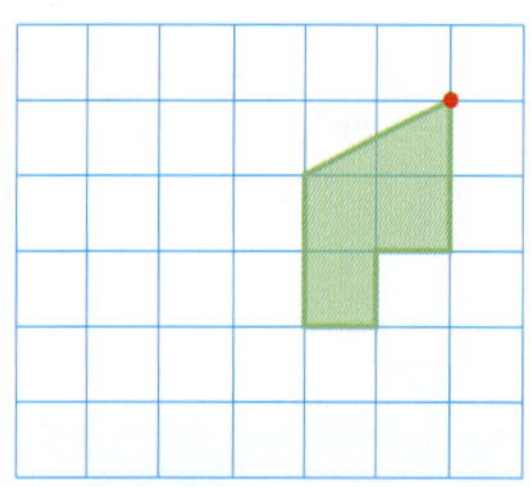

i scale factor 4

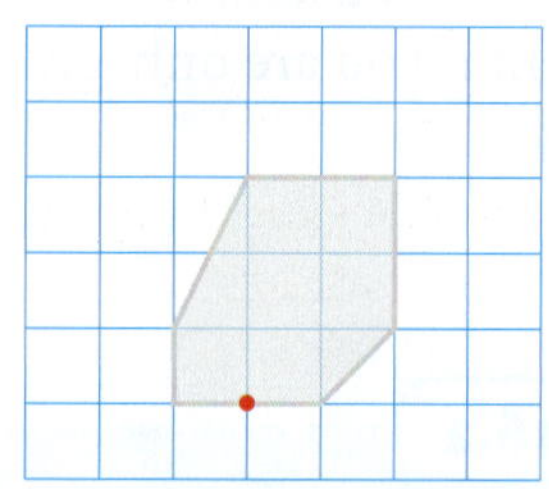

2 The vertices of this triangle are at (2, 2), (2, 3) and (4, 2).

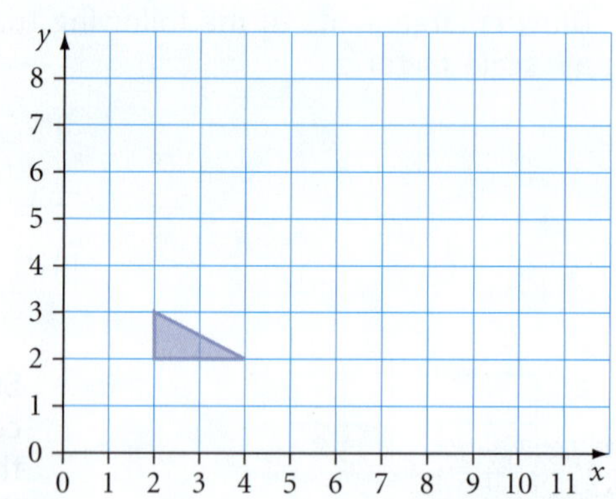

a Copy the diagram onto squared paper.
Mark with a dot the centre of enlargement at (1, 1).
Enlarge the triangle with scale factor 3 from the centre of enlargement.

b Write down the coordinates of the vertices of the image.

3 The vertices of this trapezium are at (3, 2), (7, 2), (5, 4) and (4, 4).

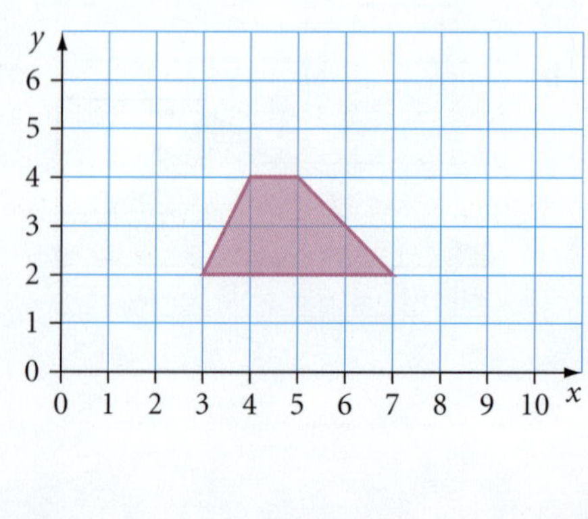

a Copy the diagram onto squared paper.
Mark with a dot the centre of enlargement at (5, 2).
Enlarge the trapezium with scale factor 2 from the centre of enlargement.

b Write down the coordinates of the vertices of the image.

For question **4** work in a group of three or four.

i On your own, draw the enlargement for part **a** only of the question.

ii Compare your diagram with the other members of your group. Discuss the different approaches that you each used to draw the enlargement and decide which ones are correct.

iii Repeat the process for part **b**, and then part **c**.

4 Copy each of these shapes onto squared paper.
Enlarge each one, using the given scale factor and centre of enlargement.

a scale factor 2

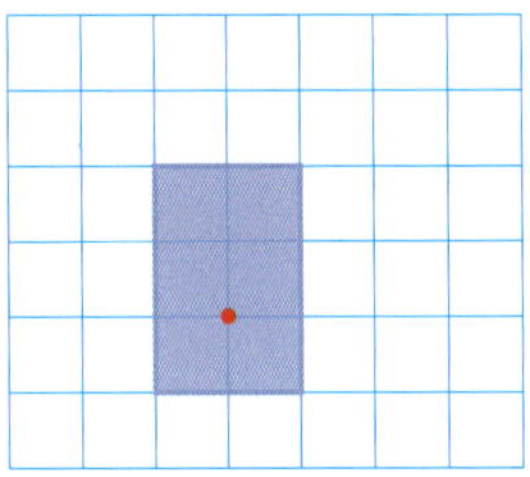

b scale factor 3

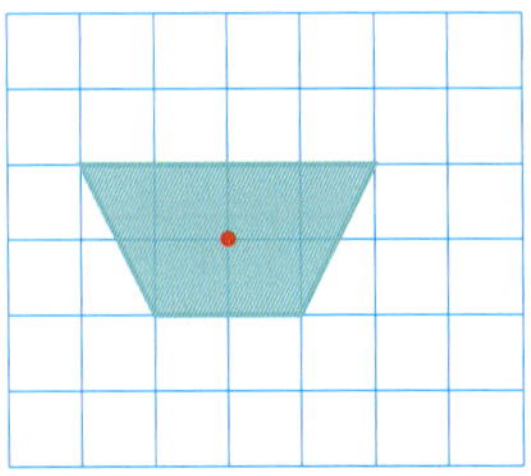

c scale factor 4

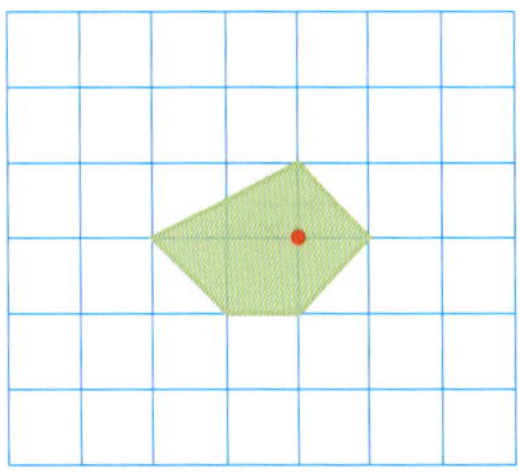

For question **5** work in a group of three or four.

i Copy the diagram for each part.

ii For part **a** only, write down the coordinates of the centre of enlargement and the scale factor.

iii Compare your answer with those of the other members of your group. Discuss the different approaches that you each used to work out the coordinates and scale factor and decide whose answers are correct.

iv Repeat the process for part **b**.

5 Each diagram shows an object and its image after an enlargement.
For each part, write down scale factor and the coordinates of the centre of enlargement.

a

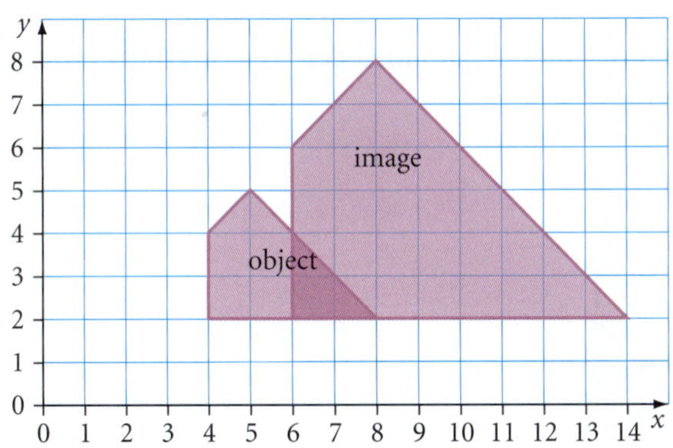

b

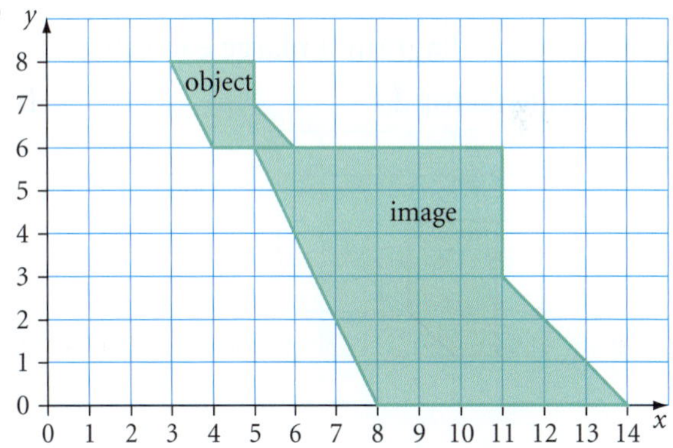

Summary

You should now know that:

- ★ An enlargement of a shape is a copy of the shape that changes all the lengths but keeps the same proportions. All the angles stay the same.
- ★ The scale factor tells you how the lengths of the shape change and also how far from the centre of enlargement the image is.

You should be able to:

- ★ Transform 2D shapes by rotation, reflection and translation, and by simple combinations of these transformations.
- ★ Understand and use the language and notation associated with enlargement.
- ★ Enlarge 2D shapes, given a centre of enlargement and a positive integer scale factor.

End-of-unit review

1 Copy each diagram. Add the mirror line with the given equation. Reflect the shape in the mirror line.

a

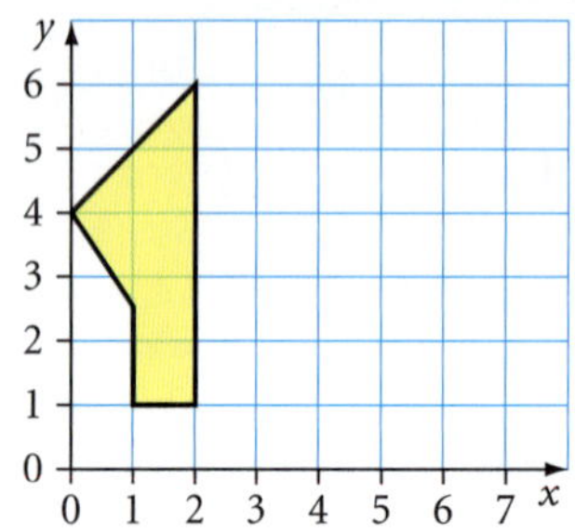

mirror line $x = 4$

b

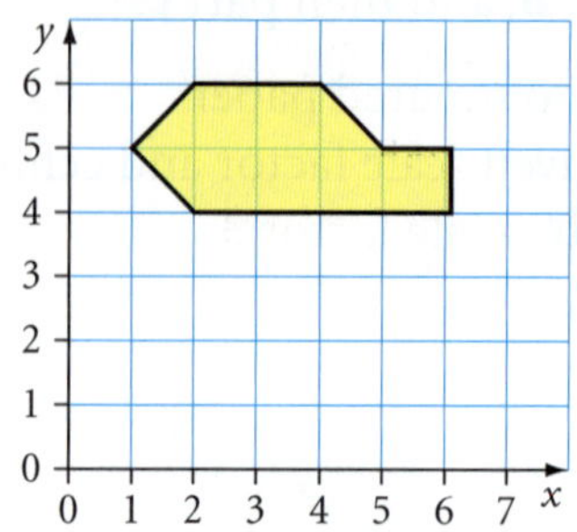

mirror line $y = 3.5$

2 Copy each diagram. Use the information you are given to rotate the shape.

a

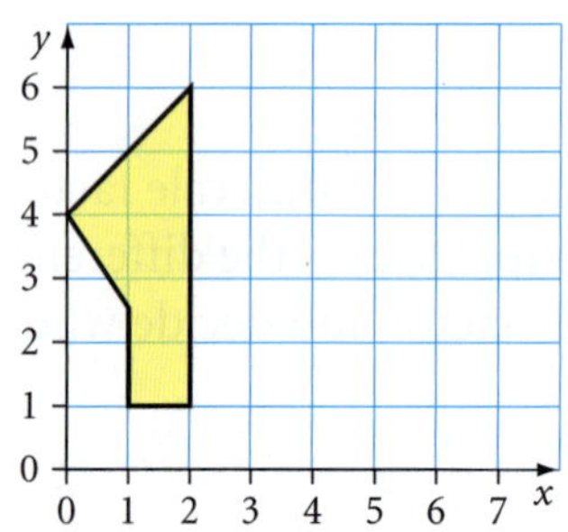

180°
centre (4, 4)

b

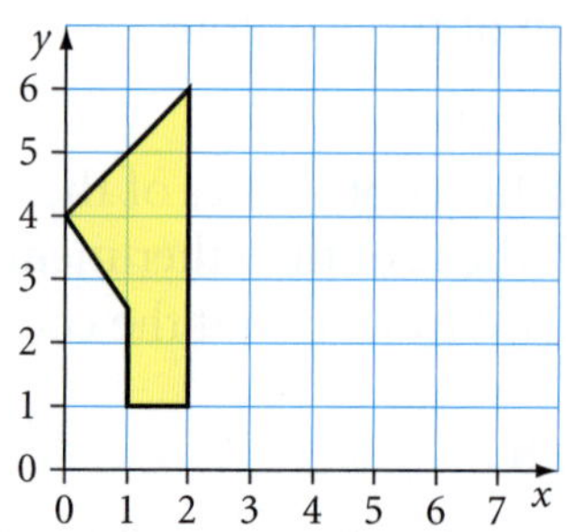

90° anticlockwise
centre (3, 3)

3 Copy each diagram. Enlarge each shape using the given scale factors and centres of enlargement.

a scale factor 2

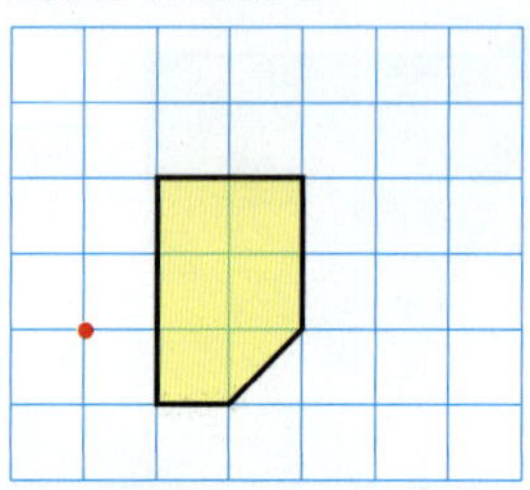

b scale factor 3

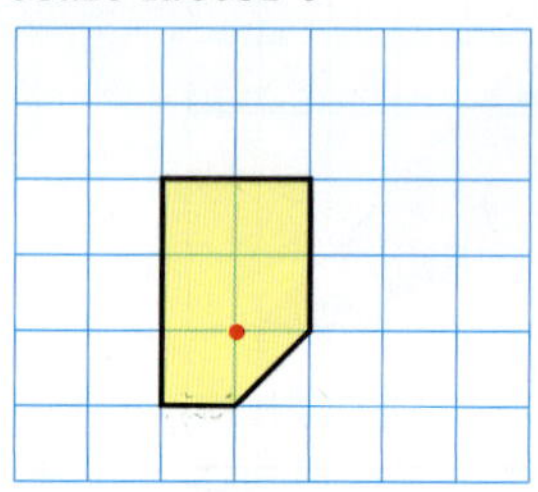

4 The diagram shows a triangle A. Make three copies of the diagram. Draw the image of A after each combination of transformations. Use a different copy of the diagram for each part.

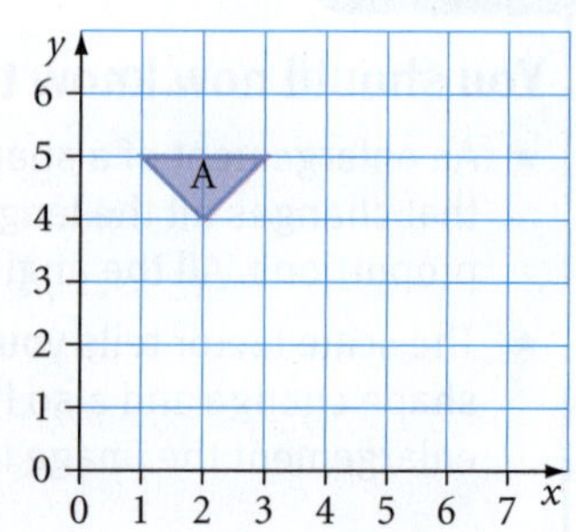

a A translation 3 squares right and 2 squares down followed by a reflection in the line $y = 3$. Label the image B.

b A rotation of 90° clockwise, centre (3, 3) followed by a translation 1 square left and 1 square down. Label the image C.

c A reflection in the line $y = 3$, followed by a reflection in the line $x = 4$, followed by a rotation of 180°, centre (5, 3). Label the image D.

17 Area, perimeter and volume

A circle is a set of points that are all the same distance from a fixed point, called the centre.

Do you remember the names of the different parts of the circle?

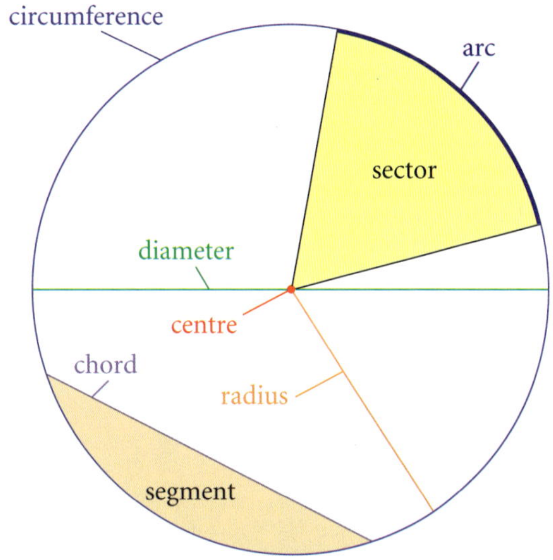

Key words

Make sure you learn and understand these key words:

π, pi
perpendicular height
compound shape

It is a curious fact that for every circle, if you divide the length of the circumference by the length of the diameter, you will always get the same number: 3.141592653589... This number has been given the name **pi** (pronounced 'pie') and is also known by the symbol π.

π

Pi is a mathematical constant – it stands for one particular number. Pi has an infinitely long sequence of numbers after the decimal point, which is why we usually use the approximation of 3.14.

The existence of the constant pi means that we can use it in formulae about circles. In this unit you will learn two formulae that are used with circles.

The first formula, $C = \pi d$, you use to find the circumference of a circle.

The second formula, $A = \pi r^2$, you use to find the area of a circle.

It is thought that the number pi was used by the ancient Egyptians and Babylonians in about 1900 BCE. However, it is the ancient Greek mathematician Archimedes of Syracuse (287–212 BCE) who is largely thought to be the first to calculate an accurate estimation of the value of pi.

The Welsh mathematician William Jones was the first to use the Greek letter π to represent the number. Jones was born on the Isle of Anglesey in North Wales. In 1706 Jones published his now famous book, *Synopsis palmariorum mathesios*, in which the symbol π was used.

You may have a π button on your calculator, but in this unit you will use a common approximation for π, which is 3.14.

In this unit you will use the formulae for the circumference and area of a circle. You will also learn how to work out the areas of triangles, parallelograms and trapeziums, as well as surface areas and volumes of solid shapes.

17.1 The area of a triangle

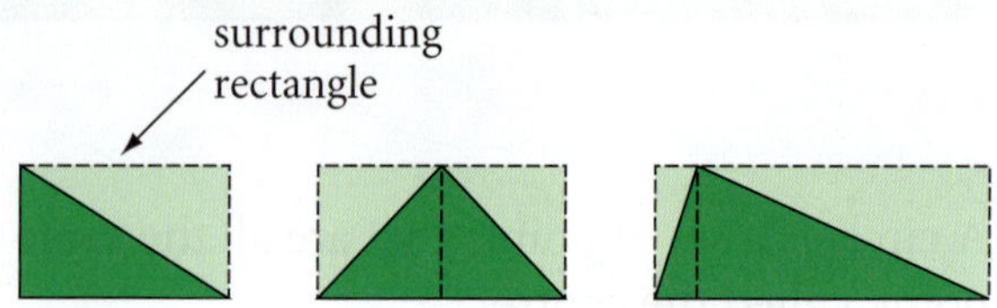

The area of a triangle is always half of the area of the rectangle that surrounds it, as these diagrams show.

You find the area of a rectangle by multiplying the base by the height. So, the area of a triangle will be a half of the base multiplied by the height.

You can write the formula as: area = $\frac{1}{2} \times$ base $\times$ height

or simply: $A = \frac{1}{2}bh$

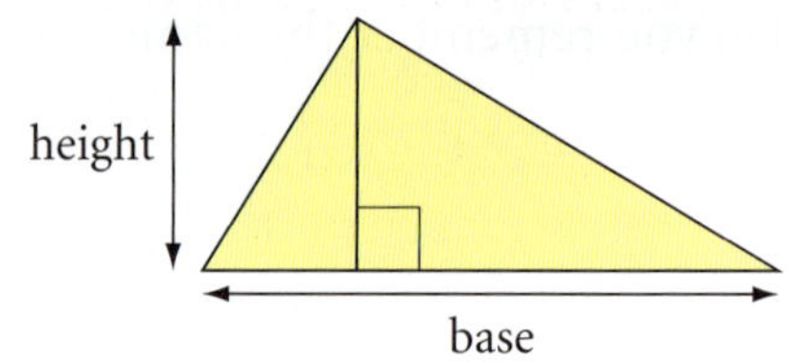

Note that the height measurement of the triangle <u>must</u> be the **perpendicular height**, from the base to the opposite vertex.

The height must be at right angles (90°) to the base.

Worked example 17.1

a Work out the area of this triangle.
b Check your answer using estimation.

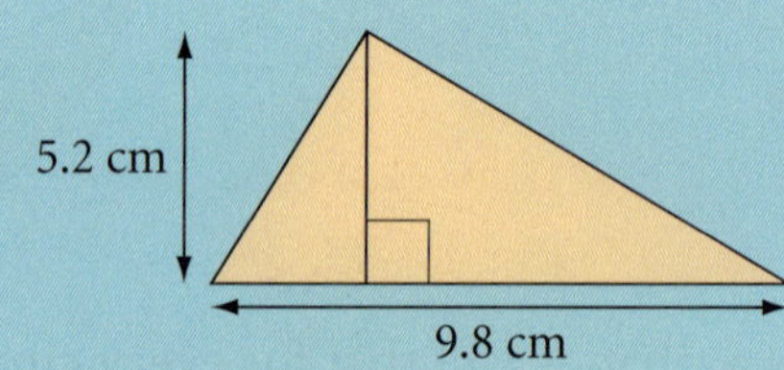

a	$A = \frac{1}{2}bh = \frac{1}{2} \times 9.8 \times 5.2$	Write down the formula, then substitute the values of b and h.
	$= 25.48\ \text{cm}^2$	Work out the answer. Remember to include the units (cm²).
b	$5.2 \rightarrow 5$ and $9.8 \rightarrow 10$	First, round the base and height to the nearest whole number.
	$A = \frac{1}{2} \times 10 \times 5 = 25\ \text{cm}^2$	Use the rounded numbers to work out an estimate of the area. 25 is close to 25.48, so the accurate answer is probably correct.

Exercise 17.1

1 **a** Work out the areas of each triangle.

i

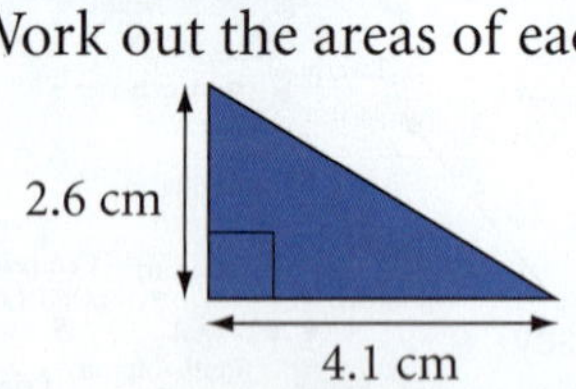

ii

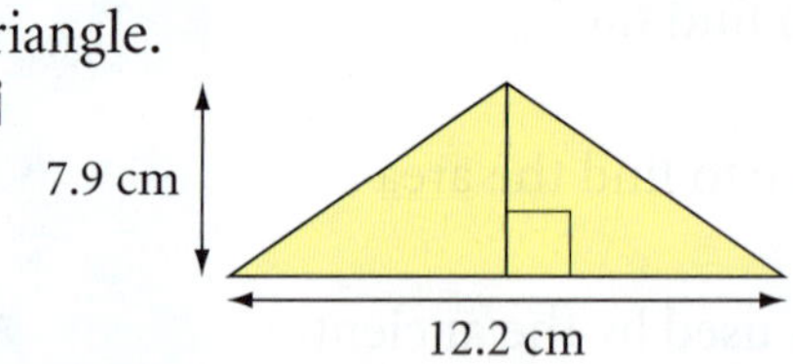

iii

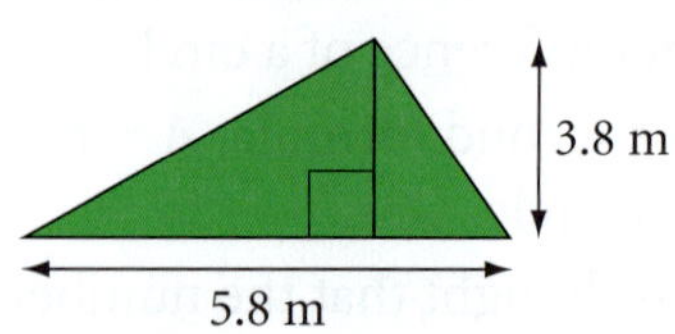

b Use estimation to check each answer in part **a**.

2 The length of the base of a triangle is 8.2 cm.
The area of the triangle is 39.77 cm².
Shen works out that the perpendicular height of the triangle is 7.9 cm.

a Without using a calculator, explain how you can tell that Shen is wrong.
b Work out the perpendicular height of the triangle.
c What mistake do you think Shen made?

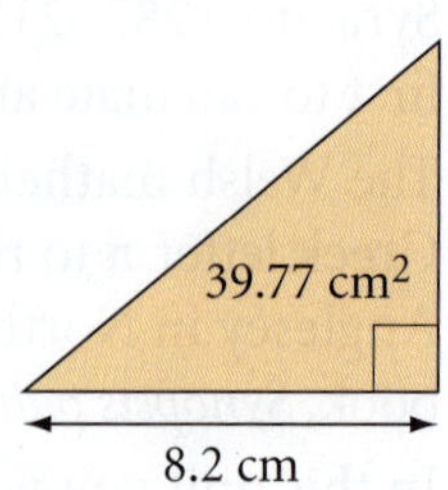

17.2 The areas of a parallelogram and trapezium

Look at this parallelogram.

Imagine you cut off the triangle from the left end of the parallelogram and moved it to the right end. You would have made a rectangle.

So the area of the parallelogram is the same as the area of the rectangle with the same base and height.

You can write the formula for the area of a parallelogram as:

area = base × height

or simply $A = bh$

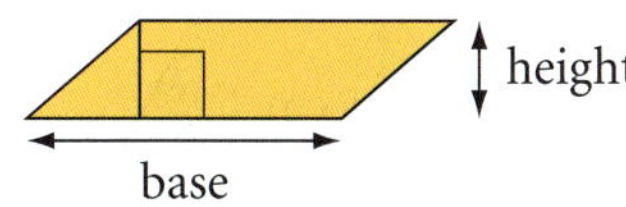

Note that the height measurement of the parallelogram must be the perpendicular height.

Now look at this trapezium.
The lengths of its parallel sides are a and b.

Its perpendicular height is h.

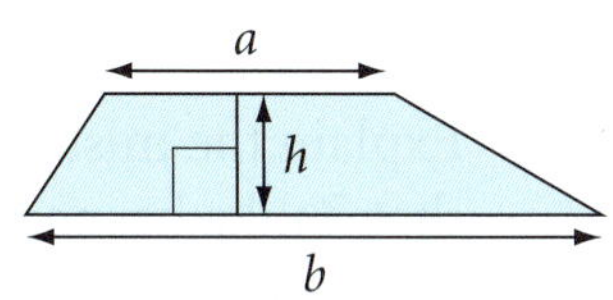

Two trapezia can be put together like this to make a parallelogram with a base length of $(a + b)$ and a height h.

The area of the parallelogram is:
area = base × height = $(a + b) \times h$

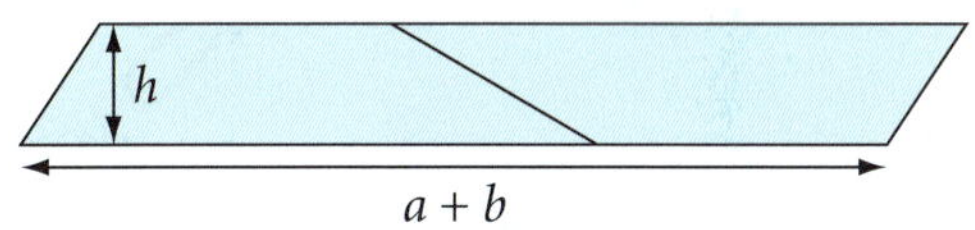

The area of one trapezium is half the area of the parallelogram.

So, the area of a trapezium is: $A = \frac{1}{2} \times (a + b) \times h$

Note again, that the height measurement of the trapezium must be the perpendicular height.

'Trapezia' is the plural of trapezium.

Worked example 17.2

Work out the area of each shape.

a

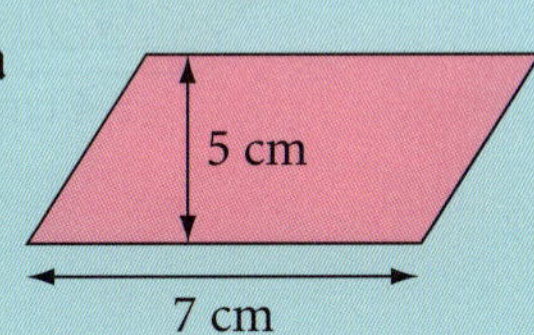

b

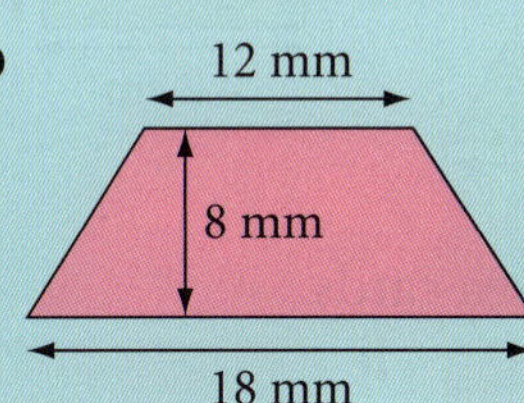

a	$A = bh = 7 \times 5$	Write down the formula, then substitute for b and h.
	$= 35\ \text{cm}^2$	Work out the answer, and remember to include the units (cm^2).
b	$A = \frac{1}{2} \times (a + b) \times h$	Write down the formula.
	$= \frac{1}{2} \times (12 + 18) \times 8$	Substitute the values of a, b and h.
	$= \frac{1}{2} \times 30 \times 8$	Work out 12 + 18 = 30 first, then work out $\frac{1}{2}$ of 30 = 15.
	$= 15 \times 8$	Finally work out 15 × 8.
	$= 120\ \text{mm}^2$	Remember to include the units (mm^2) with your answer.

Exercise 17.2

1 Work out the area of these parallelograms.

a 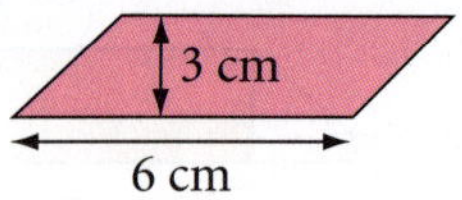

b 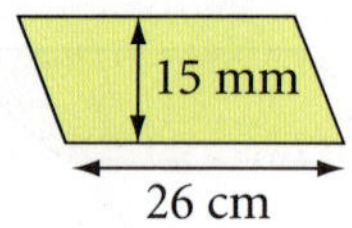

c 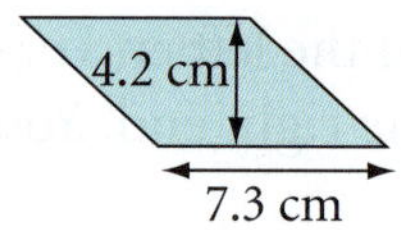

2 Work out the area of each trapezium.

a 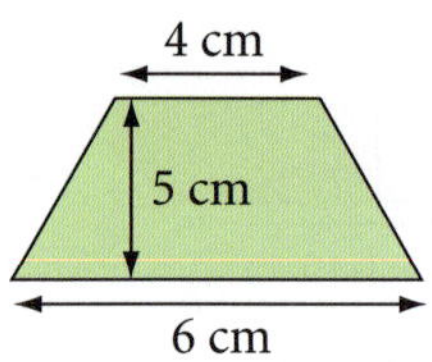

b 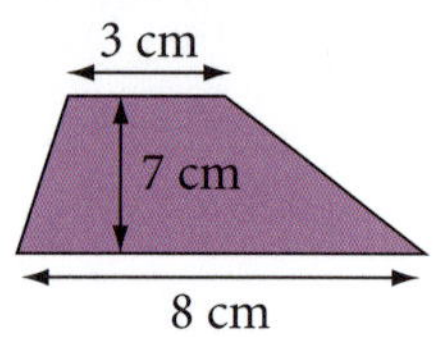

c 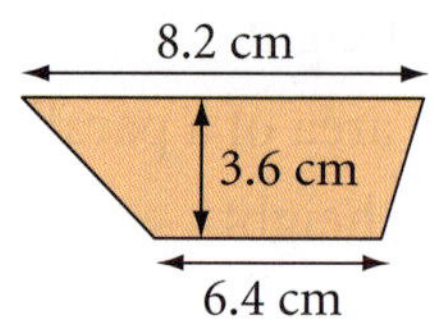

3 This is part of Zalika's homework.

a Explain the mistake that Zalika has made.

b Work out the correct answer for her.

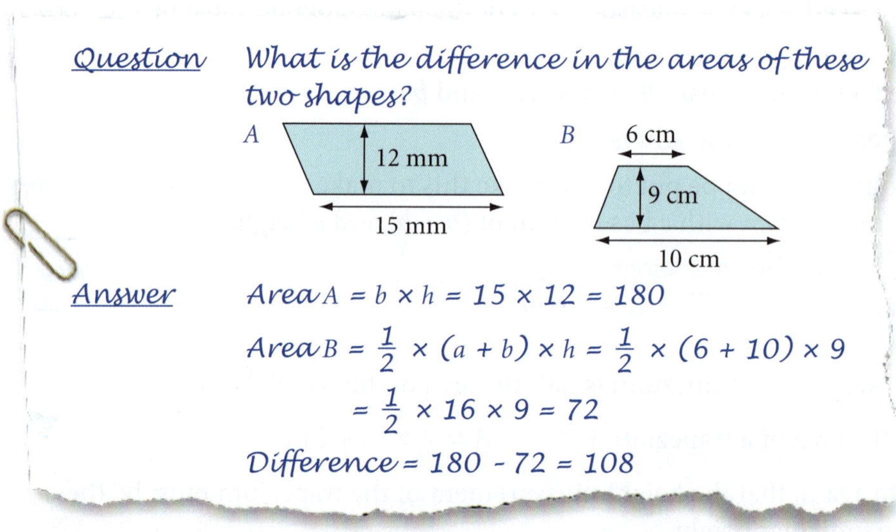

Question — What is the difference in the areas of these two shapes?

A: 12 mm, 15 mm

B: 6 cm, 9 cm, 10 cm

Answer — Area A = $b \times h = 15 \times 12 = 180$

Area B = $\frac{1}{2} \times (a + b) \times h = \frac{1}{2} \times (6 + 10) \times 9$

$= \frac{1}{2} \times 16 \times 9 = 72$

Difference = $180 - 72 = 108$

4 Here are four shapes A, B, C and D.

A 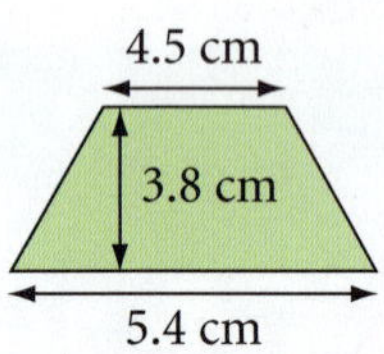

B 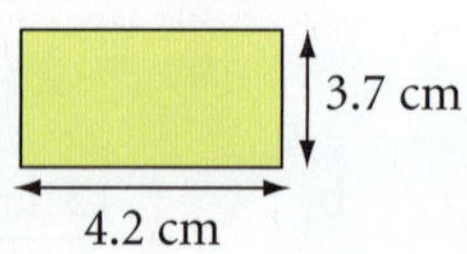

C 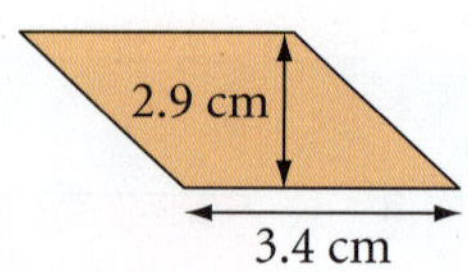

D 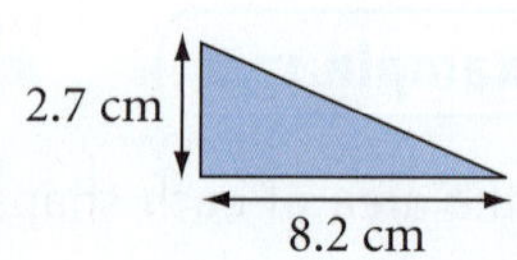

Here are five area cards.

i 9.86 cm^2 **ii** 18.81 cm^2 **iii** 24.48 cm^2 **iv** 15.54 cm^2 **v** 11.07 cm^2

a Using only estimation, match each shape to its area card.

b Use a calculator to check that you have matched the shapes and the area cards correctly.

c Sketch a shape that has an area equal to the area on the card you haven't matched.

5 A parallelogram has an area of 832 mm^2.
It has a perpendicular height of 2.6 cm.
What is the length of the base of the parallelogram?

6 A trapezium has an area of 1500 mm^2.
The lengths of its parallel sides are 4.8 cm and 5.2 cm.
What is the perpendicular height of the trapezium?

17.3 The area and circumference of a circle

The circumference of a circle is the path of points that are all the same distance from the centre.

You can work out the length of the circumference (perimeter) of a circle, with the formulae:

$C = \pi d$ where C is the circumference and d is the diameter of the circle.

You can also use:

$C = 2\pi r$ where C is the circumference and r is the radius of the circle.

Remember that diameter = 2 × radius, which is why there are two versions of the formula.

The one you use depends on the information you are given.

- When you are told the diameter, use $C = \pi d$.
- When you are told the radius, use $C = 2\pi r$.

From the rules of algebra:
$C = \pi d$ means $C = \pi \times d$
$C = 2\pi r$ means $C = 2 \times \pi \times r$

You can work out the area of a circle, with the formula:

$A = \pi r^2$ where A is the area and r is the radius of the circle.

In the area formula you must use the radius.

When you are told the diameter, calculate the radius (radius = diameter ÷ 2), then use the formula.

From the rules of algebra:
$A = \pi r^2$ means $A = \pi \times r^2$
$r^2 = r \times r$
A common mistake is to work out r^2 as $r \times 2$ instead of $r \times r$.

Worked example 17.3

Work out: **i** the circumference **ii** the area of a circle with **a** radius 4 cm **b** diameter 3 m.

Use $\pi = 3.14$ and round your answers correct to 1 decimal place (1 d.p.).

a i $C = 2\pi r$ — You are given the radius, so write down the formula you are going to use.
$= 2 \times \pi \times 4$ — Substitute $r = 4$ into the formula. You don't need to write 3.14 for π.
$= 25.12$ — Work out the answer.
$= 25.1$ cm — Round your answer correct to 1 d.p. and remember to write the units, cm.

ii $A = \pi r^2$ — Start by writing down the formula you are going to use.
$= \pi \times 4^2$ — Substitute $r = 4$ into the formula. You don't need to write 3.14 for π.
$= \pi \times 16$ — Work out 4^2 first.
$= 50.24$ — Work out the answer.
$= 50.2\ \text{cm}^2$ — Round your answer correct to 1 d.p. and remember to write the units, cm².

b i $C = \pi d$ — You are told the diameter so write down the formula you are going to use.
$= \pi \times 3$ — Substitute $d = 3$ into the formula.
$= 9.42$ — Work out the answer.
$= 9.4$ m — Round your answer correct to 1 d.p. and remember to write the units, m.

ii $A = \pi r^2$ — Start by writing down the formula you are going to use.
$r = d \div 2$ — You know the diameter, but you need the radius, so work out the radius first.
$= 3 \div 2 = 1.5$
$A = \pi \times 1.5^2$ — Substitute $r = 1.5$ into the formula.
$= \pi \times 2.25$ — Work out 1.5^2 first.
$= 7.065$ — Work out the answer.
$= 7.1\ \text{m}^2$ — Round your answer correct to 1 d.p. and remember to write the units, m².

Exercise 17.3

1 Work out the circumference of each circle.
Use $\pi = 3.14$. Round your answers correct to 1 d.p.

a radius = 6 cm **b** radius = 5 m **c** radius = 12 cm
d diameter = 14 cm **e** diameter = 9 m **f** diameter = 3.5 m

2 Work out the area of each circle.
Use $\pi = 3.14$. Do not round your answer.

a radius = 3 cm **b** radius = 7 m **c** radius = 2.5 cm
d diameter = 18 cm **e** diameter = 11 m **f** diameter = 6.4 m

3 This is part of Ahmad's homework.
Use Ahmad's method to work out
i the perimeter
ii the area of a semicircle with:
a diameter = 20 cm
b diameter = 15 m
c radius = 8 cm
d radius = 6.5 m
e diameter = 8.6 cm
f radius = 3.2 mm.
Use $\pi = 3.14$.
Round your answers correct to 1 d.p.

Question Work out the perimeter and area of this semicircle.

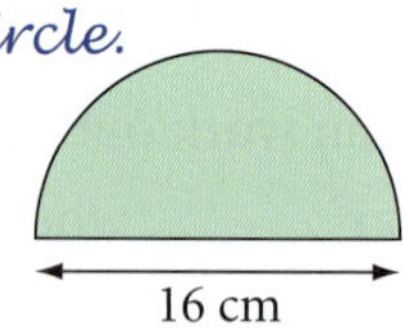

Answer

Perimeter = half of circumference + diameter
$= \frac{1}{2} \times \pi \times d + d$
$= \frac{1}{2} \times \pi \times 16 + 16$
$= 25.12 + 16 = 41.12$ cm

Area = half of area of circle
$= \frac{1}{2} \times \pi \times r^2$
$= \frac{1}{2} \times \pi \times 8^2$
$= \frac{1}{2} \times \pi \times 64$
$= 100.48\ \text{cm}^2$

4 The diagram shows a semicircle and a quarter of a circle.
Read what Xavier says.

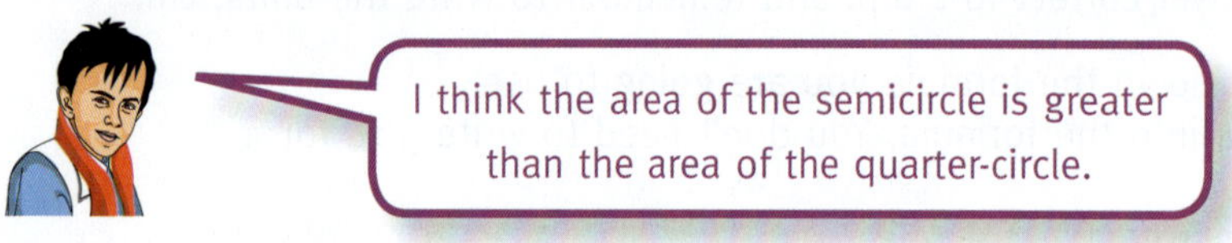

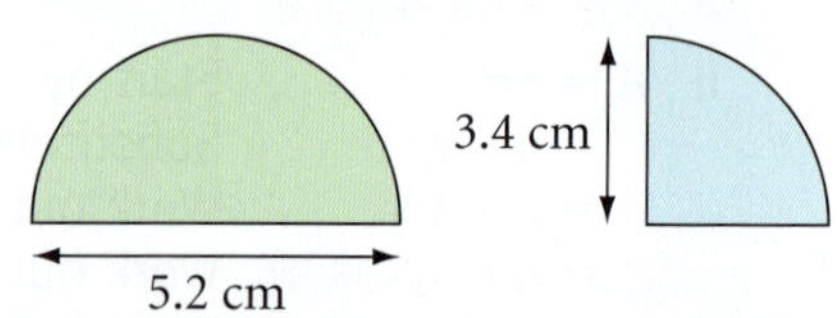

Is he correct? Show working to support your answer.

5 The diagram shows a semicircle and a quarter of a circle.
Read what Tanesha says.

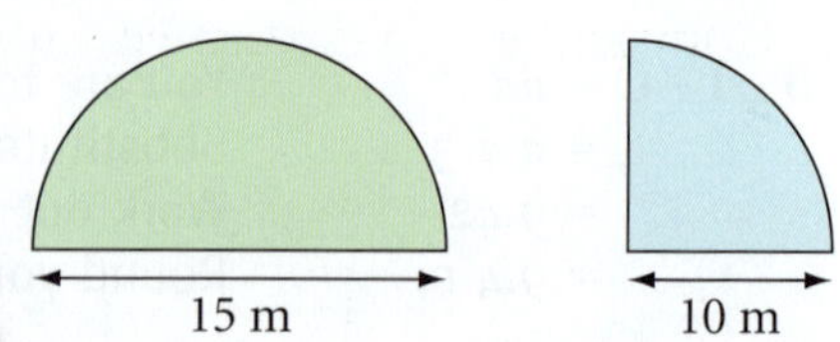

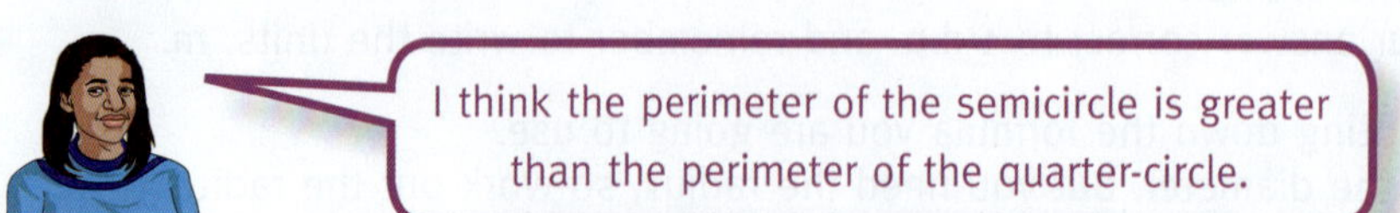

Is Tanesha correct? Show working to support your answer.

17.4 The areas of compound shapes

You can already work out the areas of simple shapes such as rectangles, triangles, parallelograms, trapezia and circles.

A **compound shape** is a shape that is made up of simple shapes.

Use this method to work out the area of a compound shape.

1 Divide the compound shapes into simple shapes.
2 Work out the area of each simple shape.
3 Add or subtract the areas of the simple shapes to get the area you need.

Worked example 17.4

Work out the areas of these shapes.

a

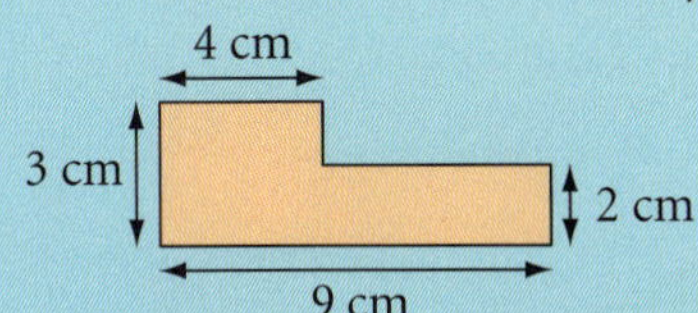

b

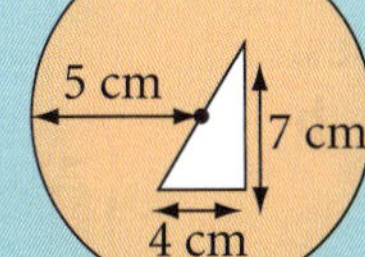

a

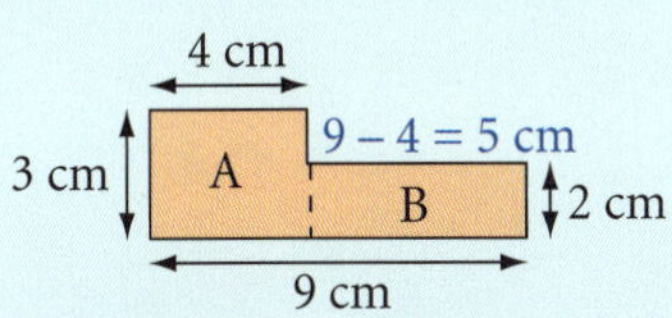

Divide the shape into two rectangles, A and B. You know the length and width of rectangle A. You know the width of rectangle B, but not the length, so start by working out 9 − 4 = 5 cm.

Area A = $l \times w$ = 3 × 4 = 12 cm^2 — Work out the area of rectangle A.

Area B = $l \times w$ = 2 × 5 = 10 cm^2 — Work out the area of rectangle B.

Total area = 12 + 10 = 22 cm^2 — Add together the areas of the rectangles to get the area of the compound shape.

b Area of circle = $\pi r^2 = \pi \times 5^2$ = 78.5 cm^2 — Work out the area of the circle. Use π = 3.14.

Area of triangle = $\frac{1}{2}bh = \frac{1}{2} \times 4 \times 7$ = 14 cm^2 — Work out the area of the triangle.

Shaded area = 78.5 − 14 = 64.5 cm^2 — The orange-shaded area is the area of the circle minus the area of the triangle.

Exercise 17.4

1 Copy and complete the working to calculate the areas of these compound shapes.

a

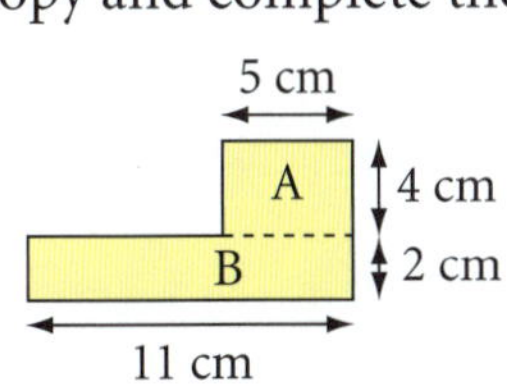

Area A = $l \times w = 5 \times \square = \square$

Area B = $l \times w = 11 \times \square = \square$

Total area = $\square + \square = \square$ cm^2

b

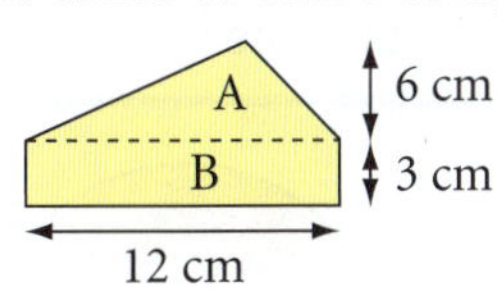

Area A = $\frac{1}{2} \times b \times h = \frac{1}{2} \times 12 \times 6 = \square$

Area B = $l \times w = \square \times \square = \square$

Total area = $\square + \square = \square$ cm^2

2 For each of these compound shapes, work out:
 i the missing lengths shown by □
 ii the area of the shape.

a

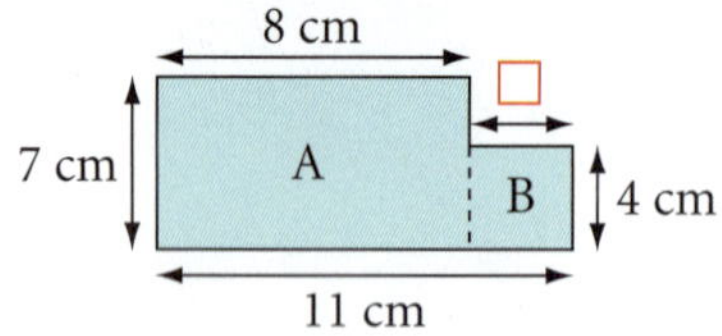

b

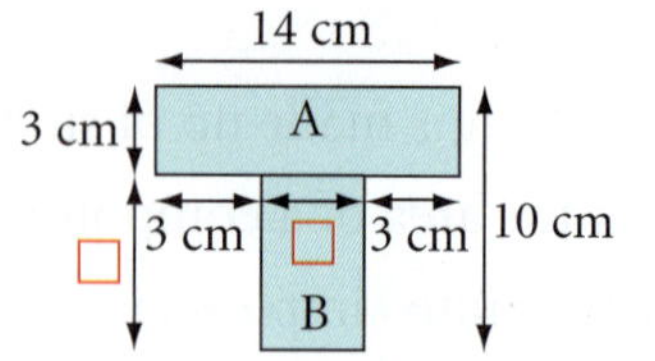

c

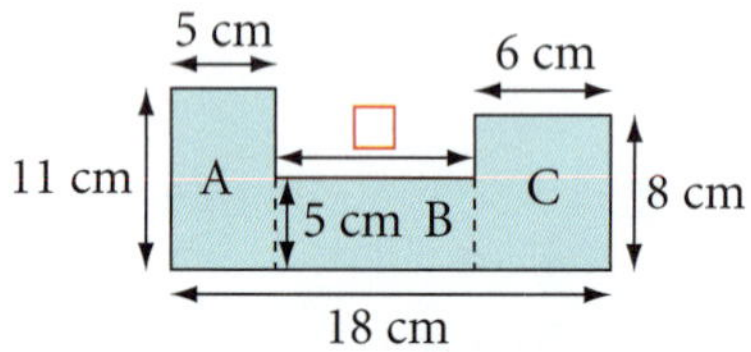

d

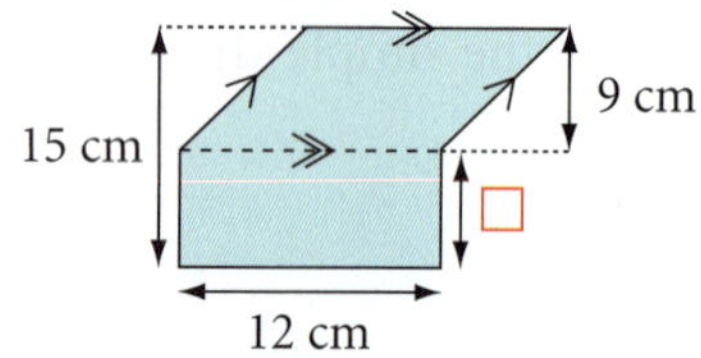

3 Work out the areas of these compound shapes.

a

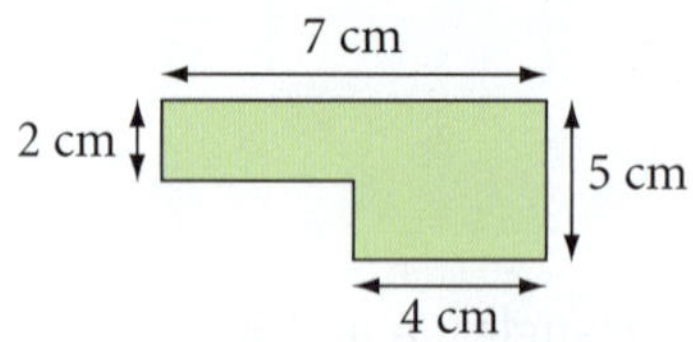

b

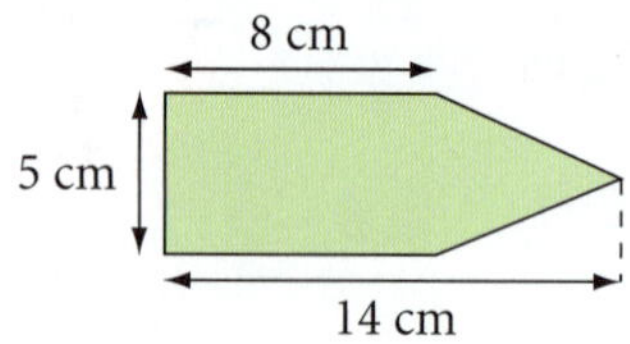

c

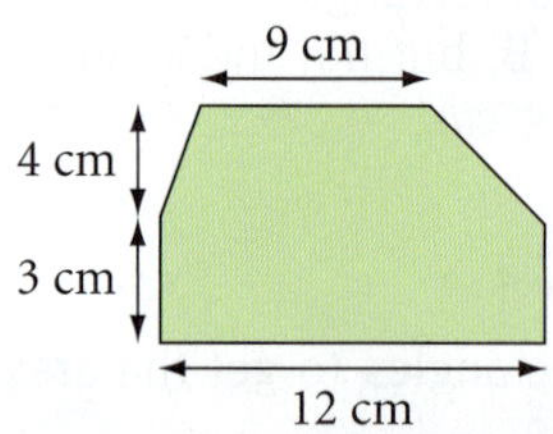

d

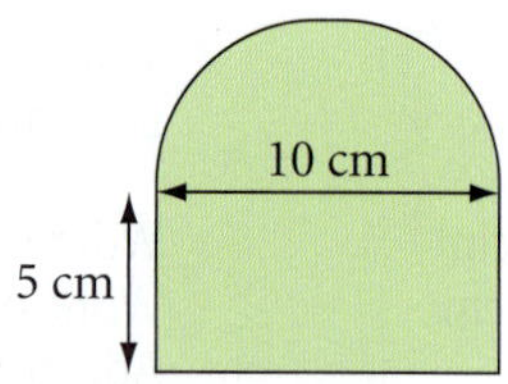

4 Work out the area of each shaded region.

a

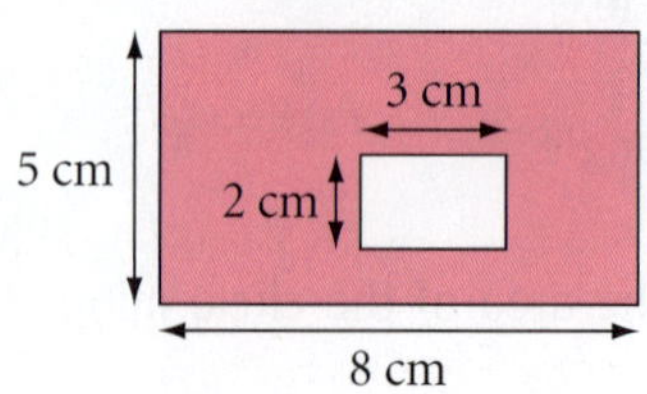

b

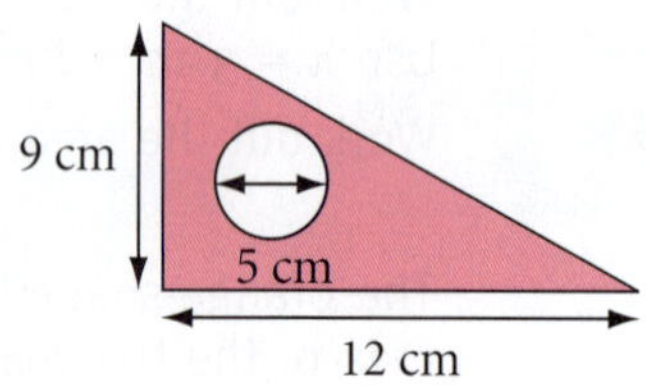

c

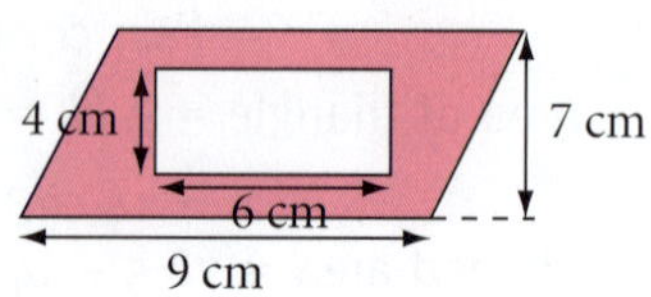

5 Razi draws these two shapes.
Read what Razi says.

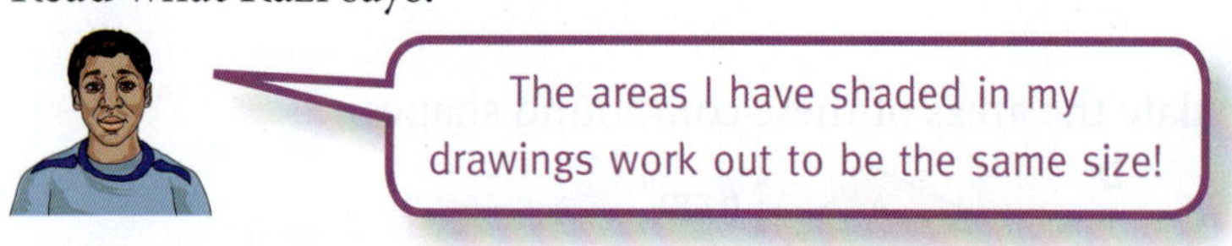

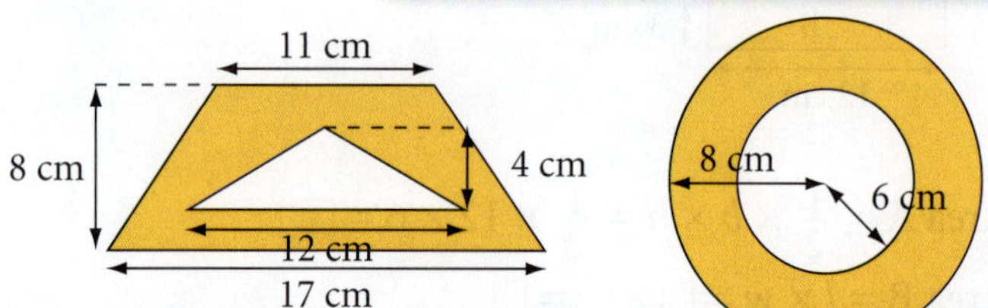

Is Razi correct? Show clearly how your worked out your answer.

17.5 The volumes and surface areas of cuboids

Do you remember the formulae for the volume and surface area of a cuboid?

For a cuboid with length l, width w and height h:

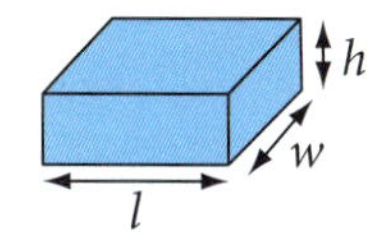

volume = length × width × height

or $V = lwh$

surface area = 2 × length × width + 2 × length × height + 2 × width × height

or $SA = 2lw + 2lh + 2wh$

Remember: when you use these formulae, the measurements for length, width and height must be in the same units.

Worked example 17.5

a Work out the volume and surface area of this cuboid.

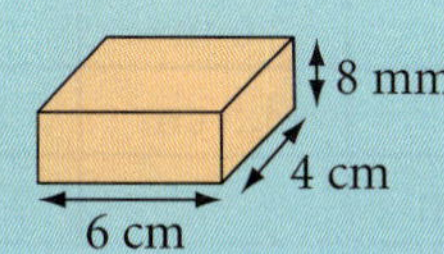

b A cuboid has a volume of 60 cm³.
The length of the cuboid is 5 cm.
The height of the cuboid is 4 cm.
Work out the width of the cuboid.

a 8 mm = 0.8 cm — The height of the cuboid is given in mm. Change this to cm so that all the measurements are in the same units.

$V = l \times w \times h$ — Write down the formula you are going to use for the volume.

$V = 6 \times 4 \times 0.8$ — Substitute the numbers into the formula.

$= 19.2\ \text{cm}^3$ — Work out the answer and remember the units (cm³).

$SA = 2lw + 2lh + 2wh$ — Write down the formula you are going to use for the surface area.

$= 2 \times 6 \times 4 + 2 \times 6 \times 0.8 + 2 \times 4 \times 0.8$ — Substitute the numbers into the formula.

$= 48 + 9.6 + 6.4$ — Work out all the multiplications.

$= 64\ \text{cm}^2$ — Work out the answer and remember the units (cm²).

b $V = l \times w \times h$ — Write down the formula you are going to use for the volume.

$60 = 5 \times w \times 4$ — Substitute the numbers that you know into the formula to make an equation, with w as the unknown.

$60 = 20 \times w$ — Simplify the right-hand side of the equation; $5 \times 4 = 20$.

$w = \frac{60}{20} = 3\ \text{cm}$ — Divide 60 by 20 to work out the value of w. Remember to include the units (cm) in your answer.

Exercise 17.5

1 Work out the volume of each cuboid.

a

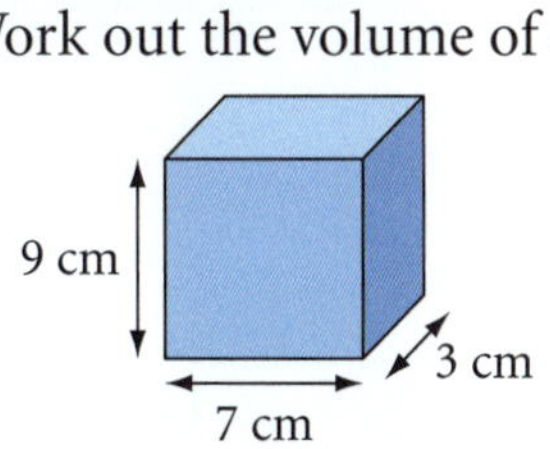

b

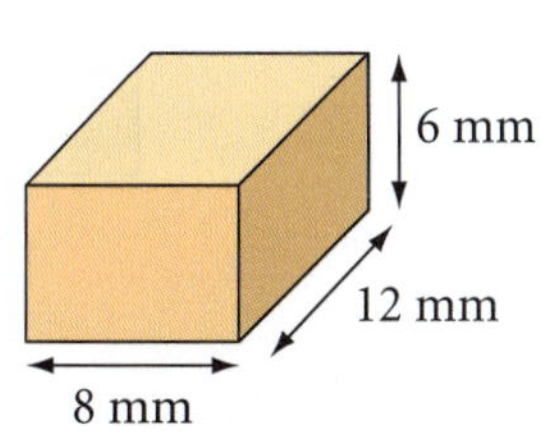

c

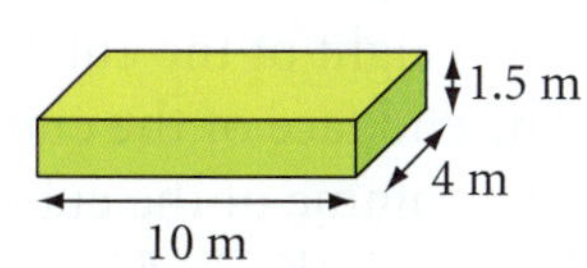

2 Work out the surface areas of the cuboids in question **1**.

3 Work out the volume of each cuboid.

a
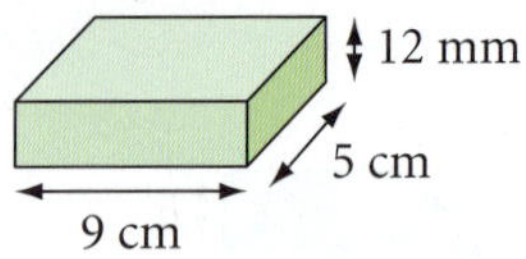

b
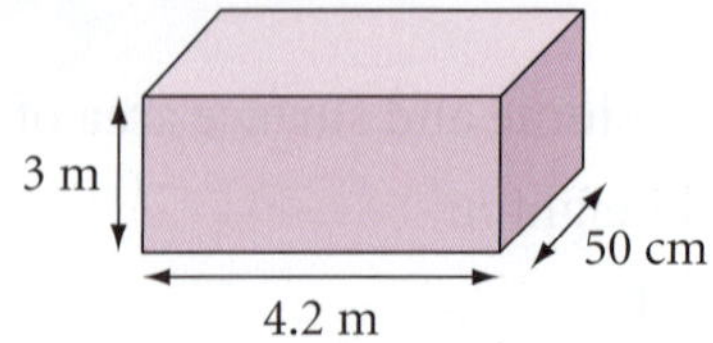

c
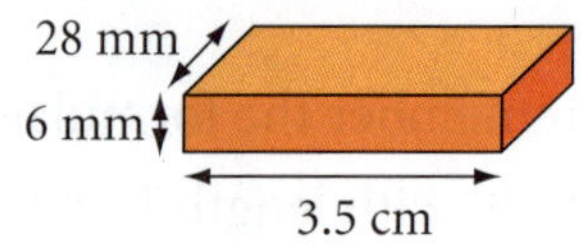

4 Work out the surface areas of the cuboids in question **3**.

5 The table shows the volume and dimensions of some cuboids.

	Length	Width	Height	Volume
a	4 cm	8 cm	7 cm	
b	10 cm	5 cm		300 cm^3
c	12 mm		6 mm	648 mm^3
d		2 m	6 m	96 m^3
e	4.2 cm		3.5 cm	14.7 cm^3
f	3.6 cm	5 mm		2160 mm^3

Copy the table and fill in the missing values.

6 Here are three cuboids A, B and C.

A
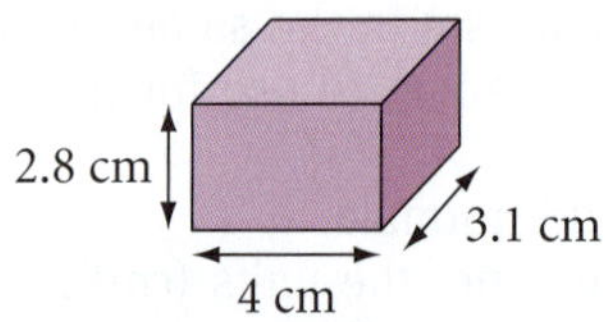

B
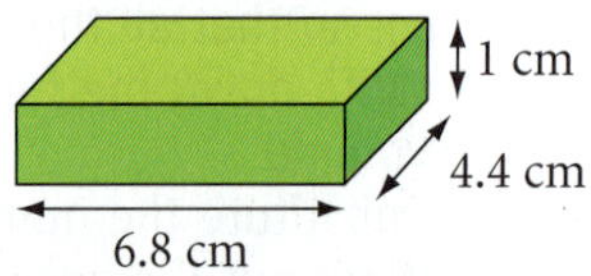

C
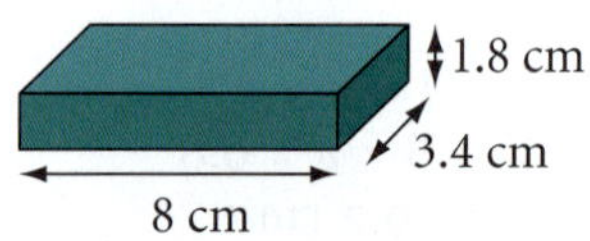

Here are four volume cards.

i 48.96 cm^2 **ii** 34.72 cm^2 **iii** 24.24 cm^2 **iv** 29.92 cm^2

a Using only estimation match each cuboid to its volume card.
b Use a calculator to check that you have matched the cuboids and the volume cards correctly.
c Sketch a cuboid that has a volume equal to the volume on the card you haven't matched.

7 The diagram shows a cuboid.
The length of the cuboid is 14 cm.
The width of the cuboid is 8 cm.
The volume of the cuboid is 672 cm^3.
Work out the surface area of the cuboid.

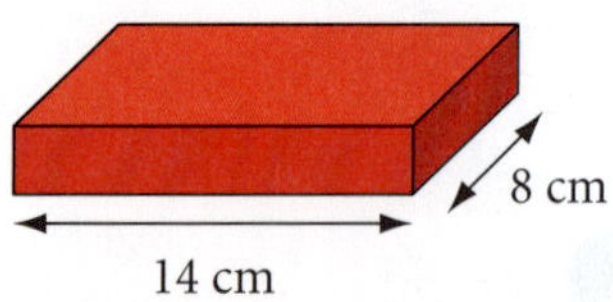

8 The diagram shows a cuboid.
The height of the cuboid is 45 mm.
The end face of the cuboid is a square.
The volume of the cuboid is 162 cm^3.
Work out the surface area of the cuboid.

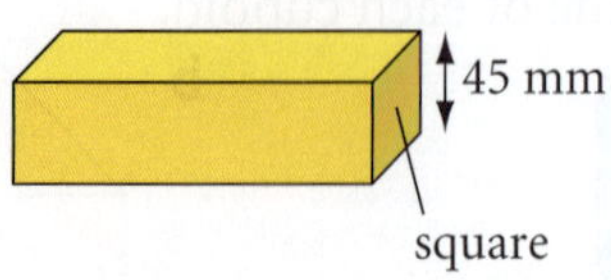

17.6 Using nets of solids to work out surface areas

You learned how to draw the nets of some 3D solids in Unit 8.
You can use the net of a 3D solid to help you work out its surface area.

> The surface area of a solid is the total area of all its faces.

Worked example 17.6

The diagram shows a triangular prism.

a Sketch a net of the prism.
b Work out the surface area of the prism.

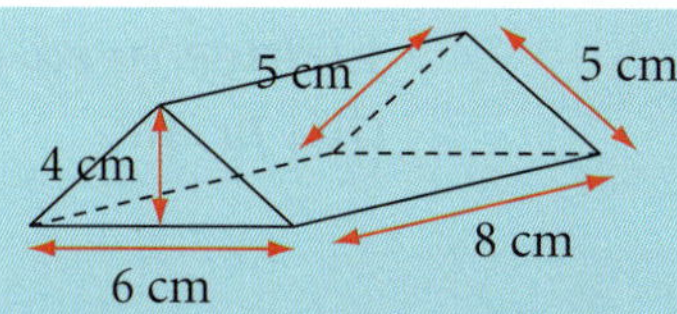

a

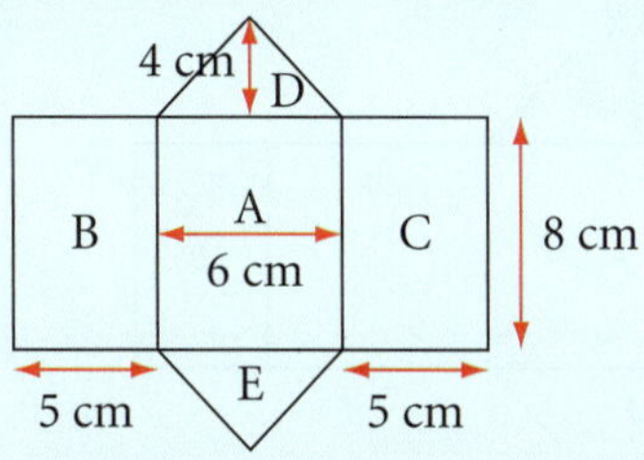

The prism has a rectangular base (A), measuring 8 cm by 6 cm.
It has two rectangular faces (B and C) that measure 8 cm by 5 cm.
It has two triangular faces (D and E), each with a base length of 6 cm and a perpendicular height of 4 cm.

b Area A = $l \times w = 8 \times 6$
$= 48\text{ cm}^2$ — Work out the area of rectangle A.

Area B = $l \times w = 8 \times 5$
$= 40\text{ cm}^2$ — Work out the area of rectangle B. Note that C has the same area as B.

Area D = $\frac{1}{2}bh = \frac{1}{2} \times 6 \times 4$
$= 12\text{ cm}^2$ — Work out the area of triangle D. Note that E has the same area as D.

Total area $= 48 + 40 \times 2 + 12 \times 2$ — Remember to include 40×2 and 12×2.
$= 48 + 80 + 24$ — Add the areas together.
$= 152\text{ cm}^2$ — Remember the units (cm^2).

Exercise 17.6

1 For each of these solids:
  i sketch a net
  ii work out the surface area.

  a triangular prism (isosceles)

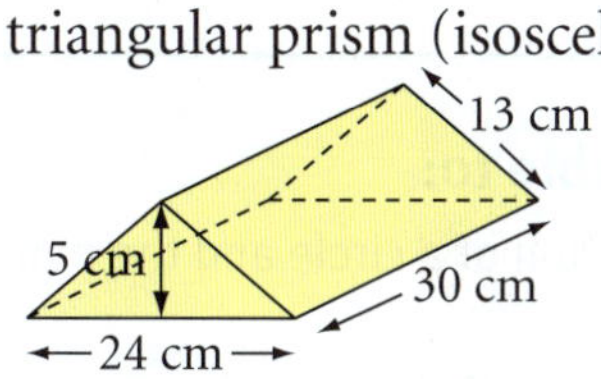

  b triangular prism (right-angled triangle)

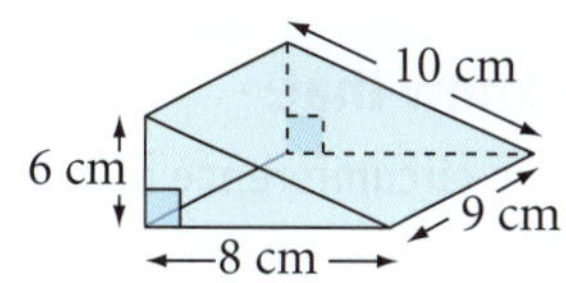

  c square-based pyramid (all triangles equal in size)

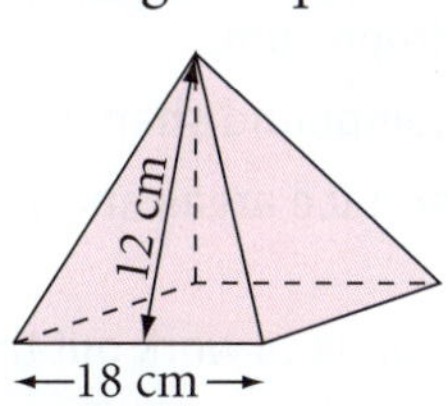

  d triangular-based pyramid (all triangles equal in size)

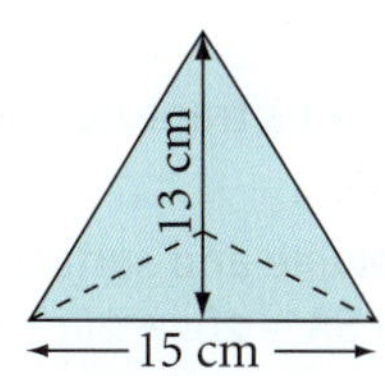

2 This is part of Dakarai's homework.
Dakarai has made several mistakes.

a Explain the mistakes that Dakarai has made.

b Work out the correct answer for him.

Question Work out the surface area of this prism.

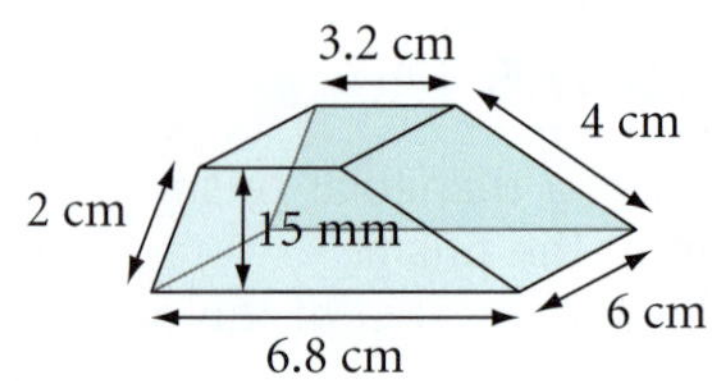

Answer

Area A = $2 \times 6.8 = 13.6\ cm^2$

Area B = $6 \times 6.8 = 40.8\ cm^2$

Area C = $4 \times 6.8 = 27.2\ cm^2$

Area D = $3.2 \times 6.8 = 21.76\ cm^2$

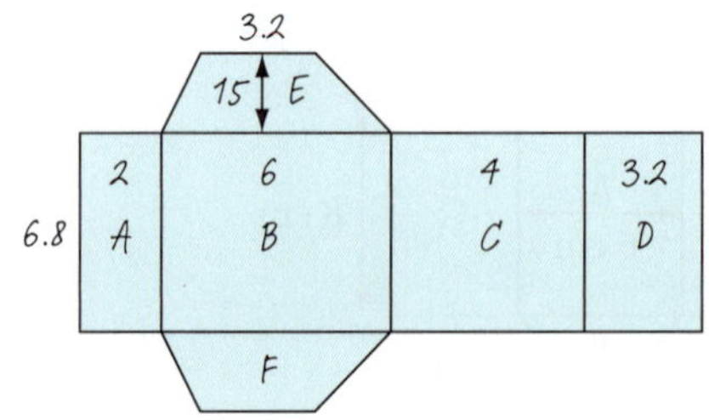

Area E = $\frac{1}{2} \times (3.2 + 6) \times 15$

$= \frac{1}{2} \times 9.2 \times 15 = 69\ cm^2$

Area F = area E

Total surface area = $13.6 + 40.8 + 27.2 + 21.76 + 69 = 172.36\ cm^2$

3 Mia draws a cube of side length 48 mm.
She also draws a triangular prism with the dimensions shown.
Mia thinks that the cube and the triangular prism have the same surface area.
Is Mia correct? Show clearly how you worked out your answer.

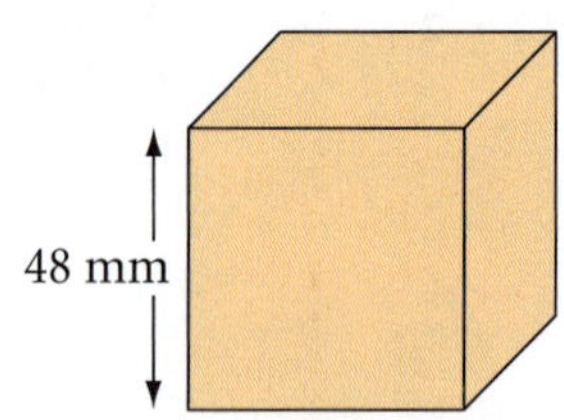

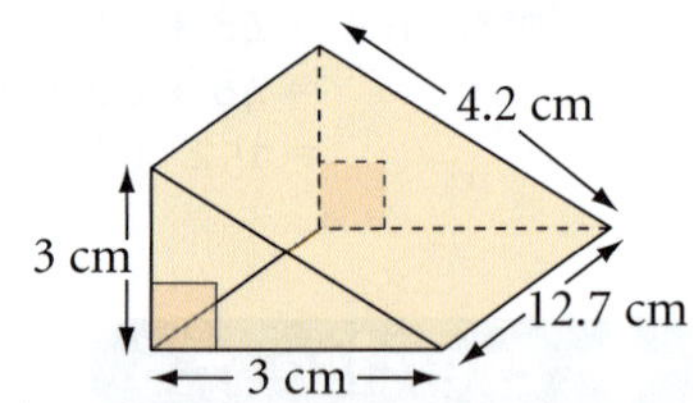

Summary

You should now know that:

★ The formula for the circumference of a circle is $C = \pi d$ or $C = 2\pi r$.

★ The formula for the area of a circle is $A = \pi r^2$.

★ The formula for the area of a triangle is $A = \frac{1}{2}bh$.

★ The formula for the area of a parallelogram is $A = bh$.

★ The formula for the area of a trapezium is $A = \frac{1}{2} \times (a + b) \times h$.

★ The formulae for the volume and surface area of a cuboid are $V = lwh$ and $SA = 2lw + 2lh + 2wh$.

You should be able to:

★ Know the definition of a circle and the names of its parts.

★ Know and use formulae for the circumference and area of a circle.

★ Derive and use formulae for the area of a triangle, parallelogram and trapezium.

★ Calculate areas of compound shapes.

★ Calculate lengths, surface areas and volumes of cuboids.

★ Use simple nets of solids to work out their surface areas.

End-of-unit review

1 Work out the area of each of these shapes.

a

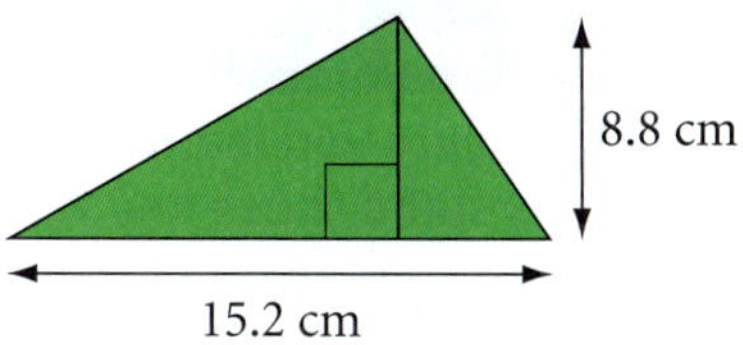

b

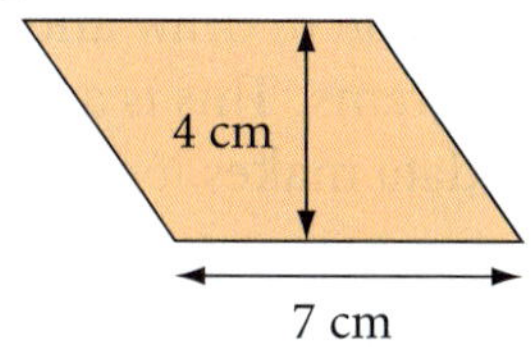

c

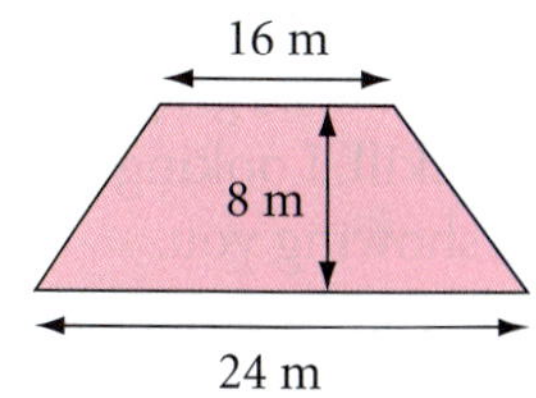

2 Work out: **i** the circumference **ii** the area of these circles.

a radius = 4 cm **b** diameter = 12 cm

Use $\pi = 3.14$.

Round your answers correct to 1 d.p.

3 Show how you would check your answers to question **1**, using a single number instead of π.

4 A circular tile has a circumference of 48.2 cm.
Work out the diameter of the tile.
Give your answer correct to the nearest millimetre.

5 Work out the area of each of these compound shapes.

a

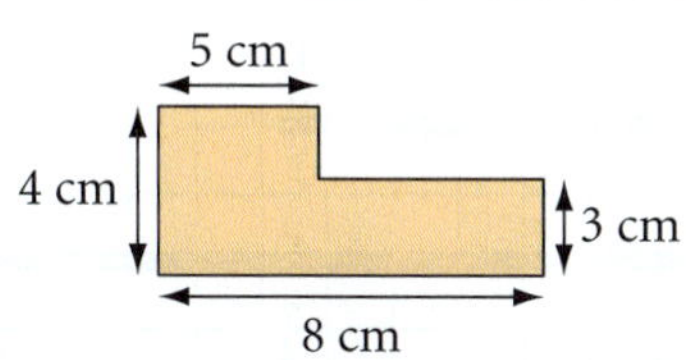

b

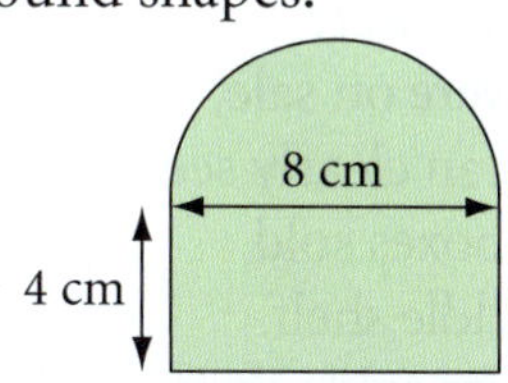

6 Work out the area of the pink-shaded region.

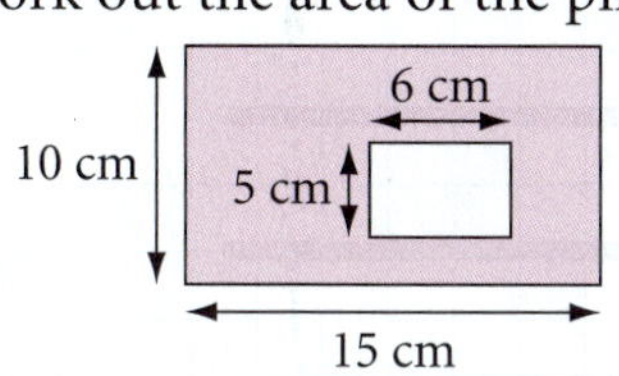

7 Work out:

a the volume

b the surface area of this cuboid.

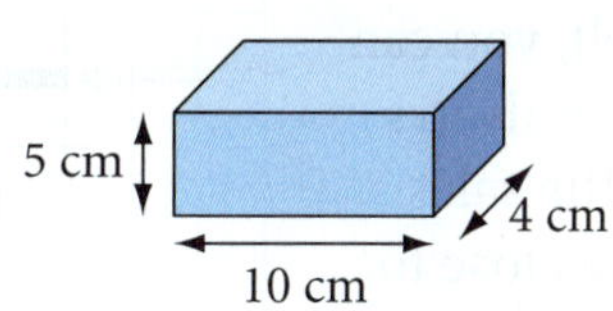

8 The diagram shows a cuboid.
The height of the cuboid is 1.2 cm.
The end face of the cuboid is a square.
The volume of the cuboid is 5760 mm^3.
Work out the surface area of the cuboid.

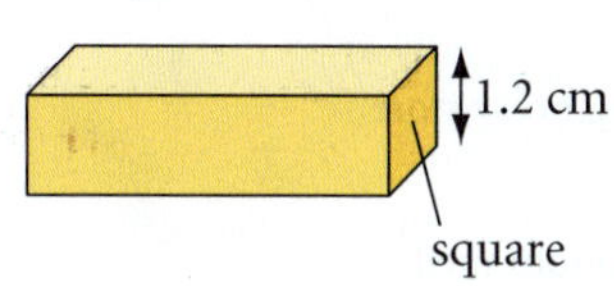

9 **a** Sketch the net of this shape.

b Use your net to work out the surface area.

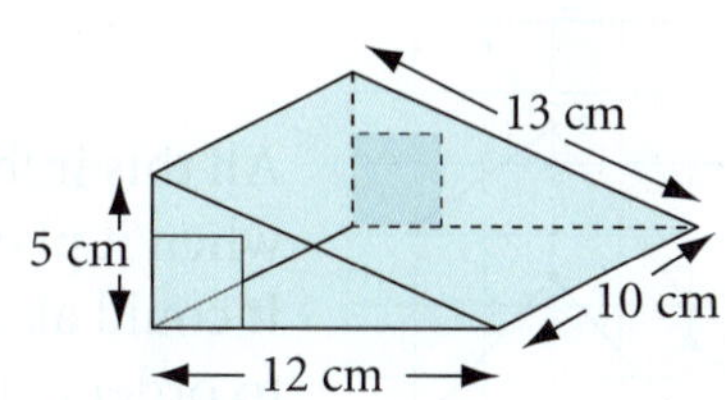

18 Interpreting and discussing results

When you study statistics, you need to be able to draw and understand charts, graphs, tables and diagrams. This is a very important skill. Looking at a 'picture' of data makes it easier to see what it is showing you.

Key words

Make sure you learn and understand these key words:

line graph
trend
stem-and-leaf diagram

For example, look at the table on the right. It shows the number of boxes of breakfast cereal sold at a grocery store each month from January to June. It also shows which shelf the boxes were on when they were on sale in the store. There is a lot of information in the table but it is difficult to understand just by looking at it. However, when the data is put into a bar chart showing the total monthly sales, you can now see that May had the largest number of sales by quite a long way. Total sales in all the other months were all very similar.

Number of boxes of breakfast cereal sold						
	Jan	**Feb**	**Mar**	**Apr**	**May**	**Jun**
Top shelf	30	33	28	23	44	22
Middle shelf	32	52	46	40	65	51
Bottom shelf	26	10	20	35	24	14

Sales of breakfast cereals according to position on shelves

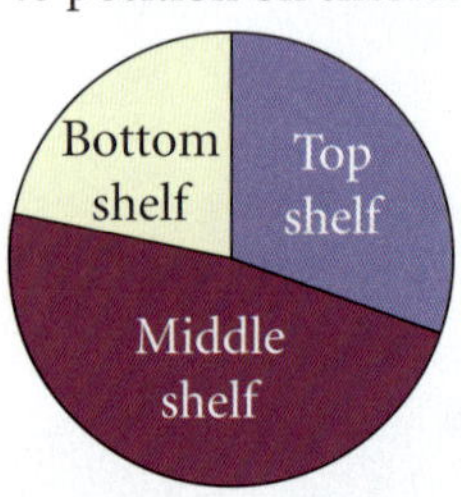

A pie chart that just shows the shelf where the cereals were placed, when they were on sale, is also helpful. You can clearly see that nearly half the boxes sold had been on the middle shelf. The fewest boxes were sold when they were on sale on the bottom shelf.

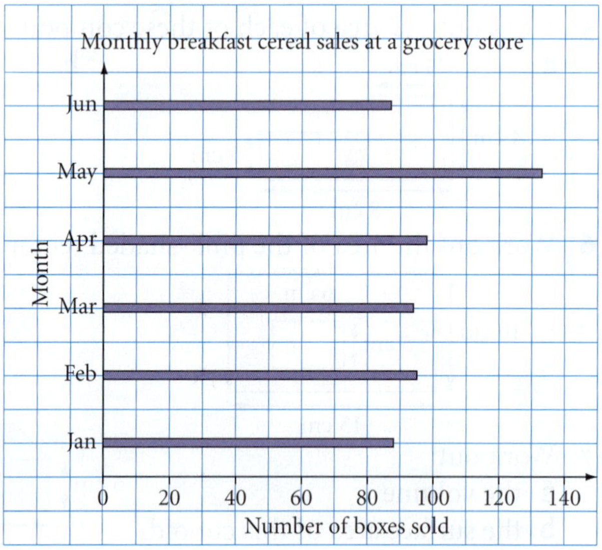

When the data is put into a line graph showing the monthly sales and the positions on the shelf, you can see that the sales from the middle shelf were always greater than sales from the other shelves. The sales from the top and bottom shelves were quite close to each other on some occasions.

Monthly breakfast cereals sales at a grocery store from May to June

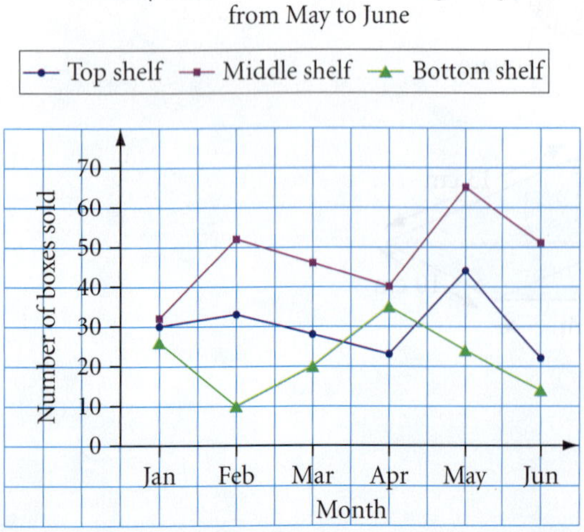

All this information could be important to a grocery store when it plans where to place items to get maximum sales. It could also help the store decide in which months it needs to order extra stock.

In this unit you will learn how to draw and interpret frequency diagrams, pie charts, line graphs and stem-and-leaf diagrams. You will also learn how to draw conclusions from data that is presented in different ways.

18.1 Interpreting and drawing frequency diagrams

Frequency diagrams show how often particular values occur in a set of data. One example of a frequency diagram is a bar chart. In bar charts, bars can be used to represent frequency.

When you draw a bar chart for discrete data you should make sure that:
- the bars are all the same width
- there is equal gap between the bars
- you write the data groups under each bar
- you give the frequency diagram a title and label the axes
- you use a sensible scale on the vertical axis.

When you draw a bar chart for continuous data you should make sure that:
- the bars are all the same width
- there are no gaps between the bars
- you use a sensible scale on the horizontal axis
- you give the frequency diagram a title and label the axes
- you use a sensible scale on the vertical axis.

Worked example 18.1

a The frequency diagram shows how many pieces of fruit the students in class 8T ate in one week.

i How many students ate 4–7 pieces of fruit?

ii How many more students ate 8–11 pieces of fruit than 12–15 pieces?

iii How many students are there in class 8T?

b The frequency table shows the masses of 20 teachers, measured to the nearest kilogram.
Draw a frequency diagram to show the data.

Mass, m (kg)	Frequency
$60 < m \leqslant 70$	3
$70 < m \leqslant 80$	8
$80 < m \leqslant 90$	6
$90 < m \leqslant 100$	4

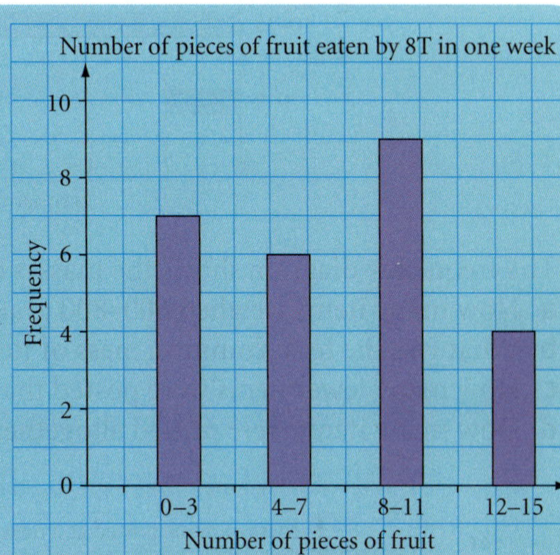

a **i** 6 students — The bar for 4–7 has a height of 6 on the frequency axis.

ii $9 - 4 = 5$ students — The frequency for 8–11 is 9 and the frequency for 12–15 is 4. Subtract one from the other to find the difference.

iii $7 + 6 + 9 + 4$
$= 26$ students — Add together the frequencies for all the groups.

b

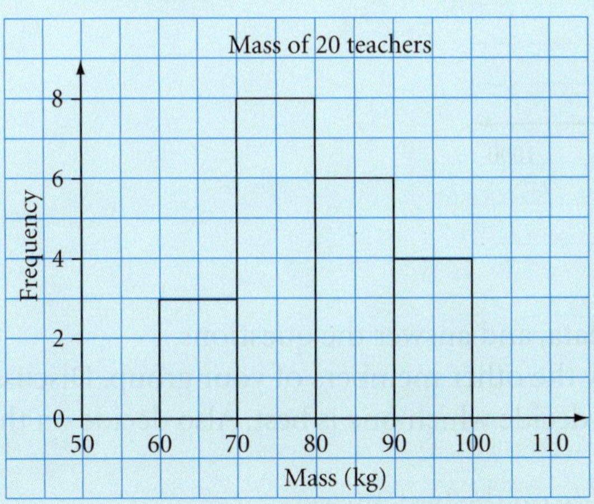

The bars are all the same width and, as the data is continuous, there are no gaps between them.
The horizontal and vertical axes both have a sensible scale.
The frequency diagram has a title and the axes are labelled.

Exercise 18.1

1 The frequency diagram shows the number of phone calls made by all the employees of a company on one day.

  a How many employees made 10–19 phone calls?
  b How many more employees made 30–39 phone calls than 0–9 phone calls?
  c How many employees are there in the company?
  Explain how you worked out your answer.

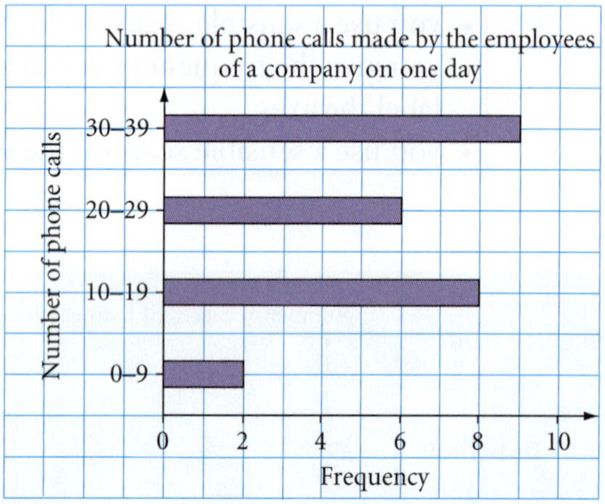

2 The frequency diagram shows the masses of the items posted at a post office on one day.

  a How many items weighed 600–800 grams?
  b What was the least common mass of items posted?
  c How many fewer items were posted that weighed 0–200 g than 400–600 g?
  d How many items were posted altogether? Explain how you worked out your answer.

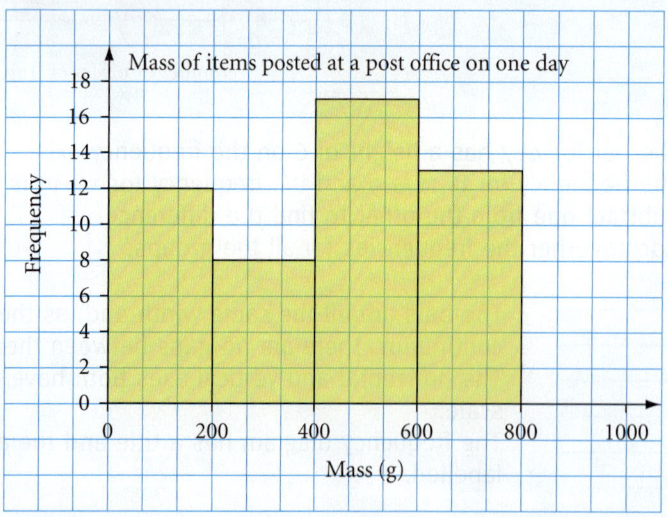

For questions **3** to **5** work in a group of three or four.

i On your own, draw a frequency diagram to show the data, and answer the questions.

ii Compare your frequency diagram with those drawn by the other members of your group. Discuss the different scales that you each used for the axes and decide which one is best. Also decide on the best title and labels for the axes.

iii Compare your answers to the questions and again decide on the best answers.

3 The frequency table shows the number of cups of coffee sold each day in a coffee shop during one month.

Number of cups of coffee sold	Frequency
0–19	2
20–39	3
40–59	6
60–79	12
80–99	5

a Draw a frequency diagram to show the data.
b Which month do you think your frequency diagram represents? Explain your answer.
c Read what Jake says.

Is he correct? Explain your answer.

4 The frequency table shows the speeds of cars passing a speed camera on one day. The speeds are recorded in kilometres per hour (km/h).

Speed of car, s (km/h)	Frequency
$50 < s \leqslant 60$	2
$60 < s \leqslant 70$	3
$70 < s \leqslant 80$	6
$80 < s \leqslant 90$	12
$90 < s \leqslant 100$	5

a Draw a frequency diagram to show the data.
b The speed limit is 80 km/h. How many cars were travelling over the speed limit?
c Read what Harsha says.

Is she correct? Explain your answer.

5 Here are the heights, in centimetres, of some plants.

25	32	30	26	34	22	33	34	31	28
39	20	27	33	37	32	25	24	30	29

a Draw a frequency diagram to show the data.
Use the class intervals $20 \leqslant h < 25$, $25 \leqslant h < 30$, $30 \leqslant h < 35$ and $35 \leqslant h < 40$.
b How many of the plants are at least 25 cm high?
Explain how you worked out your answer.

18.2 Interpreting and drawing pie charts

A pie chart is used to display data to show how an amount is divided or shared. The angles in all the sectors add up to 360°. When you draw a pie chart you must make sure that each sector is labelled and the angles are drawn accurately.

Worked example 18.2

a 90 people were asked what type of holiday they had last year. The table shows the results of the survey.

i Draw a pie chart to represent the data.

ii What percentage of the people went on a beach holiday?

Type of holiday	Number of people
Activity	32
Beach	27
City break	24
Other	7

b The pie chart shows where the 90 people went on holiday last year.

i What fraction of the population went to Spain?

ii What percentage of the population went to Greece?

iii How many people went to 'Other countries'?

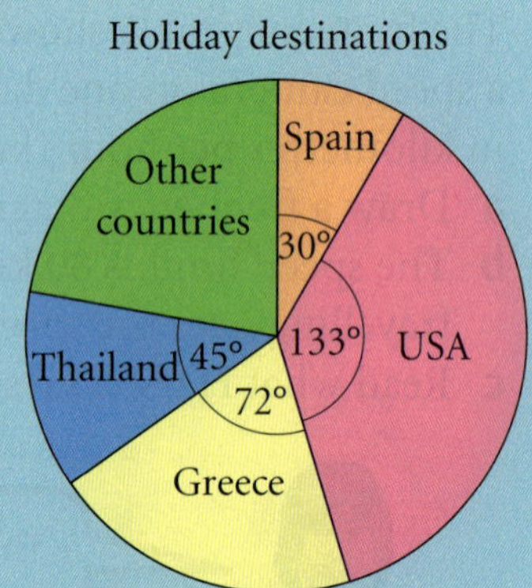

a

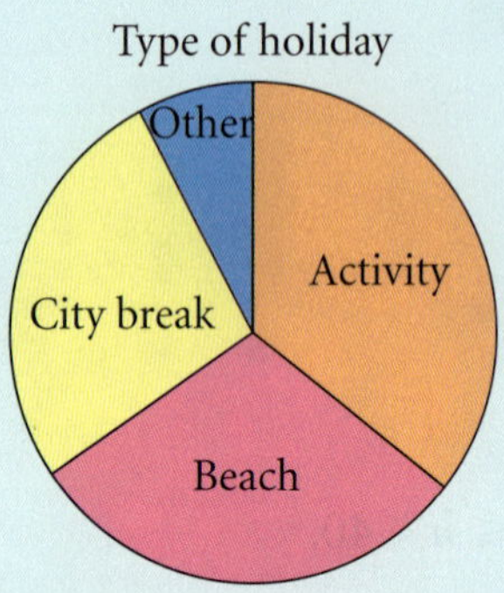

First, work out the number of degrees per person.
$360° \div 90$ people $= 4°$ per person.
Work out the number of degrees for each sector.
Activity: $32 \times 4° = 128°$ Beach: $27 \times 4° = 108°$
City break: $24 \times 4° = 96°$ Other: $7 \times 4° = 28°$
Check the total of all the sectors is 360°.
$128° + 108° + 96° + 28° = 360°$ ✓
Draw the pie chart. Remember to use a protractor to measure each sector accurately. Give the pie chart a title and label each sector.

b i $\frac{30}{360} = \frac{1}{12}$ — 30° out of 360° represents Spain. Cancel the fraction to its simplest form.

ii $\frac{72}{360} \times 100 = 20\%$ — 72° out of 360° represents Greece. Multiply by 100 to get the percentage.

iii $30 + 133 + 72 + 45 = 280°$ — Add up the degrees that are shown for the four countries.
$360 - 280 = 80°$ — Subtract this total from 360° to find out how many degrees are left.
$\frac{80}{360} \times 90 = 20$ people — 80° out of 360° is for 'Other countries'. Multiply the fraction by 90 to work out the number of people.

Exercise 18.2

1 The table shows the favourite flavours of ice cream of the 30 students in class 8A.

Favourite flavour	Vanilla	Strawberry	Raspberry	Chocolate	Caramel
Number of students	6	9	5	8	2

- **a** Draw a pie chart to represent the data.
- **b** What percentage of the students chose vanilla as their favourite flavour?

2 The pie chart shows the four makes of car sold by a garage in June. Altogether they sold 180 cars in June.

- **a** Which make of car was the most popular?
- **b** What fraction of the cars sold were Toyota?
- **c** What percentage of the cars sold were Vauxhall?
- **d** How many of the cars sold were Ford?

Make of cars sold in June

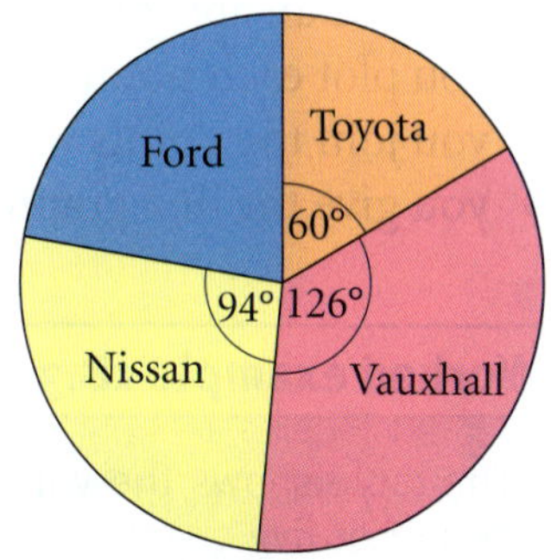

3 The pie charts show the results of a survey about the type of chocolate preferred by men and by women.
480 men took part in the survey.
600 women took part in the survey.

- **a** How many men chose plain chocolate?
- **b** How many women chose plain chocolate?
- **c** Hassan thinks that more men than women like milk chocolate. Is Hassan correct? Show how you worked out your answer.
- **d** The 'Caramel' sector for men and women is the same size. Without doing any calculations, explain how you know that more women than men chose 'Caramel'.

Men's favourite chocolate

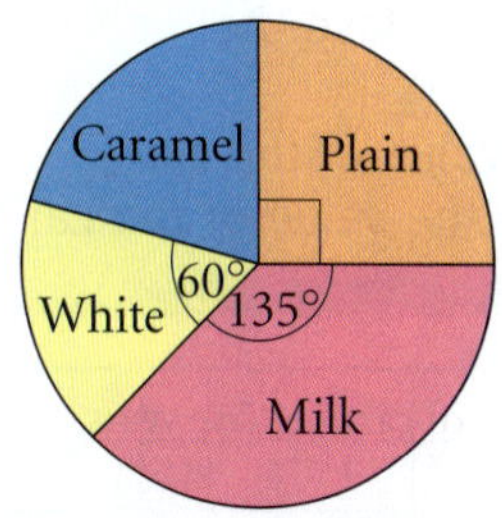

Women's favourite chocolate

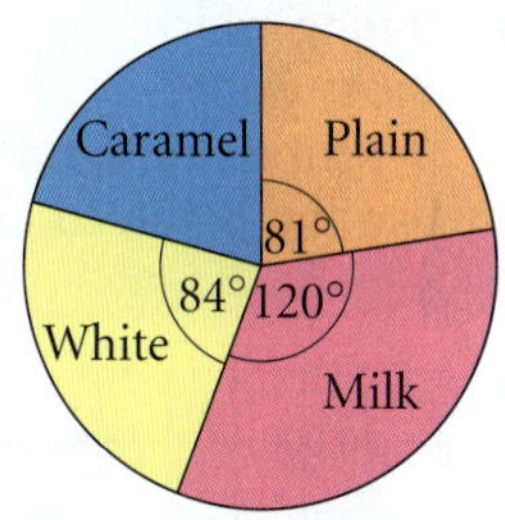

For questions **4** and **5** work in a group of three or four.

- **i** On your own, answer each part of the question. Show all your working.
- **ii** Compare your answers and workings with those of the other members of your group. Discuss the different methods that you each used to answer the questions and decide which one is best.

4 The pie chart shows the results of a survey on students' favourite subjects.

- **a** What fraction of the students chose Science?
- **b** 60 students chose Maths.
  - **i** How many students chose Languages?
  - **ii** How many students chose Other?
  - **iii** How many students took part in the survey?

Favourite subjects

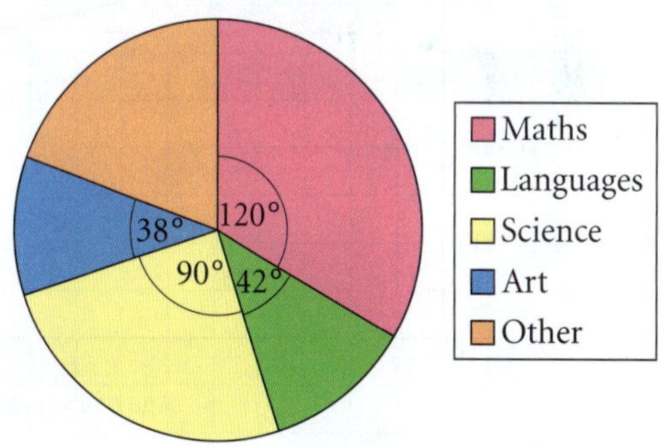

5 The pie charts show the favourite sports of the students in two schools.
There are 1600 students in Pembroke School.
There are 1100 students in Milford School.
Which school had the larger number of students choosing tennis as their favourite sport?
Show your working.

Pembroke School Milford School

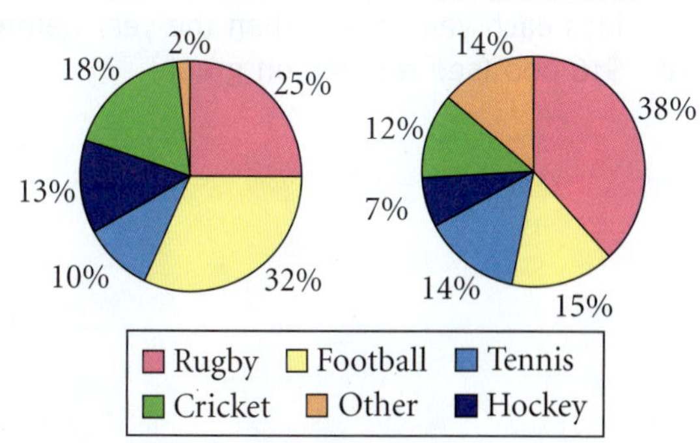

18.3 Interpreting and drawing line graphs

A **line graph** is a series of points that are joined by straight lines.

They are usually used to show **trends**, which tell you how data changes over a period of time.

When you draw a line graph, make sure that:
- you put time on the horizontal axis
- you use an appropriate scale on the vertical axis
- you plot each point accurately
- you join the points with straight lines
- you give the line graph a title and label the axes.

Worked example 18.3

The table shows the value of a car over a period of five years.

Age of car (years)	0	1	2	3	4
Value of car ($)	25 000	20 000	17 000	14 900	13 400

a Draw a line graph to show the data.
b During which year did the car lose the most value?
c Describe the trend in the value of the car.
d Use the graph to estimate the value of the car after $2\frac{1}{2}$ years.

a

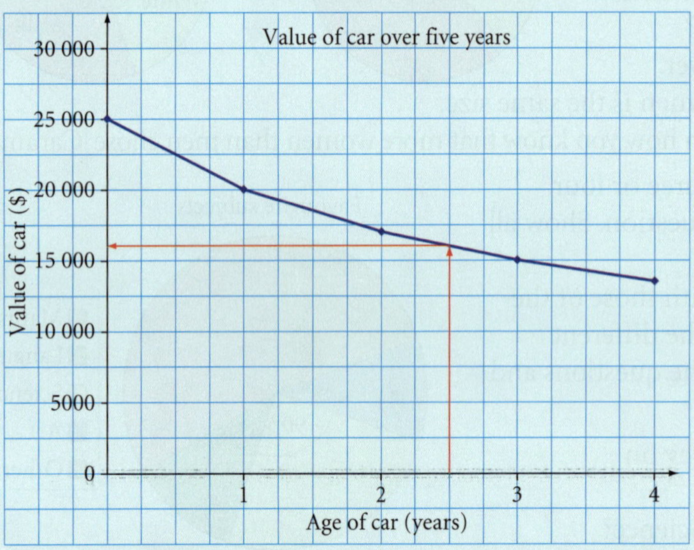

Age of car (years) goes on the horizontal axis.
Value of car ($) goes on the vertical axis.
The vertical axis has a sensible scale that is easy to read.
All the points are plotted accurately and are joined with straight lines.
The graph has a title and the axes are labelled.

b During the first year.

The greatest loss is $5000 in the first year.

c The car goes down in value every year, but the loss each year is less than the year before.

The losses are $5000, $3000, $2000 and $1500 so each year's loss is not as bad as the year before.

d $16 000 (see red line on graph)

Read up from $2\frac{1}{2}$ on the horizontal axis to the line, then across to the vertical axis to read off the value.

Exercise 18.3

1 The line graph shows the profit made each year by a company over a six-year period.

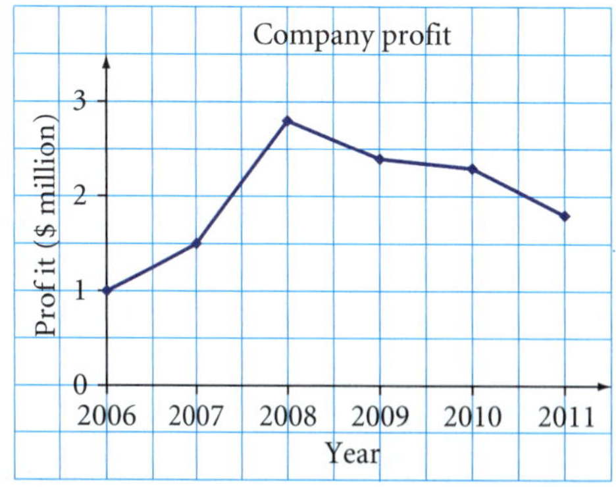

   a How much profit did the company make in:
      i 2006   ii 2007?
   b In which year did the company make the largest profit?
   c Between which two years was the greatest increase in profit?
   d Between which two years was the greatest decrease in profit?
   e Describe the trend in the company profits over the six year period.

2 Ian records the sales of skateboards at his shop each month for one year.
The data is shown in the line graph.

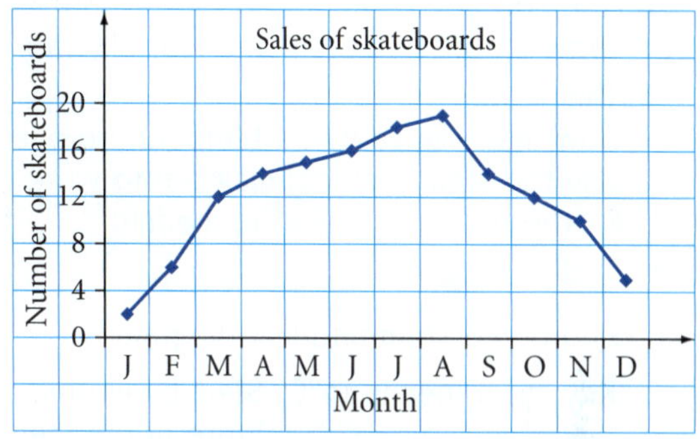

   a How many skateboards did Ian sell in:
      i March   ii May?
   b In which month did he sell the most skateboards?
   c Between which two months did his sales double?
   d Describe the trend in skateboard sales over the year.

3 The line graph shows the value of a house over a ten-year period.

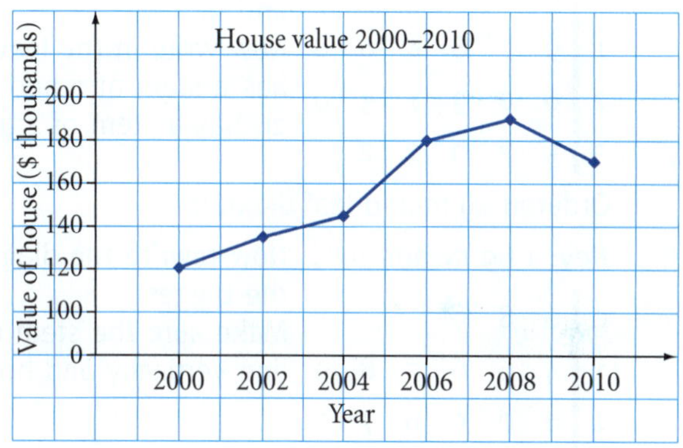

   a What was the value of the house in:
      i 2000   ii 2010?
   b In which year did the house reach its greatest value?
   c Between which two years was the greatest increase in the value of the house?
   d Describe the trend in the value of the house over the ten-year period.
   e Use the graph to estimate the value of the house in: i 2003   ii 2009.

For questions **4** and **5** work in a group of three or four.

i On your own, draw a line graph to show the data, describe the trend in the data and answer the question.

ii Compare your line graph, description and answers with those of the other members of your group. Discuss the different scales that you each used in your graph and the descriptions you gave. Decide which one is best. Check you gave the same answers to the questions.

4 The table shows the number of people staying in a guest house each month for one year.

Month	Jan	Feb	Mar	Apr	May	Jun	Jul	Aug	Sep	Oct	Nov	Dec
Number of people	8	6	11	15	17	20	24	26	18	14	8	7

Between which two months did the number of people at the guest house change the most?

5 The table shows the average price of silver over a 25-year period.

Year	1985	1990	1995	2000	2005	2010
Average price of silver ($)	6.10	4.80	5.20	5.00	7.30	20.20

In which five-year period did the price of silver change the most?

18.4 Interpreting and drawing stem-and-leaf diagrams

A **stem-and-leaf diagram** is a way of showing data in order of size.

When you draw a stem-and-leaf diagram, make sure that:

- you write the numbers in order of size from smallest to largest
- you write a key to explain the numbers
- you keep all the numbers in line vertically and horizontally.

Key: 2 | 3 means 23 cm

2 | 3 4 7 8
3 | 0 6 7 7 8
4 | 1 9 9

stem — leaves

Worked example 18.4

Here are the temperatures, in °C, recorded in 20 cities on one day.

9	19	26	35	6	17	32	20	30	16
14	16	18	29	27	8	25	32	20	32

a Draw an ordered stem-and-leaf diagram to show this data.

b How many cities had a temperature over 28°C?

c Use the stem-and-leaf diagram to work out:

i the mode **ii** the median **iii** the range of the data.

'Ordered' means you write the numbers in order of size from smallest to largest.

a Unordered stem-and-leaf diagram

Key: 1 | 9 means 19°C

0 | 9 6 8
1 | 9 7 6 4 6 8
2 | 6 0 9 7 5 0
3 | 5 2 0 2 2

Start by writing a key. You can use any of the numbers to explain the key.

Write in the stem numbers. In this case they are the tens digits, 0, 1, 2 and 3.

Now write in the leaves, taking the numbers from the table above. So 9 has a stem of 0 and 9 as the leaf. 19 has a stem of 1 and 9 as the leaf. 26 has a stem of 2 and 6 is the leaf. Complete for all 20 temperatures.

Ordered stem-and-leaf diagram

Key: 1 | 9 means 19°C

0 | 6 8 9
1 | 4 6 6 7 8 9
2 | 0 0 5 6 7 9
3 | 0 2 2 2 5

Now rewrite the diagram with all the leaves in order, from the smallest to the biggest.

Make sure the stem numbers are in line vertically and that the leaves are in line vertically and horizontally.

b 6 cities — You can see that 29 °C, 30 °C, 32 °C, 32 °C, 32 °C and 35 °C are all over 28 °C.

c **i** mode = 32 °C — You can see that 32°C is the temperature that appears most often.

ii median = 20 °C — There are 20 temperatures, so the median temperature is the average of the 10th and 11th. These are both 20 °C, so the median is 20 °C.

iii range = 35 − 6 = 29 °C — You can easily see from the diagram that the highest temperature is 35 °C and the lowest is 6 °C. Subtract them to find the range.

Exercise 18.4

1 Shen listed the playing times, to the nearest minute, of some CDs. He recorded the results in a stem-and-leaf diagram.

Key: 4 | 5 means 45 minutes

4 | 5 5 7 9
5 | 0 2 5 6 8 9
6 | 1 2 4 6 7

a How many CDs did Shen list?

b What is the shortest playing time?

c How many of the CDs had a playing time longer than 60 minutes?

d Work out:

i the mode **ii** the median **iii** the range of the data.

2 The stem-and-leaf diagram shows the heights, to the nearest 0.1 cm, of some seedlings.

a How many seedlings were measured?

b What is the height of the tallest seedling?

c How many of the seedlings had a height less than 4.5 cm?

d Work out:

i the mode **ii** the median **iii** the range of the data.

Key: 2 | 3 means 2.3 cm

Stem	Leaf					
2	3	5	9			
3	0	1	8	9	9	
4	5	5	5	7	7	8
5	2	3	6	6		
6	0	1	1	3		

3 A company keeps records of the number of jars of strawberry preserve they produce each day. The stem-and-leaf diagram shows the number of jars of preserve produced each day for one month.

a Which month does the stem-and-leaf diagram represent? Explain how you worked out your answer.

b What is the smallest number of jars of preserve produced in one day?

c On how many days did the company produce fewer than 135 jars of preserve?

Key: 11 | 2 means 112 jars of preserve

Stem	Leaf							
11	2	4	6	8				
12	0	0	1	2	4	5	6	9
13	1	4	4	5	8	9		
14	2	4	7	7				
15	0	1	1	3	6	8		

4 These are the masses, in kilograms, of 25 adults.

73	62	85	71	64	89	80	59	72	69	78	60	64
82	58	92	69	59	75	95	61	90	64	73	86	

a Draw an ordered stem-and-leaf diagram to show this data.

b How many of the adults weighed less than 80 kg?

c Use the stem-and-leaf diagram to work out:

i the mode **ii** the median **iii** the range of the data.

5 These are the file sizes, in kilobytes (kB), of 30 files on Greg's computer.

101	128	117	109	154	139	166	155	115	145	135	162	117	168	125
131	140	160	151	125	152	108	139	130	165	158	103	130	110	148

a Draw an ordered stem-and-leaf diagram to show this data.

b How many of the files are larger than 150 kB?

c Use the stem-and-leaf diagram to work out:

i the mode **ii** the median **iii** the range of the data.

6 The students in class 8B took a test. The stem-and-leaf diagram shows their scores out of 40.

a What percentage of the students had a score greater than 32?

b What fraction of the students had a score less than 25%?

c Any student scoring less than 40% must re-sit the test. How many students do not have to re-sit the test?

d What is the mean score?

Key: 1 | 8 means 18

Stem	Leaf									
0	6	8	8	9	9					
1	8									
2	5	6	8	8	9					
3	0	1	2	3	3	5	6	7	8	8
4	0	0	0	0						

7 The stem-and-leaf diagram shows the price of the same book in 12 different stores.

a In what fraction of the stores is the price less than \$6.50?

b In what percentage of the stores is the price greater than \$7?

Key: 5 | 65 means \$5.65

Stem	Leaf						
5	65	95					
6	20	25	45	49	60	75	99
7	05	20	25				

18.5 Drawing conclusions

So far you have drawn several different types of diagram, chart and graph. You have also read information from these diagrams, charts and graphs. It is important that you can also use the information you find to draw conclusions and make observations.

Worked example 18.5

a Mia makes necklaces. She sells them on the internet. The stem-and-leaf diagram shows the price of the necklaces she sells in one week. Mia makes a profit if the mean price is greater than \$7.50. Does Mia make a profit this week?

Key: 6 | 25 means \$6.25

Stem	Leaf					
6	30	45	85	95	99	
7	00	05	59	63	68	70
8	25	45	99			

b The bar charts show the number of goals scored by two soccer teams in 30 matches. Xavier thinks that 'The Blues' score more goals on average then the 'The Reds'.

i Explain how Xavier could be right.

ii Explain how Xavier could be wrong.

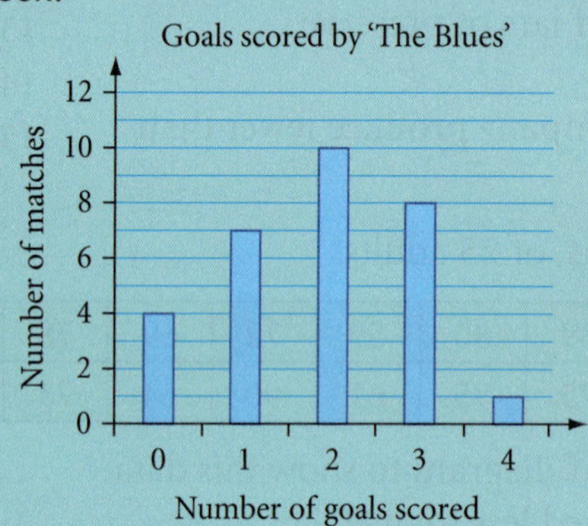

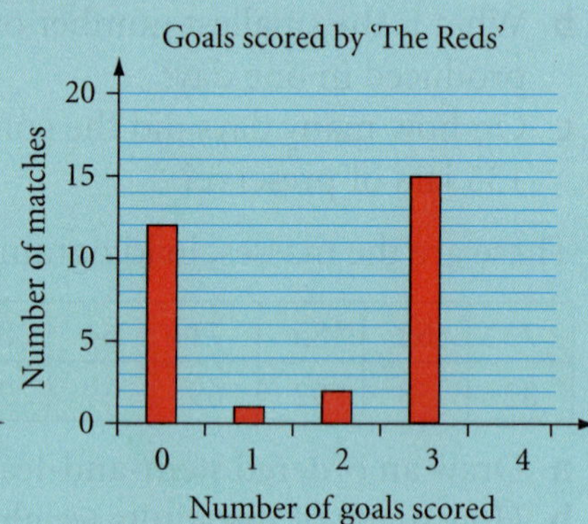

a Total of all prices = 6.30 + 6.45 + ... + 8.99
= \$103.88
Mean = 103.88 ÷ 14
= \$7.42
No, she hasn't made a profit as the mean price is less than \$7.50.

First calculate the mean by adding together all of the prices of the necklaces she sold. Then divide the total by the number of necklaces she sold (14). Compare the mean price with \$7.50 and decide whether she has made a profit or not. Give an explanation of your decision with your answer.

b i Total number of goals scored by Blues
$7 \times 1 + 10 \times 2 + 8 \times 3 + 1 \times 4 = 55$
Mean = 55 ÷ 30 = 1.83 goals per match
Total number of goals scored by Reds
$1 \times 1 + 2 \times 2 + 15 \times 3 = 50$
Mean = 50 ÷ 30 = 1.67 goals per match
Blues mean > Reds mean, so Xavier is right.

Xavier uses the word average so this could be the mean, median or mode. Work out the mean for each team.

You can see that the mean for The Blues is greater than the mean for The Reds, so Xavier is right.

ii Blues mode = 2, Reds mode = 3
Blues mode < Reds mode, so Xavier is wrong

Compare the modes and you can see that Xavier is wrong.

Exercise 18.5

1 Mr Lopez makes pottery vases. He sells them on the internet. The stem-and-leaf diagram shows the prices of the vases he sells in one week.
Mr Lopez makes a profit if the mean price is greater than $25.50.
Does Mr Lopez make a profit this week?
Show your working.

Key: 24 | 20 means $24.20

Stem	Leaves						
24	20	33	79	80	90		
25	05	25	50	70	70	99	99
26	40	45	60	65	90		

2 The bar-line graphs show the number of goals scored by two hockey teams in 25 matches.
Tanesha thinks that Allerton score more goals on average than Batesfield.

a Explain how Tanesha could be right.

b Explain how Tanesha could be wrong.

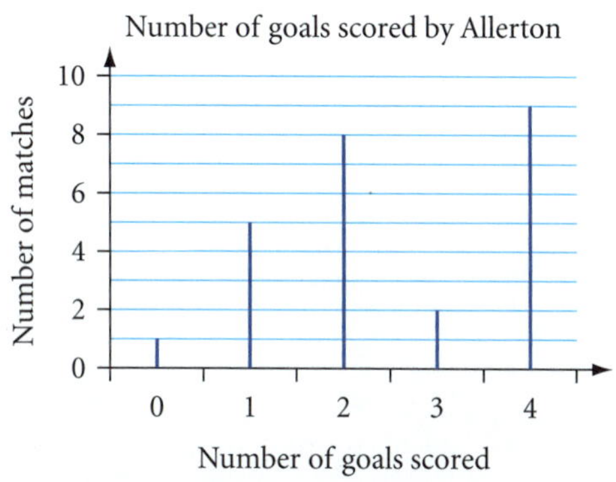

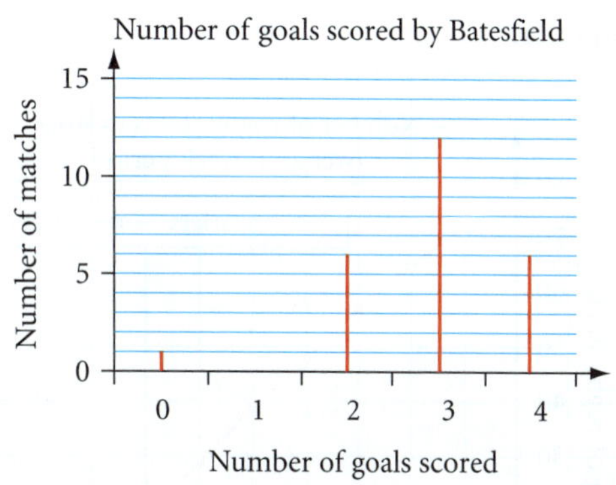

3 The students in class 8P ran the school cross-country (long-distance running) course in their PE lesson.
The frequency diagram shows the time taken by the students in class 8P to complete the course.
The PE teacher says: 'If 60% of you finish the course in less than 15 minutes, you can all go early for lunch.'
Do class 8P go early for lunch?
Show your working.

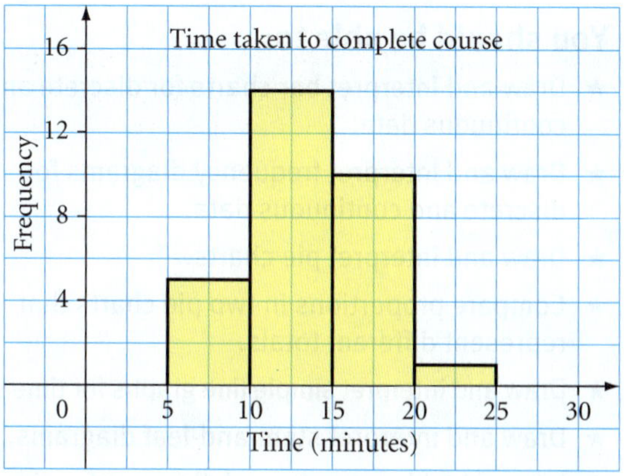

For question **4** work in a group of three or four.

i On your own, answer each part of the question.

ii Compare your descriptions, answers and explanations with those of the other members of your group.
Discuss the different descriptions and explanations you gave and decide which ones are best.

4 A sports shop sells the rugby shirts of two teams, Scarlets and Dragons.
The line graph shows the number of rugby shirts the shop has in stock each week over an 8-week period.

a Describe the trend in the sales of:

  i Scarlets rugby shirts

  ii Dragons rugby shirts.

b Do you think that the shop has enough Scarlets rugby shirts in stock for week 9? Explain your answer.

c Do you think that the shop has enough Dragons rugby shirts in stock for week 9? Explain your answer.

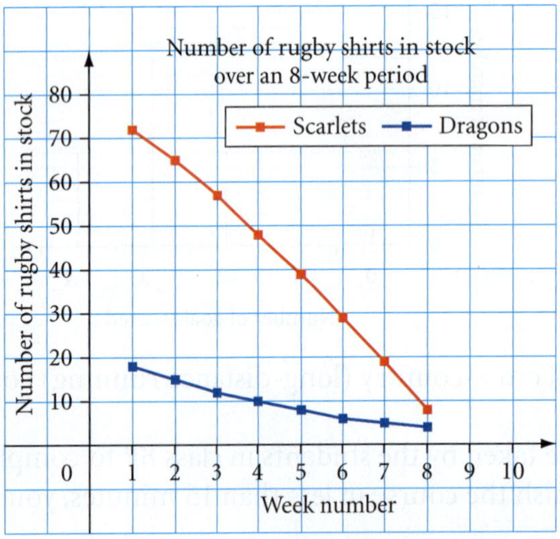

Summary

You should now know that:

★ A bar chart is an example of a frequency diagram in which the bars represent discrete or continuous data.

★ In a frequency diagram, bars can represent discrete or continuous data.

★ A pie chart is a way of displaying data to show how an amount is divided or shared. The angles in all the sectors add up to 360°.

★ A line graph is a series of points that are joined by straight lines. Line graphs are usually used to show how data changes over a period of time.

★ A stem-and-leaf diagram is a way of showing data in order of size.

You should be able to:

★ Draw and interpret bar charts for discrete and continuous data.

★ Draw and interpret frequency diagrams for discrete and continuous data.

★ Draw and interpret pie charts.

★ Compare proportions in two pie charts that represent different totals.

★ Draw and interpret simple line graphs for time series.

★ Draw and interpret stem-and-leaf diagrams.

★ Interpret tables, graphs and diagrams for discrete and continuous data, and draw conclusions, relating statistics and findings to the original question.

End-of-unit review

1 The frequency diagram shows the masses of the items posted by an internet company in one week.

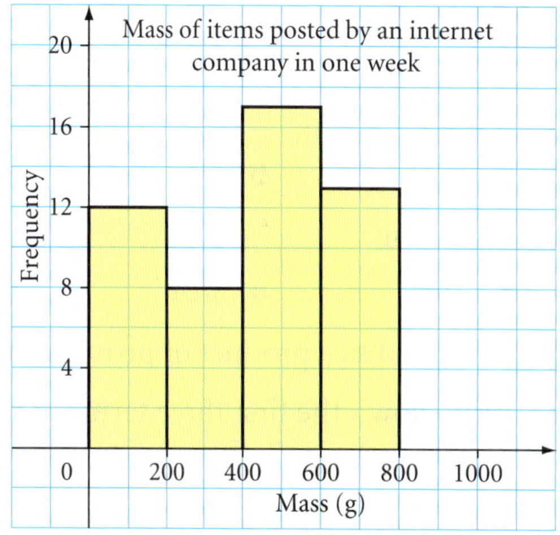

a Why are there no gaps between the bars of this frequency diagram?
b How many items weighed 600–800 g?
c What was the most common mass of items posted?
d How many more items were posted that weighed 0–200 g than 200–400 g?
e How many items were posted altogether?

2 The frequency table shows the number of MP3 players Gio sold each day in his shop during one month.

Number of MP3 players sold	Frequency
0–9	3
10–19	5
20–29	12
30–39	8
40–49	2

a Draw a frequency diagram to show the data.
b Can you tell which month your frequency diagram represents? Explain your answer.
c Gio says: 'The frequency diagram shows that that the highest number of of MP3 players sold in one day was less than 50.'
Is Gio correct? Explain your answer.
d Draw a pie chart to represent the data.
e On what percentage of days in the month were between 20 and 29 MP3 players sold?

3 The students in class 8T took a test. These are the results, marked out of 50.

28	12	50	28	24	39	46	27	18	50	49	28	36
45	34	43	8	28	36	37	18	39	29	38	9	

a Draw an ordered stem-and-leaf diagram showing their scores out of 50.
b What percentage of the students had a score greater than 35?
c What fraction of the students had a score less than 25?
d Any student scoring less than 40% must re-sit the test.
How many students do not have to re-sit the test?
e Read what Zalika says.

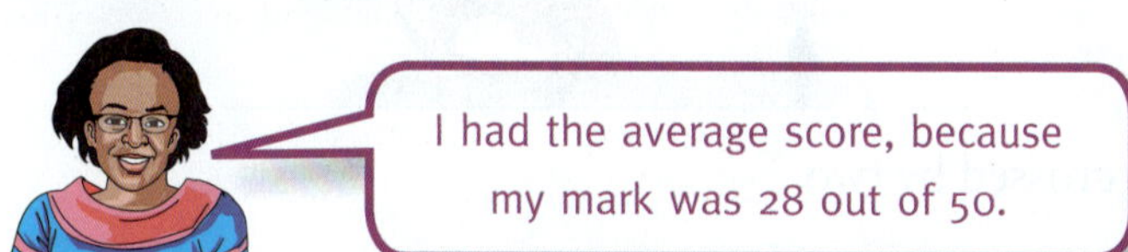

i Show that Zalika could be correct.
ii Show that Zalika could be wrong.

End-of-year review

1 Work these out.
a $7 + -3$ **b** $7 - -5$ **c** $-7 - -7$ **d** -7×-3 **e** $-70 \div 10$

2 Work out.
a $\sqrt{144}$ **b** $\sqrt[3]{64}$ **c** the highest common factor of 144 and 64.

3 Write 450 as a product of prime numbers.

4 Write down the first three terms of the sequence described.
The first term is 7; the term-to-term rule is 'add 3'.

5 Look at the sequence of numbers.

6 12 18 24

a Write down the next number in the sequence.
b Write down the term-to-term rule.
c Write down the position-to-term rule.

6 Work out the value of the expression $2n + 1$ when $n = -5$.

7 Write the number 10 000 000 as a power of 10.

8 Round each number to the given degree of accuracy.
a 8785 (nearest 100) **b** 183 890 (nearest 10 000) **c** 3 601 111 (nearest million)
d 17.81 (nearest whole number) **e** 59.52 (1 d.p.) **f** 7.176 (2 d.p.)

9 Work out $84 \div 0.2$.

10 Which metric units would you use to measure:
a the length of a basketball court **b** the area of a label on a can of beans
c the mass of a woman **d** the volume of a large jug?

11 The diagram shows a man standing next to a dinosaur.
Estimate the height of the dinosaur.

12 The diagram shows a pair of parallel lines crossed by two intersecting transversals.
a Work out the size of angle *a*. Give a reason for your answer.
b Work out the size of angle *b*. Give a reason for your answer.
c Work out the size of angle *c*. Give a reason for your answer.
d Work out the size of angle *d*. Give a reason for your answer.
e Work out the size of angle *e*. Give a reason for your answer

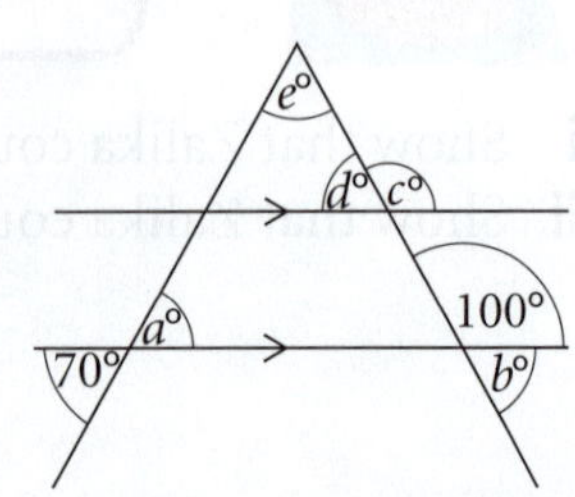

13 Some elephants were born in captivity. They were weighed and the results, measured to the nearest kilogram are shown.

75	101	90	82	97	79	88
92	84	94	107	89	93	80

a Copy and complete the grouped frequency table.

b How many of the elephants had a mass of more than 90 kg but not more than 100 kg?

c How many of the elephants had a mass of more than 90 kg?

d How many of the elephants had a mass of 90 kg or less?

e Altogether, how many elephants were weighed?

f Is the mass of an elephant discrete data or continuous data?

g Is the number of elephants measured discrete data or continuous data?

Mass, m(g)	Tally	Frequency
$70 < w \leqslant 80$		
$80 < w \leqslant 90$		
$90 < w \leqslant 100$		
$100 < w \leqslant 110$		
	Total	

14 The table shows some fractions, decimals and percentages. Copy the table and complete it.

Fraction	$\frac{1}{4}$				$\frac{4}{5}$				$\frac{6}{25}$
Decimal		0.6		0.2		0.5		0.08	
Percentage			30%				64%		

15 Work out these additions and subtractions.
Write each answer in its simplest form and as a mixed number where appropriate.

a $\frac{1}{4} + \frac{5}{8}$ **b** $\frac{2}{3} - \frac{1}{4}$ **c** $2\frac{5}{6} + 3\frac{1}{4}$ **d** $4\frac{1}{2} - 2\frac{5}{9}$

16 Work out these multiplications and divisions.
Write each answer in its simplest form and as a mixed number where appropriate.

a $\frac{1}{3} \times \frac{1}{7}$ **b** $\frac{1}{4} \div \frac{2}{5}$ **c** $\frac{5}{8} \times 9$ **d** $9 \div \frac{5}{8}$

17 These two triangles are congruent.

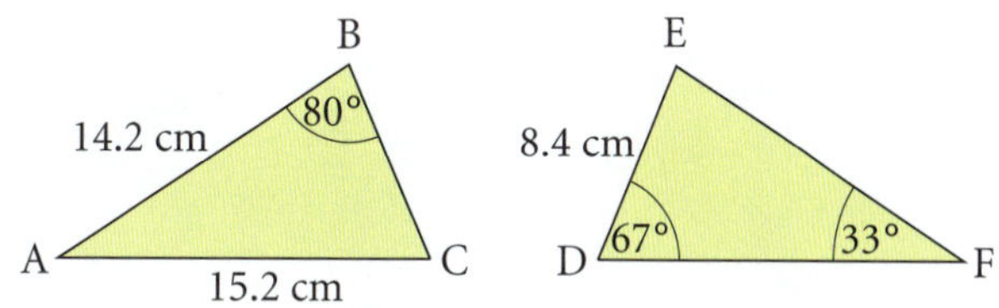

a What is the length of the side: **i** EF **ii** BC **iii** DF?

b What is the size of **i** $\angle$ACB **ii** $\angle$DEF **iii** $\angle$BAC?

18 Draw a sketch of the net of this triangular prism.

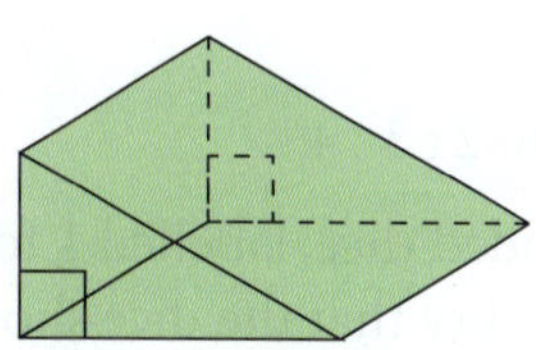

19 Simplify these expressions.

a $3a + 7b + 5a - 2b$ **b** $3x^2 + 7y + 9 - x^2 + 5y$

20 Expand and simplify $6(3w + 1) - 4(w + 5)$.

21 Work out the values of x and y in this diagram.
All measurements are in centimetres.

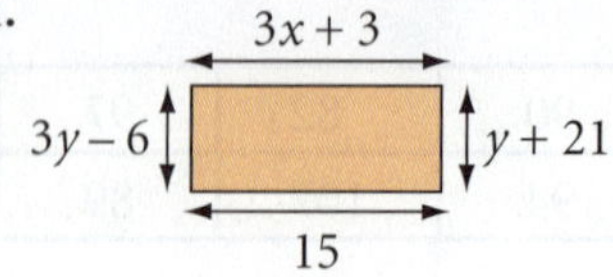

22 This frequency table shows the times 40 people waited to be served in a café.

Time (minutes)	5	6	7	8	9	10	11
Frequency	6	13	7	3	6	0	5

a Work out the modal waiting time.
b Work out the median waiting time.
c Work out the mean waiting time.
d Find the range of the waiting times.

23 The table shows how many people went to a cinema on two days.

	Adults	Children	Total
Monday	120	180	300
Tuesday	140	135	275

a What percentage of the audience on Monday were adults?
b Work out the percentage decrease in the number of children who went to the cinema on Tuesday compared to the number who went on Monday.

24 Draw an arc with a radius of 6 cm and a centre angle of 40°.

25 Using only a ruler and compasses, make an accurate copy of this triangle.
Show your construction lines.

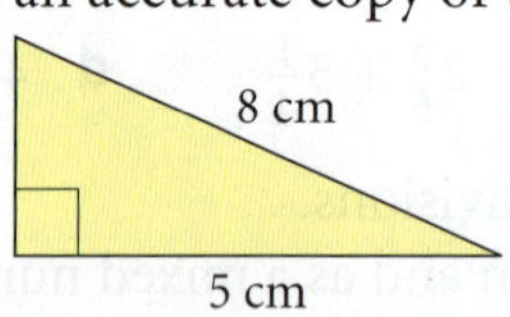

26 Copy these axes and use your grid to draw the graph of $y = 3x - 2$.

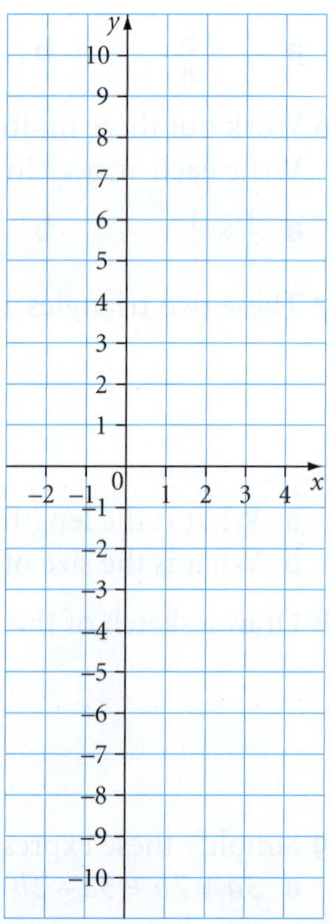

27 Share \$180 in the ratio 2 : 3 : 4.

28 Jamilia throws an 8-sided dice, labelled 1 to 8.
a What is the probability that the dice shows a 2?
b What is the probability that the dice does not show a 6?
c The dice is thrown 50 times and lands on an odd number 28 times.
Work out the experimental probability of getting an even number.

29 The diagram shows a triangle A. Make three copies of the diagram. Use a different copy of the diagram for each part of the question.

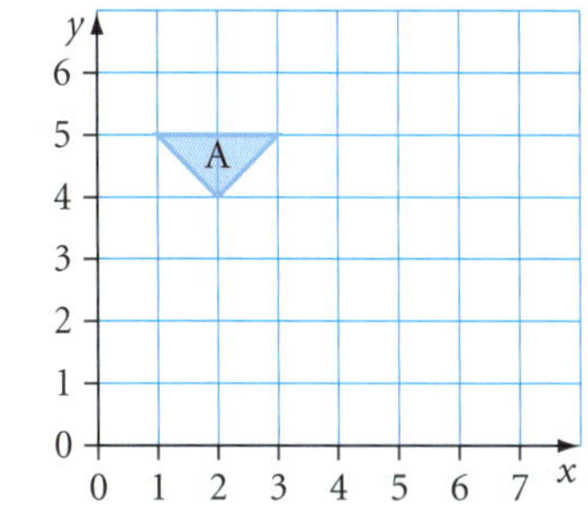

- **a** Draw the image of A after translation 3 squares right and 2 squares down. Label the image B.
- **b** Draw the image of A after rotation of 90° clockwise, centre (3, 3). Label the image C.
- **c** Draw the image of A after reflection in the line $y = 3$, followed by a reflection in the line $x = 4$. Label the image D.

30 Zahir is driving from his home in Dhaka to his sister's house in Mymensingh.
Anika is driving from her home in Mymensingh to her brother's house in Dhaka.

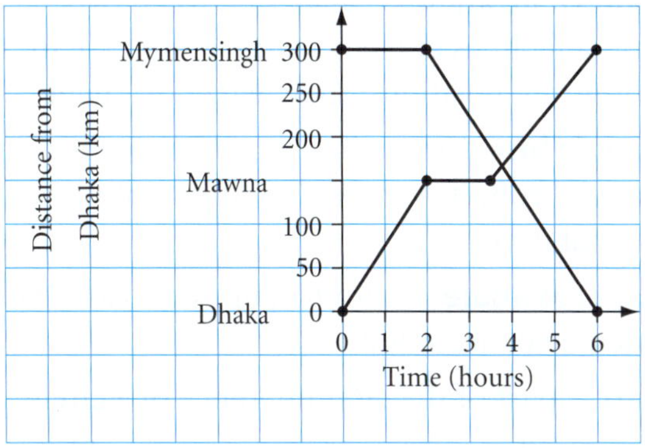

- **a** How long did Zahir take to get to Mawna?
- **b** How long did Zahir stop at Mawna?
- **c** How long did Anika take to get to from Mymensingh to Dhaka?
- **d** How far were the cars from Dhaka when they passed one another?
- **e** How can you tell from Zahir's graph that he drove faster before his stop than after?

31 A circle has a radius of 4 cm.
Work out

a the circumference **b** the area.

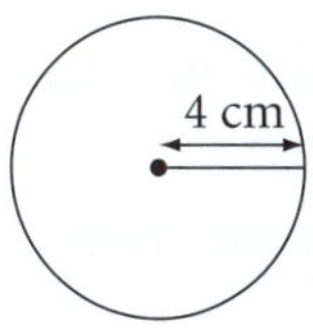

32 The diagram shows a cuboid.

- **a** Work out the volume.
- **b** Sketch a net of the cuboid.
- **c** Use the net to work out the surface area of the cuboid.

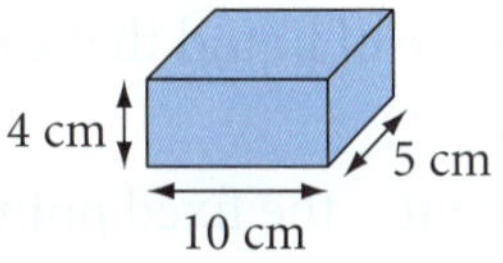

33 The students in class 8Z took a test. These are the results. The maximum score was 40.

23	38	33	32	40	15	26	9
28	40	33	11	21	23	33	

- **a** Draw an ordered stem-and-leaf diagram showing their scores out of 40.
- **b** How many of the students had a score greater than 25?
- **c** What fraction of the students had a score less than 25%?
- **d** Any student scoring less than 30% must re-sit the test. How many students do not have to re-sit the test?
- **e** Sami says: 'I had the average score of 33 out of 40.'
  i Show that Sami could be correct. **ii** Show that Sami could be wrong.

Glossary and index

π, pi the value of the circumference of any circle divided by its diameter; it is approximately 3.14 165

algebraically using algebra 24

alternate angles angles between two parallel lines and a transversal that are in opposite positions; they make a Z-shape 51

angle bisector a line drawn through an angle from its vertex, dividing it into two equal parts 124

approximate round a number to a suitable degree of accuracy 41

arc part of the circumference of a circle 120

area the amount of surface covered by a flat shape 45

at random *see* random

average a representative value; mode, median and mean are examples 103

bisect divide a line or angle into two equal parts 88

capacity the volume of liquid that can be put into a container 45

centre of enlargement the fixed point of an enlargement 161

chord a line segment between two points on the circumference of a circle 120

circumference the perimeter of a circle 120

class a group in a set of continuous data 105

class interval the width of a group or interval in a grouped frequency table 66

collect like terms gather, by addition and subtraction, all like terms 96

combination of transformations two or more transformations carried out one after another 159

common denominator a denominator used to add or subtract fractions with different denominators, by producing equivalent fractions; the lowest common denominator is the lowest common multiple of the denominators of the fractions being added or subtracted 74

common factor a number that divides into other numbers without remainder 11

common multiple a number that is a multiple of two different numbers 11

compound shape (or composite shape) a shape made up from simpler shapes 171

congruent identical in shape and size 84

construct (algebra) use information to write a formula 99

continuous data data that can take any value within a given range 65

corresponding angles (in parallel lines) angles between two parallel lines and a transversal, which are in the same relative positions 51

corresponding angles (in polygons) angles that are in the same relative position in two or more similar or congruent shapes 84

corresponding sides sides that are in the same relative position in two or more similar or congruent shapes 84

cube the result of multiplying three 'lots' of the same number together; the cube of 5 is 125 because 5 cubed = $5^3 = 5 \times 5 \times 5 = 125$ 15

cube root the number that produces the given number when cubed; the cube root of 125 = $\sqrt[3]{125} = 5$ 15

decrease make or become smaller or fewer in number 113

degree of accuracy the level of accuracy in any rounding 36, 62

derive construct a formula or work out an answer 27

diagonal a line segment joining non-adjacent vertices of a polygon 88

diameter a line segment between two points on the circumference of a circle (or on the surface of a sphere) that passes through its centre 120

direct proportion two or more quantities are in direct proportion if, when one increases or decreases so does the other, with the ratio of the quantities staying the same 145

discrete data data that can only take specific, exact values, but cannot have in-between values 65

enlargement a transformation that increases the size of a shape to produce a mathematically similar image 158

equal class intervals class intervals, in grouped data, that are all the same size 66

equation two different mathematical expressions, both having the same value, separated by an equals sign (=); also a way of labelling a straight line on a grid 24, 30

equivalent calculation a calculation that gives the same answer 39

expand (brackets) multiply all parts of the expression inside the brackets by the term alongside the brackets 98

experiment a repeatable process, such as rolling a dice 62

experimental probability a probability estimated from data collected in an experiment 154

expression a collection of symbols representing numbers and mathematical operations, but not including an equals sign (=) 26

external angle an angle outside a triangle, or other polygon, between an extended side and the side next to it 54

factor a whole number that will divide into another whole number without a remainder; 6 and 8 are factors of 24 11

factor tree a diagram used as a method for finding prime factors 13

formula (*plural* **formulae**) an equation that shows the relationship between two or more quantities 27

frequency table a table that lists the number of times a specific value or item occurs in a set of data (its frequency) 66

function a relationship between two sets of numbers 24

function machine a diagram that shows the steps in a function 24

highest common factor (HCF) the largest number that is a factor of two or more numbers 11

hypotenuse the side opposite the right angle, in a right-angled triangle 84

image a shape after a transformation 158

improper fraction a fraction in which the numerator is larger than the denominator 75

increase make or become larger or greater in number 113

index (*plural* **indices**) a number used to show a power; in 3^4, 4 is the index 15, 32

input a number to be acted upon by a function 24

integer a number from the set of whole numbers …, −3, −2, −1, 0, 1, 2, 3, … 8

interview a conversation in which one person (the interviewer) asks another (the interviewee) questions 62

inverse the operation that has the opposite effect; the inverse of 'add 5' is 'subtract 5' 8

kilometre (km) one thousand metres (1000 m) 47

length measurement of a line, usually in metres 45

line graph a series of points that are joined by straight lines 184

line segment a part of a straight line between two points 122, 134

line symmetry property of a shape that can be divided by a line segment (or mirror line) into two congruent halves, one being the mirror image (or reflection) of the other 86

linear expression an expression with at least one variable, where the highest power of any variable is 1 26

linear sequence a pattern of numbers in which the difference between consecutive terms is the same 19

lowest common multiple (LCM) the smallest possible common multiple of two numbers; 24 is the lowest common multiple of 6 and 8 11

map the process of changing an input number to an output number by the use of a function 18

mapping diagram type of diagram that represents a function 24

mass the amount of substance in an object; sometimes the word 'weight' is used in everyday speech 45

mean an average of a set of numbers, found by adding all the numbers and dividing the total by how many numbers there are in the set 103

median the middle number when a set of numbers is put in order 103

method of collection the way in which data is collected, such as survey, experiment or observation 62

metric units measurements based on multiples and divisions of ten; the most commonly used units of measurement 45

midpoint the centre point of a line segment 122, 134

mile measure of distance, approximately 1.6 or $\frac{8}{5}$ of a kilometre 47

mixed number a number expressed as the sum of a whole number and a proper fraction 75

modal class the class with the highest frequency 105

mode the most common number or value in a set 103

multiple the result of multiplying a number by a positive integer; the first few multiples of 3 are 3, 6, 9, 12, …, … 11

mutually exclusive two outcomes are mutually exclusive if they cannot both happen at the same time 152

net a flat diagram that can be folded to form the faces of a solid 90

***n*th term** the general term of a sequence; using algebra to write the position-to-term rule, where *n* represents the position number of the term 23

object a shape before a transformation 158

observation primary data collected by recording things that are seen 62

output the result after a number has been acted upon by a function 24

parallel lines having the same perpendicular distance continuously between them 51

percentage a fraction written out of 100, as 'percent'; a quarter is 25% 111

perpendicular bisector a line drawn at 90° to a line segment, dividing it into two equal parts 122

perpendicular height the height of a shape or object measured at 90° to its base 166

population the total set of people, things or events being investigated 62

position-to-term rule the rule that allows any term in a sequence to be calculated, given its position number 19

power a number written using an index; 3 to the power 4 is written as $3^4 = 3 \times 3 \times 3 \times 3 = 81$ 15, 32

powers of 10 the number 10 being multiplied by itself a number of times 32

prime *see* prime number

prime number a number with exactly two factors, 1 and itself; 7, 13 and 41 are primes 11

proof an argument to show a particular statement or fact is true 54

prove give a proof 54

questionnaire a set of written questions with a choice of answers 62

radius (*plural* radii) a line segment from the centre of a circle to its circumference (or from the centre of a sphere to its surface); the length of this line segment 120

random describes a situation where outcomes are equally likely 150

range the difference between the largest and smallest number in a set 103

ratio an amount compared to another amount, using the symbol : 141

recurring repeating; in a recurring fraction, a digit or group of digits is repeated forever 73

reduction decrease 113

reflect transform a shape, producing the mirror image of that shape 158

right angle, hypotenuse, side (RHS) condition that construction of a right-angled triangle is possible, given the lengths of the hypotenuse and one other side 126

rotate transform a shape, moving or turning each point of the shape around a fixed position through the same angle 158

rotational symmetry the property that means that a shape can be rotated a fraction of a whole turn and still look the same as it does in its initial position 86

round make an approximation of a number, to a given accuracy 36

sample a selection from a large population 62

scale the ratio between the lengths on a scale drawing and the actual lengths represented 92

scale drawing an accurate drawing in which lengths in the drawing are in a given ratio to lengths in the original 92

scale factor the ratio by which a length is increased (or decreased) 161

sector part of a circle, the edges of which are two radii (plural of radius) and an arc 120

segment part of a circle, bounded by an arc and a chord 120

simplify (a ratio or fraction) divide all parts of the ratio (or fraction) by a common factor 141

simplify (an expression or equation) gathering, by addition and subtraction, all like terms to express each term in its simplest form 96

square the result of multiplying a number by itself; the square of 5 is 25 because 5 squared = $5^2 = 5 \times 5 = 25$ 15

square root the number that produces a given number when squared; the square root of 25 = $\sqrt{25} = 5$ (or -5) 15

side, side, side (SSS) condition that construction of a triangle is possible, given the lengths of all three sides 126

statistics study and use of data; values calculated from a set of data 103

stem-and-leaf diagram a way of displaying data like a horizontal bar graph but with a set of digits forming the bars 186

survey a method of collecting information by asking questions or observing 62

term-to-term rule a rule to find a term of a sequence, given the previous term 19

terminating ending; a terminating decimal has a finite number of decimal places, it does not go on forever 73

theoretical probability a probability found using equally likely outcomes 154

transform move a shape by reflection, rotation or translation; change a shape by enlargement 158

translate transform a shape, moving each part of the shape the same distance in the same direction 158

transversal a line crossing parallel lines 51

trend a pattern in a set of data 184

two-way table a table displaying data, with rows and columns usually showing different variables 66

unitary method solving direct proportion problems by first calculating the value of a single item 145

units of measurement names of units given to measure something. For example, length is often measured in units called metres (m); mass is often measured in units called kilograms (kg) 45

variable a symbol, usually a letter, that can represent any one of a set of values 26

volume the space occupied by a solid or 3D shape 45